RELOCATING TELEVISION

For over half a century, television has been the most central medium in Western democracies – the political, social and cultural centrepiece of the public sphere. Television has therefore rarely been studied in isolation from its socio-cultural and political context; there is always something important at stake when the forms and functions of television are on the agenda. The digitization of television concerns the production, contents, distribution and reception of the medium, but also its position in the overall, largely digitized media system and public sphere where the internet plays a decisive role.

The chapters in this comprehensive collection are written by some of the world's most prominent scholars in the field of media, communication and cultural studies, including critical film and television studies. *Relocating Television* aims to describe, analyse and interpret a highly complex process of change. Avoiding the technology fetishism and technological determinism so prevalent in writing about digitization and digital media, each article seeks an understanding of a key element in or aspect of the process. The book in its entirety thus delivers a critical account of the digitisation process as a multifaceted whole.

Relocating Television offers readers an insight into studying television alongside the internet, participatory media and other techno-cultural phenomena such as DVDs, user-generated content and everyday digital media production. It also focuses on more specific programmes and phenomena, including *The Wire*, MSN, amateur footage in TV news, Bollywoodization of TV news, YouTube, fan sites tied to e.g. *Grey's Anatomy* and *The X Factor*. *Relocating Television* will be highly beneficial to both students and academics across a wide range of undergraduate and postgraduate courses including media, communication and cultural studies, and television and film studies.

Jostein Gripsrud is Professor in the Department of Information Science and Media Studies at the University of Bergen, Norway, and leader of the DigiCult research group. He has published extensively in several languages on theatre, popular literature, film history, television, journalism, popular music, media and cultural policy and relevant social and cultural theory for all of these media, genres and cultural forms. Previous publications include *Television and Common Knowledge* (1999), *Understanding Media Culture* (2002), and *Media, Markets and Public Spheres* (co-edited with Lennart Weibull, 2010).

COMEDIA

Series Editor: David Morley

Comedia titles available from Routledge:

RELOCATING TELEVISION

Television in the digital context

Edited by
Jostein Gripsrud

Routledge
Taylor & Francis Group

LONDON AND NEW YORK

First published 2010
by Routledge
2 Park Square, Milton Park, Abingdon, Oxon, OX14 4RN

Simultaneously published in the USA and Canada
by Routledge
771 Third Avenue, New York, NY 10017

Routledge is an imprint of the Taylor & Francis Group, an informa business
Editorial selection and material © 2010 Jostein Gripsrud
Individual chapters © 2010 the Contributors

Typeset in Garamond by Taylor & Francis Books
Printed and bound in Great Britain by the MPG Books Group

British Library Cataloguing in Publication Data
A catalogue record for this book is available from the British Library

Library of Congress Cataloging in Publication Data
Relocating television : television in the digital context / edited by Jostein
Gripsrud.
p. cm. – (Comedia)
Includes index.
Originally presented as papers at a symposium organized by the DigiCult
research group in Paris in collaboration with the Institut Francais de Presse at
the Université de Paris II in October , 2008.
1. Television broadcasting–Technological innovations–Congresses. 2.
Digital television–Congresses. 3. Digital media–Congresses. 4. Television
programs–Social aspects–Congresses. 5. Television broadcasting–Social
aspects–Congresses. 6. Television and politics–Congresses. I. Gripsrud, Jostein,
1952-
PN1992.5.R45 2010
302.23'4–dc22
2009046869

ISBN13: 978-0-415-56452-6 (hbk)
ISBN13: 978-0-415-56453-3 (pbk)
ISBN13: 978-0-203-85137-1 (ebk)

CONTENTS

CONTENTS

TABLES AND FIGURES

Tables

Figures

CONTRIBUTORS

Ib Bondebjerg is a professor in the Department of Media, Cognition and Communication and Director of the Centre for Modern European Studies at the University of Copenhagen, Denmark. He is the editor of *Northern Lights: Film and Media Studies Yearbook* (2000–9) and is on the editorial board of *Studies in Documentary Film*. He is the author of *Film and Modernity: Film Genres and Film Culture in Denmark 1940–1972* (2005, in Danish) and *Narratives of Reality: The History of the Danish TV-Documentary* (2008, in Danish), and the editor of *Moving Images, Culture and the Mind* (2000) and *Media, Democracy and European Culture* (2008).

John Bridge is working on his doctoral dissertation at the University of California, Los Angeles. He is part of the Cinema and Media Studies department.

Nick Browne is Professor and Chair of the Cinema and Media Studies Program and Director of the Moving Image Archive Studies Program at UCLA. He is currently working on the economy of cultural prestige in American cinema.

Charlotte Brunsdon is Professor of Film and Television Studies at the University of Warwick. Her books include *Screen Tastes: Soap Opera to Satellite Dishes* (1997), *The Feminist, the Housewife and the Soap Opera* (2000) and *London in Cinema* (2007).

Christa Lykke Christensen is Associate Professor in the Department of Media, Cognition and Communication at the University of Copenhagen, Denmark. In her book *Visuelle følelser* [Visual Emotions] she examines young people's perception of visual media, discussing the relationship between cognition and emotion. She is head of a network on 'Experts and Expertise' at the University of Copenhagen, and is currently working on a project on lifestyle as TV entertainment. See http://www.media.ku.dk for further information.

John Corner is Visiting Professor in Communication Studies at the University of Leeds and an editor of the journal *Media, Culture and Society*.

Recent work includes a historical study of documentary journalism and *Public Issue Television* (co-authored with Peter Goddard and Kay Richardson, 2007). With colleagues, he has just started a funded research project into the cross-generic mediation of British political culture.

John Ellis is Professor of Media Arts at Royal Holloway, University of London. Between 1982 and 1999 he produced over 100 documentaries for television, mainly for Channel 4 in the UK, through Large Door Productions. He is chair of the British Universities Film & Video Council (http://www.bufvc.ac.uk). He is the author of *TV FAQ* (2007), *Seeing Things* (2000) and *Visible Fictions* (1982), and is writing a book on documentary for publication by Routledge in 2011. A detailed bibliography can be found at: http://www.rhul.ac.uk/media-arts/staff/ellis.shtml.

Barbara Gentikow is Professor in the Department of Information Science and Media Studies at the University of Bergen, Norway. She works principally in the field of media use, including qualitative empirical studies, and has authored books on media literacy and the appropriation of digital television in Norway.

Todd Gitlin is Professor of Journalism and Sociology, and chair of the PhD program in communications, at Columbia University. He has authored a number of publications, including *The Whole World Is Watching*, *Inside Prime Time* and *Media Unlimited*. His next book is *The Chosen Peoples: America, Israel, and the Ordeals of Divine Election* (Simon & Schuster, September 2010), co-authored with Liel Leibovitz.

Peter Golding is Professor of Sociology at Loughborough University, where he was Head of Social Sciences from 1991 to 2006 and Pro-Vice-Chancellor for Research 2006–9. He is an editor of the *European Journal of Communication* and is Honorary Chair of the European Sociological Association Media Research Network. His most recent books are *Researching Communications: A Practical Guide to Methods in Media and Cultural Analysis* and *European Culture and the Media.*

Jostein Gripsrud is Professor in the Department of Information Science and Media Studies at the University of Bergen, Norway, and leader of the DigiCult research group. He has published extensively in several languages on theatre, popular literature, film history, television, journalism, popular music, media and cultural policy and relevant social and cultural theory for all of these media, genres and cultural forms. Previous publications include *Television and Common Knowledge* (1999), *Understanding Media Culture* (2002), and *Media, Markets and Public Spheres* (co-edited with Lennart Weibull, 2010).

Anne Jerslev is Senior Lecturer in the Department of Media, Cognition and Communication at the University of Copenhagen, Denmark. She has published a number of books, most recently *Det er bare film. Om unges videofællesskaber og vold på film* [It's only a movie. Young people's video communities and violence on film] (2000) and *Vi ses på tv. Medier og intimitet* [See you on TV. Media and Intimacy] (2004). Anne has also edited several anthologies in Danish and English, most recently *Performative Realism* together with Rune Gade (2005).

Peter Larsen is a professor in the Department of Information Science and Media Studies, University of Bergen, Norway. He is also the Director of the research project Photography in Culture at the Norwegian Research Council (2003–7). He has published a number of books on textual analysis, semiotics and visual culture, his latest English publication being *Film Music* (2007).

Erlend Lavik is an associate professor at the Department of Information Science and Media Studies at the University of Bergen. He completed his PhD on the relationship between classical and postclassical Hollywood cinema – entitled 'Changing Narratives: Five Essays on Hollywood History' – in 2008.

David Morley is Professor of Communications in the Department of Media and Communications, Goldsmiths College, University of London. His most recent book is *Media, Modernity and Technology: The Geography of the New* (2006).

Graham Murdock is Reader in the Sociology of Culture at Loughborough University. His main interests are in the sociology and political economy of culture. He has written extensively on the organization of the mass-media industries, and on the press and television coverage of terrorism, riots and other political events. His current work is on advertising and on the social impact of new communications technologies.

Helle Sjøvaag is a PhD candidate in the Department of Information Science and Media Studies at the University of Bergen, Norway. Her dissertation investigates changes in the news market as a result of digitalization processes, and the effect this has on journalism as an institution. Central to the work is a combination of social contract theory, structuration theory and gate-keeping theory.

Lynn Spigel is the Frances E. Willard Chair of Screen Cultures at North-western University, USA. Her books include: *TV by Design: Modern Art and the Rise of Network Television* (2009); *Welcome to the Dreamhouse: Popular Media and Postwar Suburbs* (2001) and *Make Room for TV: Television and the Family Ideal in Postwar America* (1992). She has co-edited numerous collections including *Television after TV: Essays on a Medium in Transition* (2004).

Daya Kishan Thussu is Professor of International Communication at the University of Westminster in London. Among his key publications are *Internationalizing Media Studies* (2009); *News as Entertainment: The Rise of Global Infotainment* (2007); *Media on the Move: Global Flow and Contra-Flow* (2007); *International Communication – Continuity and Change*, 2nd edition (2006) and *War and the Media: Reporting Conflict 24/7* (2003). He is the founder and Managing Editor of the journal *Global Media and Communication*.

William Uricchio is Director of the MIT Comparative Media Studies Program and Professor of Comparative Media History at Utrecht University in the Netherlands. He has held visiting professorships at Stockholm University, the Freie Universität Berlin, the University of Science and Technology of China, and Philips Universität Marburg. His most recent books include *Media Cultures* (2006) and *We Europeans? Media, Representations, Identity* (2009). He is currently completing a manuscript on the concept of the televisual from the seventeenth century to the present.

PREFACE

Jostein Gripsrud

The digitization of television concerns the production, contents, distribution and reception of the medium but also its position in the overall, largely digitized media system where the internet now plays an important role. Some prophets of the digital era, such as Nicholas Negroponte, have declared that television is going to die. The personal computer will deliver all mediated public communication. Some have even, in a more utopian vein, claimed that broadcasting in the traditional centralized sense will be replaced by a considerably more egalitarian system of communication where the distinction between production and reception is blurred and participation is the key term.

But there is always a complex pattern of continuity and breaks as new media technologies are born. Television is not going away in the foreseeable future. It will change, however, as it survives in some degree and in a kind of osmosis and symbiosis with the internet and the mobile phone. What goes on is a restructuring of the entire public sphere. Less than ever can television be studied and understood in isolation from its context. This book is about these processes.

Among the authors are some of the world's most prominent scholars in the field of media, communication and cultural studies, including critical film and television studies. All chapters aim to describe, analyse and interpret a highly complex process of change. Avoiding the technology fetishism and technological determinism so prevalent in writing about digitization and digital media, each chapter charts and seeks an understanding of a key element in, or aspect of, the process. The book in its entirety thus delivers a critical account of the digitization process as a multifaceted whole.

The editor is leader of the research group DigiCult at the University of Bergen, Norway, and the chapters in this book were originally presented as papers to a symposium that DigiCult organized in Paris in collaboration with the Institut Français de Presse at the Université de Paris II in October 2008. DigiCult is short for Democracy and the Digitization of Audiovisual Culture. The group has had a diverse dossier of projects, central among them an ambitious theoretical project on the public sphere, but the group has lately concentrated much of its work on issues related to the medium of television. This involves asking questions concerning anything from the impact of digitization on television production and aesthetics to the structure(s) and productive practices of what we used to call audiences; from the analysis of the internet as a 'broadcasting' audio-visual medium to the ties between digitization and cultural globalization; from digitization's consequences for the representation of politics in television and other media to the general implications of the radical changes in the status of photography for the news genre across media.

All of these questions – and more – are dealt with in this book. It is divided into four parts. The first of these, The Medium of Television: Changes and Continuities, contains four chapters that in different ways address major issues relating to digitization as a historical process. The editor presents public-sphere theory as an overarching theoretical perspective on the political, social and cultural role of television, explores the extent to which digitization entails a redefinition of 'broadcast TV', suggests ways in which a relocation of TV in the now largely digital public sphere may be understood, and points to the challenge of increasing class differences with respect to the participation in democratic processes. William Uricchio then offers a very different but largely compatible approach to the question of television's historical role by looking at television as 'time machine', i.e. exploring the changing specificity of television as a medium in terms of its representation of time and history, starting from Raymond Williams' now classic observations and analysis of US TV flow decades ago and ending with television's 'pas de deux' with the internet and the 'participatory turn' as represented by YouTube. John Corner then investigates the status of television in the light of how digitization changes the general conditions of 'public seeing'. His chapter addresses the relationship between television and digital culture through an analysis of digitization's revived public profile of the still image. The photograph's newly expanded ways of setting up relationships of seeing, of brokering between world and subjectivity, of offering space for the contemplative gaze, provide a productive comparison and contrast with traditional televisual modes and offer a way into understanding the broader contexts of audio-visual change. The last chapter in this section is Nick Browne's contribution to a historical shift in the tradition of textual analysis in film, television and media studies. His chapter is a 'close reading' of the homepage of Microsoft Nation, MSN, and treats the internet as an audio-visual medium and showing what the historical process called 'convergence' may be about in practice. The analysis is about the design, significance and function of this one page, starting with a simple formal analysis of just a few elements: shape, dimension, colour and layout, and ending up with the multimedia character of this particular page – including its direct link to the cable channel MSNBC and from that to television, the media in general and the social system at large.

The book's second section, Changing Genres, follows up on Browne's textual analysis and comprises six chapters that deal with genres and particular programme texts that are important ingredients in what today's digital channels offer their audiences. Together they show the intricate interplay between change and stability, and between technological, financial and cultural factors in the development of actual programme material. Using three instances of television police/crime drama, Charlotte Brunsdon deals with the question of how television critics should write about television in the age of digital availability – not least in the age of watching television series by way of DVD box-sets. While it is hard to determine a satisfactory answer at a general level, the chapter indicates some necessary considerations about critical contexts and modes of viewing through a discussion of its specific examples: *The Wire* (HBO 2002–7) and *Law and order* (BBC 1978). Erlend Lavik then takes a closer look at *The Wire* from a different angle. He starts out from the observation that the relationship between technology and aesthetics has been a key area of study for film and television scholars, especially since the breakthrough of digital technologies in the early nineties. The emergence of the DVD format, internet forums and non-linear editing equipment is commonly considered to underlie important recent developments such as narrative complexity and the so-called MTV style. Still, Lavik points out, *The Wire*, the critically acclaimed television series that is arguably the most innovative of all, enjoys a curiously conflicted and contradictory relationship with these fashionable tendencies. Lavik argues that the show's originality in certain respects might paradoxically be seen to stem from a return to rather old-fashioned narrational and stylistic conventions. In other words, digitization does not necessarily change everything.

Daya K. Thussu's chapter is, on the other hand, about very clearly observable changes in quite another genre: news. But the changes are only indirectly tied to digitization, by way of increased competition between a rapidly increased number of channels and forms of convergence related to concentration of capital: India has more than 40 dedicated news channels, and so India has one of the world's most competitive broadcast-news markets. The chapter maps the tendency among news networks to veer towards infotainment, partly as a result of newly emerging synergies between entertainment conglomerates – both national and global – and news networks. This 'Bollywoodization' of TV news, the chapter argues, is transforming the public sphere in the world's largest democracy. Helle Sjøvaag and John Bridge then examine a highly significant global trend in the production of news: the increasing use of amateurs' photos or footage in newscasts – the ubiquity of digital cameras turns ordinary people into reporters for broadcast media. The assassination of Benazir Bhutto on 27 December 2007 was a major event that prompted heavy media coverage across the world. Bridge and Sjøvaag analyse how established news media (CNN and NBC in the US; NRK and TV 2 in Norway) used amateur footage of the assassination in its reporting. The editing of such footage into the news and the discursive variations by which newscasters introduce, contextualize, and explain events through the amateur lens can help reveal how professional news organizations relate to the increasing flood of amateur footage in the news.

Moving us to a related genre, Ib Bondebjerg discusses how recent journalism and documentary formats show interesting trends towards new players and hybrid forms. His chapter takes a closer look at new online media in some of their typical forms and asks what democratic developments and new voices and genres might be expected from them – if any. The chapter argues against both extreme pessimism and extreme optimism, opting instead for a pragmatic look at the new media environment as a place for new forms but within an already existing social, cultural and economic framework. Online media and user-driven factual and documentary content and formats do not in and of themselves lead to a radically new media democracy – but they open up both new spaces and new conflicts.

Christa Lykke Christensen's contribution then starts from the fact that in the digital era, i.e. since the late 1990s, lifestyle programmes have dominated early prime time in several countries' public-service channels. Programmes about house, garden, vacation, fashion, body, health and pets intend to inform, advise and entertain. Christensen looks at different categories of lifestyle programmes, primarily focusing on dimensions of entertainment and the motivation for watching: competence, daydreaming, wishes for change. She also points out how public-service broadcasting has supplemented its educational function with a function of *updating*, and how the previous cultural educative function has changed with lifestyle programming in that such programming has a more instrumental character: it may serve as a manual and a guide to market-related lifestyles – supported by webpages on the internet.

The interplay between television and the internet is a key topic in the book's third section, Reception: Figures, Experience, Significance. Barbara Gentikow addresses this issue by investigating to what extent the uses and understandings of television change in households that also have computers hooked up to the internet. Drawing not least on three empirical studies she conducted in Norway between 2004 and 2007, Gentikow shows that the radical consequences of digitization predicted by some were not easy to find – continuities from pre-digital times seem to be at least as important as changes. What has changed, however, is, as was touched upon for example in Christensen's piece on lifestyle programmes, the kind of support a particular TV programme can get from other media: the internet really makes a difference here. In Peter Larsen's chapter, 'The grey area', the focus is on the multitude of internet discussion arenas that have emerged during the last decade, from the early Usenet groups and email lists to the current chat groups, blogs, boards and other forms of internet publishing. These are compared to the 'discussion groups' that were an essential part of the 'classical' cultural public sphere. During the late 1990s most television networks and channels established internet sites devoted to major shows. In addition to these 'official' sites, a few eager fans of a given show would create their own sites. Today the official sites are elaborate constructions, and the fan sites have changed correspondingly into complex discussion arenas. Larsen's chapter gives an overview of one such discursive universe: the one that has ABC's prime-time drama *Grey's Anatomy* as its centre. Anne Jerslev then follows with an analysis of the debate on Danish public-service television's site for the Danish version of the internationally successful show format *X Factor*. It was a large debate site, but still only one of the hundreds of sites where the show was discussed. The degree of viewer commitment is striking. As in other internet discussions, there is an abundance of exclamation marks and capital letters through which writers communicate strong affects. It is as if writers are primarily eager to raise their own voice and let go. Debates marked by strong disagreement may support feelings of relatedness to a programme but, as this analysis shows, the creation of loyal viewers is no uncomplicated task.

Viewer commitment of quite a different kind is the topic of John Ellis' contribution 'The digitally enhanced audience: new attitudes to factual footage'. It starts from an observation that was also central to John Corner's and Bridge/Sjøvaag's chapters – that digital technologies have made the production of recorded images a routine experience for people who used mainly to be their consumers. Ellis argues that this has changed the general cultural understanding of moving images, and then deals with the consequences in terms of viewers' reactions to images of distant suffering. There exists a continuum between a mundane sofa interview on a light topic on breakfast TV and massacre footage. In each case the footage is interrogated in almost the same instant as it is felt. Televisual witness involves a complex to and fro between seeing, believing and feeling in today's active, knowledgeable viewers. The compassion and pity experienced, most of the time, on witnessing traumatic footage should, therefore, be considered as subsets of a more general emotional process: the process of empathy.

The issue of digital media's impact on the public and on public discourse is dealt with in a different manner in Todd Gitlin's contribution, 'Digital media, television and the discourse of smears', which can be said to explore the relationship between the phenomenology of digital media and the experience of politics. The author opens the chapter by raising the issue of the degree to which screened media in the digital age represent a break with previous developments in media culture – and, specifically, American media culture – or whether what digital media do is rather to continue along the same lines, only faster. He then goes on to take a closer look at incidents in the last presidential campaign, in which the internet – by way of television – became an important source and channel for the smearing of candidates.

While also referring to historical evidence of smearing in US politics, Gitlin argues that digital media are particularly well suited for 'a discourse of insinuation and falsehood', since they 'specialize in the production of impressions' which 'circulate easily'. This is now simply part of the reality in which politics is played out these days. The problem is not the technology, it is about morality.

Peter Golding's chapter 'The cost of citizenship in the digital age' opens the fourth and final section, Critical Perspectives. Golding assesses the implications of digitization for democracy, especially for the capacity for citizens to participate as informed and therefore autonomous in democratic processes. The major themes addressed are the changing contribution of television to political communication with growing digital provision; the fragmentation of the market for media outputs; the commoditization of information and its impact on citizenship, a theme moving beyond the media to other cultural spheres; the growing prominence of 'culpability' as an organizing principle for the transmission of news about public affairs; and the continuing salience of the 'digital divide' despite constant attempts to dismiss it both analytically and politically.

Graham Murdock takes a compatible but quite different point of view in his 'Networking the commons: convergence culture and the public interest', which suggests a way to make use of the positive possibilities of the digital era. Arguing for the political importance of cultural expression, Murdock analytically describes the ways in which the internet's 'gift economy' or culture of sharing has increasingly been exploited and colonized in ever-new ways by commercial forces. While criticizing, for instance, Henry Jenkins for naïvely celebrating the new ways in which cultural industries relate to their customers, audiences and fans, Murdock goes on to argue that – and describe how – public-service broadcasting (at least in Europe) can play a central role in the building of an alternative and counterweight to the commercialization of public culture.

Lynn Spigel presents a very different, more broadly sociological take on digitization's social implications in her chapter 'Smart homes: digital lifestyles practiced and imagined'. Whereas Thorstein Veblen in 1899 famously argued that the Victorian bourgeoisie were obsessed with 'conspicuous consumption' (or the desire to display their wealth and leisure), Spigel argues that twentieth-century ideals of middle-class life stress the need for residents to be seen working all the time – even when, for example, watching TV or listening to music. Her chapter explores how television, music and web-access are networked together in contemporary designs for residential smart homes (or homes designed around internet connectivity) which function as vessels for current ideals of work, play and gender in post-feminist, post-industrial culture. Looking at designs for home offices, media rooms and smart kitchens, she argues that smart homes are based on 'conspicuous production'.

The book's final chapter, David Morley's 'Television as a means of transport: digital technologies and transmodal systems' then takes theoretical reflection on the process of digitization one or several steps further out into the social landscape surrounding television and the media in general. It concerns ideas of digitization, de-territorialization, the disembedding of social life from material space, time–space compression and the much advertised 'death of geography'. It relates these matters to the presumed role of technology in globalization and to current theorizations of the changing relations of the virtual and the actual. These issues are exemplified in relation to a BBC News project designed to generate stories about the global economy by monitoring the progress of a container box with a GPS transmitter attached to it as it is shipped around the world. In this context, the chapter also argues for a reconsideration of the relations of communications/media and transport studies!

As should be evident from this overview of its contents, this book covers a lot of ground, theoretically as well as empirically, and suggests a plurality of approaches and perspectives on the phenomena under scrutiny. One might say it raises a lot of questions. That is an important quality in itself. But it also suggests some answers, makes some distinctions and formulates critiques of previous work. The editor is of the opinion that the book's brilliant and hard-working contributors have made this a landmark collection in the study of television in the digital era – and hopes that readers will agree.

Part I

THE MEDIUM OF TELEVISION
Changes and continuities

1

TELEVISION IN THE DIGITAL PUBLIC SPHERE

Jostein Gripsrud

Introduction

The digitization of media and communication is part of the digitization of society, i.e. the introduction of digital technology in all parts and sectors of society, from global stock markets to local health care. It is a very complex process which affects all levels and parts of the industries, institutions, arenas and actors that sustain public life in democratic societies, as well as the everyday lives and living conditions of all. The consequences are bewilderingly diverse and difficult to describe and understand in a comprehensive way – as once demonstrated by Manuel Castells (1996).

The digitization of television is of special importance. Television was the central element in the media-based public sphere in the last half of the twentieth century. It gathered by far the largest audience; it was the medium that all other forms of public communication had to relate to. Television was the key link between society's public life and the private lives of citizens. Peter Dahlgren has talked about an 'integration of television and political culture' and claimed that 'to a significant extent, the official political system exists as a televisual phenomenon' (Dahlgren 1995: 45). If digitization radically changes television, then the political, social and cultural features of our societies are undergoing changes of considerable importance. This chapter and this entire book are intended as material for further reflection on the issue.

The metaphor of a 'relocation' of television assumes a spatial way of thinking, and the metaphorical space thus indirectly referred to in the book's title is that which is now commonly referred to as the public sphere. In the following, I will first try to sketch the historical development of the public sphere and show why and how it is important to the understanding of the socio-cultural role of television (and other media) and its destiny in digital times. I will then try to define key terms such as 'broadcasting' and 'television' in order to say something about broadcast television's position and characteristics in a digitized public sphere. I discuss features such as inter-activity and TV's relations with the internet, before going into how the structure of the public sphere changes as the internet and the multitudes of channels in digital television establish new possibilities for various kinds of minorities. Finally, I attempt to conclude – and point to the issue of social class and a 'digital divide' along the lines of class divisions as a major con-cern in the era of a digitized public sphere.

The public sphere

In historical terms, Jürgen Habermas defined the public sphere, a key element in modern democracy, as follows:

> The bourgeois public sphere may be conceived above all as the sphere of private people come together as a public; they soon claimed the public sphere regulated from above against the auth-orities themselves, to engage them in a debate over the general rules governing relations in the basically privatized but publicly relevant sphere of commodity exchange and social labor. The medium of this political confrontation was peculiar and without historical pre-cedent: people's public use of their reason (*öffentliches Räsonnement*).
>
> (Habermas [1962]1989: 27)

The empirical version of the 'classic' bourgeois public sphere from around 1750 onwards was not least characterized by there being few participants. The three criteria for full participation were male gender, property and education in the sense of *Bildung*. Women, servants and certain other people considered to be of a lower class could participate to some extent in the cultural or literary part of the public sphere if they were literate, but they were not allowed entry into the political public sphere. The establishment of public school systems, the spread of literacy, the growth of industries and the emergence of organizations characteristic of industrial capitalism greatly increased the number of participants. The introduction of universal suffrage marks the transition to a democratic society where all adults are recognized as, in principle, autonomous equals.

But this reform was also part of the public sphere's structural change – what Habermas called its 're-feudalisation'. First, it was invaded by orga-nized movements based in the (private) economic sphere (organizations for labour and capital that openly declared they defended certain interests instead of debating the common good). The political outcome of that was, in Europe and elsewhere, a welfare state which interfered much more directly in the private realm. So the public sphere was squeezed between this active state and the forces based in the economic sphere. It became a space for the proclamation of truths and decisions arrived at behind closed doors (as in feudal societies) instead of being a space where truths and decisions emerged from open deliberation. With the development of mass media as commercial enterprises driven more by financial interests than convictions, public life turned into staged entertainment. Citizens largely stopped being participants. Instead they became consumers of the spectacles organized by media and the political establishment.

This gloomy diagnosis was not quite adequate, as Habermas himself later conceded (Habermas 1992). Another problem with Habermas' 1962 version of public-sphere theory was its emphasis on the unity of the public sphere. From the beginning there was not only the differentiation between a political and a cultural ('literary') public sphere. While the government, the parliamentary assembly and institutions such as national theatres continued to constitute central arenas in the public sphere, industrialization brought a new social complexity. Multitudes of new informal social spaces and formalized organizations constituted a new, similarly multifarious set of public spheres with genres of discourse ranging from drama and poetry to educational prose and political propaganda. Some of these would qualify as what Nancy Fraser has called 'subaltern counterpublics', i.e. 'parallel discursive arenas where members of subordinated social groups invent and circulate counterdiscourses to formulate oppositional interpretations of the identities, interests and needs' (Fraser 1992: 123). To the extent that their participants or members were historically excluded from full participation in the central political and/or cultural public sphere, through suffrage laws in the political and sheer social prejudice in the cultural realm, these counterpublics would often tend to regard themselves as training camps and waiting rooms for aspiring future participants in the 'proper', national public sphere (cf. Gripsrud 1981 and 1997).

The general public sphere still has a politically central arena, at the centre of which one finds what Fraser (1992: 134) calls 'strong publics', i.e. 'publics whose discourse encompasses both opinion formation and decision making', such as sovereign parliaments and the Supreme Court. These are few, and have few participants. The 'weak publics' (ibid.) that are 'only' involved in the formation of a public opinion that may influence the strong publics, are innumerable and have all citizens as participants. The structure of the public sphere is now described by Habermas (1996) as a complex network that 'branches out into a multitude of overlapping international, national, regional, local, and sub cultural arenas' (1996: 373), exemplified by public spheres within popular sciences, religion, art and literature, feminism and other 'alternative' political orientations. Parts of the mass media operate close to the strong publics, but for the most part they belong in what Habermas likes to call the 'wild' part of the public sphere: 'At the periphery of the political system, the public sphere is rooted in networks for wild flows of messages – news, reports, commentaries, talks, scenes and images, and shows and movies with an informative, polemical, educational, or entertaining content' (Habermas 2006: 415). The public sphere is further differentiated into different levels based on the 'density' of communication, and the complexity and scope of organization – 'from the episodic publics found in taverns, coffee houses, or on the streets; through the occasional "arranged" publics of particular presentations and events, such as theatre performances, rock concerts, party assemblies, or church congresses; up to the abstract public sphere of isolated readers, listeners, and viewers scattered across large geographic areas, or even around the globe, and brought together only through the mass media' (1996: 374). All of these public spheres remain 'porous' in their relation to one another, and so discourses circulate even if they also are changed in accordance with shifting contexts.

Digitization adds considerably to this complexity by offering plentiful opportunities for further differentiation between special interest groups and an endless number of minorities (we all belong to some). On this background we might ask: What is the role of broadcasting?

Broadcasting, modernization and democracy

In his *Television: Technology and Cultural Form* (1975) Raymond Williams argues that broadcasting media arrived at a time when political and economic power and resources were concentrated and centralized more than ever before, while on the other hand the population at large was marked by modernization processes Williams summed up in the term *mobile privatisation*. Mobility was

> only in part the impulse of an independent curiosity: the wish to go out and see new places. It was essentially an impulse formed in the breakdown and dissolution of older and smaller kinds of settlements and productive labour. The new and larger settlements and industrial organisations required major internal mobility, at a primary level, and this was joined by secondary consequences in the dispersal of extended families and in the needs of new kinds of social organisation.
>
> (Williams 1975: 26)

People were experiencing dissolution of older, more stable communities and a much higher degree of both social and geographical mobility. They were increasingly living in nuclear families or as singles, without strong ties to their neighbourhoods, more closed-off in relation to their surroundings, i.e. more private, in 'the apparently self-sufficient family home' (Williams 1975).

Broadcasting appeared as a communication technology perfectly suited to this sort of society, at a time when class cleavages and class struggle were very pronounced features. According to Williams, it was 'a new and powerful form of social integration and control' (1975: 23). It could secure the communication of socially essential information from the centre to the periphery while also producing a common socio-cultural identity in nation states, an 'imagined community' (Anderson [1983]1991) based in shared experiences that were also more simultaneous than the experience of news-papers had been, even if they were also doing the same thing: 'Day in day out radio, television and newspapers link these two incommensurate human temporalities: the historical life of societies and the lifetimes of individuals' (Scannell 2000: 21). Thus broadcasting also, and not least, produced the cultural conditions for a civic culture, i.e. semiotic and emotional conditions for citizens' active, informed participation in democratic processes. In other words, as I have argued elsewhere (Gripsrud 1998), broadcasting was not just about top-down control and ideological manipulation. It was also a socio-cultural form suitable for democracy, i.e. for the benefit of citizens as much as for Government or Capital.

A brief analysis of the meanings of the word 'broadcasting' is useful here. It clearly reflects a centre–periphery structure. It originally meant sowing by hand, in the widest possible (half) circles. But 'broadcasting' is thus as a metaphor also tied to optimistic modernism. It is about an effort to produce growth in the widest possible circles, the production, if the conditions are right, of a rich harvest. The metaphor presupposes a bucket of seeds, i.e. the existence of centralized resources intended and suited for spreading. In the formulation of broadcasting policies between the World Wars, the interest in broadcasting as a means of securing equal access to resources necessary for informed and therefore autonomous participation in political, social and cultural life played a very important role in many countries. It underlies the formula of the first Director General of the BBC, Sir John Reith, for the BBC's mission – 'to inform, educate and entertain', and we find some of the same in the US, for instance in the 1927 Radio Act, which was to regulate the Federal Radio Commission's allocation of frequencies. It contained a formulation which has lived on: all broadcasters must operate in accordance with 'the public interest, convenience, and necessity'. The phrase was elaborated on by the commission in a 1928 statement, in which it was said that

> broadcasters are not given these great privileges by the United States Government for the primary benefit of advertisers. Such benefit as is derived by advertisers must be incidental and entirely secondary to the interest of the public ... the emphasis must be on the interest, the convenience, and the necessity of the listening public, and not on the interest, convenience or necessity of the individual broad-caster or advertiser.
>
> (Hoynes 1994: 38)

In other words, the democratic potential of broadcasting was also perceived from the beginning in the US. An explanation of why something in the way

7

of European-style public-service broadcasting never happened in the US would not be about the idea being so strange. It would rather be about cultural reasons for resisting the model – and class reasons: the distribution of social and political power.

A critique of broadcasting as a top-down socio-cultural integration in service of the ruling powers is related to a critique which takes for granted that two-way communication, dialogue, is more democratic than a basically one-way form such as broadcasting (for important modifications of its monologue nature, see the section on interactive TV below). But as argued by John Durham Peters in his *Speaking into the Air* (1999), it is not necessarily so: broadcasting (along with other 'one-way' forms of mass communication) is about dissemination, about speaking 'into the air', aiming for anyone and no one in particular, like Jesus: 'The practice of the sower is wasteful. He lets the seeds fall where they may, not knowing in advance who will be receptive ground, leaving the crucial matter of choice and interpretation to the hearer, not the master ... ' (Peters 1999: 5). Broadcasting thus allows a freedom for its public which strictly 'dialogical' forms of communication deny. Moreover, they address people in a certain way. Their schedules and programme output are constructed so that they 'appear to speak to each one of us personally ... and yet, at the same time, are available in the same way to anyone who cares to watch or listen' (Scannell 2000: 22).

The democratic potential of broadcasting is enhanced when it operates as a public service, and diminishes with its degree of commercialization. This has been argued or regarded as an a priori fact in a large number of scholarly publications over the last few decades (e.g. Garnham 1983; Murdock 2005). But it has recently also been argued on the basis of hard data from a large-scale, comparative study of media and broadcasting systems in four different countries – the US, the UK, Denmark and Finland (Curran et al. 2009). The study convincingly shows that (1) the overall levels of public knowledge are higher and (2) the difference in knowledge between people with different levels of education is very significantly smaller in countries where public-service broadcasting is quite strictly regulated and not funded by advertising (Finland and Denmark) than in countries with very lax regulation of commercial forces in broadcasting (US – the UK is placed in an intermediary position).

Defining 'broadcast television'

If we are now to understand what happens to television in digital times, we need to decide what it is. We need, not least, a working definition of *broadcast* television, the classic form of television associated with public-service institutions in Europe and the networks in the US.

In current US media studies, 'broadcast television' seems most often to denote over-the-air, terrestrial television, while cable and satellite TV is not counted as broadcasting (cf. for instance Banet-Weiser et al. 2007; Lotz 2007). While this may be in line with US industry terminology, it makes less sense when considering the fact that many or most people in a number of countries actually watch broadcast television via satellite and/or cable. Some American film and television scholars, therefore, go against the main trend these days and claim that 'broadcast TV' stands for network programming, whichever technology delivers it:

> Network programming can be received over the air, by cable, by satellite etc. It is a term indifferent to technological specification. It can be either analog or digital.
>
> (Nick Browne, personal communication, 21 September 2001)

So for the US case, broadcast television refers to a type of programming and to a distribution structure that at the outset reached major segments of the US audience by means of local, affiliated stations.

I, for my part, very much agree that broadcasting cannot be defined by the technology of distribution, what is known as the 'channel' in traditional mass-communication models. Neither is it defined by the platform on which it is listened to and/or watched, where 'platform' means 'the technology which allows the viewer to receive electronic content' (Griffiths 2003: 57), i.e. computers, mobile phones, PAs, flat-screen TVs or whatever. Broadcast TV can be watched on all of these.

Broadcasting is instead, as suggested by Williams, a cultural form where audio-visual material is disseminated (cf. above) in a continuous, sequential form – a flow – from some central unit to a varying number of anonymous people who receive the same material at the same time – or, with the time zones in the US, PVRs, etc. in mind: roughly the same time. In other words, broadcasting is a 'push'-type form of communication, not a 'pull': it does not deliver discrete items on demand to specific individual subscribers when they order them. The fact that there is now machinery available – DVRs – that can make broadcast material available to viewers as discrete items at any given time is an important development – but the items in question were transmitted and received (by the DVR) as broadcasts.

Consequently, when I watch digital BBC television delivered through old French telephone wires and my internet router, it is still broadcast television. On the other hand, I can, instead of pushing the TV button, push the VOD button on my remote control and order movies and TV shows whenever I like. My present system (Orange, France) delivers these items immediately and allows me to watch them as many times as I like for 24 hours. I am then not watching television. I enjoy the digital version of watching a rented videocassette.[1] This distinction between television and VOD services is in line with the 2007 European Union directive concerning 'Audiovisual Services' – a directive that replaced the previous 'Television Without

Frontiers' directive of 1989 and 1997: the new directive distinguishes, within the new category of 'audiovisual services', which was created to be independent of the method of broadcasting, between 'linear services, which are traditional television services, the Internet and mobile telephone services, which "push" content to viewers, and non-linear services, i.e. on-demand television, where viewers "pull" content from a network ("video-on-demand", for example)'.[2]

The TV set has long since become a multipurpose screen for audio-visual texts – first we had VCRs and video cameras, now also DVD players, gaming machinery, computers and more. We could perhaps propose to change its name to, for instance, 'the AV set' – 'I just turned on the AV' – but such renaming is rarely feasible. The box will be called TV for the foreseeable future, and so the television function of the screen is in a sense privileged for historical reasons.

Furthermore: television means 'seeing at a distance'. The idea of live transmissions of sound and moving images from public events to people's homes was fundamental to early visions of the medium as well as the early experience of it (see Gripsrud 1998). It is still a distinct, if only partial, feature of any terrestrial, broadcast television channel. In principle, then, any technology that allows for seeing what is taking place simultaneously at some other location can be called television. There was person-to-person television available as DIY sets well before the Second World War (Allen 1983: 114f) – the present equivalent would be webcam conversations. For about the same number of years there has also been closed-circuit TV of various kinds, such as surveillance systems. These forms share the capacity for liveness with broadcast television. They are, however, not broadcasting – their 'audiences' are highly specific, and they do not have any schedule.

This does not mean that TV channels only qualify as such if they exclusively contain live programming. It means that they have a potential for this. All traditional PSB and US network channels are thus television channels, since their coverage of news, sports, special events, etc. is regularly transmitted live. But it is also possible to say that television more generally relies on a watered-down notion of simultaneity that John Ellis has called 'currency', i.e. a form of near or imitated simultaneity which is more general:

> [D]irect address is still a basic component of the repertoire of TV presenters, and comprises not just the adoption of a person-to-person intimacy, but also the assumption that the presenter and the audience occupy the same moment in time. Words like 'we', 'now', 'here', 'in a moment', 'today', 'this week' are routinely used to indicate this co-presence between TV show and audience. This relationship is no longer one of literal co-presence as shows are routinely taped before the transmission time and edited to provide

pace and eliminate errors. Co-presence has developed into a sense of currency. TV shows may not be live, but they are current. They explicitly claim to belong to the same historical moment that their audiences are living. TV programmes are temporarily meaningful, designed to be understood by their contemporary audiences, which is why old TV looks so odd, and resists nostalgia ...

(Ellis 2007: 154)

In other words, TV channels address their audiences, even when airing pre-recorded material, in ways that imitate liveness, e.g. in all the instances of direct address both inside and between programmes. References are constantly made to the current socio-cultural situation and to current events or issues. Since viewers in addition also bring the assumption of liveness with them from their watching traditional television on the same piece of hardware, even channels that never go live, such as Discovery or Animal Planet, might well be experienced as imbued with television's characteristic liveness. One could imagine a new term applied to them – 'broadcast video channels' – but the borderlines between the categories are in practice too unclear for such a distinction to be practical.

A subscription channel such as HBO in the US will, as I understand it, now and again carry live 'events' programming. It might be argued, however, that HBO is not a broadcast channel, since it requires a specific subscription. They know quite precisely who (names and addresses) and what sort of people (educated, middle-class, more or less well-to-do) form their audience. But it is available to anyone who is able and willing to pay a certain sum for it. Access is not restricted to certain ethnicities, hair colours or people with a password and a username. The same goes for access to channels such as Discovery, Animal Planet, the History Channel, which, as a rule, are bought as part of larger 'packages' of channels from cable, satellite or internet suppliers. They also distribute their contents as flow, i.e. sequentially according to a schedule viewers cannot influence directly. Thus, if the principle of broadcasting, and the key feature of television, is interpreted generously, all these channels with scheduled 'push' programming may be seen as broadcast television, even if they differ in terms of the liveness (television) and dissemination (broadcasting) principles.

Diversity vs. fragmentation

Digital channels take up much less space than analogue ones and so, consequently, there is room for many more channels within the spectrum – even if it is decided by governments or regulators that there should also be room for quite a few of the much more demanding high-definition channels and/or interactive services. In addition, one might say that the multichannel systems of broadcast radio and television are doubled, since all these channels are now also available on the internet, along with a lot of additional material of various kinds, older programming via on-demand services, etc.

The enormous growth in the number of television channels, in conjunction with the endlessly diverse sites and uses of the internet, has already diminished the average audience size of the traditional broadcast television channels. This means that the attention-drawing power of these central elements in the mediated public sphere is weaker. It does not at all, however, mean that it has completely disappeared (see below). For the functioning of the public sphere and democracy, it is also important that these developments radically expand the possibilities for specialized public spheres, both political and cultural. Furthermore, digital recording and distribution technologies advance both new genres of expression and new channels for communication between citizens, in part across national borders, and between citizens and decision-makers. Individuals and groups now probably have better chances than ever both for developing their group identities as subaltern counterpublics and for talking back to authorities and institutions of power. And, importantly, digitization and the internet in particular enrich the everyday life of those who have access, enable forms of escape from local and national parochialism, and thus set the mobile individual freer than s/he has ever been in the history of modernity. Consequently, there are many reasons for optimism and we shall return to some of them later.

But there is also a pessimistic view, which is that the internet and a digitized TV/radio system radically increase not primarily a positive diversity but rather a destructive fragmentation of the public. The fear of fragmentation frequently voiced by media and communication scholars and other intellectuals is sometimes clearly related to old fears of modern society 'falling apart' or becoming 'atomized', not least as an effect of the expansion of mass media (cf. Gourd 2002: 257f). The notion of 'mass society' that developed in the late nineteenth century was one in which atomized (mobile and privatized) masses were more easily manipulated by ruthless, anti-democratic forces – and Hitler's success suggested these fears were not entirely unfounded. The more recent worries over the consequences of digitization are, as a rule, somewhat less drastic, but also well worth taking seriously. Here are Todd Gitlin's 1998 formulations on the public sphere in the era of the World Wide Web:

> Does it not look as if the public sphere, in falling, had shattered into a scatter of globules, like mercury? The diffusion of interactive technology surely enriches the possibilities for a plurality of publics – for the development of distinct groups organized around affinity and interest. What is not clear is that the proliferation and lubrication of publics contributes to the creation of a public – an active democratic encounter of citizens who reach across their social and ideological

differences to establish a common agenda of concern and to debate rival approaches.

(Gitlin 1998: 173)

Cass Sunstein, philosopher of law, has in his *Republic.com* (2001) and *Republic.com 2.0* (2007) elaborated on these worries and presented a dystopian vision of the public being divided into narrowly defined special interest groups communicating exclusively within themselves, avoiding counter-arguments and thus, according to research in social psychology that Sunstein refers to, moving in an extremist direction.

If this were the case, it would not just increase the possibilities for clashes between extremist groups and other violent events. It would also mean that the possibility for building a strong public opinion which can really have an effect on will-formation and decision-making in the political centre is reduced. Most importantly, perhaps, it might lead to an erosion of a common ground for debate. The radically diversified digital media system might be one where specific groups' chances for self-presentation increase – while the chances that other groups are presented to them are reduced (Gourd 2002: 251). General debates, involving most or all people in some way, may become much more difficult to achieve. In fact, 2009's debate over health care in the US may serve as an illustration (cf. Garber 2009): groups get their information from radically different and often dubious sources so there is little common ground for debate. Mutual distrust is widespread and the same can be said of ignorance about the subject matter of the debate. Furthermore, the central political system may well lose much of its legitimacy and stability if it is perceived as being without basis in some shared, comprehensive public sphere (Gourd 2002: 257).

Even if no progress is achieved without loss, many would say this price is too high. There is a need for some sort of central stage, if only a circus-like system of multiple rings, to make the public sphere, and thus democracy, work. The question is how to achieve something like that – and in what form. What would be broadcast television's place in it?

The end of broadcast television?

Prophets mesmerized by digital information and communication technologies and their possibilities have for over 15 years proclaimed that the end of broadcast television is imminent. The most drastic of visions were about the total disappearance of television, such as this one by right-wing 'techno-utopian intellectual' (according to Wikipedia) George Gilder (1993):

> The computer industry is converging with the television industry in the same sense that the automobile converged with the horse, the TV with the nickelodeon, the wordprocessing program with the

typewriter, the computer-aided design program with the drafting board and digital desktop publishing with the Linotype machine and the letterpress.

Such a view is simply uninformed. It is contradicted by all the experience we so far have about how media systems (and the arts) adjust to arrivals of newcomers. Photography was not the end of painting; neither theatre nor books were replaced by the movies; radio was not killed by television. For that matter, the electric guitar did not kill the acoustic version, it promoted it.

But there have also been other, related but slightly more sophisticated, prophecies. 'The idea that ten years from now people are going to be comfortable sitting in front of a television set – my instinct and our focus groups tell me they're not', Senior Vice President of NBC Interactive Bon Meyers said to reporters in 1996. 'My little focus group at home sure isn't – they expect a TV to act like a PC', he continued, in an interview entitled 'The end of TV as we know it. Forget HDTV. Forget interactive television. Forget the 500-channel universe. Instead start thinking PCTV' (Rose and Brown 1996). This vision was directly inspired by the once-leading digital prophet in the US, the founder of MIT's Media Lab, Nicholas Negroponte, who predicted the complete downfall of broadcast networks in favour of narrowcasting and totally individualized choices – to be enjoyed on PCs. In *Wired* 1.01. of March/April 1993, he wrote the following:

> As intelligence in the television system moves from the transmitter to the receiver, the difference between a TV and a personal computer will become negligible. It can be argued that today's TV set is, per cubic inch, the dumbest appliance in your home. As the television's intelligence increases, it will begin to select video and receive signals in 'unreal time'. For instance, an hour's worth of video – based on a consumer's profile or request – could be delivered over fibre to an intelligent TV in less than five seconds. All personal computer vendors are adding video capabilities, thereby creating the de facto TV set of the future.
>
> (Negroponte 1993)

While Negroponte here correctly foresees the development of TiVo and other PVR varieties, and while it is true that millions of people these days now and then watch television on their computer screens, his core idea that the personal computer will become the TV set of the future is wrong. He did not foresee that the US in 2006 would be the world leader in the spread of HDTV sets, with 10 per cent of households having bought this equipment.[3] He, more generally, did not foresee the explosive sales of large, flat-screen TV sets that are used for broadcast TV, digital games and watching DVDs – but *not* for banking, ordering pizzas or airline tickets, or emails. In short, the TV set has become a multipurpose screen, but it is extremely rare to use it as a screen for services specifically associated with the internet. People maintain a division between labour and leisure in the uses of TV and the PC so that TV is exclusively associated with leisure, while the PC is also associated with work or work-like personal activities (see also Barbara Gentikow's contribution in this volume).

This is one important reason why several studies, at least in Europe, show that the rapidly increasing use of computers and the internet has not lead to a reduction in the total time spent on television. In fact, the tendency is rather the opposite, at least in some countries: Norwegians have never watched more television per day than now, even if Norway is also very near the world top in terms of the distribution of broadband connections, home computers, internet activity and, for example, Facebook membership. The average Norwegian's viewing of television on an average day was up roughly half an hour from the mid nineties to the middle of the following decade, and the average viewing time on an average day among those who were actually watching TV went up almost 40 minutes and hit 3 hours for the first time in 2006. (The same year, people in Japan and the US were averaging 4.5 hours, while the figure was 3.5 hours a day for the UK, and only 2.5 in Sweden.)[4] At the same time, from 2000 to 2006, the average use of the internet per person in Norway, on an average day, rose from 18 minutes to almost an hour, and from almost an hour to one and a half hours if you exclude those who never used the internet. And this is in a country where 79 per cent of the population had internet access from their homes in 2006, when 63 per cent had a broadband connection at home – compared to just over 50 per cent with broadband at the end of 2006 in the UK[5] and an official 50.8 per cent in the US in October 2007.[6]

It seems evident, then, that increased use of the internet, and a growing number of households getting a broadband connection, does not necessarily lead to a reduction in the viewing of broadcast TV – provided it offers something worth watching. But the internet is increasingly important as an arena in the public sphere (see below) even if it also seems as if its significance depends on whether its sites and activities are registered and highlighted by the traditional media – especially television. In the US, an extremely diverse, large population, used to multitudes of TV channels for decades, is now also offered myriads of 'public sphericules' on the internet. Still, even if the internet was of great importance, television played the key role in the 2008 election campaign by constructing and providing overview and distributing attention to some web activities and not to others. Television's continued centrality is also indicated by, for instance, Barack Obama's appearances, at a time when he needed to address directly as many citizens as possible about his promised health reform, on five Sunday-morning talk shows on 20 September 2009 and also, in a first for an acting president, on David Letterman's late-night talk show the following day. TV is still very much the central stage of the public sphere, even if this stage, of course, is composed of a number of channels. The reason is, simply, that it is still the only medium that can draw several tens of millions of viewers at one and the same time. And it does so not only for presidents, and not only for news. It still does so also for drama series – and advertisers.

Interactive television and democracy

Broadcast television may not be dying, but it *is* changing – adapting to the new situation in various ways. It more than ever appears definable as 'an entertainment machine with news' (Gripsrud 1995). There is certainly more entertainment and infotainment on at prime time, even on European public-service channels (cf. Peter Golding's chapter in this volume).

Another development related to digitization is the increased use of 'interactivity' as an integrated feature of programmes. This has been seen as a very welcome democratization of the previously authoritarian, paternalistic and monologue medium. Formats relying on interactivity vary dramatically, ranging from *Pop Idol* (and *American Idol*) and other 'reality' shows, via US CNN's *Talk Back Live*, to Norwegian public-service broadcaster NRK's video jukebox show *Svisj*, where the choice of clips is decided by text-message requests from viewers and accompanied by viewers' text messages such as 'I love you, baby', 'anybody out there ready to party?', and so on.

So how democratic are these or other forms of digital interactivity? Bordewijk and Kaam (1986) argued that any communication process can be described and understood based on the distribution of power over the production and distribution of information between what they call the 'information consumer' on the one hand, and the 'information centre' on the other. In the case of television, that is to say the distribution of power between viewers and TV station or channel. They suggest that two questions can be asked to determine the nature of the communication in question in terms of the distribution of power: (1) Is the information distributed, produced and owned by a central information service or by an individual information consumer? (2) Is the selection and distribution of the information controlled by a central information service or an individual information consumer?

Building on this idea, Danish media scholars Thomas Bøgelund and Tove Arendt Rasmussen (2001: 2) have constructed a table which offers the four logically possible categories of interactive television programming. Table 1.1 is my version of that table.

Bøgelund and Rasmussen say the lines between their four categories should not be taken as absolute: there are gradual transitions between them and they are frequently mixed.

Very briefly put, the four categories can be defined as follows: *transmission* is the classic version of broadcasting, where the listener or viewer's only possible and necessary (physical) activity is to turn the radio or TV off or on.

16

Table 1.1 Forms of interactive television

	Content delivered by TV	*Content delivered by viewer*
TV controls selection of content and time of viewing	*Transmission* TV → Viewer	*Registration* TV ← Viewer (TV → Viewer)
Viewer controls selection of content and time of viewing	*Consultation* TV → Viewer (Viewer → TV)	*Conversation* Viewer ←→ Viewer

Traditional feedback to broadcasters via letters, telephones, demonstrations and (now) emails, and so on, is not included since it takes place outside of the TV medium. *Registration* is when information from viewers is collected or registered and used in a particular programme – for example an answer from viewers to a question about how much money they give their kids to spend each week. The answers could be delivered via telephone, email, text messages, fax or set-top boxes. *Consultation* is when viewers decide when to watch a programme on PVRs or the internet. *Conversation* is what goes on, for instance, on the websites of popular reality shows, where the connection between viewers is provided by a TV channel but where viewers interact directly while also possibly, as in the case of *Big Brother*, watching the show's web transmissions.

Bøgelund and Rasmussen (2001: 3) refer to Laurel (1990), who suggests that one might measure how interactive a TV programme is by looking at *frequency* – i.e. how often viewers are allowed to interact; *extension* – i.e. how many choices are available; and *influence* – i.e. how much viewer's choices actually impact what goes on. This is a highly useful suggestion, since it can show how very limited real interaction and viewer impact is in almost all cases in almost all four of the above categories. Even what may seem to be the most radical of the four, 'conversation', does not influence the content of the show in question at all. The most radical possibilities in terms of real viewer influence may actually be found in the category of 'consultation', since this is the most adequate box for the late-night video-clip jukebox show with intimate text messages that I mentioned above. Another possible example might be the pornographic shows on late-night European cable, which allow viewers to text message (or telephone?) peep-show type instructions to scantily clad women.

What is most striking here is (a) the relatively trivial and/or pseudo-democratic nature of so many of the programmes that are marked by interactivity of these sorts, (b) the fact that any form of interactivity ultimately is controlled by the broadcaster, and (c) that the most powerful of all forms of interaction with broadcasters has a long and interesting history and little or nothing to do with digitization: telephones, letters, demonstrations, letters to the editor, mobilizing the press, organizing consumer boycotts, and so on. These often very effective, partly direct and partly public-sphere-based forms of feedback are, as a rule, overlooked in the literature on interactivity. The same goes for the many decades of telephone-based radio programmes, the use of telephone, letters and vox-pop interviews in TV programmes and the scores of other ways in which both radio and television, throughout most of their history, have established dialogues with their audiences.

The really new thing is the internet. Television is no longer the only audio-visual technology in the homes of us mobile and privatized people.

The internet

Much of the discourse on the internet has been exalted, utopian, and revolutionary. One characteristic example is the postmodern theorist Mark Poster, who in his 1997 piece on 'Internet and the public sphere' said:

> The 'magic' of the Internet is that it is a technology that puts cultural acts, symbolizations in all forms, in the hands of all participants; it radically decentralizes the positions of speech, publishing, film-making, radio and television broadcasting, in short the apparatuses of cultural production.
>
> (Poster 1997: 211)

Over a decade later, the idea that the internet has 'radically decentralized' all the 'apparatuses of cultural production' clearly appears as an exaggeration. But the point Poster makes is not totally wrong, since the internet, together with the digitization of the technologies for writing, photography, sound recording and more, has without doubt lowered the threshold for new entrants into cultural production in different media. The significant expansion of the number of producers is absolutely an important development – in particular since these producers can distribute their products on the internet for free or at a very low price and so actually *reach an audience*. While people have always photographed, played the guitar, made amateur movies and had all kinds of culturally productive hobbies, they have never before had the possibility now offered by the internet to have their output exhibited to anonymous audiences of varying sizes. It can be done on various individually managed websites, or it can be done on privately owned and operated collective sites like YouTube and MySpace. In both cases it clearly resembles broadcasting. Not only is there the one-to-many structure, much of what one finds there are excerpts from television programmes. But it is a 'pull' type of technology with no scheduling and so it is something other than broadcast television: an internet-specific Video on Demand service.

The internet's reputation as a democratic, popular counterweight to top-down, scheduled television is exaggerated, though. Most internet traffic these

Table 1.2 Top 10 global web parent companies, home and work

Rank	Parent	Unique audience (000)	Active reach %	Time per person (hh:mm:ss)
1	Google	349,662	84.10	2:46:34
2	Microsoft	312,576	75.18	3:09:59
3	Yahoo!	237,129	57.03	2:22:42
4	Facebook	185,449	44.60	5:18:12
5	Ebay	159,086	38.26	1:38:04
6	Aol llc	136,611	32.86	2:21:21
7	Wikimedia foundation	136,376	32.80	0:15:13
8	News corp. Online	132,467	31.86	1:22:39
9	Interactivecorp	112,610	27.08	0:13:53
10	Amazon	111,517	26.82	0:22:45

Source: Nielsen NetView.

days is to sites owned and run by major institutions or corporations. As early as 2001, 45 per cent of the top five websites in 26 countries were affiliated with Microsoft, according to an analysis of Nielsen NetRatings data (Lake 2001). In today's Norway, six out of the 10 most popular websites (as measured by the number of individual users each day) are owned by the same, nationally dominant and internationally active media corporation, Schibsted. And Table 1.2 shows Nielsen Net Ratings' list of the 10 parent companies of the most visited websites in August 2009.

In other words, it has been a while since the internet was primarily about grass-roots communication and participatory culture. The concentration of capital and competence characteristic of media markets generally now also structures much of the internet. In addition to the really big corporate players in Europe, Japan and elsewhere, there are the banks, the insurance companies, the oil companies, the car companies, the hotels, the restaurants and so on. And smart business initiatives that only exist on the net, such as Second Life. It was already estimated several years ago that '90 percent of all Web pages are for financial gain' (Schuler 2004: 69). Then there are all the big sites based in the public or non-profit civil-society sector: government sites, those of universities, museums, and so on. After all of this, what remains in terms of space for non-profit newcomers with a mission is quite limited. It is *not* easy to actually reach a larger audience on the internet without somehow achieving cooperation with one or more of the big players.[7]

This is, importantly, not the whole truth about the internet. It remains a fact that it offers people previously inconceivable opportunities for making available to the public any kind of cultural product or political utterance, for communicating and organizing across great distances and even on a global scale, for accessing enormous cultural resources such as archives, museums, internationally renowned newspapers and other media, and so on. It therefore seems obvious to me that it may be said to add historically new and highly valuable forms of publicness to the traditional public sphere.

Television and the digital public sphere: a preliminary conclusion

The fundamental social conditions that, according to Raymond Williams, made broadcasting so socially relevant and valuable generally remain: we still have centralized political and economic power on the one hand and see-mingly ever-more mobile, privatized people on the other. There is still a need for a focus, a limited set of central arenas in a comprehensive, general public sphere, if such people and their opinions on public matters are to influence political decision-making. Mobile and privatized people also need a sense of community that broadcasting and its 'currency' can provide – something to talk about, shared rituals and major events, shared frames of reference, shared knowledge. And nation states are not at all dead, even if in some respects they are quite different and weaker than they used to be. Broadcast television will therefore continue to exist for as long as we can now reasonably claim to see into the future and continue to deliver information, education, enter-tainment and identity components.

But television does not remain the same. Traditional broadcast media must now relate to and rely on not only print media and the music and motion-picture industries; they also have to take into account the internet. The internet is not only an increasingly important channel or platform for the distribution of broadcast radio and television. It is also a sound-and-video-on-demand service of enormous proportions, offering material that has already proved able to become a shared reference in various communities, and also to help constitute new ones – the obvious examples being sites such as YouTube and MySpace. But there are also many more that may be said to act as some kind of centre to many (very many) anonymous listeners, viewers, readers and users. In that, they resemble broadcasting institutions though they cannot be counted as such since they lack the schedule, the flow, the 'push'-type of delivery.

Television channels have long since discovered that their websites are very useful in tying viewers to them, in forming virtual communities linked to certain programmes, in communicating additional material and further information tied to particular news or documentary programmes and much, much more. The sort of symbiosis now developed between television and the internet is evidenced in the fact that some of the most intense person-to-person, egalitarian communicative activities, once seen as a hallmark of the internet as such, are actually public conversations about TV shows (see for instance Jenkins 2006, Chapters 1 and 2, about *Survivor* and *American Idol* respectively; and Peter Larsen's contribution to this volume, on *Grey's Anatomy*). These websites may, in interesting ways, be reminiscent of the salons of the arts in the classical public sphere. But contrary to those eighteenth- and nineteenth-century forums, these websites will tend to be either run or 'infiltrated' by production companies and networks, which regard them primarily as tools for marketing.

The most important question concerning television and the internet is what the outcome of the new, digitized situation will be for the structure of the public sphere. The World Wide Web provides users with access to innumerable websites, thus potentially completely splintering the public. But looking only at the number of websites available would be a classic technological-determinism-type mistake. As I have argued, in reality the web is used in much more concentrated and hierarchical ways than are often imagined.

Similarly, broadcast television's viewers may now at any given time be distributed across several hundred channels, or watching whatever suits them off-schedule and without the ads by using their PVRs. This is certainly a problem for advertisers, since it has been estimated that 'in the 1960s an advertiser could reach 80% of US women with a spot aired simultaneously on CBS, NBC and ABC. Today an ad would have to run on 100 channels to have a prayer of duplicating this feat' (Bianco 2004).[8] But it may be less of a problem for those whose primary interest is to maintain a functioning general public sphere, towards which all weak publics and all subaltern counterpublics gravitate in order to effectively critique or influence decisions affecting all of society. So far it seems that viewers flock regularly to a quite limited number of channels, but only very rarely visit the many dozens of others. Any one of the traditional US networks can, even now, on a good day, with a good show, draw about 30 million people at once. In the course of a week, most Americans will have watched a network channel or two, or three – the number here is not so important.

Consider this analogy: a European public sphere is now, in the scholarly literature, often defined as a space where national public spheres make up the infrastructure but where there is more or less simultaneous discourse on European issues; a space which is 'a pluralistic ensemble of issue-oriented publics that exists once the same issues are discussed simultaneously and within a shared frame of relevance' (Lingenberg 2006: 123, quoting Eder and Kantner 2000: 315). The coherence of multi-channel national public spheres, in multi-ethnic societies, can arguably be maintained along similar lines. Cass Sunstein's warning against 'cyberbalkanization' is still worth considering. But the continued existence of a relatively centralized and uniting broadcast television system along the lines just presented, together with a degree of centralization on the internet, are among the reasons why the danger should not be overestimated. The positive possibilities for increased diversity may in fact seem closer to realization.

A case in point is Graham Murdock's proposition that countries with a functioning public broadcaster, in particular, should strive to construct a 'digital commons' by pooling the digital resources of several public-sector institutions, thus linking public broadcasting with public universities, libraries, museums, parks, festivals, and so on, creating a significant non-commercial space as a counterweight to the rampant commercialization of the World Wide Web (Murdock 2005). This is by no means a utopian idea; it is just a good one.

The question of class

The most serious problem for a functioning public sphere may be of a different nature: the digitization of the public sphere may entail greater differences between social classes. Peter Golding's contribution in this volume contains many examples of the importance of class. I will here provide a couple more.

With two colleagues, I conducted a survey in the autumn of 2008 on a representative sample of the more than 25,000 students in all institutions of higher education in Bergen, Norway. We were struck by the consistency and clarity of our findings concerning solid links between students' social backgrounds, their choices of studies and their uses of digital media. Those with lower-class backgrounds in vocational programmes (nursing, engineering and teaching) were much less active on the web than other groups with more resourceful backgrounds and choices of longer, more academic studies. The use of the web as a source for news and other politically relevant informational material was clearly for the most part a characteristic of students from resourceful backgrounds, especially from homes where cultural capital was a more important part of their total resources than economic capital (Gripsrud, Hovden and Moe, forthcoming).

On the basis of national empirical research, Nick Couldry, Sonia Livingstone and Tim Markham (2007) have expressed concern about a lack of 'public connection' in an increasing proportion of the population. Public connection is the minimal precondition of at least periodical attention to what goes on in the central processes of democracy, in the political public sphere. There are many signs that such a connection may be lacking among increasing numbers of people in the Western world. Voter turnout down towards around 50 per cent in national elections was long unimaginable in Western Europe, but is now not very uncommon there and quite normal in the US. Sixty per cent of UK citizens now agree that 'people like me have no say in government', only 8 per cent trust 'any politician to tell the truth' always or most of the time – while 52 per cent 'almost never' trust them to speak truthfully (Couldry et al. 2007: 180).

Such a lack of interest and confidence is matched also in the use of the various media. Only 49 per cent of the UK population now 'normally read a daily morning paper' and only 12 per cent use the internet as a 'regular' news source, i.e. between two and five days per week (ibid.). Several studies reveal that, even for its most frequent and active users, the internet is rarely used as a source of information on news and current affairs (2007: 181–82). Many of the respondents in Couldry, Livingstone and Markham's study were very updated, interested in and knowledgeable about celebrities or sports, but they found no signs that such interests ever lead to interest in the central political processes of the country (2007: 182–83).

The main point in this context is that Couldry, Livingstone and Markham's study represents an approach to the issue of media and the public sphere which in a sense starts outside of the media themselves, in general social and political problems. This makes for a more comprehensive view of the social situation in which the media operate, including the internet. Such an approach is still very useful, as it was when applied by the two principal sources of inspiration for this article: Raymond Williams started his theorization of television with the general processes of modernization, and Habermas' wide-angled classic was a piece of historical sociology which, for instance, pointed out that the expanding market economy was the driving force behind the establishment of a modern public sphere. What we need to do in order to grasp the real significance of today's media developments, with a view to the functioning of a democratic public sphere, is to start by situating ourselves and our media in a wider socio-historical context and study our chosen area of special interest against that background.

The author would like to thank John Ellis and Nick Browne for their comments on an earlier draft of this article.

Notes

1 The immediate delivery is very different from the NVOD (Near Video On Demand) systems I discussed in my contribution to Spigel and Olsson 2004 – which was written in 1999.
2 http://europa.eu/legislation_summaries/audiovisual_and_media/l24101a_en.htm.
3 http://www.ofcom.org.uk/media/news/2007/12/nr_20071213.
4 Ibid.
5 Ibid.
6 http://www.consumeraffairs.com/news04/2008/01/ntia_broadband.html.
7 Here I can also draw on my own experience as the first editor of a web magazine devoted to issues related to the freedom of speech and the freedom of information, *Vox Publica* (http://www.voxpublica.no).
8 This does not mean that 'the masses' or 'the mass market' have disappeared, only that alternative ways to do 'mass advertising' must be – and have been – found (Nunes and Merrihue 2007).

References

Allen, Jeanne (1983) 'The social matrix of television: invention in the United States', in E. Ann Kaplan (ed.) *Regarding Television: Critical Approaches – an*

Anthology, American Film Institute, Los Angeles: University Publications of America, pp. 109–19.

Anderson, Benedict ([1983]1991) *Imagined Communities*, London and New York: Verso.

Banet-Weiser, Sarah, Chris, Cynthia and Freitas, Anthony (2007) *Cable Vision: Television Beyond Broadcasting*, New York and London: New York University Press.

Bianco, A. (2004) 'The vanishing mass market', *Business Week*, 12 July, pp. 61–74.

Bordewijk, L. Jan and Kaam, Ben van (1986) 'Towards a new classification of TeleInformation Services', *Inter Media*, vol. 14.

Bøgelund, Thomas and Rasmussen, Tove Arendt (2001) 'Interaktivt TV i medie-landskabet', article first published by Center for Journalistik og Efteruddannelse, http://www.update.dk/cfje/vidbase.nsf/(VBFriTekstMultiDB)/ 97CB23546477BD0AC1256A07002EF21B?OpenDocument. Accessed 26 September 2009.

Castells, Manuel (1996) *The Information Age: Economy, Society, and Culture*, vols. 1–3, Oxford: Blackwell.

Couldry, Nick, Livingstone, Sonia and Markham, Tim (2007) *Media Consumption and Public Engagement: Beyond the Presumption of Attention*, Basingstoke and New York: Palgrave Macmillan.

Curran, James, Iyengar, Shanto, Lund, Anker Brink and Salovaara-Moring, Inka (2009) 'Media system, public knowledge and democracy: A comparative study', *European Journal of Communication*, vol. 24, no. 1, pp. 5–26.

Dahlgren, Peter (1995) *Television and the Public Sphere: Citizenship, Democracy and the Media*, London, Thousand Oaks, New Delhi: Sage Publications.

Eder, Klaus and Kantner, Cathleen (2000) 'Transnationale resonanzstrukturen in Europa. Eine kritik der rede von öffentlichkeitsdefizit', in M. Bach (ed.) *Die Europäisierung nationaler Gesellschaften*, Wiesbaden: Westdeutscher Verlag, pp. 306–31.

Ellis, John (2007) *TV FAQ: Uncommon Answers to Common Questions about Television*, London: I.B. Tauris.

Fraser, Nancy (1992) 'Rethinking the public sphere: a contribution to the critique of actually existing democracy', in Craig Calhoun (ed.) *Habermas and the Public Sphere*, Cambridge, MA and London: The MIT Press, pp. 109–42.

Garber, Megan (2009) '"Now don't you let the government get a hold of my medicare" ... and other absurdities of fact-free town halls', 12 August 2009, *Columbia Journalism Review*, http://www.cjr.org/campaign_desk/now_dont_you_let_the_government.php. Accessed 29 September 2009.

Garnham, Nicholas (1983) 'Public service vs. the market', *Screen*, vol. 24, no. 1, pp. 6–27.

Gilder, George (1993) 'Life after television, updated', 23 February 1993, in *Forbes ASAP*, http://www.seas.upenn.edu/~gaj1/tvgg.html. Accessed 29 September 2009.

Gitlin, Todd (1998) 'Public sphere or public sphericules', in J. Curran and T. Liebes (eds) *Media, Ritual and Identity*, London and New York: Routledge, pp. 168–74.

Gourd, Andrea (2002) *Öffentlichkeit und digitales Fernsehen*, Wiesbaden: Westdeutscher Verlag.

Griffiths, Alan (2003) *Digital Television Strategies: Business Challenges and Opportunities*, Basingstoke and New York: Palgrave Macmillan.

Gripsrud, Jostein (1981) 'La denne vår scene bli flammen ...' Perspektiv og praksis i og omkring sosialdemokratiets arbeiderteater ca 1890–1940. ('Let this stage be the flame ...' Perspectives and Practices in and around the Worker's Theatre of the Social Democratic Labour Movement 1890–1940), Oslo: Universitetsforlaget/Norwegian University Press.

Gripsrud, Jostein (1994) 'Intellectuals as constructors of cultural identities', Cultural Studies, vol. 8, no. 2, pp. 220–31.

Gripsrud, Jostein (1995) The Dynasty Years: Hollywood Television and Critical Media Studies, London and New York: Routledge.

Gripsrud, Jostein (1997) 'La Norvège ou l'invention d'un peuple "pur"', Liber. Revue internationale des livres, no. 31, juin, 1997 (Supplément au numéro 118 d' Actes de la recherche en sciences sociale).

Gripsrud, Jostein (1998) 'Television, broadcasting, flow: key metaphors in television theory', in D. Lusted and C. Geraghty (eds) The Television Studies Book, London: Edward Arnold.

Gripsrud, Jostein (2004) 'Broadcast television: the chances of its survival in a digital age', in Lynn Spigel and Jan Olsson (eds) Television After TV: Essays on a Medium in Transition, Durham, NC and London: Duke University Press, pp. 210–23.

Gripsrud, Jostein, Hovden, Jan F. and Moe, Hallvard (forthcoming) A Cultural Elite? Students, Class and Cultural Preferences 1998–2008 (preliminary title).

Habermas, Jürgen ([1962]1989) The Structural Transformation of the Public Sphere, Cambridge, MA and London: The MIT Press.

Habermas, Jürgen (1992) 'Further reflections on the public sphere', in: Craig Calhoun (ed.) Habermas and the Public Sphere, Cambridge, MA and London: The MIT Press, pp. 421–61.

Habermas, Jürgen (1996) Between Facts and Norms: Contributions to a Discourse Theory of Law and Democracy, Cambridge, MA: The MIT Press.

Habermas, Jürgen (2006) 'Political communication in media society: does democracy still enjoy an epistemic dimension? The impact of normative theory on empirical research', Communication Theory, vol. 16, pp. 411–26.

Hoynes, William (1994) Public Television for Sale: Media, the Market and the Public Sphere, Boulder, San Francisco, Oxford: Westview Press.

Jenkins, Henry (2006) Convergence Culture: Where Old and New Media Collide, New York and London: New York University Press.

Lake, David (2001) 'Worldwide Web domination – Microsoft's dominance is becoming apparent as Web ratings firms begin measuring traffic in other countries', 6 August, The Industry Standard, http://findarticles.com/p/articles/mi_m0HWW/is_30_4/ai_77826056. Accessed 5 March 2008.

Laurel, Brenda (1990) 'Interface agents: metaphors with character', in Brenda Laurel (ed.) The Art of Human–Computer Interface Design, Reading, MA: Addison-Wesley.

Lingenberg, Swantje (2006) 'The audience's role in constituting the European public sphere: a theoretical approach based on the pragmatic concept of John Dewey', in N. Carpentier et al. (eds), Researching Media, Democracy and Participation, Tartu: Tartu University Press.

Lotz, Amanda (2007) The Television Will Be Revolutionized, New York and London: New York University Press.

Murdock, Graham (2005) 'Building the digital commons. Public broadcasting in the age of the Internet', in G. F. Lowe and P. Jauert (eds) *Cultural Dilemmas in Public Service Broadcasting*, Göteborg: Nordicom, pp. 213–30.

Negroponte, Nicholas (1993) 'HDTV: What's wrong with this picture?', March/ April, *Wired*, http://www.wired.com/wired/archive/1.01/negroponte.html. Accessed 29 September 2009.

Nunes, Paul F. and Merrihue, Jeffrey (2007) 'The continuing power of mass advertising', *MIT Sloan Management Review*, vol. 48, no. 2, pp. 63–71.

Peters, John Durham (1999) *Speaking into the Air: A History of the Idea of Communication*, Chicago: University of Chicago Press.

Poster, Mark (1997) 'Cyberdemocracy: Internet and the public sphere', in D. Porter (ed.) *Internet Culture*, New York and London: Routledge, pp. 201–17.

Rose, F. and Brown, E. (1996) 'The end of TV as we know it. Forget HDTV. Forget interactive television. Forget the 500-channel universe. Instead start thinking PCTV.' 23 December, *Fortune*, http://money.cnn.com/magazines/fortune/fortune_archive/1996/12/23/219864/index.htm. Accessed 3 March 2008.

Scannell, Paddy (2000) 'For-anyone-as-someone structures', *Media, Culture & Society*, vol. 22, no. 1, pp. 5–24.

Schuler, Douglas (2004) 'Reports of the close relationship between democracy and the internet may have been exaggerated', in Henry Jenkins and David Thorburn (eds) *Democracy and New Media*, Cambridge, MA and London: The MIT Press, pp. 69–84.

Spigel, Lynn and Olsson, Jan (eds) (2004) *Television After TV: Essays on a Medium in Transition*, Durham, NC and London: Duke University Press.

Sunstein, Cass (2001) *Republic.com*, Princeton, NJ and Oxford: Princeton University Press.

Sunstein, Cass (2007) *Republic.com 2.0*, Princeton, NJ and Oxford: Princeton University Press.

Williams, Raymond (1975) *Television: Technology and Cultural Form*, New York: Schocken Books.

2

TV AS TIME MACHINE

Television's changing heterochronic regimes and the production of history

William Uricchio

Most of the existing scholarly literature on television texts focuses on particular programmes. This chapter, however, will consider television's dynamics as a larger textual composite. At a moment when, to invoke Raymond Williams, television's technology and cultural form are very much in transition, the medium's fast-changing textual mix and our access to it merit closer consideration. In considering this mix, I will focus on a particular aspect of television's temporality that in effect makes it a time machine, allowing viewers to experience a distinctive kind of time, and possibly even notion of history. Television's temporal regime has been in flux since the start of the broadcast era, and I am interested above all in how changing configurations of time and the (re-)sequencing of programming units themselves constitute key elements of the medium's relationship to historical representation. I am interested in using medium-specific attributes to explore television's changing role as a site for the personal construction of historical meaning and as a vehicle for public history. Although the broad contours of this short narrative – the shift over the past 60 years from relatively stable and widespread textual sequences to highly variable and personalized constellations – will not be surprising, by limiting my focus to the interplay of certain televisual logics, I hope to at least shed some light on an under-illuminated aspect of television's historical capacities.

Narrowing the field

VI [Channel 7 news desk] (Announcer 2)
A mayor in Alameda County is working for a proposition to ban further apartment-construction in his city. But his wife and six daughters are working for the other side. Reporter (film of street in city; cars and houses): The proposition is being voted

on tomorrow. The issue is legal and environmental. Further development, it is said, will reduce open spaces and lead to extra traffic pollution.

VII Woman (film: hand-spraying from can; table dusted). Liquid Gold furniture polish; brings new sparkle to your furniture; it's like meeting an old friend again.

VIII Man (film clip): The 6:30 movie is *Annie Get Your Gun*. Betty Hutton as the sharpest–shooting gal the Wild West ever saw.

(Williams [1974]1992: 95)

This excerpt from Raymond Williams' 'medium-range' analysis of a broadcast sequence from San Francisco's Channel 7 on 12 March 1973 (5:42pm) traces a series of shifts in time, space, voice and mode of address. From a live news desk, to a presumably recently filmed location report, to an 'evergreen' studio-shot advertisement, to a clip from George Sidney's 1950 film with a recent voice overlay, a few seconds of television time yields quite an experiential range. While read as 'disruptive' to a cultural outsider like Williams, the sequence flows along quite well for native viewers.[1] Williams' close-range analysis goes a step further, demonstrating the art of segue so important in the broadcast era. While not discussed by Williams, who was more interested in perceived temporal continuities, the recycling of these elements further complicates the story. Texts, as cultural artefacts, carry associations, so how might we think about the repositioning of those elements (texts and their associations) into new contexts? The 1973 broadcast of a 1950 film might come inscribed with particular meanings for a viewer who first saw it at the cinema 23 years earlier; or, repositioned in a broadcast environment where the promo for *Annie Get Your Gun* follows a report of a shooting by a woman, it might take on a whole new meaning. The advertisement for Liquid Gold might normalize domestic divisions of labour in 1973, or, shown in a different era, might be appreciated for documenting early 1970s lifestyles or critiqued as an instrument for maintaining gender inequality. While hypothetical examples, they point to the role of sequence, context and association in the construction of meaning, and the tensions inherent in ordering and reordering the bits of time, space and event that they constitute. For better or worse, the English word 'history' suffers from semantic ambiguity, referring among other things to the events of the past as well as to the meanings and emplotted representations of those events from a later point in time; both to the infinity of detail bound up in any one occurrence and to the inherently partial rendering and interpretation of that occurrence; both to history as inexorably shackled to the particularities of time and place, and to history as the violent repositioning and recontextualizion of the past to reflect the needs of the present. Although we can explore television's relationship with history through any number of lenses, including those used for other audio-visual media, I contend that its distinction as a historical medium – and as a time machine of sorts – may be found in its constant remix of representational and temporal elements. Television's audio-visual relationship to past events (the *resemblance* that it shares with photography, film and recorded audio – and its status as *trace*, which distinguishes it from the printed word) (Kittler 1999) is complicated by its distinctive engagement with time, characterized by the 'liveness' effect (Bourdon 2000) (*immediate, continuous* and *co-existant*).

Much ink has been spilled on the notion of representation in the pas de deux of television and history. However, the more medium-specific notions of the 'liveness effect' and televisual flow have either been absent from such discussions or have formed the basis for critique. Television, so the argument goes, contributes to a *loss* of history because 'liveness' and 'flow' keep the viewer trapped in an endless unfolding of a (simulated) present, too interested by what comes next to ever reflect upon deeper sets of connections; television effectively flattens the appearances of the past into the ongoing fabric of the present. This view recalls the notion of distraction associated with late-nineteenth-century urbanization and modernity and articulated in very different ways by critics such as Benjamin (1936), Horkheimer and Adorno (1947), this time as a condition of the medium's existence (a problem already hinted at in 1935 by one of television's earliest observers, Rudolf Arnheim [1935]1969). A few, including Arnheim, have even argued that the very terms of television's encounter with the world ('live' iconic and indexical representations) are the source of its undoing. This argument, the 'seeing is believing' critique, claims that television falsely empowers its viewers, encouraging them to equate what they see 'with their own eyes' through the medium with what they experience in the world, blurring the line between two experiential domains and encouraging viewers to feel that they 'know' what they have only partially seen.

Superficiality, distraction and confusion, it seems, emerge from a medium that by its nature and cultural logics is nothing short of anti-historical. If we add to this television's reach as a popular representation system and the scale of its viewing public, the implications of these various concerns can be quite dramatic, even dangerous. Several scholars, however, have gone against the grain, using these same issues to demonstrate television's importance as a site of history. For example, John Ellis (1999) has argued that television provides 'a vast mechanism' for processing the raw data of daily life into narrativized and coherent forms, while Paddy Scannell (1966, 2004), attending to broadcasting's temporal regime, has made a compelling case for the relevance of 'mediated subjectivity' to modern historical consciousness. These and other scholars have explored the implications of television's temporality – the way, for instance, that broadcasting (including radio) is not just 'live' in the sense of immediate but also in the sense of an 'always already present' that can punctuate anything that is being broadcast (including recorded material), and in the sense that television's co-existent, continuous, 24/7 feed renders the medium into something like an accomplice, companion and ongoing reference point. These factors greatly complicate the simple airing of historical texts by situating their meaning, qualifying the status of any particular programme, and bearing on the very construction of subjectivity.

The time of television

Heterochronia describes that aspect of television's temporality that accounts for its specificity as a medium, distinguishing it from other textual engagements with history. The term heterochronia traditionally refers to certain medical pathologies characterized by irregular or intermittent times (the pulse), or erratic developmental sequence (organ growth). This notion of displacements in time or the vitiating of sequence was picked up by Foucault as something of a temporal extension of his notion of *heterotopia*. This latter term denotes for Foucault sites with a multiplicity of meanings, defined by uncertainty, paradox, incongruity and ambivalence; sites for which he suggested a temporal corollary (heterochronia) best exemplified by long-term accumulation projects such as libraries and museums (Foucault [1966]1970, 1998). Evocative as much for its weak definitional status as for its promise, heterochronia is a term I would like to define between its diagnostic roots (the vitiating of sequence, displacements in time) and Foucault's institutional setting. Like a library or museum, 'a place of all times that is itself outside of time', television is a temporal aggregate, an accumulation of visions, tastes, forms and ideas gathered together into one place (Foucault 1998: 182). Like a museum or library, television is a space of endlessly recombinatory artefacts. Unlike them, however, and this is a crucial distinction from Foucault's meaning, television's recombinatory process plays out as a linear sequence *over time*, not outside it.

Consider the difference between collage and montage: a similar principle (the compositing of differently sourced artefacts) works to a very different effect along a durational axis. Collage radically uproots and recombines visual elements from various provenances and with different histories. The resulting whole is greater than the sum of its parts, and many collages exploit the dissonance of source, materiality and referenced temporality to great effect. But montage, the *durational* assemblage of divergent materials, relies upon sequence and ever-changing context for its effect. In cinematic terms, the principles of montage found early articulation through Lev Kuleshov, briefly the teacher of Eisenstein and a great influence on Pudovkin, Vertov and other Soviet filmmakers. Just after the Russian revolution, at a time of minimal film imports and poor production resources, Kuleshov experimented with the recombinatory effect of film editing, recutting found footage to construct new meanings. By intercutting footage of an actor's face with a bowl of soup, a coffin and a girl, he was able to construct a nuanced performance for audiences who read identical images of the actor's face as expressing hunger, loss and quiet joy. The 'Kuleshov effect', as the results of this and other experiments became known, demonstrated that shot sequence and context were far more determining than expected, and that shot content and meaning, long considered self-evident and relatively stable within the painterly and photographic tradition, were in fact highly malleable.

Kuleshov's insights gave voice to a temporal recombinatory practice that is older than the film medium, evident for example in nineteenth-century programming of magic lantern exhibitions, where showmen learned to build – and to rework – stories from the slides that they happened to have. But these early practices, particularly as they appeared through film's first decade or so, actually made use of recombinatory logic in a double sense. First, in the hands of filmmakers such as Edwin S. Porter and D. W. Griffith, the sequence of shots was manipulated to construct overall textual meaning (just as Kuleshov would later theorize and experimentally demonstrate). Second, the positioning of Porter's, Griffith's and others' films into full programmes (complete with lantern slides, actualities and other narratives) could itself radically transform the meanings of individual films. Here, the programmer (usually the projectionist) could, through simple manipulation of film sequence, comment upon or build different frameworks of coherence for a particular film. This meta-level of recombination was not discussed by Kuleshov, and indeed largely took residual form in exhibition practice (a routine programme with previews, a short or two and the feature). But it was seized upon by television (and radio), where programmatic recombination would emerge as the economic lifeblood of the industry in the form of the rerun. And it provides one of the keys to television's distinctive engagement with history.

Libraries and museums are heterochronic both in the sense of latency (their collections reflect acquisitions drawn from very different times) and the activity they engender (the practice of browsing, of encountering chance sequences of texts produced over different times, of wandering and thus activating very different contexts and meanings). But they differ from television in several ways: in terms of the fullness of their potential latency (television's temporality is of necessity active, and even though choices must be made, televisual flow is unstoppable); and, at least during the broadcast era, in terms of the agency that structures sequence (the programmer rather than the individual browser or flâneur) and in terms of the public scale of the experience (mass rather than individual). We shall shortly consider the profound transformations of the structure of television's temporality and audiences (and thus the logics of television's heterochronic regime) symbolized by the remote control device and digital access systems such as TiVo and IPTV.

Heterochronia, in the sense of displacements in time or the vitiating of sequence, is a televisual constant, and it can be found on many different levels. As just suggested, it drives the textual logic of individual programmes (à la Kuleshov), and enjoys variation across programme and genre forms, from news to drama, from argument to chronicle. But there is something more to televisual heterochronia. Its programme logics turn on a triad of elements: sequence, interpenetration and repetition.

- *Sequence* pertains to the careful orchestration particularly relevant during broadcast-era programming (but residually present as well in its successor regimes), in which the programme day addressed a changing constituency of viewers, and in which the programme 'line-up' was designed to enhance the chances of continuous viewing. Sequence, as well, speaks to the notion of temporal contiguity and thus contextualization that is the driving force of both the Kuleshov effect and programmatic historical framing (and in this, it remains highly relevant, even for the self-programmer of YouTube segments).
- *Interpenetration* can be found in the practice of parsing out particular programmes over time and over the broadcast schedule (e.g. weekly or daily series, where the programme day and our lives are interpenetrated) and of fragmenting individual programmes with advertisements and announcements of various sorts, effectively constructing a meta-text beyond the control of the individual text's author. Far more egregious in commercial television settings, interpenetration also refers to the practice of using programme 'bumpers' and 'hooks' (displaced micro-programme elements) to keep viewers watching. The effect, paradoxically, is both to rupture engagement with a particular programme and to interconnect programme elements into a larger whole. But the punctuation of programme sequence is not always subtle: a well-timed advertisement for aspirin during the evening news can undercut the most serious economic reports, as can an unfortunately timed advertisement for gasoline following news of the latest evidence of global warming.
- *Repetition* refers to the recycling of footage, programmes and programme units, whether in a single-channel environment or across channels. Examples range from heavily circulated iconic footage (the collapse of the World Trade Center), to advertisements (where frequency of repetition is part of their persuasive logic), to programme segments (CNN Headline News' repetition of news stories and sequences on a 30-minute rotation), to entire programme reruns (whether repeated or syndicated).

While interpenetration and repetition may seem at odds with an ideal viewing experience, they are central to the notion of television as a larger textual system (as opposed to programme texts). Moreover, they bear heavily on the (re-)construction of textual meaning and reflect the current state of television's economy. Interpenetration brings textual elements of a different temporality and intent into the primary textual domain. They can be assimilated as part of a larger text (an aspirin ad can be read as inadvertently commenting upon the latest bad news from Afghanistan), or bracketed out as a minor annoyance (and ignored), but in either case they redefine the temporality of the primary text and thus the viewing experience and meanings. Repetition, in turn, invariably takes place in a new cultural present, serving variously to reactivate the past of the primary text (recalling original impressions upon first seeing the programme or, through the text, its fuller cultural moment), or to recast it through the knowledge that has since been acquired. In this context, Marx's (1942) opening words in 'The Eighteenth Brumaire of Louis Bonaparte' ('Hegel remarks somewhere that all great, world-historical facts and personages occur, as it were, twice. He has forgotten to add: the first time as tragedy, the second as farce.') take on new meaning.

Technology and cultural form

If some televisual images have an epistemological slipperiness about them, sliding from trace of a historical event to a historical interpretation of that event (and positions in between), the temporal situation of those images would seem to play a crucial role in fixing and holding them fast (even if only momentarily). I've suggested that the notion of heterochronia helps us here, by calling attention to television's pervasive fabric of displaced and recombinatory temporalities. Heterochronia helps us to account for something like the Kuleshov effect, except played out not only within the programme text but on a meta-textual, 'televisual' dimension as well. Ever-changing sequences of images and programmes selectively activate the uncertainty, paradox, incongruity and ambivalence of any one text within it. An awareness of televisual heterochronia helps us to explore the role of sequence, interpenetration and the repetition and recombination of programmes and programme elements as *themselves* constituting sites of meaning-making. This is not to suggest that producers' intended meanings are completely evacuated or overwritten by the meta-textual flow of programme sequence; rather, it is to argue that the medium's particular form of heterochronia plays an important and potentially determining role in conceptually framing any given text. Because these processes play themselves out with displaced, irregular and ever-changing temporal elements, they are particularly well suited to generate tensions (and meanings) of a historical nature. The interpenetration of particular programme units can frame a particular programme unit as historical artefact; or it can reframe an orthodox historical interpretation, fundamentally changing its reading. The frisson between programme units – ever-changing with regard to sequence and lived historical context (in the case of programme repetition) – is itself a key element in the construction of history.

So, as previously stated, in contrast to the library with its latent form of heterochronia, television's recombinatory structures necessarily play out over time. Our access to that time, however, is very much in flux, complicating easy generalizations. Although televisual time has certain distinguishing characteristics (*immediate, continuous* and *co-existant*), the actual textures and experiences of these characteristics are themselves historically contingent. In order to help specify the kinds of recombinatory practices that television and its viewers engage in – the key elements, after all, in the medium's historical claim – we need to understand the broad trends in television's technologies, programme sequencing and user interfaces.

The notion of flow, one of the most developed discursive strands in television studies, touches directly upon this point (see Uricchio 2004). Closely associated with Raymond Williams' path-breaking contribution to the study of television, the concept has gone on to support very different arguments and, in the process, has helped both to chart shifts in the identity of television as a cultural practice and to map various undulations in the terrain of television studies (see Williams [1974]1992; Gripsrud 1998; Uricchio 2004). It has been deployed perhaps most consistently in the service of defining a televisual 'essence', adhering to Williams' description of flow as 'perhaps the defining characteristic of broadcasting, simultaneously – as technology and as a cultural form' (Williams [1974]1992: 8). It has been used to describe the structure of textuality and programming on macro-, meso- and micro-levels. And it has given form to the viewing experience, serving as a framework within which reception can be understood (variously activated in terms of larger household regimes and the logics of meaning-making).

I would like to call upon this concept because it offers a concise way to locate the changing contours of the televisual *dispositif*, that is the historically specific constellation of technologies, logics and practices that constitute the medium. Roughly speaking, we can distinguish three periods, the first of which is the television-broadcast era, which began in most Western nations around 1950 and, at least in the US, ended in the mid- to late 1970s shortly after Williams published his book. Williams experienced a form of broadcast television largely dependent on limited VHF and UHF transmissions, with between three to six channels available in most urban American markets. Viewed over television sets that required manual tuning (and often manipulation of the antenna), conditions were ripe for the dominance of the television programmer, who orchestrated a continuous flow of texts, keeping viewers pinned to their seats. Scarcity also meant that America's 'big three' broadcasting companies enjoyed massive audience share, and that broadcasting could work in the service of a consensual project. Programme sequence was essentially under the control of the broadcasters, with viewers having few other options at their disposal. And with controlled sequence and few other options, the broadcast era was characterized by a finely crafted, relatively stable and largely programmer-defined heterochronic order of the sort analysed by Williams.

By the mid- to late 1970s, change was in the air. New regulations for the diffusion of cable service transformed cable from a community service into a business. Meanwhile, the Domestic Communication Satellite Rules allowed private satellite distribution, ending the monopoly of the Communications Satellite Corporation. Time Incorporated's Home Box Office, Ted Turner's Atlanta independent WTCG and Pat Robertson's Christian Broadcasting Network, to mention but three of the cable operators that expanded exponentially in the late 1970s and early 1980s, grew in the space provided by these regulatory changes. On the programming front, new opportunities for the recycling of old broadcast (and film) texts proliferated as cable stations sought ways to fill air-time, and television's economic logics increasingly turned to syndication, reruns and endless self-reference (Kompare 2005). Old classics found new contexts, whether through happenstance or programming strategies – from thematic packaging like the History Channel to *Nick at Nite*'s recasting of classics as camp (Spigel 2001). The videocassette recorder (VCR) also entered the American home in rapidly increasing numbers, effectively unshackling viewers from television programmers' sequencing logics.

The widespread appearance of the remote control device (RCD) emblematizes this era. It stands in synergetic relation to the radical increase in television channels, the availability of cable and satellite service, and the introduction of the VCR, with 'the click of a button' facilitating viewer mobility among the 'older' broadcasts and the 'newer' programming sources. And, most importantly, it signals a shift away from the programming-based notion of flow that Williams described, to a viewer-centred model. In this new regime – the era of 'narrowcasting' – not only was the once mass audience fragmented, but it gained a greater degree of agency in arranging its own programme sequence, in shaping its own patterns of interpenetration (zapping through advertisements, switching channels) and, thanks to the VCR, in defining its own course of programme repetition and recycling. Indeed, the breakup of the mass audience and the rise of more robust forms of individual agency seem implicit in one another. With the shift in agency from the network's programmer to the individual, and with greater control over television's recombinatory potentials, a new experience of television's underlying temporality – and heterochronic potentials – was born.

Today, the affordances of digitalization have radically displaced control and sequence. Control has shifted to an independent sector composed of meta-data programmers and filtering technologies (variously constructed as search engines in the case of IPTV and adaptive interfaces in the case of intelligent DVR-based systems such as TiVo). The ability of viewers to exercise their own agency over programme sequence – and even textual production and distribution – has greatly increased. Thanks to intensified

convergence and the television medium's own shift from over-the-air broadcasting to a variety of alternate carriers (cable, satellite, video-on-demand
systems and the internet), content has been loosened from any particular
distribution model. The results of digitalization can be seen in new kinds of
interfaces between viewer and programme such as TiVo, in internet protocol
distribution systems and video portals such as Hulu and YouTube.

The overarching trend from the early 1950s to the present seems clear:
from television as a one-way, coherent, programmer-controlled flow to television as bidirectional, fragmented, user-controlled experience; from mass
audiences to atomized viewers; from a site of public memorialization to an
increasingly personal site of private and public expression. This fabric of
changes has left unchallenged television's temporal characteristics of immediacy and continuity, but it has fundamentally transformed the experience of
sequence, interpenetration and repetition. The shifts in agency, in scale
and directionality have significant implications for the concept and experience of televisual heterochronia ... and wider cultural implications in terms
of public memory.

The future of television history

I have argued that the disjunctions, discontinuities and endless recombinatory possibilities of televisual flow lead to a medium-specific dimension of
(meta-)textual production, and thus of meanings ... and, potentially, historical
meanings. This process works in tandem with the textual units constructed
by programme-makers – documentaries, dramatic fictions, advertisements,
news, programme bumpers, promos – effectively transforming any particular
text's original meaning and epistemological status. My point is relatively
straightforward: although something like the associational logic captured by
'the Kuleshov effect' is axiomatic when we think about the grammar of
time-based texts and the manner in which individual shots accrete into
meaningful utterances, our approaches to the study of television have usually
failed to extend these insights into the relationship of programme elements
to one another. Instead, we (and our archives) tend to focus on individual
texts, plucked from their environment, stripped of their advertisements and
framing context, freed from notions of repetition or interpenetration or larger
programme sequence, and exempted from any consideration of the particular
heterochronic regime of which they are a part. As a result, television texts are
analysed very much like film texts; and while we have long since abandoned
the notion of stable meanings, we have for too long assumed the existence of
the stable text. This approach has of course yielded a wide range of insights;
and yet, particularly when we are considering how texts – and how the
medium generally – engages with history, the larger heterochronic dimension is also vitally important. It helps to account for the variable status of a
particular shot or programme – either as history in the sense of interpretation

or as trace of the past – and for the embedding of ever-shifting bits of recorded time into new contexts. Television's complex temporality renders it into a history generator.

The twist regarding this general effect is that television's configurations of technology and cultural form have morphed over time. The situation today is indeed quite different from that of the broadcasting era, with the medium's broad definitional contours very much in a state of contention. Yet television – even when distributed through the internet – has maintained its roots in the twin definitional logics of a particular representational order and temporal order ('live' in the sense of potentially immediate, continuous and co-existent). And more than simply changing, these televisual configurations have accreted, and exist side by side: for example, it is still possible to view programmer-dominated, broadcast-like television over the internet, still possible to experience 'old' cable, and, at the same time, to experience new DVR-generated television flow.

And what about the latest reconfiguration of the medium? Contemporary viewers enjoy several affordances unavailable to earlier generations. *Access* to content continues to expand greatly, with global television increasingly coming on line and massive archival digitization projects enhancing access to the televisual (and filmic) past. *Agency* is also shifting, although to more than one model. We are becoming much more dependent on programme meta-data and on search engines, and can see increasing signs that social-recommendation systems will play an important role in how we imagine navigating the medium. At the same time, the blurring of producers and users and the active distribution of the results promise even greater variation of content. Most importantly, users can control the flow of programme elements, constructing contexts and playing with the ensuing meanings. Together, these affordances in the areas of access and agency enable viewers to look beyond their regions or nations, assessing the world from outside a long-controlled viewing position. They can ask how particular situations have evolved, and have the means to investigate the before and after of those developments. Historical memory has new compilers, new sites of accretion, new pathways, as users navigate a soup of textual possibilities, either refashioning their own texts or recombining contexts and causal sequences of texts to express new meanings. The shift underway is from the art of selection (the broadcast and cable eras) to the art of aggregation, and the far more active reassembly of sequence. And if we complicate this by factoring in the increasing importance of cross-platform prowling, the possibilities are daunting.

As television – a medium with a long history of entanglements with other media, from the telephone to film to the radio – continues its latest pas de deux with the networked computer, the direction of flow is changing. In our online world, we read *and* write; we download *and* uplink; we consume *and* 'cut and paste' *and* produce. YouTube, of course, emblematizes this participatory turn (and television's increasingly close relationship with the internet), and I would like to close by briefly noting its implications for the television and history relationship (Uricchio 2009). Although mainstream television is flirting ever-more intently with user-generated content (*America's Funniest Home Videos*, BBC's *Video Diaries* and citizen journalism forms such as *CNN: I-Reports*), much YouTube content is predicated upon the viewer/user's reappropriation and recontextualization of existing televisual and film material. Indeed, many videos literalize the associative and often transgressive reading practices that I have been arguing are inherent in televisual heterochronia. Original programme texts are disassembled, recycled, remixed with materials of other provenance and recast as new texts. And YouTube provides a site for their distribution, for further recycling, and for commentary. I am not claiming that YouTube and its ilk are more or less historical in nature than earlier forms of television, but rather that their heterochronic order is accessible, manipulable and more capable of being reordered than earlier forms. They offer tangible evidence of the kinds of recombinatory reading practices that have long accompanied television's temporality. YouTube offers ample evidence of creative appropriation and recombination, whether we look to the thousands of short family histories that integrate interviews with photographs, film and video images clipped from the web, or the videos on world war, recast and remixed into new entities. As well, YouTube, as a larger composite of viewer-organized videos, offers users an opportunity to assess and assemble their own evidence and construct their own arguments regarding historical developments. As a heterochronic ensemble, the videos assembled under a rubric such as 'the Bay of Pigs' include diverse sources (interviews, Cuban-sourced footage, US propaganda, period news and advertisements, and so on) and temporalities that permit nuanced insights into the situation based on sources long unavailable to the US public. Not only do viewer-produced videos function as explicit forms of historical inscription, the very assemblages of clips under a particular rubric are capable of having historical potential.

My point here is to counter fears of the inevitability of social fragmentation. As we consider the accretion of videos around new topics, and the pace of user remixing and sequence intervention, we are witnessing nothing less than the emergence of grass-roots *lieux de mémoire*, places marked and commemorated by communities of interest, not nation states or national broadcasting companies. If we add to this process of accretion the many user comments that ensue, we have evidence of robust forms of 'bottom-up' historical engagement and meaning-making. In a world with historical re-enactors, amateur genealogists and local historians, the production of grass-roots history is nothing new. But the repurposing of televisual texts, their recombination and resequencing, suggests signs of a *critical* engagement and an acute awareness of the ambivalence and limits of historical evidence.

This participatory turn, even though it is by and large uncontrolled, undocumented, and unacceptable as professional scholarly history, would nevertheless seem to have advantages over the mere consumption of historical fare, sensitizing its lay practitioners to the pitfalls and challenges of representing and assessing the past. The end of history? No, just a new and potentially more active turn in its engagement by people who, when they watch television and embrace the heterochronic environment it provides, presumably deploy some of the same active, recombinatory logic.

Note

1 A proviso is in order. Television's institutional practices tend to be culturally and historically specific in terms of programme source, mix and the manner in which that programming is presented (foreign texts dubbed in the US, subtitled in the Netherlands, read by a single voice in Poland). Such specificities have implications for the construction of public and collective memory. For reasons of brevity, I will be using US commercial television as my default.

References

Arnheim, Rudolf ([1935]1969) 'A forecast of television', in R. Arnheim *Film as art*, London: Faber and Faber, pp. 156–63.

Benjamin, Walter ([1936]1969) 'The work of art in the age of mechanical reproduction' in Hannah Arendt (ed.) *Illuminations*, New York: Schocken.

Bourdon, Jérôme (2000) 'Live television is still alive: on television as an unfulfilled promise', *Media, Culture & Society* 22:5, pp. 531–56.

Ellis, John (1999) 'Television as Working-Through', in J. Gripsrud (ed.) *Television and Common Knowledge*, London: Routledge, pp. 55–70.

Foucault, Michel ([1966]1970) *The Order of Things: An Archaeology of the Human Sciences*, New York: Pantheon Books.

Foucault, Michel (1998) 'Different spaces', trans. R. Hurley, in M. Foucault, *Essential works of Foucault 1954–1984*, Vol. 2, London: Penguin, pp. 175–85.

Gripsrud, Jostein (1998) 'Television, broadcasting, flow: key metaphors in TV theory', in C. Geraghty and D. Lusted (eds) *The Television Studies Book*, London: Arnold, pp. 17–32.

Horkheimer, M. and Adorno, T. ([1947]2002) *Dialectic of Enlightenment: Philosophical Fragments*, G. S. Noerr (ed.), trans. E. Jephcott, Stanford: Stanford University Press.

Kittler, Friedrich (1999) *Gramophone, Film, Typewriter*, Stanford: Stanford University Press.

Kompare, Derek (2005) *Re-Run Nation: How Repeats Invented American Television*, New York: Routledge.

Marx, Karl (1942) 'The Eighteenth Brumaire of Louis Bonaparte', in *Selected Works*, Vol. 2, London: Lawrence and Wishart.

Scannell, Paddy (1996) *Radio, Television and Modern Life*, Oxford: Blackwell.

Scannell, Paddy (2004) 'Broadcasting historiography and historicality', *Screen* 45:2, pp. 130–41.

Spigel, Lynn (2001) *Welcome to the Dream House*, Durham, NC: Duke University Press.

Uricchio, William (2004) 'Television's next generation: technology/interface culture/flow', in Lynn Spigel and Jan Olsson (eds) *Television After TV: Essays on a Medium in Transition*, Durham, NC: Duke University Press, pp. 232–361.

Uricchio, William (2009) 'The future of television? in Pelle Snikkars and Patrick Vonderau (eds) *The YouTube Reader*, London: Wallflower Press.

Williams, Raymond ([1974]1992) *Television: Technology and Cultural Form*, Hanover: Wesleyan University Press.

3

'CRITICAL SOCIAL OPTICS' AND THE TRANSFORMATIONS OF AUDIO-VISUAL CULTURE

John Corner

In this chapter I want to raise some questions about the ways in which images are encountered, perceived, understood and (often) questioned as a result of the radical transformation of visual culture within digital contexts. This will involve attention to aspects of the changing culture of photography since it seems to me that, in engaging with the implications of the digital, television scholarship can benefit considerably from a closer, comparative attention to what has happened to photography as it has become transformed over the last 15 years or so. This transformation has clearly affected its practices of production and has completely reconfigured its modes of distribution, display and consumption. More broadly, it has generated what I think can be seen as a new, critical appreciation of how images mean and of the complexity of the processes both of production and of consumption involved in the production of meaning. Along with other developments, without directly 'subverting' the use of images, it has brought about a degree of *instability* in visual meaning. It has served to 'unstick' the image from the world a little – not detaching it completely but pulling it over into the more openly contentious realms of culture and of politics. It is this process I want to highlight in my title term 'critical social optics', with its emphases on critical engagement and the sociality (both in awareness and in the terms of their distribution) of emerging modes of the image.

Television remains, in most countries, the dominant public medium. Its versions of mobile visibility, its kinetic (and aurally supported) renderings of the world, have been given expanded reach through the digital applications that other chapters in this book will explore. Whatever the changes it undergoes, its semiotic commitments to flow, sequence, process, action and narrative design are likely to continue, albeit with modifications. However, within this context I want to open up some questions about the revived public profile of the still and silent image, whose distinctive, provocative

41

ways of setting up relationships of seeing, of brokering between world and subjectivity, of 'holding' time and 'giving' time, provide, as I have suggested, a useful comparison with television's characteristic modes of 'capturing' the real, and of promising knowledge to viewers. I also want to note here how the cultural contexts of viewing, into which much factual television now 'goes out' and works, are also changing, partly as a result of the broader shifts, the new patterns of production, circulation and use, apparent in visual mediation.

The new Routledge journal *Photographies* provides just one indication of the kind of revised agenda of theory and inquiry generated around digital change and the culture of the image. In the editorial to its first issue, it noted that:

> One thing seems certain: there is now more photography, possibly of more kinds, than ever before. We are dealing with a truly expanded field where deep continuities run alongside unforeseen and radical transformation.
>
> (Editorial 2008)

Over the last two decades, photography, far from being dispatched into a more marginal, residual position within media culture by the developments of new technology, has become a more dominant and influential feature of the mediascape. Most dramatically, it has wholly reconfigured the character of self-documentation in the private sphere, its digital possibilities and applications bringing about a shift in private visual culture that has continued with accelerated pace the revolution in 'seeing ourselves' (and, of course, 'seeing others') that popular photography first introduced in the late nineteenth and early twentieth century.

How have the new shifts impacted upon the character of photography as a mode of public communication, as a mode of 'seeing the social' and 'seeing the political'? First of all, it is immediately clear that the radical changes to photography in what I have called private visual culture have often had direct implications for public visual culture. This is most obviously true in respect of the use of photography within photoblogging, where the private/public fusions that are defining of 'blogs' as a genre are given an open articulation.[1] It is also clearly true in respect of the important role photographs play within social-networking sites such as MySpace and Facebook, where precisely the uncertain borderlines between 'private' and 'public' have been the source of pleasure, insight, embarrassment and even legal prosecution.[2]

But what of more direct uses of the photograph as an agency of public and political knowledge? With its widely discussed characteristics of silence and stillness, characteristics imparting both its semiotic strength and its limitations, how does the photograph figure within a public culture that might be thought to be moving ever-more emphatically towards a commitment to the semiotics of sound and movement, to the hectic modalities of representation characterized, for instance, in 'reality television' and in the new modes of 'infotainment'?[3] In what ways has its significatory and ideological profile shifted, revealing new possibilities both for deception and for knowledge, within the emerging terms of technological application? How far does that 'critique of photography' (and especially of documentary photography) developed in the 1970s and 1980s transfer to the newer modes of production and display?[4]

I want to pursue some of these questions by looking at examples of recent high-profile 'public photography' and exploring how digital applications have worked to thicken and extend the exchange of viewers' critical discourse around the still image at the same time as providing photographers with a new platform for displaying their images and for telling stories about them and about the contexts of their taking. Images have thus become more thickly 'narrated' both by those who produce them and by those who view them. Following up on the point made earlier, by using the phrase 'critical social optics', I mean to signal both a concern with the construction of the image as an aesthetic, artefactual object of engagement and perhaps of pleasure, and a broader address to the political and cultural consequences of connecting viewers to the world photographically. As photography takes its myriad digitalized routes through political, social, institutional and psychological space, it has become newly 'foregrounded', more sharply marked *as a social practice*. In a later section, I discuss further the consequences this carries for our understanding of the transformation of television.

Case study: the World Press Photo award

In 2007, the annual World Press Photo award for the best news picture of the previous year was given to the American photojournalist Spencer Platt of Getty Images for a photograph taken on 15 August 2006 in Beirut. ('World Press Photo of year award 2006' brings up a number of options on a Google 'images' search, involving over 50 websites in June 2009. Worldpressphoto. org itself includes an opportunity both to see the image and to hear Spencer Platt talking about it.) The 15 August was the day after the ceasefire in the conflict between Israel and Hezbollah forces in the Lebanon, a conflict that had resulted in the Israeli shelling of parts of Beirut.

The photograph shows five young people – four women and one man – seated in a moving red convertible against a background of devastated buildings and heaped debris from the shelling. The bottom half of the frame is tightly around the group in the car, running from the windscreen along to the folded canopy at the rear. The upper half of the frame is dominated by the damage on the far side of the street down which the car is driving left to right. A few standing figures can be seen in front of the debris, some apparently speaking on mobile phones. The picture cuts off the visible fore-ground after revealing only the first few inches of the car's nearside but a strong perception of the out-of-frame foreground is signalled by the fact that four of the car's occupants, all but the man driving, are looking towards this foreground, two at an angle to the line of the camera and two looking directly in its direction. One of the women on the back seat is holding a handkerchief to her face, one appears to be taking a photo (or perhaps sending a text) on a camera phone. Four of the car's occupants are wearing sunglasses.

The shiny red colour of the car, the resonance of open-topped driving and the sense of youthful style conveyed by the clean, neat appearance of those seated inside, with the woman on the front seat in a white T-shirt, and two of those in the back in black dresses, are all in striking contrast with the setting. Crucially, the position of the photographer is higher than road level, allowing a perspective that gives the car's interior a depth from nearside to offside within which its occupants can be more clearly and fully seen. We look into the car as well as perceive it against its background.

The caption initially given to the picture was 'Affluent Lebanese drive down the street to look at a destroyed neighbourhood in southern Beirut' with an added date. However, the contrastive force of the image was picked up and amplified more explicitly by other users (one Dutch newspaper used the caption 'The Cool People VS. Hezbollah'). A website writer noted, more critically still and elaborating on the caption:

> The 'Young Lebanese' happen to be a sports car full of women who have clearly devoted a lot of energy to trying to look sexy in a global-celebutard sort of way. It's like they were hoping to be hounded by paparazzi, but ended up instead in a war photographer's viewfinder.
>
> ('One Photograph That Sums it All Up',
> Veryshortlist.com, 22 February 2007)

When it was awarded the top prize in February 2007 by World Press Photo (an independent, non-profit foundation supporting international photo-journalism and based in Amsterdam), the chairwomen of the panel offered a more nuanced reading, noting how it was 'a picture you can keep looking at. It has the complexity and contradiction of real life, amidst chaos. The photograph makes you look beyond the obvious.' (Cited at http://www.lensculture.com. 'World Press Photo Winners for 2006'.) On the website OpenDemocracy.net, the writer Mai Ghoussoub (2007) picked up the theme of contradiction after having the image emailed to her by a friend. She observed how the picture 'looked disturbing and even repellent to most viewers' but went on to note her own fascination with it and the way its meaning for her centred on 'the metaphor it creates about war photography', about 'voyeurism' and 'the act of taking photos in tragic situations'. She also mentioned another friend's suggestive comments about how the image of these young people together in a convertible seemed to connect connotatively with a classic Hollywood iconography of youth, glamour and fate. To many viewers of the image, this will be seen as a plausible pickup on the cultural echoes (even down to the Monroe-like profile of the woman in the white sweater and dark glasses at the front of the car).

Negative readings of the image as showing 'disaster tourism' circulated alongside more complex, or positive ones, with controversy surrounding the award in a number of countries, both among professional and amateur photographers and more widely. For example, Lebanese photographer Samer Mohdad claimed that the giving of the prize was 'an insult to all news photographers who have risked their lives to cover this horrible war.' (Cited in 'Award Winning Photograph Puts Subjects on the Defensive' mesarabies.blog, 22 February 2007.) A Toronto gallery owner and photography festival organizer posted a note on the site of the Canadian magazine *Walrus* raising questions not only about the values of the people in the photograph but, by metaphoric extension, about those of society in general:

> At first glance, this photograph is an indictment of the five youths in the car. Clearly the children of privilege, they seem to be on an innocuous Sunday drive. Their bright red sports car and fashions show them as the 'in crowd'. What is it that shields them from the devastation that surrounds them? Is it the shiny car, their money, or their attitude? It is the latter notion which troubles me the most because it isn't the attitudes of these five that disturbs me, but our own. Although we are informed of the world's problems and hold opinions for solutions, or at the very least we express exasperation at the improbability of finding answers to many specific issues from regions with systemic hatred, we are sheltered in our own islands of affluence.
>
> (Stephen Bulger, *Walrus* website, 28 August 2007)

Questions were inevitably raised about the conditions of the photograph's taking and Platt was quite quick to establish its 'authenticity' and his own relationship of integrity towards what it depicted. His account, in interview, was posted on a number of websites, and a crucial passage went as follows:

> This was the first morning that we were able to really survey what had happened here. And I saw out of the corner of my eye, coming at me at a fairly decent speed, a car that really stood out from everything else. It was clean. Nothing in the neighborhood was clean. It was like 9/11, the day after ... I had very little time to focus, to compose. I snapped, I suppose, about five images, four

of which were completely and totally ruined because there was a gentleman standing in front of me and his arm was in the picture.

(Platt 2007)

He went on to note that he took 400 images that day, editing them down in his hotel room to 30, which he sent through, and which included the car photo. Reflecting on the difficulties in making sense of the image, he commented:

> There's a lot of ambiguity to the image, who the women are, what they're thinking, what kind of background do they come from? I hear a different interpretation of it every day, and I'm somewhat sympathetic with them all.
>
> (Platt 2007)

In a short presentation placed on the World Press Photo website after the award had been made, he elaborated on the range and scale of interpretations:

> You go online and there are 12, 15, 20 different interpretations from 20 different nationalities and backgrounds, about what they think about it, what they feel about it, what they think the photographer was trying to say.
>
> (worldpressphoto.org, 2007)

In further comment during a telephone interview with the BBC, reported on the BBC website, Platt moved to a slightly different take on the people in the car from the dominant concern with whether or not they were 'disaster tourists'. He placed them as possible victims, but victims seen in a new way:

> The picture challenges our notion of what a victim is meant to look like. These people are not victims, they look strong, they're full of youth.
>
> (Cited in Ghattas 2007)

Few published interpretations had taken the 'victim' route, even in speculation or as a perceived challenge to stereotypical readings. In the context of the developing controversy around the image, Platt elaborated on this view (complicating it with some further, rather revealing, judgements aligning political power and spending power) in an interview with Getty Images CEO Jonathan Klein (posted on YouTube):

> In the media ... you are you used to seeing people from the Middle East that are not empowered. And these people have power.

These are beautiful, sexy looking people that look like they have
some spending power. And these people represent a dynamic in a
very important part of the Middle East.

(Klein 2007)

In a development that is not too surprising given the level of international
media interest, the people in the car were found and interviewed by the press
(German and Belgian journalists were involved initially, with the account
rapidly being distributed to other news outlets and websites). In the process,
they gave their own story of the background to the image. Four of them
were actually residents in the area depicted who had had to flee because of
the shelling. This was their first trip back, to check on their apartment and
belongings. The car itself had been previously used to transport medication
to refugees taking shelter in central Beirut. One of them noted of the image:

It's an interesting picture, but there were so many more that reflected what really happened here ...
But it's true that there were people who did come to the area just to
have a look at the destruction ...
It's the caption that went with the picture that made it famous and
that's what's upsetting, the caption reinforces the cliché.

Another commented:

I understand why the picture won. It's about the contrast between
destruction and glamour. But it's the wrong image of the war and it
sanitizes it.

(Both cited in Ghattas 2007)

The implication from these interviews is also that none of the people in the
car had any idea that the picture had been taken until its publication in
Paris Match in September 2006. They had not noticed Platt at all.

What this example highlights is that familiar capacity of photography to
be both powerful and indeterminate. This combination can be found in other
media of course, but photography's lack of *propositionality*, its much discussed
status as an apparent representation of a given moment rather than an
explicit discourse *about* that moment, gives its way of being 'open to interpretation' a very distinctive character. The circuits of the web are providing a
new and prominent platform for the display of photographic practice, for its
special ways of bringing us close to the 'look of things' and, at the same
time, an active critical forum, a space of exchange, for debating the photograph's problematic and contestable 'iconicity', its often implicit (sometimes
beguiling, sometimes deeply objectionable) ways of producing knowledge
and encouraging judgements.

47

While not having the space to develop a second case study of comparable length, I would like to mention here the World Press Photo award winner for the following year, taken in 2007 and awarded in 2008 (as with the Beirut photo, there are many websites carrying this image as 'World Press Photo of Year Award 2007', with worldpressphoto.org itself an obvious choice). Once again, the critical social optics of 'seeing conflict' are involved. This image, taken by the British photographer Tim Hetherington, working for *Vanity Fair*, shows a young US soldier leaning back against the earth wall of a darkened military bunker in Afghanistan. His upturned helmet is cradled against his chest by his left hand and his right hand diagonally covers his upper face, leaving the left eye visible, in a gesture of exhaustion and stress. The background details of the image (military equipment, netting and so on) are reduced in definition by the overall darkness of the scene, giving the soldier (and especially his face) strong focus. The official caption was 'American soldier resting at bunker, Korengal Valley, Afghanistan, 16 September' but other websites have variations on this; for instance, the BBC website reproduces it with the slightly more interpretative caption 'An exhausted American soldier in Afghanistan's Korengal Valley'. Hetherington was working at the time with the writer/reporter Sebastian Junger (author, among things, of the 'faction' bestseller and then film, *The Perfect Storm*). He has noted how the image was taken spontaneously (in his acceptance speech he described it as 'a snatched moment ... I had no idea what the soldier was thinking or feeling') (Hetherington 2008a). He and Junger were resting in the bunker at the time and using its protection against the possibility of further Taleban fire on what had been an 'intense day'. Hetherington also comments:

> At the time I took the picture, I remember seeing the image on the back of the digital camera, showing it to Sebastian. I knew it was good.
>
> (Hetherington 2008a)

The idea of 'exhaustion' was carried further, into an implicitly political interpretation, by the Chairman of the jury, Gary Knight, who observed that 'this image shows the exhaustion of a man – and the exhaustion of a nation' (worldpressphoto.org). The broader view stops short of offering a more precise reading of the terms of 'national exhaustion', leaving the specific attitude taken towards America and the war relatively 'open'. In his acceptance speech, Hetherington commented 'It's said the man portrayed shows the exhaustion of a nation. Some people see it as propaganda for the war, others as an indictment of the war. But it doesn't need to be either ... it's about a young man stuck on the side of a mountain in Afghanistan.' Hetherington went on to say how the soldier in the picture was now 'proud of it', as were his family, although the soldier was unhappy with the news that it had been used on placards at an anti-war protest in Nashville (Hetherington 2008b).

Clearly, keeping the meanings of the image contained around the soldier himself rather than playing them into frameworks for assessing the war is virtually impossible, as I found when I showed this image to my students and asked for their immediate interpretations. The iconicity of a sole human figure in a posture of fatigue against a darkened background immediately works symbolically as well as naturalistically. Similarly, the photograph has sufficient figurative ambiguity to afford a resource both for pro-war and anti-war readings, as student opinion also showed.[5] It is a photograph that one might imagine the US Army being quite comfortable with, as well as the anti-war movement. Since Hetherington was working at the time as an embedded journalist, this is not at all surprising.

Aesthetically, the very darkness of the image was central to critical responses, for some critics the indication of a technical/compositional flaw, but for others quite the reverse, conveying the enriching suggestions of chiaroscuro. In a detailed and perceptive posting on the photo website Foto8 (Broomberg and Chanarin 2008) a writer noted how the 'blurred focus and pixelated JPEG compression make this image feel accidental and urgent ... for some members of the jury it was also "painterly"'.

Unlike the 'Beirut' image, the Afghanistan photograph, although deeply ambivalent, did not become strongly controversial for *what* it depicted, only *formally*, for its choice as the winner against more sharply defined, attractively composed images on the shortlist.

Temporality, instability, relocation: digital visual culture and television

Just where the routine professional work of photojournalism and photo-documentary is now placed within these newer circuits of distribution, promotion, commentary and critique, within the emerging digital spaces and times, is uncertain. This is particularly so since the power and centrality of television journalism is in most countries defining for visual public knowledge. Nevertheless, the single image remains one dominant media mode, both realist and expansively symbolic, for engaging with the world, perhaps most notably in the traditional form of the front-page photograph. Disasters, wars, domestic political affairs and various kinds of 'scoop' are given a focalizing, condensing and often figurative projection through this practice. Web photography continues and then extends the practice, not only in relation to the scale of image availability and its subsequent informal distribution but also in relation to the huge increase in representational scope, including image–text combinations, given by the use of site-based 'gallery' folders containing multiple images and perhaps involving slideshow formats. These widely used formats permit the control of individual image engagement by the viewer or can be clicked to provide a time-sequenced route determined by the photographer, with opportunities for narrative development and voice-over commentary that allow closer proximity to television/video.[6] The emerging forms of web publication take place in what is still a 'second tier' of mediation, below that of mainstream television, newspapers and magazines. The attention they receive is therefore demographically skewed, although we know that the social profile of web use, including its relation to mainstream media, is now rapidly changing and that mainstream media themselves are sensitive to this, as they are to the wider circulation of images brought about by digital photography.[7] A much wider take-up of what had become 'newsworthy' images clearly happened with the World Press Photo award images, carrying them digitally well beyond their first, selective print publication.[8]

I have suggested that the new contexts for photography include thickened possibilities both for explanation, commentary and critique. In that sense, they not only give added projection to the distinctive qualities of the still image as a mode of mediated perception and knowledge but also create a broader and more varied forum for debating the image in both highly specific and also more general terms and according to a number of criteria, both substantive-realist and formal. The photograph as 'public document' thus itself becomes the object of a certain (constrained but significant) public discourse and the *debatability* of photography, not just photographic practice, is given a novel, expanded scope.

Let me return to the comparison with television and the essentially different organization of temporality with which this medium works. In his suggestive account of television's ontological character, Richard Dienst (1994) makes some general observations on this theme:

> ... time is the substance of television's visuality, the ground of its ontology, and the currency of its economy. Television has been analysed as a machine for the prodigious regulated construction and circulation of time. Its limited morphology of representation obeys strictly temporal constraints ... An adequate conceptualisation of time as an open-ended process of composition and decomposition is a precondition for any homology between televisual images and exchange value, not to mention any discussion of how television's systemic *visuality* accounts for the contingent subjective processes of *visibility*.
>
> (Dienst 1994: 159)

As in photography, this play-off between visuality and visibility, between an aesthetic/representational order and particular forms of perception, of social seeing, is both central and complex. Like many theorists of television, Dienst is primarily concerned with television's difference from cinema in respect of its significatory regime, although no discussion of representational temporality is complete without some reference to photographic orders of 'stillness'. Pursuing some comments of Deleuze, Dienst argues for the way in which still time in television is always located within the terms of 'automatic time':

> Hence still time is not a moment of capturing a picture and making an object of it, as in photography. Televisual stills are created by switching away from a picture, pushing past one towards another, by halting a movement or adding a different one. And these stills do not add up or follow one another: each turns over and disappears from view.
>
> (Dienst 1994: 161)

Perhaps Dienst might have given a little more sustained attention to photography, although at the time he was writing the full implications of the digital changes in photography's identity, particularly the terms of its web circulation, were only just appearing. It has, of course, been a regular move in critical analysis of television to somehow, if only figuratively, 'stop' television, to 'interrupt' its ceaseless and prolific, pointed yet also incidental and accidental, flow of meanings. We can compare this glut of noisy images in motion with the mute, often enigmatic, restraint of what is presented in many photographs, even when accompanied by a caption and set within a framing news item or feature. Photographs present themselves to us, in Dienst's terms, as that which has been made into an object, an artefact, even if nowadays we often see them on screens rather than hold them in our hands. Television's energies of mobile and noisy depiction, its active rendering of an active world, resist such objectifying; its picturings are therefore often passed off as naturalistic in a way that photography's often mesmerically unnatural stasis (what Barthes suggestively terms its – to him, endlessly fascinating – properties of 'arrest') and its silence serve to block. However compellingly truthful a photograph can seem to be in the intensity and detail of its referential 'capture' (a capture offered for our full engagement, if we wish to give it), it has a good deal of the truthfulness of art in its way of being true to life. Television actualities, by contrast, are often resolutely keen to repress their aesthetic status. This repression even carries over into the aesthetics of much television fiction, a point that has often been made in a contrast with cinema, indicating a difference that clearly owes much to the very different conditions of screening and reception within which the two systems operate.

Nevertheless, increasingly set within a visual culture offering more scope for the exercise of scepticism and criticism, one in which sites like YouTube are able to circulate opportunities for specifically critical *re-seeing* and even for parody, television programmes will find it less easy to premise their truth claims on a self-evident visual naturalism. Even in the debates of the late nineties about UK reality television, there were signs that fresh resources of critical assessment were feeding into popular viewing perceptions (see Ellis 2005).

Certainly, I believe that the long-running and intensive debate about the 'adequacy to the real', the social sufficiency, of television's news and documentary portrayals is given a further, instructive point of reference by the photographic practices and the discourses of photographic comment that have been encouraged by digital platforms.[9] What is beyond dispute is that these practices and discourses require attention in any proper assessment of digital culture's character and direction, including the directions now being taken by television, and of the impact upon the shifting conditions of 'public seeing'.

Notes

1 Chris Cohen (2005) provides an illuminating account of the aesthetic and social drives at work here. See *The New York Times'* new photoblog 'Lens' (lens.blog. nytimes.com) for an indication of how mainstream media can work to relay elements of the photographic blogosphere as well as contribute to it.

2 As I write, the latest British narrative of 'public' embarrassment follows the appearance on Facebook of details of the family life, accompanied by photographs, of the next head of the Secret Intelligence Service. They were placed there by his wife, on her own page, and then quickly removed by authorities following discovery by the press. Photographs of him playing football on a beach, in swimming trunks, make a dramatic contrast with the fact that his predecessor began his period of office publically unnamed and with no public images of him allowed.

3 As well as the formative discussions of photography's semiotics contained in the work of Barthes and Sontag (notably Barthes 1984 and Sontag 1979), there are many illuminating studies of photographic temporality. A recent, important collection is Green and Lowry 2006.

4 An influential example of this would be Martha Rosler's classic essay (1981, revised and expanded 1989).

5 Some students found reading the soldier's primary circumstances (routine tiredness after being on watch, total fatigue, utter despair?) difficult, quite apart from making the move from this particularity to a broader symbolic level (the war, America, etc.). Quite a few read the image as showing a soldier representing the physical toll of 'doing his duty', a reading that could move into patriotic, affirmative directions at least as easily as critical ones.

6 See Langton (2009) for a very recent account of the continuing possibilities and constraints for photojournalism, written from the perspective of a practitioner.

7 Here, one example would be the routine use made by television news programmes of images sent in by 'eyewitnesses', now including video images captured on phone cameras. Another, broader, example of this expansion and multi-layering of visual culture would be the regular call by some popular

television magazine programmes, including holiday series and even the weather slots of regional news, for viewers to send in their own images as part of an informal 'competition' to get a possible showing on the programme.

8 Of course, the most important and widely discussed instance of a photo-digital record (here, a private one) receiving major public circulation is the Abu Ghraib 'prisoner abuse' photographs of 2004. Among the commentaries and critical literature, Susan Sontag's 'Regarding the torture of others', first published in *The New York Times* (Sontag 2004), and widely reprinted, is an essential point of reference. A very recent discussion is Andre Gunthert's (2008). This includes attention to the issue of why, in an age of supposed scepticism towards the integrity of the digital image, these images were read immediately and widely as 'true'. For a suggestive analysis of the paradoxes of veracity at work in digital culture, see Fetveit (1999).

9 I have recently discussed the history of debate about documentary 'adequacy' (Corner 2008).

References

Barthes, R. (1984) *Camera Lucida*, London: Fontana.

Broomberg, A. and Chanarin, O. (2008) 'Unconcerned but not indifferent', *Foto8*, 5 March 2008.

Cohen, C. (2005) 'What does the photoblog want?', *Media, Culture & Society* 27.6, pp. 883–901.

Corner, J. (2008) 'Documentary studies: dimensions of transition and continuity', in T. Austin and W. de Jong (eds) *Rethinking Documentary*, Maidenhead: Open University Press/McGraw-Hill 2008, pp. 13–28.

Dienst, R. (1994) *Still Life in Real Time*, Durham, NC: Duke University Press.

Editorial (2008) *Photographies* 1.1, pp. 1–8.

Ellis, J. (2005) 'Documentary and truth on television: the crisis of 1999', in A. Rosenthal and J. Corner (eds) *New Challenges For Documentary*, Manchester: Manchester University Press, pp. 342–60.

Fetveit, A. (1999) 'Reality TV in the digital era: a paradox in visual culture', *Media, Culture & Society* 21.6, pp. 787–804.

Ghattas, K. (2007) 'Lebanon war image causes controversy', http://news.bbc.co.uk/1/hi/world/middle_east/6385969.stm. Accessed 13 August 2009.

Ghoussoub, M. (2007) *Beirut and Contradiction: Reading the World Press Photo Award*, 13 February 2007, http://www.opendemocracy.net/conflict-Literature/world_press_photo_4342.jsp. Accessed 14 August 2009.

Green, D. and Lowry, J. (eds) (2006) *Stillness and Time: Photography and the Moving Image*, London: Photoforum/Photoworks.

Gunthert, A. (2008) 'Digital imaging goes to war: the Abu Ghraib photographs', *Photographies* 1.1 pp. 103–12.

Hetherington, T. (2008a) *Picture Power: Tim Hetherington*, 14 February 2008, http://news.bbc.co.uk/1/hi/world/south_asia/7240590.stm. Accessed 13 August 2009.

Hetherington, T. (2008b) Acceptance Speech, http://www.rethink-dispatches.com/essays/world-press-photo-acceptance-speech-amsterdam-april-27th-2008/. Accessed 13 August 2009.

Klein, J. (2007) 'Jonathan Klein interviews Getty photographer Spencer Platt', http://www.youtube.com/watch?v=iQQIp2PEr-s. Accessed 14 August 2009.

Langton, L. (2009) *Photojournalism and Today's News*, Malden, MA: Wiley-Blackwell.

Platt, S. (2007) *Through The Looking Glass*, http://www.onthemedia.org/transcripts/2007/05/04/04. Accessed 13 August 2009.

Rosler, M. ([1981]1989) 'In, around, and afterthoughts on documentary photography'. The revised version is in R. Bolton (ed.) *The Contest of Meaning*, Cambridge, MA: The MIT Press, pp. 303–41.

Sontag, S. (1979) *On Photography*, Harmondsworth: Penguin.

Sontag, S. (2004) 'Regarding the torture of others', *The New York Times*, 23 May 2004.

4

MSN, INTERFACE

Nick Browne

We can begin with the blue field that is eclipsed when the computer successfully boots up. It is not, as I will try to show, a screen, a window, or a portal but the ground for any display of information whatsoever. Blue is the field that palpitates between the appearance of simulated life, after booting up, and the void of information absence, negation, or implosion. Nearly all the drive characteristics, addresses, and memory of the computer are activated by the system configuration that grounds itself on this blue field. Even its acronym, BSOD (Blue Screen of Death), provokes anxiety in its community of users and its actual appearance is met with convulsions and despair. This blue field is the most feared colour in the Microsoft world, occurring whenever something has gone terribly wrong, when the system encounters a fatal error, or when the system fails absolutely.

1. Happily, my topic is not catastrophe, but the colour blue of the homepage of Microsoft Internet Explorer, MSN, and the Microsoft Nation. The homepage is in fact the face and indeed the flag of that nation and the foundation on which Microsoft asserts its distinctive claims to sovereignty. Like the pyramids, its construction and maintenance required billions of dollars and years of effort by thousands of people. But unlike the pyramids, the details of its monumentality change daily. Though we are obliged to acknowledge the distinctive claims to local sovereignty evident in design and language of the page in China, Norway, the UK, or France, MSN is the homepage of dozens of discrete electronic states and constitutes, in its full assemblage, a veritable and virtual United Nations. For millions of users the day starts and ends in the space of its embrace. This is simply to say that the look and design of MSN's homepage is at the same time a complex icon of national identity and a kind of supernational, multicultural grammar of significant informational form. For these reasons, I propose to study the design, significance, and function of this single page. Necessarily, I will restrict myself to an analysis of a single instance; for convenience, the American one. I propose then, at the outset, a simple formal analysis of the page with just a few elements: shape, dimension,

colour, and layout. We can move from there to the larger, less obvious schemes.

2. For the Pythagoreans, remember, beauty inhered in proportions, in ratios. Though the heritage of the concept is complex, the classical golden ratio, height to width, is 1 to 1.62 (roughly 3 to 5). The extent to which Renaissance scholars and artists employed this ratio in painting, architecture, and book design is a subject of continuing debate. It may not be clear, however, that the designers of home computers, both desktops and laptops, had this ratio in mind when framing their world. What we actually see as the dimensions of the typical computer screen, height to width, until it recently went widescreen, was 1:1.33 (3 to 4). History shows that this is, in fact, the precise ratio of the 35mm silent-film image, later formally adopted as the official, classical Hollywood standard and the same proportion, until recently, of the standard US television screen. Indeed, this ratio is nearly identical to that of a sheet of standard American business stationery. This modern ratio, to which the proportions of the computer screen conform, constitutes, in effect, a definite formal paradigm which, for lack of a better term, we might designate as the 'Corporate Ratio', the CR for short. Let's then designate this new 3 to 4 ratio as the enshrined ratio of Western, commercial, and representational civilization in the twentieth century.

The ratio of the Microsoft Network homepage, however, is different from that of the frame of the computer screen, both because of some margins and bars and because the page extends into an area below the frame-line of the computer screen. The display presented by the computer screen is that of a landscape format. The full homepage cannot be seen in its entirety in a single glance. To view the full homepage, the user must scroll down to see what, adopting a term from old media, is 'below the fold' – about 60 per cent of the page. The page, as distinguished from the screen, is modelled on the portrait – the vertical dimension is dominant. However, if the homepage were rotated on its side, 90 degrees, and seen in a fully unscrolled manner, the ratio of the full, extended homepage would conform, almost exactly, to the 1 to 1.62 ratio of the Greek ideal. What area does this screen frame? On a standard laptop, the MSN homepage is about 27cm × 40cm; that is about 11in. x 18in. The surface that supports MSN information is about 1,100 square centimetres, about one and a third square feet. A page of a newspaper, edge to edge, for example *The New York Times*, is 12in. × 22in. and contains about 20 per cent more information area than the homepage.

To sum up, the frame of the computer screen has the same ratio as the image of the classic Hollywood cinema, the television screen, and the standard sheet of writing paper. The ratio of the unscrolled homepage, laid on its side, is nearly identical to the ratio of the Pythagorean golden rectangle. The computer screen and the MSN homepage, in other words, constitute two different paradigms for the presentation or display of information – one modern and one ancient. But, we must ask, is this duplex format beautiful?

3.   The layout of the homepage page consists of three vertical columns capped top and bottom by three horizontal bars. The centre and right columns are of the same width; the left column is about half the width of the other two. Inside these columns (in mid-2009) were 19 rectangles, the building blocks of the page. With their headings, we might call these units, for lack of a more precise term, 'chapters'. They are irregular, both in size and alignment (with respect to chapters in adjacent columns). The centre and right columns appear on a flat white surface and are separated by a thin blue line that delineates a border. The white columns in turn are superimposed on a blue background that decreases in saturation from top to bottom of the page. The topics are standard: 'news', 'sports', 'money', 'entertainment', 'health', and 'shopping', as well as 'today's picks', 'msn and you', 'A list searches', advertisements, and so on.

What we have called the chapters consist of two basic geometrical figures – rectangles, about twice as long as they are high, and squares. There is considerable uniformity. Each has a printed heading in bold typeface and four or five one-line, bulleted, story items. Three quarters of the chapters incorporate a photograph, in every case located in its own enclosure in the upper left of the chapter frame. Most chapters have a pair of buttons on the upper right that permit expansion or contraction of the listed items. Several chapters incorporate smaller boxes with a green 'go' button allowing the user to 'find' or 'get' additional information on the referenced topic. The left column incorporates some specific MSN operations – Hotmail accounts, tools for customizing content, and, notably, the option, with a screen and controls, to select and play from a catalogue of videos. The left column, unlike the other two, is set on a blue background. Two top horizontal panels, one blue, one white, extend continuously across the page with six clusters of topics organized alphabetically, from 'Air Tickets' to 'Yellow Pages'. The bottom panel has a similar design, with segregation of options by headings – 'features', 'go to', and 'services'. Both the top and bottom horizontal panels present an open search box.

The overall look of the homepage is of a loose, even casual amalgam of irregularly sized boxed, bordered units irregularly aligned in columns, consisting of combinations of text and image, whose dominant colour scheme varies from blue on white to white on blue. The colour blue, the ultimate support, is modulated for contrast and emphasis. Even the photographs are figured according to this regime. The typeface and size, whether in blue or white, is nearly uniform. There are small touches of black, green, and red. The font style, a Microsoft-commissioned typeface, Verdana 8.5, is designed to be readable in the graphic environment characteristic of standard computer screens.

4.   The MSN homepage is the congenial face, the façade of Microsoft Internet Explorer. The design of the search engine is hidden in complex, invisible algorithms. The purpose of Internet Explorer, the browser, is to

control and to monopolize the user's access to the world available on the internet. The homepage assists by mapping the world in familiar, user-accepted categories. The central business strategy of integrating the browser with the operating system enforced the restrictions on interoperability, annihilated competitors, and positioned Internet Explorer as the dominant browser, in control of nearly 80 per cent (prior to the ascendency of Google) of the world's searches.

Microsoft's replacement of the original MS_DOS text-based interface by the Xerox–Apple 'graphical user interface' in the late 1980s constituted the radically new paradigm of the user–computer interface for the general population. The point-and-click hypertext system, with its convenient windows, menus, and icons, established the current paradigm by enhancing the sense of user power and control while reducing user effort. The audible click is perhaps the most gratifying sound in this new universe of work. Every picture and line of text, regardless of specific content, is integrated as a hook into the substratum of a wider, denser, deeper, more declarative, commercial network. The homepage itself, however, disguises this purpose and presents just two chapters, less than 10 per cent of the page area, designated as 'advertisement'. However, each bulleted story, whether news, service, or lifestyle, constitutes points of attachment that lead the user to related commercial services. The segregated, horizontal panels at the top and bottom of the page are plainly lifestyle directories, sites for social comparison, celebrity, self-refashioning and gratification. A story on uncharted islands, accompanied with pictures, for example, promised escape to deserted beaches in French Polynesia, but led directly to the frequently consulted MSN Travel section and to a page crowded with ads and sponsored links for flights, hotels, and cars. An unsolicited offer to help the user find related articles leads to new pages and new links. These new pages, in turn, have three columns – the left is the directory, the middle the article proper, the right a full vertical column of associated ads. Overdetermination of the routes to consumption, that is enforced territorialization of uninhabited space through an itinerary of established links/routes to other Microsoft-owned or affiliated sites; that is, self-reference is, where possible, the preferred model of commercial occupation. Indeed, it is the model for the entire network and, in this branching, networked, recursive way, the Microsoft universe is integrated, evolves, and is held together.

5.   Whatever the apparently casual appearance of the homepage, its most striking and fundamental functional feature is this – every chapter, picture, line, and word is integrated into an architecture built on a graphical interface activated by a mouse and nearly every mark on the page is a hypertext link to another site. A click on 'weather' leads to an ad for automobile insurance performed by a break-dancing skeleton. The homepage is keyed to the restricted array of hypertext links. Indeed, user-initiated search is only possible by activation of an archaic, mechanical apparatus, the

typewriter keyboard. This organized, preselected set of topical categories, their stories, and the skeins of affiliation and entailment constitute a veritable map of the world according to Microsoft. Its chapters and boxed panels are its continents. Every site in this universe, whatever its self-presentation, is sold, bought, and sponsored. Within this paradigm, information is organized, packaged, and displayed. In this respect, the MSN homepage is a corporate representation of the larger commercial world that Microsoft integrates. The page reflects the face and the psyche of the public as a more or less integrated array of social subjects – that is, as a nation. 'Network' and 'national' thus become substitutable terms. In this way, the public sphere as a universe of discourse is reduced to a union of potential consumers, a market, a universe of networked consumption.

American commercial television as a temporal, linear medium required obligatory viewing of ads as the price for the privilege of moving towards and viewing the next segment of the story. In television logic, the network sells consumers to advertisers and the circuit is completed only after a temporal delay when the product is purchased at the supermarket. Like television, the stories and pictures on the MSN homepage are simply points of attraction or adhesion between two domains: the public and the world of commerce. However, with the internet, the opportunities for commercial linkage are exponentially expanded and patterns of consumption, and of reading, are fundamentally altered. With e-marketing, the temporal distance between the ad and the execution of the purchase is the time needed to click the mouse. The MSN homepage brings together newspaper columns, stories, and format with television's means of attracting audience attention in a uniquely direct, effective, innovative commercial medium. In this sense, the point-and-click system represents a simple but profound elaboration on the mediated system that contracts the space between desire/need and its material attainment that commercial television successfully introduced and exploited. Cross-media, synergistic platforms intensify this commercial network at nodal points of attraction.

6. For these reasons, the area framed by the MSN homepage, though small, is some of the most valuable real estate on the face of the planet. It is, moreover, not a stand-alone entity. It is legally and institutionally allied as a business and a presentational form with a cable television channel, MSNBC, and indirectly with CNBC, the Consumer News and Business Channel, promoted as 'America's Business Channel'. This channel is structured to include significant content participation with the Dow Jones Corporation and *The Wall Street Journal*. These financial institutions interpenetrate, support, and feature each other in the construction of the American financial landscape. CNBC, the cable channel, is notable for its innovative stylization of visual format, with active, horizontal bars at the top and bottom of the TV screen. Throughout its various format transformations – of set, logos, graphics, and printed texts – the show has been dominated by the colour

blue, a deep blue. Blue, of course, in today's action and thriller movie genres, is the new noir. It's the colour of the elevator shafts, wiring, and the secret and often dangerous restricted spaces of computer and communications centres, the offices of the police and CIA, warehouses, and headquarters of multinational banks. In the movies it's the colour of the rarely seen insides of modern, tall commercial buildings in New York, Los Angeles, and European capitals. It is a colour that carries a narrative and emotional edge. It is serious and dangerous. It is the colour of international intrigue and the world of high finance. Word, Windows, and Internet Explorer make blue the sign and banner of the Microsoft universe as well. I think it is no secret – blue is the colour of money. We might even say blue is the colour of our era.

Part II

CHANGING GENRES

5

BINGEING ON BOX-SETS

The national and the digital in television crime drama

Charlotte Brunsdon

As G2 launches a new column on the delights of box setting, Tim Lusher celebrates the piggy pleasures of gorging yourself on your favourite TV shows.

> *The Guardian*, 6 March 2009, *G2*, p. 9,
> [launching a column called 'Your next box set']

I miss the communal effort that goes into watching scheduled television – the knowledge that by switching on the kettle during the adverts I am contributing to the surge in the national grid ... TV in real time means you are forced to wait a week between episodes ... It also, more poignantly, means that you age along with the characters. Watching five boxed sets in a month, you surface a little fatter, slightly dazed, and behind on your correspondence.

> Morven Crumlish, *The Guardian*, 28 May 2009, p. 33

Graeme Turner and Jinna Tay have recently asked whether it is possible 'any longer' to 'claim a characteristic socio-cultural function for the medium [television] at all?'[1] They ask this question in the introduction to a book in which they successfully problematize what they characterize as an over-simple 'end of broadcasting/rise of broadband narrative' (2009: 8), partly through the straightforward method of extending the discussion of what is happening to television beyond the US/Europe context which has been for-mative for television studies. This leads them to argue that '[n]otwithstand-ing the internationalization of the media industries, these days the answer to the question, "What is television?" very much depends on where you are' (2009: 8). So while in the US a television scholar can comment in 2006 that 'the materially based distribution of television on DVD seems nearly anti-quated in comparison with the internet-based developments of recent months',[2] in Britain (just to stay with the Anglophone axis), as my first epigraph shows, it is only in 2009 that a national newspaper has begun to review DVD box-sets.

One of the things that television, in its many contemporary forms, continues to be, is a story-telling technology. Some of these stories have always remained local, some have been widely exported, and some, in this mobility, such as *Dallas* and *Dynasty*, in the 1970s and 1980s, have proved foundational for television studies.[3] As Turner has pointed out, even if one does not want to go all the way with the 'end of broadcast television' narrative, television studies is now confronted with what he characterizes as 'the increasingly contingent relationship between television, broadcasting and the nation-state' (Turner and Tay 2009: 55). Recognition of the contingency of this relationship is difficult for television studies, because so much television scholarship has been occupied with what television tells us about something else, which is usually, in one way or another, the cultures in which it is produced and viewed, or in Turner and Tay's terms, its 'characteristic socio-cultural function'. I want to explore what this greater contingency might mean in relation to television crime drama, which is one of the fictional genres often selected to demonstrate television's contribution to understandings of the public sphere.[4]

Milly Buonanno has recently pointed to the contradictoriness of a period in television's history which has been influentially characterized as 'abundant' by John Ellis. Buonanno points out that the abundance of channels is accompanied by the continuing inelasticity of time, the relative scarcity of content, and the passage from free to subscription television.[5] In this context, she observes that one of the consequences of the relative scarcity of content is that television sets up 'a living museum of itself' through 'the incorporation of the history of the medium in the more advanced forms of its present'.[6] One of the manifestations of television's 'living museum of itself', in addition to nostalgia shows and reruns, is the release of old television on DVD, a format which, as Derek Kompare has shown, 'finally enabled television to achieve what film had by the mid-1980s, namely, a viable direct-to-consumer market for its programming'.[7] Barbara Klinger and Matt Hills have demonstrated the significance of the DVD format to fan cultures, while other scholars, such as James Walters, have welcomed the increased opportunity for aesthetic analysis of television.[8] My interest lies in what the DVD box-set does for the messy, cross-disciplinary set of practices known as television studies. As well as being a material object, the DVD box-set can be treated as a methodological palimpsest which, in its portability and its textual form, embodies some of the current challenges to the founding national and textual assumptions of television studies.

Bingeing on box-sets

The impressive speed with which the DVD has penetrated the domestic has been accompanied by the adoption of new metaphors to describe home DVD viewing. Most notable has been the emergence of the somatic metaphor of 'bingeing' to describe the domestic viewing of multiple episodes sequentially.[9] This popular usage offers a rather more complex apprehension of what has happened to television than may first appear, especially if considered in relation to the previously widespread characterization of regular viewing as 'addiction'. Addiction, a metaphor prominent in the twentieth century in relation to soap-opera viewers, and particularly 'housewives', condenses judgements about television fiction and its viewers. It proposes an involuntary, non-cerebral relation to the medium, an out-of-control habit. The contempt for television and its viewers in this metaphor was often shared by cinema scholars, who have, however, in the twenty-first century, suddenly flocked to the medium to explore US 'quality' television in forms such as *The Sopranos* and *The Wire*. There is in this scholarship often a stress on the way in which television has become more cinematic, or at least less televisual. Kompare has suggested that DVD box-sets 'provide the content of television without the "noise" and limitations of the institution of television' (2006: 352). This new, good television, in contrast to old, bad, addictive television is not broadcast network television, but television which one either pays to see, or watches on DVD. Instead of being associated with housebound women, this new television is young, smart, and on the move, downloaded or purchased to watch at will.

It is in these discursive contexts, in which certain kinds of non-broadcast television viewing are signs of distinction, that we find the metaphor of 'bingeing' on serial drama. This is an activity, as can be discovered through any reading of the popular press, or everyday conversation, performed by many types of people: women who have broken up with their boyfriends, students avoiding writing essays, and footballers sequestered before an important match. This verb, with all its connotations of an uncontrollable, excessive consumption, ironically reconnects the prestige dramas, marketed as being superior to 'television', with the addiction metaphors that have always been used to characterize the consumption of television drama. Favourite serials can now be consumed not with the regular 'injection' of addiction, each episode with its beginning and ending, with their concomitant feelings of anticipation and loss, but in an endless 'more'. And this *more*, the metaphor implies, induces eventual feelings of nausea and self-disgust, producing a body bloated with favourite fiction.

Thus the move from addiction to bingeing offers a very economical, popular description of what in the academy are called 'changing modes of delivery' and the shift away from the unquestioned dominance of broadcast television. The metaphors demonstrate the shift from something which is rationed temporally (broadcast television), and which you must therefore get a fix from regularly, to something more like a box of chocolates which you purchase and consume in your own time. But there is also a recalibration of agency and the location of badness. For bingeing describes bad television *watching* ('piggy pleasures'), as opposed to the watching of bad television, and has been imported into descriptions of television viewing from the now extensive vocabulary of bad eating and bad drinking. So it is both a moral and a somatic metaphor, and perhaps it is not too far-fetched to say that it has contemporary neoliberal connotations in its implied good opposite: self-disciplined non- or limited TV watching. To binge on television drama is to abandon aspiration, to be stuck on the sofa in the living room. However, in this naming of a practice which involves surrender to temptation, perhaps popular culture also tells us something about bingeable television. Can 'bingeability' also be seen as a textual property?

One aspect of DVD bingeability is evidently a digital form of the complex pleasures of narrative, in which one is caught in the contradictory desire to find out what happens next and for the story not to end. Buonanno, discussing the temporal organization of television series and serials, reminds us that distinguished literary scholars such as Peter Brooks and Frank Kermode have considered the torments and pleasures of seriality and the sense of an ending: '[W]e can see therefore that the two deep-rooted structures of modern popular fiction are made up by acknowledging and satisfying desires that pull readers in two different directions: on the one hand, the protraction of the *same* story, a device adopted by the *feuilleton* and the novel in instalments; on the other hand the start of a *new* story, a task assumed by a series of novels' (2008: 124). It is the lure of 'the same' and 'the new' that is promised by so many DVD compilations, and which transposes the national-broadcast order of waiting, in which we must return to view at an externally imposed time, to an individually chosen moment. The ambivalence towards this 'out of time' viewing which Morven Crumlish expresses in the epigraph, with its gains of personal convenience and loss of sociality, has been characterized by Amanda Lotz as the further erosion of the 'network-era cultural forum function of television' in the USA.[10]

But for the viewer to want to view in this way, the fictional world must be imagined and realized with sufficient intensity to make it hard to resist returning. That is, there are aesthetic preconditions, often associated with production values, script, and performance, which reward return. But the programme must also have a predictability, a promise of a repeated pleasure, which has been most adequately theorized, in the study of film and television, in relation to genre and the promise of 'repetition with difference'.[11] The nausea implicit in bingeing comes from the disturbance of the temporal control of this repetition, the failure to understand that a little forgetting is a necessary part of the pleasure of 'more'. Without this forgetting, generic pleasure becomes not repetition with difference, but repetition with too much of the same.

It is this delicate balance of development and recognition, which can only be explored properly in relation to specific programmes, which is economically alluded to in the metaphor of 'bingeing'. This suggests some areas for further study in the textual organization and management of narrative which is produced with a box-set in mind, as opposed to the temporality of tele-vision produced in earlier regimes, to which I will return below.[12] However, the sequestered autonomy of binge viewing, the implied squandering of time and money, points to a paradox at the heart of the new, valorized 'not television' DVD television. Matt Hills has argued convincingly that these modes of viewing and circulation shift DVD television towards the contexts of auteur-based valorization, while at the same time reinforcing the deva-luation of 'ordinary' television. But, despite this valorization within tradi-tional aesthetic discourse, there is, in this metaphor of bingeing, the trace of a persistent cultural shame at absorption in an audio-visual, fictional world. This feeling, while it takes a specific historical form in relation to DVD viewing, seems to me to be clearly related to the feelings expressed by viewers and readers of other popular fictions (see, for example, the extensive feminist scholarship on soap-opera and romance reading), and thus suggests that there are structures of feeling in play here which are not technology specific. Here I also agree with Hills that 'we should refrain from overstating the differences made by new media and by DVD culture' (2007: 53), although he is concerned mainly with cult/fan viewers and the ways in which DVD packages have worked to intensify their relationship with both programmes and programme producers. But in the separation of the tele-vision text from the 'noise' of television, which permits these different, intense engagements, something else is lost too, the socio-historical context, and it is that to which I now wish to turn. For, in the context of television crime fiction, I am interested in the question of what it is now appropriate to include in a critical analysis, and I will demonstrate the problem with two examples which have a rather recalcitrant relation to 'bingeability', one a twenty-first-century US programme, and the other a 1970s British one.

Local stories 1: Baltimore

Perhaps inevitably in a paper written in the early twenty-first century on television crime drama, I will use a comment made by David Simon, the creator of the acclaimed crime drama *The Wire* (HBO, 2005–8) for the first example. Simon is writing in a liberal British newspaper, in 2008, about the international success of his Baltimore-set drama:

> When I read reviews and commentary on *The Wire* in the British press, I'm usually moved to a peculiar and conflicted place. I'm gratified by the incredible amount of verbiage accorded our little drama and I'm delighted to have the fundamental ideas and arguments of the piece discussed seriously.
> But at the same time, I'm acutely aware that our dystopian depic-tion of Baltimore has more appeal the farther one travels from America. *The Wire* is, of course, dissent of a kind and it is true that

there are many of my countrymen who are in fundamental disagreement with the manner in which the nation is being governed
and managed. But somehow, it sounds better to my ear when it's
my own people talking trash and calling our problems out.

At the same time, it's not just a question of standing, but of nuance
as well. I get that we've been the bull in the china shop internationally, that we've been arrogant and tone-deaf in so many arenas
for so many years ... Fair enough. We had it coming. But the
emotion in all of that sometimes leads the overseas commentary
about Baltimore and *The Wire* toward something that I don't
recognise as accurate.[13]

Simon is writing about the willingness of non-American commentators to
read the Baltimore of *The Wire* as a metaphor for the USA. The 'emotion in
all that' resentment of the US feeds into a reading of the show as illustrative
of the pervasive corruption and spiritual bankruptcy of US culture, and, at
the same time, he suggests, this reading is fuelled by a kind of vengeful joy:
'Fair enough. We had it coming.' Against this reading of the series, which
inscribes the show within an international power geometry, he proposes
something a little more situated and local. The starting point of his article is
a newspaper item about the unwillingness of Baltimore juries to convict
criminal defendants. From here, he moves into an account of *The Wire* as a
programme which deals very specifically with a particular urban environment in which the drug trade and a series of responsive policies have produced a radical distrust of, and disengagement from, every aspect of the
criminal-justice system and civic government. His argument, in which he
draws on the contrasting experiences of working in Baltimore for white and
black members of the cast and crew of the programme, is that there are
specific, traceable policies which have been enacted in Baltimore, and which
The Wire partly documents, which have real results such as the unwillingness
of jurors to convict.

So the writer of one of the definitive treatments of twenty-first-century
television crime, which is being sold on DVDs with subtitles in more than
20 languazes, wants to argue that he is telling a local story. Evidently, he
recognizes that there is more to it than that (and indeed, the very first pre-
title sequence inscribes a metonymic reading of the series in its 'This is
America' comment), but it is his desire to restore that detailed local context
which is of interest, because it can be seen as a desire – in the context of
trans-national abundance – for interpretation to stay closer to the series'
referential context, as it would have done if the show had been network-
broadcast nationally. So if we return to Buonanno, we see some of the contradictions to which she refers in practice. *The Wire*, which draws on critical
social realism to renew generic pleasures, is only possible within the US
television economy because of the specialist subscription environment

of HBO. These conditions of production have facilitated international distribution of the series as 'quality television' 'without the "noise" and limitations of the institution of television'. But it was that 'noise', that national historical broadcast noise, which would facilitate a reading of the show as a critical intervention into a particular context; a literal, rather than metaphoric, interpretation of the show.

While it is possible to binge on *The Wire*, and its complexity makes both intense and repeated viewing attractive, it is also difficult and dark, sometimes making it a relief to stop viewing. So it offers an extreme form of serial pleasures: it can be both unbearable to watch and unbearable to stop watching. It is because of this narrative intensity, and its rich, situated detail, which many of its international – and national, I would guess – viewers understand only partially, that *The Wire* travels to such critical acclaim. Its cumulative, thick description of 'the drug war' and its institutional penetration and shaping of Baltimore, in combination with the inscription of the difficulties of its viewers in the wire-tapping police, trying to make sense of what they hear, is what makes it worth trying to understand. The series produces a thoroughly imagined Baltimore, a particular narrative place generically embodied through different institutions (the drug trade on the streets, the ports, the schools, local government, and the press) in which, as criminologists have sometimes said, 'nothing works'. However, it produces this particularity with two distinctive generic strategies. First, the device of the wire itself dramatizes the role of the viewer trying to understand how one bit of narrative, and one set of characters, connect with others. The wire-tapping police, and the viewers, are both struggling with the inaudible, with slang, with identities, and with codes. The dramatic business associated with the wire, carefully established in the first series, and returned to less frequently as the seasons proceed, offers a home alignment for the viewer among certain characters within the police force. However, the rewarding complexity of the series – and its departure from some generic predecessors – depends on the serious treatment of the non-police worlds, so that it is not only in the police world that the viewer encounters intelligence, ethical behaviour, and loyalty. The second generic device which is of great importance to the unrolling of this Baltimore is the attitude to character, and, particularly, those involved in 'the game' (the drug trade). Here, the series authenticates its depiction of the optionless brutality of the game through its attitude to players (in both senses). Characters who can't hack it are eliminated without sentimentality, as we find with the flawed heroes D'Angelo, Frank Sobotka, and Stringer Bell, and this is the opposite of the predictable pleasures of the bingeable text. The dramatic fictional world of the long-form serial, in which characters generally live on, is regularly, violently, disrupted by the murder of significant characters. There is a homology between dramatic form and depicted world, and one which lends gravitas to the aesthetic project by elevating sometimes-shocking narrative realism over familiar production protocols and generic pleasures.

It is the combination of the specific and local with this generic sophistication which produces the critical context to which David Simon refers, and which he evidently finds both gratifying and frustrating. Simon's high profile as a commentator on the programme works, in accord with Hills, argument, to valorize an authorial paradigm, even, though, ironically, it is socio-cultural interpretation that this author promulgates.

Local stories 2: real-time aesthetics

My second account steps back from twenty-first-century programmes to examine a controversial and mythologized 1978 BBC series, *Law and Order*, which was released on DVD in 2008.[14] If the example of *The Wire* posits the question of the interpretative spaces of television fiction, the case of *Law and Order* also poses the questions of critical methodology across time. This drama, made 30 years ago, shares with *The Wire* the sense of criminal justice as a formal system in which police and criminals are differently positioned, rather than essentially morally opposed. This too is a world in which political considerations, careers, and self-interest determine the practices of policing. Here I am interested in the question of what changes in textual availability do to the project of criticism. But I am also interested in noting what is entailed in the type of contextually specified reading which David Simon misses in relation to *The Wire*, and which is more inaccessible the older a text is.

Law and Order comprises four 85-minute plays (shot on film), written by G. F. Newman, directed by Les Blair, and produced by Tony Garnett.[15] The series, which uses what the BBC Director of Television, Alastair Milne, called 'Garnett's usual pseudo-realistic style'[16] addresses endemic corruption in the British criminal-justice system, focusing on the arrest, conviction, and imprisonment of a fictional career criminal, Jack Lynn. Its transmission, on one of the three national broadcast networks, caused uproar. There were questions in the Houses of Parliament and the prison officers' union resolved to refuse the BBC future filming access. There was very substantial press coverage of the programme, the corruption issues raised, and the role of the BBC. The BBC took the decision, at the highest level, that the series could not be exported or repeated.[17] Since this broadcast, *Law and Order* has been almost impossible to see and is rarely analysed, even in histories of British television.[18] So in contrast to *The Wire*, *Law and Order* remained, for many years, not only a local/national treatment of the British criminal-justice system, but one which was unseen even in Britain.

I returned to *Law and Order*, preserved on 16mm film in the National Film and Television Archive, a couple of years ago, as preparation for writing a new piece on the television crime series. My methodological assumption was that without being simply reflectionist, television crime drama from the era of national-broadcast television can seen to offer an imaginative witness to how crime, law, and policing are made sense of. It may be that these series document nothing more than how those working in television imagine that criminal justice is practiced, and scholarship on the genre points to the privileging of certain aspects of the process, such as 'detection' and 'pursuit', at the expense of, for example, more televisually boring processes such as detention in custody.[19] However, the very terms of that imagination can be telling and I planned to explore Turner's 'increasingly contingent relationship between television, broadcasting and the nation-state' by contrasting the 1970s, when television was a national real-time broadcast medium, with the more recent period, the late 1990s/early twenty-first century, when the most widely watched television crime in Britain is probably a combination of *CSI: Crime Scene Investigation, Old Tricks*, and *The Bill*, watched in individualized patterns inside and, increasingly, outside 'real-time broadcasting'.[20]

I was interested in whether, on the one hand, one could profitably explore some generic shifts over a longer period, and, on the other, whether one needs a much more 'denationalized' analytic framework. If the crime genre can still be seen to articulate something in relation to its national context of production, is it the same something, or does this now work only at a meta-level, so that what we see documented are the production and distribution patterns of the industry? How significant is the increasing internationalization and mobility of the crimes portrayed? So, for example, the 'local' armed robber dominates British television crime in the 1970s – as in *Law and Order* – while the ubiquitous figures of twenty-first-century crime are the internationally mobile 'terrorist' and the 'trafficker' (of people and drugs).

This project was interrupted when my object of study changed suddenly with the announcement that the BBC was releasing the series on DVD. So, instead of having an existence which was dominated by its historical, nationally specific time of first broadcast, the programmes were set loose from their original context, and can be watched in quite different ways. The contingency of relationships between television, broadcasting, and nation state demonstrably shift, as the BBC seeks to exploit its back catalogue. As a long-unseen series, the plays were best approached through an investigation of why they were never seen again. This story is a complicated one, in which the tumultuous political climate of late 1970s Britain and the left-wing politics of many involved in television drama have to be understood in relation to the institutional politics of the BBC, and the relationship between the BBC, and the Home Office, the government department which was also responsible for the criminal-justice system and, most relevantly, the prisons. Like Baltimore, it requires close attention.

Suddenly available, *Law and Order* is recontextualized within a broadcast environment which is very much more violent, and in which portrayal of the brutal mistreatment of prisoners, both real and fictional, is widespread. A controversial media event when first broadcast, the plays were subsequently largely vindicated in relation to the Metropolitan Police. Now, it is not so much what is shown, but how it is shown which seems most striking. It is a story told with an unrelenting rhythm and pace which is dependent on viewers tied to real-time television viewing, when there were no remote controls and it was much more difficult to flick over to something less gruelling. Once *Law and Order* is available as a DVD in the twenty-first century, it becomes much easier to see how specific its aesthetic use of its mode of delivery – national-broadcast time – was. And this is more than a point that old television was slower. It is an argument that the series was dependent on its uncontrollable broadcast time for its aesthetic and social impact.

The four programmes explored the unfolding of overlapping narrative events across time, and a time which, in the weekly pattern of the original broadcasts, both endured and progressed. While the films had the look of documentary drama, the narrative structure was experimental, with each episode focused on a different protagonist (detective, criminal, lawyer) with eclectic, unsignposted overlaps between the episodes which demanded close attention from a viewer. But the withholding of narrative progression through the weekly broadcasting, the inability to find out 'what happened next' at will, gave a different quality to the inexorability of the fate of Jack Lynn, who we see, over the four plays, being first fitted up with a crime that he did not commit, then spending all his ill-gotten gains on a crooked solicitor, and finally being deliberately broken by a brutal prison regime. The real time of the broadcast – the uncontrollable time of the broadcast – recruited the duration of the viewers' hours and weeks to the unfolding narrative of the plays. The medium was the message in a way which we can perhaps see more clearly now, when it is not so in the same way, and in which its new modes of television production and distribution foster different types of story.

Unseen, the plays were history. Footloose and fancy-free in their DVD package, they now come with an informative 25-minute 'extra' about their making, which gives them some context and provides interviews with the programme-makers. But the context that can never be restored is that uncontrollable time between broadcast episodes which gave temporal force to narrative inexorability, and which allows us to see something of the aesthetics of broadcast time. The new digital availability of past programming renders visible aspects of its temporal aesthetics that we might previously have taken for granted, as well as restoring long-absent programmes. However, this new availability, in its very presence, is only the latest form of the fantasy that we can ever possess the past again.

Although now available to watch at will, *Law and Order* does not seem to me to be something on which one would describe oneself as 'bingeing', even if you watched all six hours in one go. Its recalcitrant unfolding, but overlapping, narrative, its austere aesthetics (for example, there is no music), and its political project, do not, I think, possess 'bingeability' in the way that even a series as dark as *The Wire* does, and this is because of its deployment of time and its eschewing of certain predictable pleasures. Indeed, its project is to undermine the predictable pleasures of the police series of the time. This then raises the possibility that although DVDs may make old television more available, they may not make it much more watched. It may almost never be 'convenient' for most viewers – me included – to choose to watch difficult, draining, pessimistic television drama, let alone watch a 90-minute programme all the way through without interruption.

The new formats in which television drama is available do have aesthetic consequences, particularly, as I have shown, in relation to our understanding of the deployment of time as an aesthetic resource in what is still a time-based medium. There are not just aesthetic issues, but also interpretative ones. For the canonical works of television studies and television history have told national stories, even if not always consciously. The '"noise" and limitations of the institution of television' are not just an interference in the content of television, they are – at least in part – the whisper of history, the textual traces of transmission at a particular time on a particular channel. Continuity announcements, channel idents, and advertising have, historically, been the signifiers of the relationship between broadcasting industries, television structures, and the state, and have functioned to sanction a historical and socio-cultural interpretative framework for television programmes. It is much less clear what stories will be told about television, what contexts are relevant, and how we should interpret and understand its own stories, when these constitutive connections between medium and nation are more attenuated, when the noise has been stripped away and the stories have been repackaged to travel the world.

Notes

1 Graeme Turner and Jinna Tay (eds), *Television Studies After TV* (London: Routledge, 2009), p. 5.
2 Amanda Lotz's 'Rethinking meaning making: watching serial tv on DVD', *Flow* 4.12. Vol. 4, 22 Sept 2006, http://flowtv.org. Accessed 29 May 2009.
3 Ien Ang, *Watching Dallas* (London: Methuen, 1985); Tamar Liebes and Elihu Katz, *The Export of Meaning* (Oxford: Oxford University Press, 1990); Jostein Gripsrud, *The Dynasty Years* (London: Routledge, 1995).
4 See, for example, Richard Sparks, *Television and the Drama of Crime* (Buckingham: Open University Press, 1992), and Robert Reiner, *The Politics of the Police* (Oxford: OUP, 2000).
5 Milly Buonanno, *The Age of Television* (trans. Jennifer Radice), (Bristol: Intellect Books, 2008), pp. 21–22.

6 Buonnanno, 21; on television's self-archiving, see also Tim O'Sullivan, 'Nostalgia, revelation and intimacy: tendencies in the flow of popular television', in C. Geraghty and D. Lusted (eds) *The Television Studies Book* (London: Arnold, 1998) and Lynn Spigel, 'Our TV heritage: television, the archive and the reasons for preservation', in J. Wasko (ed.) *A Companion to Television* (Malden and Oxford: Blackwell, 2005).

7 Derek Kompare, 'Publishing flow: DVD box sets and the reconception of television', *Television and New Media* Vol. 7.4 (November, 2006): 335–60, p. 337.

8 Barbara Klinger, *Beyond the Multiplex* (Berkeley: University of California Press, 2006); Matt Hills, 'From the box in the corner to the box set on the shelf', *New Review of Film and Television Studies* Vol 5.1 (April, 2007): 41–60; James Walters, 'Repeat viewings: television analysis in the DVD age', in J. Bennett and T. Brown (eds) *Film and Television After DVD* (New York: Routledge, 2008).

9 See, for example, responses to Amanda Lotz's 'Rethinking meaning making: watching serial tv on DVD', *Flow* 4.12. Vol. 4, 22 Sept 2006: Jonathan Gray heads his response 'Binge TV'; Jason Mittell refers to 'binging on DVD' (both 23 September 2006), http://flowtv.org. Accessed 29 May 2009.

10 Amanda Lotz, *The Television Will Be Revolutionized* (New York: New York University Press, 2007), p. 62.

11 Derek Kompare has shown how fundamental repetition through syndication has been for the US market for many years (*Rerun Nation*, New York: Routledge, 2005). Outside the US, with its huge domestic market, this has not been true in the same way, except to a lesser degree with US programmes, as Buonanno, for example, discusses in her Chapter 6.

12 See, for example, Dana Polan, *The Sopranos* (Durham, NC: Duke University Press, 2009), 19–31.

13 David Simon, 'There are two Americas … ' *The Guardian Weekend*, 6 Sept 2008, 25–28, p. 26

14 G. F. Newman's *Law and Order*, BBC DVD, BBC Worldwide Ltd, distributed under licence by 2Entertain, 2008.

15 Tony Garnett's distinguished career in television production has included later police dramas such as *Between the Lines* (1992) and *The Cops* (1998). G. F. Newman's television work engages with other British institutions such as the health service and he writes the successful *Judge John Deed*. Les Blair's television and film work includes *Bliss* (1995) and *Bad Behaviour* (1994).

16 Alastair Milne, Board of Management Minutes, 10 April 1978, BBC Written Archives Centre, File R78/2,0272/1.

17 There was a late-night repeat in the early 1980s, after a change of government. See Brunsdon, *Law and Order* (forthcoming) BFI/Palgrave, 2010, for full discussion of these events.

18 The only discussion is Lez Cooke, *British Television Drama* (London: British Film Institute, 2003), pp. 113–18 and Stephen Lacey, *Tony Garnett* (Manchester: Manchester University Press, 2007) pp. 107–10.

19 Sean O'Sullivan, 'UK policing and its television portrayal: "Law and Order" ideology or modernising agenda?', *Howard Journal of Criminal Justice* Vol. 44.5 (2005): 504–526; Richard Sparks, *Television and the Drama of Crime* (Buckingham: OU Press, 1992), and Robert Reiner, *The Politics of the Police* (Oxford: OUP, 2000).

20 *CSI:Crime Scene Investigation* (CBS/Alliance Atlantis) first aired in the US in 2000. *The Bill* (Thames, for ITV), which is currently broadcast twice weekly, is a community-soap-type police series, which has run in various formats on (networked) independent television since 1983. *Old Tricks* (pilot Wall to Wall/ BBC 2003; series BBC 2004–) is one of the BBC's most popular drama series and features well-known older actors such as Dennis Waterman and James Bolam in a special unit of retired policemen.

6

FORWARD TO THE PAST

The strange case of *The Wire*

Erlend Lavik

The question of how digital technology has affected the aesthetic conventions of film and television has received a lot of scholarly attention since the early 1990s. Initially the debate focused on the influence of digital special effects on storytelling in big, special-effects-heavy blockbuster movies. In the past couple of years interest has turned to the impact of the DVD format and the internet. For example, the financial importance of DVDs has likely promoted stylistic and narrational strategies that reward repeat viewings. One upshot of this is narrative complexity, a handy if somewhat loose umbrella term that encompasses quite different kinds of stories. What they have in common is that they – in varying ways and to different extents – are more cognitively demanding than films and television series from the classical era. Subcategories are not mutually exclusive and include circular narratives, network narratives, modular narratives, database narratives, forking-path plots, twist movies, and transmedia storytelling (see for example Bordwell 2006; Jenkins 2006; Mittell 2006; Ramirez Berg 2006). DVD box-sets and TiVo, meanwhile, have probably contributed to longer story arcs and tighter plotting across episodes in TV series, as these technologies allow viewers to see their favourite shows in bulk rather than in weekly instalments. The internet has reinforced some of these developments. Complex films and television series, especially those constructed as hermeneutic riddles, lend themselves well to collective puzzle-solving online. Also, the internet has proved to be the perfect arena for cultivating the kind of dedicated fandom that has been a key factor in the proliferation of transmedia storytelling. Finally, non-linear editing systems and lightweight digital cameras have likely played a part in the move towards what David Bordwell (2002) calls an 'intensified continuity' style, characterized by rapid editing and lots of camera movement.

It seems clear that we are witnessing some major new developments, and while digital technology is not their sole cause, it has undoubtedly played an important part. Against this backdrop, it is somewhat surprising that the television series perhaps most frequently described as the best, the most complex, or most innovative – *The Wire* – enjoys a curiously conflicted and contradictory relationship to these tendencies. This chapter examines *The Wire* in the context of more widely discussed trends in popular film and television, and argues that the show stands as remarkably basic compared to the stylistic and narrational flamboyance that typifies so much of today's high-end entertainment output. Indeed, its originality and critical success in certain respects paradoxically stems from a return to the long-standing traditions of documentary film-making and the classical novel.

Narrative complexity in contemporary film and television

It seems to me that the key characteristic of the narrative complexity vogue concerns the interplay between formal complexity and self-consciousness. These two concepts are obviously not congruent, but in the context of recent modifications of popular storytelling conventions, they tend to overlap and intersect to a considerable extent. Mainly, their self-consciousness frequently appears to be a function of their complexity. Numerous contemporary films and television series, not just in the USA but worldwide, come replete with formal contrivances – spectacular twists; temporal shifts; repeated actions; and byzantine, intersecting plotlines – that both call for attentive viewing and serve to foreground their cleverness, inventiveness, and, ultimately, their own construction.

Jason Mittell (2006) uses the term 'operational aesthetic' to describe such elaborate narrational flourishes. The phrase is adopted from Neil Harris's account of P. T. Barnum's feats, where spectator pleasure was not so much tied to suspense about the outcome as to wonderment at the execution. In the context of contemporary film and television, then, an operational aesthetic is a mode of engagement that invites viewers to treat texts both as story world and as formal structure. We are encouraged not just to lose ourselves in the narrative, but also to recognize it as a piece of craftsmanship. For example, as Mittell points out, the title of the television action drama *24* refers to the number of hours and episodes it takes to relate the story within the show's real-time narrative structure; thus the title actually refers to the key narrational premise and attention-grabber of the series, rather than to anything belonging to its story world. I think Mittell is right to see this as indicative of a shift within film and television in the 1990s towards greater formal complexity and self-consciousness. Other prominent examples would include the 'backwards narration' of the film *Memento*; the abrupt convergence of seemingly distant plotlines in various *Seinfeld*, *Arrested Development*, and *Curb Your Enthusiasm* episodes; and the moment of revelation in twist movies such as *The Sixth Sense* and *Fight Club*, where the introduction of a new piece of information towards the end completely changes the meaning of everything we've seen up to that point; in the process, flaunting the careful 'constructedness' of the narration.

The point is not that these tactics are brand new. Certainly, some noir films have fairly complicated plots – for example, Stanley Kubrick's *The Killing* (1956) combines temporal shifts and repeated actions – and some of Hitchcock's most famous movies, like *Vertigo* (1958) and *North by Northwest* (1959), set up a seemingly absurd narrative premise that only makes sense right at the end; in the case of television, the most obvious predecessors are probably shows such as *The Prisoner* and *The Twilight Zone*. However, what stands out today is the sheer quantity of such narratives, the refinement of some of these tactics over time, and the combination of so many of them in individual films and television series.

The documentary influence

It would seem, then, that the notion of narrative complexity that has gained purchase within film and television studies in the past couple of years tends to focus on two interrelated features. First, such texts offer a 'cognitive workout', and second, this is frequently achieved by means of narrational flourishes that draw attention to the process of narration. As Mittell puts it, such texts 'convert many viewers to amateur narratologists' (2006: 38). Thomas Elsaesser has made similar observations, though he prefers the term 'mind-game film', a phenomenon he considers 'symptomatic for wider changes in the culture's way with moving images and virtual worlds' (2008: 39). What he finds distinctive about this tendency is that 'rather than "reflecting" reality, or oscillating and alternating between illusionism/realism, these films create their own referentiality, but what they refer to, above all, are "the rules of the game"' (ibid.).

I want to argue that *The Wire* is highly complex in the first sense, but not in the second. It is an unusually demanding show to follow in the sense that it contains vast numbers of characters and plotlines coupled with very little exposition. As we will see, though, these features are rooted in old-fashioned documentary and novelistic traditions, not in the current vogue for playful and self-reflexive formal experimentation. In *The Wire* the craft component does not come to the fore, i.e. the show does not put its own complexity on display as a form of virtuosity. For example, apart from a single flashback in the very first episode, the series is entirely linear.

Still, the narrative construction of *The Wire* does sometimes overlap with the recent move towards narrative complexity, and it might be helpful to look at how it differs, despite the resemblances. Most obviously, *The Wire* has a lot in common with network narratives. In films such as *Short Cuts*, *Magnolia*, *Playing by Heart*, and *Babel*, as well as in the TV series *Heroes*, a series of seemingly quite discrete stories gradually come to intersect. Such interweaving stories are readily apparent in *The Wire* as well. But there does not seem to be any particular symmetry or grand scheme behind the network. 'Pure' network narratives, by contrast, tend to function as a kind of conundrum, structured around a movement from complete separation, via gradual revelation, to final culmination. Eventually, it all adds up to a piece of narrative architecture designed to be noticed and admired in its own right. In *The Wire* I think it is fair to say that we are not supposed to take note of or reflect on the points of contact between the various characters. The improbable 'smallness' of *The Wire*'s Baltimore is simply an accidental by-product of the show's ambition – or the artistic license required – to investigate the contemporary urban environment as a kind of ecosystem. Hence, a tactic that, on the face of it, would seem to coincide with the narrative complexity trend turns out not to be guided primarily by formal self-consciousness but rather by socio-political analysis. *The Wire* does not so much invite us to become amateur narratologists as amateur sociologists.

Another overlap has to do with the tactic of delayed exposition, a ploy for which *The West Wing* in particular has become famous. In *The West Wing* it typically occurs at the beginning of an episode, and the narration tends to call attention to the fact that some important piece of information is missing through repetition. Thus we quickly recognize this as a habitual structuring device and take it as an instance of the show's self-conscious cleverness. Its use, in other words, is fairly codified: it is used routinely, at routine moments, for routine purposes: usually to build suspense or to whet curiosity in a knowing 'game' between the show's creators and viewers. *The Wire*, by contrast, rarely brings delayed exposition to our notice, because it is used more sporadically and unpredictably, and we are actually never safe in the knowledge that an explanation will be forthcoming at all.

In other words, in *The Wire* the tactic is not a kind of formalist amusement, customarily enacting a passage from confusion to realization. Rather, it stems from a quest for documentary realism. The creator of the series, David Simon, has often quoted Frederick Wiseman – one of the key representatives of the observational mode of documentary that tends to steer clear of overt exposition and reflexive devices – as a major influence. This is a prominent feature of *The Wire*. New characters tend to be introduced with no immediate explanation of who they are or what they do. Their identity might be revealed in a throwaway line much later, or it may dawn on us slowly as they stumble on and interact with the other inhabitants of the story world that we *do* know.

Style and the rules of The Game

To a certain extent, the documentary impulse finds expression in *The Wire*'s style as well, which is unusually basic and unselfconscious in this day and age.[1] It is shot in the now outmoded 4:3 format, and rapid-fire cutting and shaky, handheld camera moves are largely absent. Camera movement is by and large subdued enough that the occasional quick dolly-in on a character in medium close-up for climactic moments registers as a point of emphasis. Thus *The Wire* does not fall into the trap of overindulging in stylistic flourishes, something that mostly serves to create a general sense of franticness whereby nothing really stands out from anything else, effectively flattening rather than heightening the dramatic range.

Moreover, there are no fantasy scenes or voice-over, hardly any montages, slow motion sequences, or even non-diegetic music, and just one example of film style mimicking character psychology (after Ziggy Sobotka shoots George Glekas towards the end of the second season). The editing, too, is kept very simple. As Joe Chapelle, co-executive producer for Seasons Three and Four and a regular director on the show, notes: 'We never even fade to black between scenes. We fade up at the beginning of the show and fade to black at the end. There's no dissolves, just cuts. Very straightforward and simple. That's a stylistic choice. Keep it lean' (Griffin 2007: n.p.).[2]

The Wire has a distinct long-lens look, which according to Chapelle is intended to create 'that feel of a voyeuristic view of the action ... that of someone observing but slightly removed from the action' (ibid.). Also, while David Simon left the creation of the show's stylistic template to producer and sometime director Robert Colesberry, it is telling that he did insist on one rule: that the camera never 'fish' for information.[3] By this he means that the camera should not act as if it knows in advance what is going to happen, for example by moving in on a character just before he or she is about to speak. This is something that Simon wishes to avoid, as it makes the text reveal its own artifice. Such camera premonition is of course absent in most documentaries, where the action is not typically staged, but rather captured on the fly.

The Wire's favoured camera move is the slow dolly shot, particularly for masters. A new scene will often begin with the camera halfway behind a wall or a door, before gradually revealing the setting and the actors, giving the impression that the camera is creeping up on the characters, catching them unawares. This eavesdropping quality is evident in the dialogue as well. Unfamiliar words and phrases – 'in the wind', 'redball', 're-up', 'suction', 'dunker', 'burner' – abound, but are rarely explained. We simply have to infer their meaning through repeated use, as we would have to do if we were listening in on other people in real life. Again Simon invokes realism to account for this:

> Less is more. Explaining everything to the slowest or laziest member of the audience destroys verisimilitude and reveals the movie itself, rather than the reality that the movie is trying to convey. The audience need not understand everything at the moment they see or hear it, and some small details need never be explained – if they get it, great, if not, that's a lot like life.[4]

Also, as in real life, important information is rarely signposted as such. This is not to say that *The Wire* is not a carefully structured piece of fiction, but the narration is exceedingly non-redundant. It requires and rewards alert viewers, as seemingly insignificant details will turn out to have great narrative importance dozens of episodes later. It is also notable that the various worlds or social strata to which we are introduced – especially the various police departments, the drug organizations, and City Hall – are intricately hierarchical, yet we are never overtly told how they are structured.[5] As in *The Sopranos*, *The West Wing*, and to a somewhat lesser degree *Deadwood* and epic films such as *The Godfather*, part of the appeal lies in piecing together the chain of command and discerning the fine-tuned relations of power that exist among the various characters. Moreover, this is an ongoing enterprise: relationships are forever changing as some characters are promoted, others demoted or killed off (changes that might well take place off-screen, between seasons).

Thomas Elsaesser's theory, that contemporary moving-image culture displays an obsession with 'the rules of the game', is highly interesting in this context because it usefully points up a key difference between the narrative complexity trend described at the outset and *The Wire*. For as everyone even remotely familiar with the show knows, 'The Game' is precisely *The Wire*'s guiding metaphor. It is used initially to designate the drug trade, but it gradually becomes apparent that it is applicable to all walks of life. This is made most explicit, perhaps, in a courtroom scene in which a proficient but unscrupulous attorney points the finger at renowned stick-up artist Omar Little for leeching off the drug trade, and he replies, pleasantly bemused: 'Just like you – I got the shotgun, you got the briefcase. It's all in The Game though, right?' ('All Prologue', Season 2, Episode 6). Ultimately, then, 'The Game' becomes a metaphor for the web of constraints that exist within and between all kinds of modern institutions: economic, political, criminal, educational, and so on.

Now, the fixation on the rules of the game in Elsaesser's mind-game films is centripetal, so that their perceived relevance 'is not mimetic (based on "realism") or therapeutic ("cathartic" in Aristotle's sense)' (2008: 35). The rules of the game in *The Wire*, by contrast, are centrifugal, pointing outwards, beyond the text. Thus, while *The Wire*, too, is obsessed with 'the game', what it seeks to lay bare are not the rules of fiction, but the underlying mechanisms that regulate and determine the kinds of moves that the individual players are allowed to make in a fictional world that is still – unfashionably and unapologetically – representational.

The novelistic impulse

Probably the most commonly floated idea about *The Wire* is that it is a 'visual novel'. This angle was promoted by Simon right from the start, and he has reiterated it in countless interviews since. He invokes Dickens, Balzac, and Tolstoy, as well as Greek tragedies, as key references. The similarities are readily apparent, especially in relation to Balzac, whose works were also panoramic and based on careful research, though *The Wire* is more fiercely funny. Dickens's interlaced plotlines also cut from the top to the bottom of society, with individuals mere cogs in some great, unmanageable societal machine. But Simon and his co-writers are less sentimental. There are no exceedingly idealistic, noble, and innocent characters in *The Wire*'s universe, though the show's portrayal of certain environments is sometimes infused with a sense of nostalgic romanticism and idealism, such as life on the pier in Season Two and the newsroom in Season Five.

It is harder to think of TV counterparts. The emergence of narrative complexity on television is commonly held to stem from a crossbreeding of episodic and serial formats but, in *The Wire*, individual instalments display virtually no unity, apart from the opening and end credits. Admittedly, on rare occasions there will be some kind of parallel or rhyming effect between the beginning and the ending of an episode. The camera move that opens 'The Wire' (Season 1, Episode 6) slowly reveals the tortured dead body of Omar's lover, Brandon, sprawled across the hood of a car, while the episode ends on a close-up of a police photograph of the same image. Also, 'Hard Cases' (Season 2, Episode 4) begins with union leader Frank Sobotka losing his temper and taking a deep breath to resume control, and ends on a similar scene in which he stares at his own reflection in the bathroom mirror, drawing breath several times to regain composure.

Still, such instances are few and far between and, more significantly, it is only at the macro-level that recognizable thematic and narrative arcs become evident. Thus *The Wire* does not really fit existing television labels very well. We might say that the show is structured somewhat like a soap opera, except that it is pretty much drained of melodrama and has far more narrative propulsion and a pre-planned ending. Alternatively, we could say that it resembles a miniseries, except that it goes on for some 60 hours, which makes that something of a misnomer.

While there are other prominent contemporary US television series that more or less conform to the one-season-equals-one-story format, such as *Heroes* and *24*, it is much harder to think of these shows as 'visual novels'. They resemble *The Wire* in the sense that there is little episodic unity, but at the same time we intuit that they are meant to be consumed in instalments. They are jam-packed with exposition, repetition, and neat summaries for those who have missed an episode or need to have their memories refreshed. Also, whereas *The Wire* unfolds at its own pace, the others are structured around a series of cliffhangers at regular intervals. In *Heroes*, there are even temporal overlaps between many episodes: a new instalment might not pick up precisely where the previous one ended; instead the cliffhanger situation will be replayed somewhat later in the ensuing episode. These conventions clearly call attention to the 'episodicity' of these shows. Each season of *The Wire*, by contrast, unfolds much more like a single, continuous chunk of narrative.

In this respect the show is in fact even more novelistic than some of its literary predecessors. Dickens's stories, of course, were published as weekly or monthly instalments. Consequently, they were divided into carefully pre-pared pieces that come to an end at climactic moments in order to lure readers back for the next segment. In *The Wire* segmentation appears almost random: There are no cliffhangers until the fifth and final season,[6] and most of the time there is a sense that episodes simply come to an end when the allotted time is up.

'Demonstrating' social critique

The Wire offers gripping human drama among flawed characters rendered with great compassion and nuance, but where the long-story format really comes into its own is in the gradual revelation of the mechanics that constrain their actions and choices. Over time we can make out a network of institutions, routines, and regulations; a city-machine not so much run by as running on people. No matter how violently individuals rage against their fate, they tend to end up unwittingly carrying out the moves laid out for them. The Game simply plays itself out, indifferently, then starts again. As Simon has stated ad nauseam, *The Wire* has raided the ancient Greek tragedies, but substituted postmodern institutions for vengeful Olympian gods, and the show clearly works as social critique. But because Simon et al. have such a broad canvas to work with, its 'messages' – for example that the police, the courts, the school system, and so on have become self-perpetuating creatures dissociated from the greater good they were supposed to serve – are somehow demonstrated more than declared. *The Wire* utilizes the long-story format to monitor institutional rules and habits, and to set up a series of subtle parallels and cyclic patterns across five seasons, so that key ideas are not so much articulated synchronically as accumulated diachronically.

The series' unique narrational strategies have inevitably shaped its reception. Because exposition is so scarce, an unusual amount of effort in online discussions goes into simply clarifying plot points, relationships, and motives. And while the show has produced its fair share of standard fan talk about favourite characters, speculation about future events, and so on, it has also engendered considerable debate on such topics as drug policy or the relationship between individuals and institutions under capitalism. Thus while media scholars in the past couple of years have tended to cele-brate the liberating and democratizing potential of audience participation per se – no matter how inane – *The Wire* has provoked deliberation on topics that plainly belong in the political public sphere.

This is no doubt due to the show's serious treatment of serious issues, as well as the promotion, criticism, and commentary constantly underlining its claim to authenticity. Clearly, then, *The Wire* is structured differently, and invites a different kind of audience engagement, from series created as hermeneutic puzzles designed to be picked apart by compulsive exegetes. Not least, many online contributions on *The Wire* revisit favourite moments for their sheer emotional impact. They tend to be taken at face value, as drama, not as clues to a riddle, as in so many other series, from *Twin Peaks*, through *The X-Files*, to *Lost*.

Obviously, I am exaggerating in order to get the point across. It is certainly possible to enjoy *Lost* as pure drama, while *The Wire* does include, for example, visual symbolism that invites careful interpretation.[7] Still, I do think there is an important distinction to be made between *The Wire* and a show like *Lost*. The latter appears more paradigmatic of the digital era in that it challenges the boundary between production and consumption, and lends itself more readily to the pleasures (and profits!) of transmediality. In this context, a show like *The Sopranos* takes up an intermediate position. Though attributes of melodrama and soap opera are perhaps more palpable than in *The Wire*, it too is grounded in social and psychological realism, however extreme. At the same time, it shares with *Lost* – though less obviously and obsessively – a preoccupation with allusions and textual clues that inspire painstakingly detailed investigations, most conspicuously, of course, in the staggering amount of online analysis of the show's controversial was-he-or-wasn't-he-killed ending.

Fuck the average viewer?

David Simon enjoys a famously conflicted relationship to the medium of television, and has repeatedly emphasized the position of the show's writers as outsiders in the business.[8] In one interview he stressed that 'none of the people who make *The Wire* are from the world of television and none of us are particularly interested in maintaining a television show for the sake of maintaining a television show. We're trying to tell a story that we believe in, that we think is relevant' (Goldman 2006 n.p.). His main grievance is that, rather than seeking out challenging material on television, audiences tend to favour the infinite repetition of easy and familiar pleasures: '[V]iewers generally don't know what is good for them as an audience, or for *The Wire*. Given their own way, they'd eat dessert all the time and leave the vegetables on the plate. So I'm afraid we are not at all open to suggestion or petition when it comes to character or story.'[9]

In the current climate of participatory culture and fan power, then, *The Wire* stands as uncompromisingly old-fashioned. An online Q&A exchange offers the clearest example. When one fan inquires whether D'Angelo – a character strangled in prison in a previous episode – 'could be brought back' since 'technically he could've just passed out and the police put him in p.c. while he recovered', Simon's answer is refreshingly dismissive: 'He could be an angel. And he could grant wishes. And ... and ... I'm sorry, I don't mean to be sarcastic, but no, he's dead. He finally reached out for his own dignity and then someone killed him. It's outrageous, and a tragic waste. I get upset just thinking about it and I'm sure you do, too.'[10]

Though few have been as outspoken as Simon about their utter disdain for television conventions, even television viewers, he is not alone among series creators in holding such views. As Jon Kraszewski has shown, it actually harks back to the very first television auteurs, who emerged in the mid-fifties, such as Rod Serling, Reginald Rose, and Paddy Chayefski, who also felt ambiguous about the medium and portrayed themselves as odd men out in the industry. These days, antagonism towards television is a prominent feature of the public personas of David Chase and David Milch, the creators of arguably the only two series comparable to *The Wire* in terms of artistic ambition and critical praise, *The Sopranos* and *Deadwood*.

It is perhaps no coincidence that all these shows aired on HBO. The creators' opinion that the medium is fixated on ratings and self-perpetuation, on milking the commercial rather than the artistic potential of the story, chimes perfectly with the company's famous slogan 'It's not TV. It's HBO.' Traditionally, television auteurs have sought to emulate cinematic conventions to improve the quality of their work. David Chase's desire to move into feature film-making is particularly well documented, and it is interesting to note that he has talked about how HBO used to push for serialization, while his goal 'was always to do a little movie every week' (Shales 2007). The balance struck between these contrasting demands resembles the mixture of serial and episodic formats popularized by shows such as *The X-Files* and *Buffy the Vampire Slayer* in the nineties. Simon is the only one who has sought to break free of television conventions by following the example of the great novelists of the nineteenth century, in the process creating one long, continuous story. As his former *Baltimore Sun* colleague and writer on the show, Rafael Alvarez, puts it: 'You know how, in a Russian novel, the reader does the work for the first hundred pages, and then it turns and you're lost in it? With *The Wire* it might be Episode 6 before it turns and you're in' (Talbot 2007). This is a radical break with the logic of television, since individual instalments end up offering little pay-off on their own, which in turn discourages the kind of casual viewing that has customarily been the medium's bread and butter.

Still, *The Wire* might not be as out of step with our digital times as it would seem. Clearly, the DVD format has brought about notable changes in television aesthetics, economics, discourses, and reception. As Derek Kompare (2006) points out, television has traditionally been a 'flow medium', aiming to sell potential audiences to advertisers. Digital technology's superior image and storage capacities have pushed it in the direction of a publishing model, where media products are sold or rented as tangible objects. The season box-set, in particular, has isolated series from the routine programming stream. In Matt Hills's words, 'TV texts are converted from being primarily moments in a schedule, designed to hold audiences or reach audiences of a specific type, to symbolically bounded objects more akin to artworks or novels' (2007: 45). The DVD format thus performs what Hills calls a 'text-function', analogous to Foucault's 'author-function', discursively constituting some texts (especially those that lend themselves to the reading strategies of fans and academics) as more distinct than others (those that are part of the 'dailiness' of television: game and chat shows, news, and so on).

The Wire is a paradigmatic example of many of the developments Hills identifies. It is probably the most critically consecrated series in television history, and has certainly buttressed the cult of the auteur. Also, while it never received very high ratings, it has been a big hit on DVD.[11] *The Wire*'s non-redundancy and lack of episodic self-sufficiency might be ill-suited to television's ephemeral flow. However, on DVD it exists as a material object, like a book, and can be watched in the manner that its complexity warrants: repeatedly and without enforced interruptions. Thus, by returning to allegedly outmoded and analogue literary predecessors, David Simon et al. may have hit upon the narrative format of the digital future.

Notes

1 The obvious exception is the surveillance footage that was inserted regularly throughout the first season in particular, but that gradually disappeared before turning up again in the final season. Personally, I find this device slightly offputting, as I think it breaks with the show's otherwise discreet visuals, and I also do not find that it hooks up very well with the other major themes in the series.
2 Actually, it is not quite true that *The Wire* has no dissolves at all. For example, the intro to 'Storm Warnings' (Season 2, Episode 10) has some, though they are quite fast and hence not very conspicuous.
3 See Simon's talk at the Annenberg School for Communication, available at http://www.youtube.com/watch?v=k8E8xBXFLKE.
4 'Exclusive David Simon Q&A', available at http://www.borderline-productions. com/TheWireHBO/exclusive-1.html.
5 Two 'org charts' – 'The law' and 'The street' – can be found on HBO's website, however.
6 One could argue that 'Stray Rounds' (Season 2, Episode 9) ends on a cliffhanger (the appearance of Brother Mouzone). In Season Five there are three cliffhangers by my count.
7 David Simon has hinted at allegorical and symbolic meanings in several interviews, most notably the significance of trains/train tracks (which accordingly has been exhaustively analysed on various internet sites).
8 Key contributors like George Pelecanos, Richard Price, and Dennis Lehane are novelists.

9 'Exclusive David Simon Q&A', available at http://www.borderline-productions. com/TheWireHBO/exclusive-20.html.
10 'David Simon Answers Fans' Questions', available at http://www.hbo.com.
11 An article in *The Daily Telegraph* from April 2009 states: 'Thanks to its complexity, many viewers prefer to download episodes or buy each series on DVD so that they can watch it undisturbed or several episodes at a time. Tellingly, all five series remain in the top 40 DVD sales charts on Amazon.co.uk, even though the first series has been available for seven years.'

References

Bordwell, David (2002) 'Intensified continuity: Visual style in contemporary American film', in *Film Quarterly*, 55. 3, pp. 16–28.

Bordwell, David (2006) *The Way Hollywood Tells It. Story and Style in Modern Movies*, Berkeley, Los Angeles, London: University of California Press.

Elsaesser, Thomas (2008) 'The mind-game film', in Warren Buckland (ed.), *Puzzle Films. Complex Storytelling in Contemporary Cinema*, Oxford: Wiley-Blackwell.

Goldman, Eric (2006) 'IGN exclusive interview: *The Wire*'s David Simon'. Available at http://tv.ign.com/articles/742/742350p1.html. Accessed 28 August 2009.

Griffin, Nick (2007) 'Inside HBO's *The Wire*', in *Creative Communities of the World*. Available at http://magazine.creativecow.net/article/inside-hbos-the-wire. Accessed 28 August 2009.

Hills, Matt (2007) 'From the box in the corner to the box set on the shelf', in *New Review of Film and Television Studies*, 5. 1.

Jenkins, Henry (2006) *Convergence Culture. Where Old and New Media Collide*, New York and London: New York University Press.

Kompare, Derek (2006) 'Publishing flow: DVD box sets and the reconception of television', in *Television New Media*, 7. 4, pp. 335–60.

Kraszewski, Jon (2008) 'Authorship and adaptation: The public personas of television anthology writers', in *Quarterly Review of Film and Video*, 25: 4.

Mittell, Jason (2006) 'Narrative complexity in contemporary American television', *The Velvet Light Trap*, 58.

Ramirez Berg, Charles (2006) 'A taxonomy of alternative plots in recent films. Classifying the "Tarantino Effect"', in *Film Criticism*, 31: 1/2.

Shales, Tom (2007) 'Who's really the boss? David Chase calls the shots', in *The Washington Post*, 9 June 2007. Available at http://www.washingtonpost.com/wp-dyn/content/article/2007/06/08/AR2007060802684_pf.html. Accessed March 2009

Talbot, Margaret (2007) 'Stealing life. The crusader behind *The Wire*', *The New Yorker*, 22 October 2007. Available at http://www.newyorker.com/reporting/2007/10/22/071022fa_fact_talbot?printable=true. Accessed 28 August 2009.

Telegraph (na) (2009) 'The Wire: arguably the greatest television programme ever made', in *The Daily Telegraph*, 3 April 2009. Available at http://www.telegraph.co.uk/news/uknews/5095500/The-Wire-arguably-the-greatest-television-programme-ever-made.html. Accessed 28 August 2009.

7

THE 'BOLLYWOODIZATION' OF INDIAN TV NEWS

Daya Kishan Thussu

The digital deluge that hit India a decade ago has transformed television news in what used to be one of the most regulated broadcasting environ-ments of any liberal democratic polity. The rapid liberalization, deregulation and privatization of media and cultural industries in the world's largest democracy, coupled with the increasing availability of digital delivery and distribution technologies, has created a new market for 24/7 news. This chapter examines the implications of the exponential growth of Indian tele-vision in the past decade, from Doordarshan – a notoriously monotonous and unimaginative state monopoly – to more than 300 digital channels, including 70 dedicated news networks, making it home to the world's most competitive news arena, catering to a huge, increasingly Westernized Indian audience, and indeed South Asian diaspora.

The growing purchasing power and lifestyle aspirations of the expanding Indian middle-class have attracted the transnational media corporations, notably News Corporation, Sony and Viacom, into India. Focusing on news media, I examine how changes in television news in India, as elsewhere, demonstrate the global trend towards infotainment – soft news, lifestyle and celebrities – and the decline in journalism for the public interest. Given the size and diversity of India's television landscape – arguably the world's most complex television system – what is happening to TV news in India is likely to have a wider impact beyond its territorial borders and its diasporic constituencies.

While news outlets have proliferated globally, the growing competition for audiences and, crucially, advertising revenue, has intensified at a time when interest in television news is waning. Audiences for peak-time news bulletins on network television have declined in the United States from 85 per cent in 1969 to 29 per cent in 2005. With the growing com-mercialization of television news, the need to make it entertaining has therefore become a priority for broadcasters. They borrow and adapt ideas from entertainment and adopt an informal style with an emphasis on personalities, storytelling and spectacle (Gitlin 2002; Hamilton 2003; Postman 1985).

Such a move has been reinforced by the takeover of news networks by huge media corporations, whose primary interest is in the entertainment business: notable examples include Viacom-Paramount (CBS News); Disney (ABC News); the former AOL-Time-Warner (CNN) and News Corporation (Fox News/Sky News and Star News Asia). The shift in ownership is reflected in the type of stories – about celebrities from the world of entertainment, for example – that get prominence on news, thus strengthening corporate synergies. In the process, symbiotic relationships between the news and new forms of current affairs and factual entertainment genres, such as reality TV, have developed, blurring the boundaries between news, documentary and entertainment. Such hybrid programming feeds into and benefits from the 24/7 news cycle: providing a feast of visually arresting, emotionally charged infotainment which sustains ratings and keeps production costs low. The growing global popularity of such infotainment-driven programming indicates the success of this formula.

'Infotainment' – a term that emerged in the late 1980s – refers to an explicit genre-mix of 'information' and 'entertainment' in television news and current-affairs programming. This new news cannibalizes visual forms and styles borrowed from TV commercials and an MTV-style visual aesthetic, including fast-paced action, in a postmodern studio, computer-animated logos, eye-catching visuals and rhetorical headlines from an, often glamorous, anchor person. Such style of presentation, with its origins in the ratings-driven commercial television news culture of the US, is becoming increasingly global, as news channels attempt to reach more viewers and keep their target audiences from switching over.

As I have discussed elsewhere, this form of journalism has been very successful: in Italy, infotainment-driven private television catapulted Silvio Berlusconi from a businessman to the office of the Prime Minister. A study of journalism in post-Soviet Russia found that the media were 'paying huge attention to the entertainment genre', while in the Chinese news world, the Phoenix channel regularly runs such soft news programmes as *Easy Time, Easy News* (Thussu 2007a).

The globalization of a market-led television news culture can be explained by what Hallin and Mancini have described as the 'triumph of the liberal model' (Hallin and Mancini 2004: 251), arguing that the 'liberal model' is likely to be adopted across the world 'because its global influence has been so great and because neo-liberalism and globalization continue to diffuse liberal media structures and ideas' (ibid.: 305).

In a market-driven broadcasting environment, Indian television news has borrowed heavily from popular cultural artefacts devised and developed by its thriving film factories – at the epicentre of which is Bollywood – the world's largest film industry in terms of the number of films produced annually (Credit Suisse 2006; Kavoori and Punathambekar 2008). They have skilfully adapted Bollywood conventions of melodrama and spectacle, peppered with song-and-dance numbers, to gain new viewers or retain existing ones at a time when many, especially younger and urban Indians, are accessing their news from other sources than television. It may not be a coincidence that many of India's television news networks are based in Mumbai, India's commercial capital and a centre of its cultural industries, particularly film and television.

Like many other countries, India too has experienced its public broadcasting being undermined by the forces of the market in a complete departure from the traditional state-controlled television. Television was introduced in India in 1959 as a means for disseminating government policies and public information. The ostensible aim of the national broadcaster Doordarshan was to educate and inform, though it remained a mouthpiece for the government of the day, reflected especially in the haphazard and unprofessional way its information bureaucrats ran news operations (Mehta 2008). The partial privatization of the airwaves started with the introduction of advertising onto the state broadcaster in the 1970s, followed by sponsored programmes, and received a boost as India opened up to transnational media corporations in the 1990s.

The gradual deregulation and privatization of television in the 1990s transformed the industry: by 2009 more than 300 digital channels were operating, including some joint ventures with international broadcasters (Butcher 2003; Kohli-Khandekar 2006; Page and Crawley 2001; Price and Verhulst 1998; Thussu 2007a and 2007b; Mehta 2008). This unprecedented growth has been spurred on by massive increases in advertising revenue as Western-based media conglomerates tap into the growing market of 300 million increasingly Westernized, educated middle-class Indians with enhanced purchasing power and media-induced aspirations to a consumerist lifestyle (Ganguly-Scrase and Scrase 2008). Cable and satellite television have increased substantially since their introduction in 1992, growing annually at the rate of 10 per cent; by 2010 cable and satellite households are likely to touch 85 million. The media and entertainment business, one of the fastest-growing industries in India, is projected to reach nearly $23 billion by 2011, according to the 2007 report *Indian Entertainment and Media Industry: A Growth Story Unfolds*, prepared by PricewaterhouseCoopers (PWC) for the Federation of Indian Chamber of Commerce and Industry (FICCI). The Indian television broadcasting market is projected to reach nearly $12 billion by 2011 (FICCI 2007).

News galore and growing

Though the entertainment segment is the largest growth area in the media, news networks have shown extraordinary expansion. In 1998 the first 24/7

Table 7.1 Main round-the-clock TV news channels

Channel	Language	Reach
NDTV 24x7	English	International
CNN/IBN	English	International
DD News	Hindi/English	International
Star News	Hindi	International
Aaj Tak	Hindi	International
Sun News	Tamil	International
Asianet News	Malayalam	International
TV9 News	Telugu	International
Tara Newz	Bangla	International
Times Now	English	National
NDTV India	Hindi	National
Zee News	Hindi	National
Sahara Samay	Hindi	National
Headlines Today	English	National
India TV	Hindi	National
Janmat	Hindi	National
Tez	Hindi	National
IBN7	Hindi	National
Teja News	Telugu	Regional
ETV2 News	Telugu	Regional
Udaya News	Kannada	Regional
Star Anand	Bangla	Regional

news channel was launched in India; there are now 70 news channels, both national and regional, and many international in reach, as Table 7.1 demonstrates. There are dedicated news networks in a dozen of the 18 state-recognized languages, several of which have large geo-linguistic constituencies, both within the country and among the diaspora.

Deregulation of the Indian television news sector (in which government allows up to 26 per cent foreign investment) has been partly responsible for this boom, as private investors – both national and transnational – have sensed new opportunities for revenue and influence in the television-news business, making India the country with the largest number of news channels in the world. Although the highly competitive news sector attracts only 4 per cent of national viewership, its share of television advertising revenue is nearer 11 per cent (Credit Suisse 2006).

The curse of three Cs: cinema, crime and cricket

As elsewhere in the world, ratings-driven television news in India is forcing journalists and news executives to go for the safety of the soft-news option. The all-news channels in India are still in their infancy, but even in their

91

early formative years one can detect emerging themes which reflect wider trends in broadcast journalism: competition is sharp, and to beat the ratings battles they increasingly show a tendency towards infotainment.

The three Cs – cinema, crime and cricket – encapsulate most of the content on Indian television news programmes. Prominent among these, and reflecting infotainment trends elsewhere in the world, is the apparent obsession of almost all news channels with celebrity culture, which in India centres on Bollywood (Nayar 2009).

Big Bollywood news on small screen

The power of Bollywood to sell television news is best illustrated by the way Rupert Murdoch's entertainment channel Star Plus employed the most famous Bollywood star to host *Kaun Banega Crorepati*, an Indian version of the successful British game show *Who Wants to be a Millionaire?*, giving its launch in 2000 extensive coverage on its sister channel Star News. The show, hosted by the Bollywood superstar Amitabh Bachchan, dramatically changed Murdoch's fortunes in India, securing an average of 40 out of the top 50 shows every week for Star Plus (Thussu 2007b).

Other networks, too, have realized the selling power of Bollywood and most now broadcast regular programmes about the glamour and glitz of Bollywood. Star News has a daily programme, *Khabar Filmi Hai* ('the news about cinema'); Zee News runs a daily bulletin called *Bollywood News*, while NDTV 24x7 has a regular programme, *Picture This*, full of film-based gossip and tabloid titbits. Such coverage also features in the main bulletins on news channels and it is not unusual, for example, to see Bollywood film music used as a backdrop for news stories. Programmes such as 'The making of ... ' a particular (usually big-budget) film or a song sequence are routinely broadcast on news channels. When a new big-budget film is released, it is invariably headline news: television becomes the battleground for marketing and promotion, with endless speculation about how a particular film might do at the box office. Most channels will also run interviews with the stars of the film – and not just within the entertainment segment but as a main news item.

Closely associated with such Bollywoodization of news is the lifestyle segment of news channels across the board, with such examples as *Nightout* (on NDTV 24x7) and *After Hours* (on Zee TV) regularly broadcasting from the glitterati party scene. The 2007 wedding of popular Bollywood actors Abhishek Bachchan and Aishwarya Rai, a former Miss World, received wall-to-wall coverage on national television. On the day of the wedding, news networks vied with each other to provide as much trivia and as many tantrums as possible, while the main news on Zee TV devoted almost the entire bulletin – 22 out of 25 minutes – to the story. A striking example of Bollywood taking over the airwaves was to be witnessed in

August 2009 when nearly 16 million people watched the finale of *Rakhi Ka Swayamwar* (*Rakhi's wedding*), a reality show featuring Bollywood starlet Rakhi Sawant.

Broadcast on NDTV Imagine, the entertainment channel of NDTV 24x7, and managed by the well-known Bollywood director Karan Johar, the 27-part reality show, in which Sawant got engaged to a Canadian citizen of Indian origin from among 16 suitors, ran from 29 June to 2 August (Sinha 2009). Sawant, a so-called item girl (a reference to an 'item number', often a sensuous song and dance feature, inserted in a film with a view to the box office), has made a career out of such appearances, augmented by her regular presence on reality television programmes and chat and game shows, and her wedding received exceptional coverage. On the final day of the show Star News, among others, devoted a half-hour programme to the story. A day before the final episode was to be aired, NDTV 24x7 featured her in its weekly debating programme *The Big Fight*, which discussed among other things whether reality TV was eroding Indian culture.

Such synergies between Bollywood and broadcast news are not unusual. The company that ran the Hindi news channel, Sahara Samay Rashtriya, is also involved in Bollywood film production and operated a film-based channel called 'Filmy'. Zee News is part of one of India's largest infotainment conglomerates, with extensive interests in the entertainment industry – apart from general-interest Zee Television, it also runs dedicated channels Zee Cinema and Zee Music, both very Bollywood-oriented. TV-18, India's leading content provider and broadcaster of business, consumer and general news, operating since 1993, has also made forays into film production with Studio 18.

Crime as continuity story

Programmes focusing on crime and criminals, presenting them as action thrillers, are another key constituent of television news channels, particularly among the Hindi-language networks. As the ratings battle has intensified, news networks have rapidly moved towards reporting sensational stories, which are becoming progressively gruesome. Murder, gore and rape are recurring themes, with the tone and tenor of stories being inevitably populist. Exposés are routine, with a good deal of hidden-camerawork being deployed to give the stories a sensational edge. The presentation draws broadly on well-known and clichéd conventions of visualization of crime and corruption, inspired by B-grade Bollywood films. Star News, for example, runs a daily dedicated programme on crime reporting: *Sansani* ('sensation' in Hindi), usually about criminal gangs, fraudsters and fixers. Although the channels claim to be presenting such stories with the public interest in mind, more often than not there is a tendency to titillate and shock. NDTV India regularly broadcasts such crime-centric programmes as

Dial 100, and *Khabardar* ('beware') while Zee News famously used the saga of a divorced woman named Gudiya, whose soldier husband had left her on suspicion of an extra-marital affair, in the ratings battle. This innocuous story was transformed into a live drama on the television screen, with audiences sending their views on SMS and emails as well as via phone-ins (Ninan 2004).

Although nationally the crime rate has in fact fallen dramatically in the past decade (Kala 2007), sensationalized crime coverage has spiralled, especially on more populist channels. Crime as spectacle was in evidence in the most dramatic form in the way news channels covered the terrorist attacks in Mumbai on 26 November 2008 and the subsequent 60 hours of hostage-taking chaos carried out by a group of terrorists in what was described by Indian journalists as 'India's 9/11'.

As news networks vied with each other to provide new angles on what was developing into a 24/7 terrorist soap opera, the compulsion of 'breaking news' encouraged some to unwittingly provide live telecast of commandos of India's elite National Security Guards being airdropped, endangering the lives of hostages and security forces. News networks discussed in detail how Bollywood bloggers such as superstar Amitabh Bachchan and one of its leading actors, Aamir Khan, posted their reflections on the attacks and their aftermath. One indication of the Bollywoodization of the coverage was that even before the tragedy – which claimed 170 lives and injured hundreds of Indian and foreign citizens – was over, reports were circulating of producers registering names, such as '26/11: Mumbai under Terror' and 'Operation Five Star Mumbai' for action thrillers based on the macabre events. Even sober networks such as NDTV 24x7 could not resist the temptation of Bollywoodization of public discourse: its flagship weekly programme *We the People*, telecast on 30 November, just hours after the end of anti-terrorist operations in Mumbai, was dominated by a panel of Bollywood personalities.

Cricket + Bollywood = 'cricketainment'

Crime reporting seems to have even affected coverage of cricket – the most popular sport in India. During the 2007 Cricket World Cup, the death of the coach of the Pakistani team, Bob Woolmer, during the tournament prompted a media frenzy, with Star News running an hour-long whodunit programme with a dramatization of likely scenarios leading to Woolmer's death, and encouraged the viewers to vote by SMS.

Media outlets recognize the primacy of cricket in India's popular culture, the colonial game having become the most important sport among Indians, cutting across class, language and even gender barriers and second only to Bollywood in its popularity. Ashis Nandy, one of India's most respected commentators, has wittily remarked that cricket 'is an Indian game accidentally discovered by the British' (Nandy 1989).

Television has transformed cricket from a gentlemen's game to a roaring business, dependent on corporate sponsorship. The live broadcast of cricket, especially the one-day matches and Twenty20 games, has been turned into a spectacle, a visual extravaganza. Cricket-related stories appear almost daily on all major networks – and not just on sports news. These include details of private lives of cricketing stars as well as regular narratives on their expensive lifestyles.

When international matches are underway, Star News runs a regular hour-long programme titled *Match ke Mujarim* ('the guilty of the match'), where ex-cricketers and commentators dissect the day's sporting action, with active participation by audiences, naming and shaming the worst-performing players on a particular day. Interactivity is central to such infotainment, as compelling coverage can lead to channel loyalty in the long run and, at the same time, provide a new revenue stream for privatized telecom networks, which benefit from this convergence.

Cricket coverage also gets good play on the elite channels: NDTV 24x7 runs two popular daily programmes: *Sports 24x7* and *Sports Unlimited*, while CNN/IBN broadcasts *LoC – Love of Cricket*. The coverage reached a heightened pitch leading up to the 2007 World Cup, with Times Now running a daily show, *The Game*; NDTV 24x7 broadcasting special episodes of 'India Questions', an hour-long interactive interview with former and current Indian cricket skipper; and Zee News airing a daily show called *Vishwayudh* ('world war'). Programmes including travelogues and contests that gave fans a chance to win World Cup tickets and for celebrities to send across their messages to Indian players, were regularly broadcast on all major channels (Majumdar 2006; Mehta 2008).

As one recent study of television news in India notes, 'the Indian television news industry has consciously ridden on the shoulders of cricket' (Mehta 2008: 197). Arguably, the networks have both shaped coverage of cricket and been shaped by it – one prominent example is the programme *Newsnight 20/20* on NDTV 24x7, which proudly proclaims that it has borrowed the format of the popular Twenty20 cricket tournaments (a fast-paced 20-overs game played by each side, which lasts just a few hours, in striking contrast to the traditional five-day test match). It covers 20 stories in 20 minutes, leaving the remaining 10 minutes in the half-hour segment for advertisements.

The entertainment experience of Twenty20 tournaments is 'enhanced' by the presence of dancing cheerleader girls at key points of the game, as well as Bollywood stars. The Twenty20 format of the game has been given a new lease of life with the establishment of the Indian Premier League (IPL), modelled after the highly commodified British soccer industry, as well as American Baseball leagues. What distinguishes the Indian experiment is the dominance of Bollywood stars in this new form of 'cricketainment'. They not only own teams but also act as brand ambassadors for the sponsors of the tournament. Current Bollywood superstar Shah Rukh Khan, for example, owns Kolkata Knight Riders, which has a brand value of $22 million, while Shilpa Shetty, who came to international prominence after her very public row on Celebrity Big Brother in Britain in 2007, owns Rajasthan Royals – the team which won the inaugural championship in 2008. Another Bollywood star, Priety Zinta, owns Kings IX Punjab. Overall, a UK-based consultancy firm Brand Finance valued the IPL brand at $2 billion (Indiantelevision.com 2009). The second season of the IPL, which took place in South Africa in 2009, drew in 122 million viewers worldwide, according to industry figures.

Bollywoodization of the public sphere?

The three Cs discussed above are indicative of a television news culture that is increasingly becoming hostage to excesses of infotainment. A study conducted by the Mumbai-based Television Audience Measurement (TAM), which monitored two leading Hindi channels, Aaj Tak and Star News, and two English networks, Times Now and NDTV 24x7, for six weeks in September–October 2008, reported that the four news channels gave 513.22 hours of programming to crime and law-and-order stories (nearly 30 per cent of all programming), followed by sports coverage, which occupied 234 hours or 13.48 per cent of air-time (Indiantelevision.com 2008).

One could argue that by overwhelming public discourse with the three Cs, national and transnational media conglomerates – in concert or in competition – are debasing the quality of public deliberations in the world's largest democracy at a time when it is integrating with the US-led neoliberal economic and political system, both as a producer and consumer of commodity capitalism. It is no coincidence that Shah Rukh Khan endorsed the largest number of brands on television during 2008, closely followed by Mahendra Singh Dhoni, the captain of the Indian cricket team.

Has the ascendance of a Bollywoodized television news lulled the capacity for critical engagement with political processes, replacing them with a newly acquired consumer fetish? Overwhelmed by television and viral advertising, is Indian society turning into what Guy DeBord called the 'Society of the Spectacle' (DeBord [1967]1977)? Television, with its visual and symbolic power, is a crucial element in promoting such a spectacle. The growing presence of what I have elsewhere defined as 'glocal Americana' is feeding into and creating a media culture in which neoliberalism is taking deep roots (Thussu 2007c). The United States, the fount of such ideology, is receiving increasing acceptance as the favoured model to follow, despite the economic downturn triggered in 2007. A 2009 survey by the Pew Global Attitudes Project found that the US image was very strong in India, with 76 per cent of Indians expressing a positive opinion of the US, compared with 54 per cent in 2002 (Pew Research Center 2009).

While this admiration for Americana and its locally cloned celebrity culture may warm the hearts of many, the 'public' aspects of India's social reality seem to have been taken over by private corporate interests, which thrive on what a new study has called 'celebrity ecology' that ensures that 'celebrity culture is the new cool of our lives' (Nayar 2009: 181). The alarming absence of rural and developmental issues on television news demonstrates that such themes do not translate into ratings for urban, Westernized viewers and are displaced by the diversion of Bollywood-driven infotainment.

What has been ignored is the potential of this hugely powerful medium to educate and inform the masses. This is particularly pressing in a country where, in 2009, nearly 40 per cent of the population is illiterate (which translates into more than 400 million people – the largest number of citizens of any country on the planet who cannot read and write). This is doubly ironic since India was the first nation in the world to use satellite television for educational and developmental purposes, through its 1975 SITE (Satellite Instructional Television Experiment) programme.

Broadcast journalism may have been in its infancy in India but newspapers have existed in the country for more than 200 years: *The Times of India* (which claims to have the largest circulation of any quality English-language daily) was established in 1838. Professionally organized and ideologically diverse, the Indian press helped create a space for democratic discourse and its sometimes adversarial role contributed to the evolution of an 'early-warning system' for serious food shortages, and thus a preventive mechanism against famine (Ram 1990).

The failings of a Bollywoodized news culture is troubling for those who care about the public-sphere role of the mass media, though some have argued that the proliferation of news networks and the freedom from government control has widened and democratized public discourse as broadcast journalists have helped give voice to the voiceless and seek accountability from political actors (Rao, 2008).

A global Bollywoodization?

Since the transnational media conglomerates are the driving force behind marketization of cultural industries, and they are getting increasingly involved in India, what is happening to television in India acquires international significance. As India integrates further into a globalized free-market economy, the Indian version of infotainment is likely to have a transnational reach, attracting new viewers beyond its traditional South Asian diasporic constituency.

Demonstrating a robust annual economic growth in the past decade, India is increasingly viewed internationally as an emerging economic and political power. One manifestation of this status is how India's popular culture is being perceived outside India, particularly within the metropolitan centres of the globe – the international success of the British-made Oscar-winning 2008 film *Slumdog Millionaire* is a recent case in point. A combination of factors, including the availability of new delivery and distribution mechanisms as well as the growing corporatization of its film factories and television industry, have ensured that Indian cultural industries have entered the global media sphere.

The scale and scope of the change, given the size of India's population and the potential of its media and entertainment industry, could have significant impact on global media, though so far this appears not to have been sufficiently recognized in academic studies of media globalization (Thussu, 2009). For a start, there is the demographic dividend: more than 70 per cent of India's billion-plus population is below the age of 30 and a sizeable segment of these young Indians is increasingly mobile, harnessing the opportunities offered by the globalization of the trade and service industries and, in particular, using their skills in the English language, the vehicle for global communication and commerce (Athique 2009; Biao 2006; Credit Suisse 2006). The mainly US-based transnational media corporations have successfully made use of this demographic, benefiting at the same time from the growing geo-political and economic convergence between the governments of India and the US.

News networks have fruitfully deployed the emerging synergies between Bollywood and Hollywood-based media and entertainment conglomerates. Global news organizations such as CNN have entered into partnerships with Indian companies – CNN-IBN, an English news and current-affairs channel, launched in 2005, in association with the TV-18 Group, while the NDTV group has strategic ties with NBC, and for two years, 2006–8, *Times Now*, owned by the *Times of India* Group, ran a joint news operation with Reuters.

The diasporic dividend is also important to keep in mind while thinking about the globalization of Indian television. The 24-million-strong Indian diaspora increasingly contributes to and benefits from Indian economic growth. It is estimated that the net worth of the Indian diaspora is $300 billion and annual contributions to the Indian economy are valued at up to $10 billion, and increasingly members of this diaspora are tuning in to Indian news channels to keep abreast of developments. NDTV 24x7 was available in 2009 to the Indian diaspora in the US (via DirecTV), the UK (BSkyB), the Middle East (Arab Digital Distribution) and southern Africa (Multi-choice Africa). Star News and Zee News, too, were available via Sky in the UK.

Indian entertainment corporations are also looking east for new markets beyond the diaspora: the success of the 2005 Chinese film *Perhaps Love* – the first musical since the 1950s and made with expertise from Bollywood – is indicative of the potential of collaborations among major non-Western cultures. The Indian media sector is benefiting from outsourcing in such areas as animation and post-production services for Hollywood and other industries. The marriage between Hollywood and Bollywood is already on the global media agenda. The globalization of Bollywood has ensured that Indian films are increasingly being watched by an international audience: Hindi films are shown in more than 70 countries – by 2008 exports accounted for more than 30 per cent of industry earnings (Kavoori and Punathambekar 2008). As the Hollywood–Bollywood synergies become better established, a Bollywoodized broadcast journalism is likely to circulate with greater visibility and volume along the world's digital superhighways, relocating and reorienting television.

References

Athique, Adrian (2009) 'Leisure capital in the new economy: the rapid rise of the multiplex in India', *Contemporary South Asia*, 17(2), pp. 123–40.

Biao, Xiang (2006) *Global 'Body Shopping': An Indian Labor System in the Information Technology Industry*, Princeton, NJ: Princeton University Press.

Butcher, Melissa (2003) *Transnational Television, Cultural Identity and Change: When STAR Came to India*, New Delhi: Sage.

Credit Suisse (2006) 'Opportunities for Hollywood in Bollywood: India Media and Entertainment Tour', *Equity Research*, 1 December.

DeBord, Guy ([1967]1977) *The Society of the Spectacle*, Detroit: Red and Black. (First published in 1967 as *La societe du spectacle* by Buchet-Chastel, Paris.)

FICCI (2007) *Indian Entertainment and Media Industry: A Growth Story Unfolds*, Mumbai: Federation of Indian Chambers of Commerce and Industry in association with Pricewaterhouse.

Ganguly-Scrase, Ruchira and Scrase, Timothy (2008) *Globalization and the Middle Classes in India: The Social and Cultural Impact of Neoliberal Reforms*, London: Routledge.

Gitlin, Todd (2002) *Media Unlimited: How the Torrents of Images and Sounds Overwhelms Our Lives*, New York: Metropolitan Books.

Hallin, Daniel and Mancini, Paolo (2004) *Comparing Media Systems*, Cambridge: Cambridge University Press.

Hamilton, James (2003) *All the News that's Fit to Sell: How the Market Transforms Information into News*, Princeton: Princeton University Press.

Harvey, David (2007) 'Neoliberalism as creative destruction', *The Annals of the American Academy of Political and Social Science*, 610(1), pp. 21–44.

Indiantelevision.com (2008) 'News channels spend highest time on crime stories', http://www.indiantelevision.com/headlines/y2k8/nov/nov106.php. Accessed 28 August 2009.

Indiantelevision.com (2009) 'SRK's Kolkata Knight Riders is top IPL brand at $22 mn: Study', http://www.indiantelevision.com/mam/headlines/y2k9/may/maymam81.php. Accessed 28 August 2009.

Kala, Arvind (2007) 'Reforms reduce crime', *The Times of India*, 15 March 2007.

Kavoori, Anandam and Punathambekar, Aswin (eds) (2008) *Global Bollywood*. New York: New York University Press.

Kohli-Khandekar, Vanita (2006) *The Indian Media Business*. Second edition. New Delhi: Sage.

Majumdar, Boria (2006) 'Cricket as entertainment', *The Times of India*, 23 October 2006.

Mehta, Nalin (2008) *India on Television: How Satellite News Channels have Changed the Way we Think and Act*, New Delhi: HarperCollins.

Nandy, Ashis (1989) *The Tao of Cricket: On Games of Destiny and the Destiny of Games*, New Delhi: Viking.

Nayar, Pramod (2009) *Seeing Stars: Spectacle, Society and Celebrity Culture*, New Delhi: Sage.

Ninan, Sevanti (2004) 'When a soldier returns ... ', *The Hindu*, 26 September 2004.

Page, David and Crawley, William (2001) *Satellites over South Asia – Broadcasting, Culture and the Public Interest*, New Delhi: Sage.

Pew Research Center (2009) 'Confidence in Obama lifts US image around the world. Most Muslim publics not so easily moved', Pew Global Attitudes Project, Pew Research Center for the People and the Press, Washington. Released 23 July 2009, http://pewresearch.org/pubs/1289/global-attitudes-survey-2009-obama-lifts-america-image?src=prc-latest&proj=social. Accessed 28 August 2009.

Postman, Neil (1985) *Amusing Ourselves to Death: Public Discourse in the Age of Show Business*, New York: Viking.

Price, Monroe and Verhulst, Stefaan (eds) (1998) *Broadcasting Reform in India: A Case Study in the Uses of Comparative Media Law*, Oxford: Oxford University Press.

Ram, Narasimha (1990) 'An independent press and anti-hunger strategies: the Indian experience,' in Jean Dreze and Amartya Sen (eds) *The Political Economy of Hunger*, Vol. I, Oxford: Clarendon Press.

Rao, Shakuntala (2008) 'Accountability, democracy and globalization: a study of broadcast journalism in India', *Asian Journal of Communication*, 18(3), pp. 193–206.

Sinha, Ashish (2009) 'Rakhi's Swayamvar tops ratings', *Business Standard*, 4 August.

Thussu, Daya Kishan (2007a) *News as Entertainment: The Rise of Global Infotainment*, London: Sage.

Thussu, Daya Kishan (2007b) 'The "Murdochization" of news? The case of Star TV in India', *Media, Culture & Society*, 29(3), pp. 593–611.

Thussu, Daya Kishan (ed.) (2007c) *Media on the Move: Global Flow and Contra-Flow*, London: Routledge.

Thussu, Daya Kishan (ed.) (2009) *Internationalizing Media Studies*, London: Routledge.

8

AMATEUR IMAGES IN THE
PROFESSIONAL NEWS STREAM

John Bridge and Helle Sjøvaag

The amateur video-capture of Benazir Bhutto's assassination

The assassination of Benazir Bhutto on 27 December 2007 prompted heavy media coverage around the world. This chapter looks at the coverage of the Bhutto assassination in the Norwegian and US media, and analyses how established news media (CNN and NBC in the US; NRK and TV 2 in Norway) used amateur footage of the assassination in their reporting. Our primary question is how amateur footage is textually embedded into the news narrative. The editing of such footage into the news and the discursive variations by which newscasters introduce, contextualize, and explain events through the amateur lens, can help to reveal how professional news organizations relate to the increasing flood of amateur footage in the news.

There are variations in how these images are incorporated into the news stories, which reveal rhetorical and narrative adaptability on the part of professional news-makers with respect to amateur materials – materials that might be said to challenge the authority and relevance of professional journalism. The case of the Bhutto assassination demonstrates two ways of incorporating such material: what we call *embedding* and *embellishing*. Our analysis reveals that CNN – a 24-hour news channel, embellishes the amateur content, while NBC, TV 2, and NRK (regular broadcasters) tend to embed the images into the prevailing frame of the news story itself.

In the US case, the following analysis will focus on the coverage of one major network, NBC, and one 24-hour channel, CNN.[1] The analysis of Norwegian media coverage includes the public broadcaster NRK (Norwegian Broadcasting Corporation) and the commercial public-service broadcaster TV 2.[2] The purpose is to describe, analyse, and compare the presentational strategies of NBC's, CNN's, NRK's, and TV 2 News Channel's coverage of Bhutto's assassination as case studies of how American and

European television news programmes incorporate amateur footage into their news narratives.

The two tapes

In the wake of Bhutto's assassination, two different amateur videos emerged from (and effectuated) the media event. We will call these the 'gun video' and the 'suspected-killer video'.

The gun video, the first to be released, is also the more disorienting of the two. It is captured on a parallel angle to Bhutto's passing motorcade, on the advancing car's left. Its definition is quite low and at the moment of the gunshot, which it frames almost imperceptibly, the image loses stability. It will take various editing techniques to render the content of this video more clear – editing techniques we will describe and analyse in what follows. Ultimately, what we see in this video is a handgun emerging out of a crowd and firing in the direction of Bhutto, who is posed standing with the upper half of her body out of the sun roof of her car.

The suspected-killer tape, which emerged a day after the gun tape, was touted as being a superior view of the assassination. It is in fact considerably more synoptic than the gun video, offering a view of Bhutto's car from the rear, off the car's right bumper. The angle is slightly high, nearly looking down on the unfolding scene. Bhutto is centred in the frame and we see her flanked by bodyguards posed on the bumpers and sides of her car. We see some movement in the crowd to the left of the motorcade – where the gun emerged in the other tape. We see Bhutto's bodyguards duck and cover. Bhutto seems to do the same (though later debate will centre on whether or not she was hit by a bullet). The crowd scatters, the tape ends.

Given the lack of information available concerning the original production of these videos, the point should be emphasized that their amateur status is more a rhetorical one than one firmly grounded in fact. So despite effusive comparisons to the JFK assassination made in the US coverage of the Bhutto killing, there is no identifiable Zapruder. Although the amateur is something of a signifying absence in the news coverage, the videos are unquestioningly presented by all the news broadcasts here surveyed as hard visible evidence – evidence with a primary claim to factuality. Such a presentation implicitly relies on the videos' status as amateur productions – events 'caught on tape'. These videos are explicitly framed as being amateur productions, even while the news producers exclude any back-story of their production and acquisition.

A survey of the five days of intensive coverage of Bhutto's assassination on US and Norwegian television reveals a rhetorical and narrative foresight on the part of the professional news-makers. Though the 'gun' tape made the US news on 29 December and the 'suspected killer' on the thirtieth, both NBC and CNN lead off on the twenty-seventh with short montages that seem almost constructed to incorporate the amateur tapes as they emerge. It is as if the news editors anticipate the inevitable revelation of amateur footage. The still images of Bhutto in her final moments, as well as a shot of the alleged murder weapon lying in a pool of blood on the ground, serve as placeholders for this eventual amateur footage: as the tapes do appear, they are seamlessly incorporated into these sequences.

The story gains 'traction' in all four broadcasters' coverage through the deliberate choice to use their assassination sequences to amplify the controversy over the precise cause of Bhutto's death. The Bhutto camp's rejection of an autopsy stoked this controversy. So did the emergence of the two amateur recordings of her moment of death. In response, the broadcasters employ textual strategies to explain the amateur images. In this way, these professional news organizations bolster their authority over the images while simultaneously stretching the duration of the media event.

Embedding amateur footage

Norwegian broadcasters and the US network NBC use various rhetorical and narrative strategies to embed the amateur footage into their coverage. The images are used as arguments supporting the narrative frames of the reports, which centre on the dispute over the cause of Bhutto's death, and the political future of the Pakistan People's Party and the country itself. Embedded amateur images function as 'witnesses' and otherwise rhetorical evidence to the topics of the news reports. As such, the tapes and images are allowed to 'speak for themselves'.

NBC's strategy is the simpler (and perhaps more traditional) of the two US networks. Their evening coverage on 31 December is perhaps their most extensive. It includes an introduction by *Nightly News* anchorman Lester Holt that underlines the controversial aspects of the event and its competing explanations. This is followed by a montage that prominently features the two amateur videos. They are each played once, with coloured circles indicating points of evidentiary interest (the gun is circled in red; the suspected killer is circled, and so on). They are replayed with these same elements highlighted through the darkening of the non-essential elements of the scene (the crowd and surrounding vehicles). The pedagogical presentation also does the work of demonstrating the aesthetic sophistication of the NBC news team. Images of autopsy reports appear on the screen. Bhutto aides who survived the attack can be heard offering voice-over recollections of the scene. A sceptical CIA spokesman appears. He shakes his head at the undetermined cause of death: 'Unfortunately this raises many more questions than it answers', he says. The question of government deception is on the table; the story is open to further coverage. NBC will get more mileage out of the amateur videos. This sequence exemplifies the strategy of embedding amateur footage into the professional news flow. NBC effaces the non-professional provenance of the two tapes by digitally enhancing them and placing them in a professionally constructed narrative.

In this example, it would seem that the ubiquity of digital video cameras does not so much mark a significant rupture for the production of news at NBC as augment pre-existing narrative strategies. The amateur quality of the imagery does receive initial attention (especially when the suspected-killer tape is first reported), but the images are rapidly embedded into the larger flow of news as Bhutto's assassination controversy gradually segues into stories about Pakistan's vexed election process.

Like NBC, both Norwegian TV channels embed rather than embellish the amateur footage of Benazir Bhutto's murder. NRK and TV 2 both focus most of their coverage on the gun tape and stills from the suspected-killer tape. Both frame the amateur-captured images within the context of the disputed cause of death, and within the political framework of the event. The first day predominantly features reaction coverage to the event, with a visual focus on events before and after the assassination. Images show the election rally where Bhutto was killed, and street riots and the general aftermath of the bomb blast. On 28 December, both channels use images from the Pakistani Interior Ministry's press conference, where their spokesperson Javed Iqbal Cheema claims Bhutto was killed by the impact of the bomb blast. Here the gun tape is introduced; however, the focus is not on the gun being fired, but on the lever where Bhutto allegedly hit her head. As such, the 'gun' tape is not itself the focus of the news; it is merely referred to and displayed as the Pakistani authorities' claim to evidence regarding the cause of death.

Later that evening, as dispute arises as to the cause of death, both channels turn their attention to the gun video's display of shots being fired from within the crowd. NRK focuses purely on the content of the clip, displaying the encircled gun repeatedly and in slow motion. TV 2 also directs viewers' attention to the highlighted handgun, but keeps cutting back and forth between the gun tape and Cheema's statement. This underscores the disputed cause of death as the narrative frame for the report. On the 29 December, both channels use still photos from the suspected-killer tape as witness to the claim that Bhutto died from gunshot wounds. NRK cuts back and forth between the gun tape and the suspected-killer stills to support the narration that 'new images show that there may have been two assassins' and that doubt has been cast on the official version of events. TV 2 also focuses on the potential effect of the new images on the stability of Pakistan.

The suspected-killer video (which appeared on 31 December) was in the Norwegian coverage only used by TV 2, and online editions of the Norwegian newspapers *VG*, *Dagbladet* and *Aftenposten*. The online newspapers make a point of the amateur origin of the suspected-killer tape. *VG* writes that, 'An amateur video seems to prove that Benazir Bhutto was hit by the assassin's bullets' (Moltubak and Tommelstad 2007). NRK makes no use of the suspected-killer tape, perhaps since it has already decreased its coverage of the story at this point. TV 2, however, continues to cover the dispute over the cause of death, and uses the suspected-killer video to illustrate this debate. TV 2 juxtaposes this new video evidence with the gun video. TV 2 also points out the amateur origin of the suspected-killer tape, and treats it as evidence that Bhutto was shot. Again, the footage is repeated throughout reports, displayed in slow motion, with highlighted areas showing Bhutto and the suspected killer and suicide bomber.

The two Norwegian channels edit the amateur images into their reports in a manner that secures the institutions' credibility. Both channels mix the amateur footage with visual content that grounds the event in a fairly predictable narrative frame. That said, both NRK and TV 2 clearly attempt to treat the amateur videos in a non-sensational manner, and succeed in doing so through taking a detached approach to the shock value of the footage. Norway has a relatively large Pakistani community and thus both channels have clearly determined the relevance of the story to be its potential political consequences.

Embellishing amateur footage

Unlike TV 2, NRK and NBC, CNN looks to sustain the amateur aspect of the videos with segments that continually refer back to the videos' status as objects to be explained or decoded. In other words, they look to get more mileage out of the novelty of the gun and suspected-killer tapes. In two similar segments airing on the afternoon of 29 and the evening of 30 December respectively, CNN brings out 'security expert' Mike Brooks as part of their coverage of the Bhutto assassination. These segments are part of what they call 'Bhutto: Frame by Frame'. Ostensibly, Brooks is there to closely analyse the two videos. He is there on 29 December to explain the gun tape to us. He stands in front of a large flat-screen television as the video is played in slow motion. With CNN correspondent David Mattingly, he points to the gun as it appears. He then goes on to tell us how close the gunman is to Bhutto and decries this as a major security failure.

There is a kind of comic absurdity in the obviousness of his analysis, but the larger point seems to be that free-floating amateur footage is meaningless without the proper framing and explanation – which CNN can expertly provide. Brooks is brought out the next day following a broadcast of the suspected-killer tape. Though CNN anchor Drew Griffin promises that 'We'll take a frame-by-frame look at the evidence to see what, if anything, it reveals', Brooks spends most of the time informing us of the pressing need for an autopsy to get to the bottom of how Bhutto died. If Brooks is no semiotician, his appearance nonetheless allows CNN to rhetorically edify its status as indispensable gate-keeper for all amateur images. Rather than downplay the oddity of these digital artefacts by incorporating them into the flow of news narrative as NBC does, CNN uses the amateur tapes to champion the network's more sophisticated aesthetic sensibility.

The digital news landscape

Television news as a genre relies heavily on images. The availability of footage is important for an event to become newsworthy in the first place (Hjarvard 1995: 22). As traditional newspapers move online, and create 'TV stations' of their own on the internet, these too become more reliant on visuals as they set their news agendas. Digital technological advances have created tools to more easily record and disseminate images. This has made the job of fast dissemination easier for journalists. In addition, it has ensured that amateur footage can now make it into the news stream faster and more easily than before. As journalists cannot be everywhere at once, citizen mobile video recordings and digital photography now add an increasingly visual element to the 'witness' status of bystanders.

The violent and the visual – especially concerning elite persons – easily reach the threshold of what is considered newsworthy (Galtung and Ruge 1965; Harcup and O'Neill 2001). The spread of digital and mobile technology certainly makes it easier for amateurs to contribute to the news agenda. It also makes it easier for news institutions to procure images of events which no professional journalists were present to record. On the other hand, this technological development also intensifies competition between news outlets.

Visual records are a primary condition for an event to become global in scale and reference. The Bhutto assassination demonstrates the role of amateur video footage as 'witness' in a news story. The most information-rich images from this event – images that saw global news circulation – were taken by people close to the event as it happened. As such, these images exist in the news stream not because professional reporters were at the scene but because amateurs who had captured the events shared these with established news organizations with the ability to reach a global audience. This signifies the extent to which such contemporary world-changing events are dependent on often contingent visual documentation to even make it onto the news agenda.[3]

Television news needs to provide citizens with information as a natural part of its social and democratic obligations in the public sphere. But news programmes and channels are also part of larger businesses that rely on favourable ratings to ensure their survival. In this sense, amateur footage is considered newsworthy in so far as it brings to the broadcaster increased ratings, a higher status among competitors and increased advertising revenues. Thus, worthy amateur footage is eagerly incorporated in the professional news stream. But answering how such footage meets the conditions for this incorporation is only an entry point into an investigation of how this amateur identity is managed by professional news at the visual-textual level.

Embodied amateur, rhetorical amateur

It is telling that the question least asked of amateur footage is who is responsible for its capture. Our study of the Bhutto coverage suggests that television news can be said to erase the embodied amateur (the living and camera-equipped witness of the event). At the same time, the same news organizations marshal the evidentiary value of the rhetorical amateur. They present the low quality of the amateur image as evidence of a shocking veracity. As such, television news treats the amateur as an unidentified and unbiased witnessing eye – something akin to a surveillance camera. In so doing, they take for granted the socially determined and embodied aspects of mobile recording technologies.

Television news tends to place the dramatic interest on the object of the video, rather than the embodied (and indeed subjective) individual behind the camera. Thus, while the amateur 'signature' – a shaky and unfocused image – is infinitely important to the claim these videos have to newsworthiness and veracity, amateur contributors to news stories are cast as accidental. Such images are captured by a universalized witness rather than by civilians who intentionally place themselves in newsworthy situations with video cameras. This should give us some pause, particularly when amateur footage emerges from such politically specific scenes as the site of Bhutto's assassination. Our misgivings here should be redoubled when the amateur footage is used to make a case for the cause of death – as it is with the Bhutto assassination.

The paradoxical positioning of the amateur figure troubles the desire to champion the amateur as the face for media democracy. This view exposes a connection between the supposed ubiquity of video-recording devices and a democratization of news-making (Friend 2006). We might be tempted to see amateur footage in the news stream as an opening for a news and public-affairs 'participatory culture' (Jenkins 2006: 290). However, as we describe in our case study, the aesthetic strategies that news editors employ to incorporate amateur contributions into news stories tend to preclude any appropriation of the televisual apparatus for citizen journalism or camcorder activism.

Indeed, the case of using amateur footage in the reporting of the Bhutto assassination is not the same as 'user-generated content', 'participant journalism' or 'produsage' (Bruns 2008). A more appropriate term for such amateur production might be John Caldwell's concept of producer-generated users (PGU). PGU describes the commercial appropriation of fans and amateur producers by professional media-makers. Caldwell describes PGU as the 'evil twin' of 'user-generated content' and details some PGU strategies: 'Producers generate faux-amateur content, buy, and distribute amateur content pro-fessionally, provide online learning in film/video aesthetics, spin blogs, and online discussions ... ' (Caldwell 2008: 337–38). In sum, the amateur is produced by the professional, and not merely in a technological sense, but also as part of the process of developing content. What begins as an embodied practice in public space (reacting to an unfolding event by recording it) becomes a presentational strategy of professional news. This transformation is achieved through framing techniques and the strategic use of the amateur 'signature' or 'look', both of which warrant further consideration if we are to better understand the place of the amateur in the production of professional television news.

The amateur look

Coverage of event-driven news such as the Bhutto assassination is increas-ingly live – or at least presented as such. Part of what characterizes these types of stories is a saturation of images that are indelible and endlessly replayed (Livingstone and Bennett 2003: 366, 375). Novel mobile recording technologies are a strong facilitator of the development of accidental jour-nalism, particularly in the dissemination of breaking news stories (Noguchi 2005). In a news market ripe with competition defined often by timeliness and immediacy (Eide 1992: 27), established news organizations are working to remain at the forefront of the competition for user-generated content, or amateur digital images of significant events. However, 'the content of such footage is rarely newsworthy in the traditional sense, and sometimes it is staged and fraudulent' (Calabrese 2000: 49).

Jon Dovey writes of camcorder cultures when he claims that, 'the low grade video image has become the privileged form of TV "truth telling", signifying authenticity and an indexical reproduction of the real world' (Dovey 2004: 558). As such, 'the camcorder text has become the form that most relentlessly insists upon a localized, subjective and embodied account of experience' (ibid.: 557). Furthermore, this change is more than technological in character, as these images that once belonged to the alternative channels now are a part of mainstream television (ibid.: 558).

In the case of the 7/7 London train bombings in 2005, mobile videos and images from inside the train cars allowed for a closer proximity to events, both for audiences and for news organizations. Thus, the significance of events grows in proportion to the immediacy and closeness of the event. Apparently true accounts of dramatic events are transmitted within minutes from witnesses to audiences, through – and this is also significant – the established audio-visual news media outlets.

The Bhutto case departs from other examples of amateur footage in the established news stream (such as the 7/7 London Underground bombings; 9/11; the Virginia Tech school shootings; and the Indian Ocean Tsunami) for two main reasons. First, there is a time lag from the time of the murder to the surfacing of amateur images displaying that murder. Second, the videos of Bhutto's death did not travel via the internet to reach established news organizations. Instead they were submitted directly to the news institutions, signifying in this case that the claim that professional journalism remains the significant gate-keeper of the news agenda is still valid.

Summary of findings

In the US media, the broadcast of these amateur videos is presented as a media event in itself. Such amateur productions seem much less a threat to US professional news production than the contemporary discourse on the democratic values of amateur news-making (with blogs, vlogs, 'convergence culture' and the like) would indicate. The television-news release of such footage is as much a story as the information it conveys. If established news sources are challenged by the ubiquity of video cameras, their ability to embed amateur footage – either self-consciously or seamlessly – into the normal news flow ensures their role as gate-keepers.

Norwegian media coverage exemplifies a seamless embedding of the amateur footage of Bhutto's assassination. The amateur tapes are not treated as events in themselves but rather incorporated into the edited flow of images of the event providing background for the journalist's voice-over. TV 2 and NRK mainly communicate the story through standard narrated news reports, supplemented with reports from Pakistan made by their foreign correspondents.[4] Herein lies both the similarity and the main difference between US and Norwegian news broadcasts on the Bhutto assassination. All broadcasters use this editing technique throughout their coverage. However, Norwegian news broadcasts seem to largely ignore the newsworthiness of the clips as a topic in itself, while US media offer this considerable attention. NBC's strategy is decidedly closer to embedding than the embellishing done by CNN. Nonetheless, CNN also trumpets the newsworthiness of the existence of the tapes, adding a dramatic layer to the events that the Norwegian news denies. Indeed, this would be the main difference between coverage in the respective countries. What is clearly at work across our entire sample, however, is a presentational savvy on the part of all the news organizations. In various ways they appropriate the amateur and use amateur footage to suit the needs of professional news narratives.

As for the extent to which these images represent a break with or continuation of the logic of the news narrative, two features in particular stand out. First, amateur footage used in reports about significant violent events is contextualized as such. These images are primarily introduced by reference to an official source – usually a news agency, another TV station or, in case of the Bhutto assassination, the official government. Furthermore, there is little or no mention of the original source; the tapes are introduced as 'amateur footage' or 'new footage'. Little doubt is cast as to the veracity or authenticity of the images or the source of the images but, rather, it is left up to the audience to trust the good judgement of the news organization in trusting other TV stations or official sources.

Second, the very existence of these amateur images is news in itself – whether it is sensationalized (as in the US) or not (as in Norway). As such, the release of the footage is as much the story as the content of the images. The use of these images shows that they hardly represent a break with the established news narrative but, rather, that they are embedded as a natural part of the source referencing that is normal in news reports. This case study demonstrates that news organizations are willing to make use of amateur footage in their news reporting, but that there are still significant differences in terms of whether they make these tapes the subject of the news themselves.

As this case study reveals, news institutions use the visual nature of amateur footage to their advantage. Whereas most newsrooms are highly preoccupied with good image quality in their reports, amateur footage need not be of professional quality. In fact the grainier the footage is, the better – to properly distinguish it from professionally filmed footage. By referring to the secondary source from which these amateur images have been procured, the TV stations here examined continue to front their own status as gatekeepers. The rhetoric of such a positioning is that audiences should trust the news judgement of the organization in question, particularly in terms of source verification and the authenticity of the images used in reports. Far from being a threat to the professional standards and practices of television news, amateur tapes find a welcoming home in news narrative and presentation. There is clearly a range of aesthetic strategies for incorporating such footage into the news stream, i.e. the embedding and embellishing techniques we have described.

This study contributes to curbing to some extent the exuberant expectations towards various forms of participatory journalism or amateur 'produsage'. We have found that, in the case of the Bhutto assassination, established news organizations tend to underplay the non-institutional nature of the amateur-captured images, rather than to hail the accessibility of visual witness evidence as a result of technological development. Three of the broadcasters we looked at (NBC, NRK, and TV 2) tended to embed amateur images into their established professional news narratives – i.e. mixing the footage into their narratives and visual frames through professional editing. One broadcaster, the news channel CNN, embellished the footage, drawing its visual properties and amateur status to the forefront while retaining its own narrative power over the images' controversial content.

The amateur can thus be defined as the invisible, uncredited witness to the event, embodied through anonymous visual imagery. The visuality and indirectness of this witness status is indeed what erases the identity of the witness itself. Whereas witnesses offering verbal statements that provide news organizations with valuable claims to truth, immediacy, and authority in the reporting of violent events are regularly identified by name, the amateur image recorders are here erased from the pool of sources referred to in the reporting of the event. Amateurs are just that – amateurs – and thus not noted as contributors to the production of professional news. News-gathering is therefore upheld by these news organizations as a professional activity performed solely by journalists.

Conclusions

We would not want to conclude, however, that the increased flood of amateur footage that emerges from world-changing events is completely without a modicum of the revolutionary potential promised by so much digital technology. Hints to this effect could be observed during the G20 demonstrations in London in early April 2009, and during the Iranian election demonstrations in June 2009. Indeed, the identification of the relevance of amateur footage in the television news stream opens up a number of questions for future research; research that could help unlock the potential for more amateur agency in the televisual public sphere. One interesting form of investigation would be to empirically delve further into the question of 'who is the amateur?' In other words, to bring an anthropological angle to the phenomenon. If we could uncover with greater clarity who the amateur producers of 'caught-on-tape' videos actually are, and what their interests and motivations are, we might develop a more complete picture of the impact that amateur footage has on television news.

Although scholars like Henry Jenkins have increased our understanding of fan communities and how they relate to the objects of their fandom, there is certainly more work to be done on the participants of major events that choose to record such events as they unfold. The obvious challenges of identifying these people as a group aside, such work could help to dispel the sense that mobile video recorders have become some kind of existential fact of life. While this notion may be a convenient lead for newscasters into an amateur-footage news item, it remains an unsatisfactory conclusion for those interested in measuring the impact of digital technology on the public sphere. This case study opens up for theorization the aesthetics of amateur and professional images. It also provides an opportunity for developing theory about the pervasiveness of the television news genre in the face of the steady growth of rival information genres.

Notes

1 Analysis of US coverage includes four broadcasts of NBC's Nightly News (a 30-minute programme) from 27 to 31 December; two of CNN's Newsroom (morning and afternoon programmes with variable run times) and five broadcasts of Evening News (a prime-time programme) from 27 December to 1 January – a total of 11 broadcasts.

2 Analysis of Norwegian coverage includes NRK's news broadcasts *Dagsrevyen* (a 30-minute evening news programme) and *Kveldsnytt* (a 15-minute evening news update) from 27 to 31 December 2007 – 10 broadcasts; and TV 2's news broadcasts *Nyhetene 18:30* (a 30-minute early evening news programme) and *Nyhetene 21:00* (a 30-minute evening news programme) from 27 to 31 December 2007 – 10 broadcasts, so 20 Norwegian broadcasts in all.

3 Alongside the Bhutto assassination as a mediated world-changing event, we would also list such things as recent terrorist attacks: 9/11, 7/7, and the like; natural disasters: the South Asian Tsunami, Hurricane Katrina; and smaller conspicuously violent incidents such as school shootings and hate crimes that are recorded and receive widespread media coverage.

4 NRK's Asia correspondent Philip Lothe and TV 2's reporter Kadafi Zaman.

References

Bruns, A. (2008) *Blogs, Wikipedia, Second Life, and Beyond: From Production to Produsage*, New York: Peter Lang.

Calabrese, A. (2000) 'Political Space and the Trade in Television News' in C. Sparks and J. Tulloch (eds) *Tabloid Tales: Global Debates over Media Standards*, Lanham: Rowman and Littlefield.

Caldwell, J. (2008) *Production Culture: Industrial Reflexivity and Critical Practice in Film and Television*, Durham, NC, and London: Duke University Press.

Dovey, J. (2004) 'Camcorder Cults', in R. Clyde Allen and A. Hill (eds) *The Television Studies Reader*, London: Routledge.

Eide, M. (1992) *Nyhetens interesse: Nyhetsjournalistikk mellom tekst og kontekst*, Oslo: Universitetsforlaget.

Friend, D. (2006) *Watching the World Change: The Stories behind the Images of 9/11*, New York: Picador.

Galtung, J. and Ruge, M. H. (1965) 'The Structure of Foreign News. The Presentation of the Congo, Cuba, and Cyprus Crises in Four Norwegian Newspapers', *Journal of Peace Research*, 2, pp. 64–90.

Harcup, T. and O'Neill, D. (2001) 'What is News? Galtung and Ruge Revisited', *Journalism Studies*, 2, pp. 261–80.

Hjarvard, S. (1995) *Internationale TV-nyheder: En Historisk Analyse af det Europæiske System for Udveksling af TV-Nyheder*, København: Akademisk Forlag.

Jenkins, H. (2006) *Convergence Culture: Where Old and New Media Collide*, New York: New York University Press.

Livingstone, S. and Bennett, W. L. (2003) 'Gatekeeping, Indexing, and Live-Event News: Is Technology Altering the Constriction of News?' *Political Communication*, 20, pp. 363–80.

Moltubak, R. D. and Tommelstad, B. (2007) 'Her treffer kulene Benazir Bhutto', vg.no, 31 September 2007. http://www.vg.no/nyheter/utenriks/artikkel.php?artid=192281. Accessed 19 September 2007.

Noguchi, Y. (2005) 'Camera Phones Lend Immediacy to Images of Disaster', Washingtonpost.com 8 July 2005. http://www.washingtonpost.com/wp-dyn/content/article/2005/07/07/AR2005070701522.html?referrer=emailarticle. Accessed 25 June 2008.

9

A NEW SPACE FOR DEMOCRACY?

Online media, factual genres and the transformation of traditional mass media

Ib Bondebjerg

In 2007 the BBC investigative journalist John Sweeny was working on a documentary on Scientology, following Scientologists around for a long time, much to their dissatisfaction. It seemed to be a case of broadcast media fulfilling their normal role of critical watchdog, trying to investigate a powerful institution in society. However, in this case the Scientologists, as a precaution, made their own documentary about Sweeny's work, and as they were closely following him around they caught him losing his temper with a Scientologist. What they captured on camera could be described as a journalist not being able to stand his own, critical, investigative methods. Scientologists put sequences of this on YouTube, so by using new online media, the Scientologists managed to put the BBC's powerful *Panorama* on the defensive. The BBC had to respond to this in the programme.[1]

In 2007 the semi-commercial Danish public-service broadcaster TV 2 was preparing to air a critical documentary programme called *Operaen – med døden i kulissen* ('the opera – death backstage') made by one of their long-established production companies, Bastard Film, and one of their most prolific investigative journalists, Miki Mistrati. The documentary went behind the scenes of the biggest Danish company, Mærsk, who financed and built the new Opera House in Copenhagen. What the film showed was that Mærsk had used cheap Chinese labour, under conditions that strongly conflicted with their ethical standards as a global company. One week before the programme was scheduled to air, Mærsk himself, who had not wished to answer questions during the programme, wrote a letter to the head of programmes at TV 2. A few days later the head of programmes axed the documentary because 'it did not meet the journalistic standards of TV 2'. The following week, however, the Danish tabloid *Ekstrabladet*, known for its critical investigative journalism, decided to put the programme on their web-TV site, and at the same time ran a journalistic series on the conflict. The public was given the opportunity to see that the quality of the programme itself was beyond doubt and that it raised a critical and important issue; the programme was embarrassing for Mærsk, and now for TV 2.

What do these two cases tell us about the new media environment and the relationship between the traditional media and the new online media? First of all they indicate that the gate-keeping functions of traditional broadcast media and mass media can be undermined and overruled, and that alternative productions and opinions have new channels that are easily accessed. Secondly, they tell us about a transition period in which the traditional media can be seen as on the defensive, not yet quite adjusted to a situation where they compete with very fast, cheap and open forms of new media. Thirdly, these cases show that the new media can be used for just about everything: they are not just instruments for grass-roots organizations and voices of dissent rejected by mainstream media, they are also a new tool for already powerful organizations and ideologies. Online technologies do not in themselves point to a new space for democracy, but they open up for the fight for public debate and access to the public in a new media environment where access, for the first time in history, is very easy for the average citizen. But it is still very much the same old fight, with old and new players positioning themselves in relation to a new media culture.

Media 2.0 – user-driven media content

Our use of media is not primarily technology-driven, but new technologies can enhance and develop forms of media use that have a clear personal and social function, and new media can make the performing of these functions faster and easier. With mobile media, for instance, local and global community functions have transcended the former restrictions of distance communication. Mobile phones, mobile computers, video-skyping and sites like Facebook have made it easier to bond with family, friends and business partners. But on a personal and social level we are still performing the ancient rituals of communication. The decentralization of these easy-to-use technologies is an increase of communicative democracy, and recent global events in both China and Iran show that authoritarian regimes have a hard time keeping the flow of visual information from on-the-spot users out of global media. But although the new mobile technologies can enhance information and aid in fights for democracy, the new media culture also shows signs of extreme centralization of economic power to multi-media companies combining all platforms, and the potential threat of 'big brother' (see Doyle 2002).

In 2008 the first online Danish internet documentary TV-serial was made under the name *Doxwise* (see http://www.myspace.com/doxwise). MySpace and the Danish Film Institute (DFI) supported a serial in 10 parts about everyday life for four very different young Danes. Each of them made a weekly video diary, and the diaries were then edited by a central director and put on the net every week for 10 weeks – in all there were 40 diary entries. The focus is very much observational, close-up, candid and often extremely intimate, but, as a whole, the diaries also represent a portrait of social differences among young Danes. The concept has since been expanded and repeated in collaboration between the DFI and the Danish broadsheet *Politiken*.

The format in itself is not revolutionary; the concept of video diaries dates back to the 1980s, and observational cinema has portrayed everyday life very closely since before that. On sites like YouTube or MySpace, there are already, globally, millions of 'documentary' programmes and series made by ordinary citizens exposing various aspects of their everyday lives. The main-stream media produce these everyday observational documentaries all the time as in-house, professional productions, and the whole phenomenon of reality TV clearly makes use of the increased interest in online interactive formats with ordinary people performing (Beattie 2004: 105ff; Dovey 2000). Many TV channels since the 1990s have also been active in user-driven and home-produced video-diary material, often under some kind of editorial control (Renov 2004: 191ff). If we add to that the internet amateurs doing it without any form of gate-keeping on all sorts of digital platforms, allowing us, in some cases, 24-hour visual access to the private home, it is fair to say that documentaries about ordinary people and everyday life have truly gone viral, but also over the top. But in the case of *Doxwise* there is an added value in the almost 'live' character of the event and in the fact that inter-active features and debates on both a more public and a more private level are tied to the site. So, in this case, user-driven actually means two things: first of all, the characters are filming their own life and, even though the editing is done by a professional director, the material and style of the footage is created by the character whose life is in focus; secondly, the viewers of these online products interact and in a sense influence the product and the context of the viewing experience.

One of the characters in the series was obviously having serious problems, involving not just his love life and social life in general but also drugs. His story generated a lively debate on the site, where people tried to comment on and influence the way he lived his life. This viewer involve-ment clearly influenced the later episodes of his story. Again, this was not a result of the technology itself creating new forms of communication and interaction: on the contrary the new technology enhanced a social community-building normally tied to established and close networks, but in this case developed between young people connected only by an online media event. In that sense we see a much stronger user-driven development in the online media, even compared to similar events in recent broadcast media genres.

When ordinary citizens set the agenda: reality and hoaxes in the blogosphere

A very old part of the media agenda and the public sphere is giving the voice to readers, both in the form of letters to the editor and in comments. By now the phenomenon of blogs and other features of personal communication through the internet has moved this form of communication out of the hands of the gate-keepers and traditional mass media. In many ways this development, and more open access to communication for ordinary people, must be saluted as a renewal of democracy. However, the chaos of communication arising from this and the loss of authority and credibility normally connected to media that are well established and have journalistic standards, ethics and accountability can also be seen as a major problem. For some, like Andrew Keen in *The Cult of the Amateur* ([2007]2008), this development is simply a disaster for politics and culture, a narcissistic cult of the individual, undermining of factual discourses and authority. Others, for instance Brian McNair in *Cultural Chaos: Journalism, News and Power in a Globalized World* (2006), see the development as a potentially positive one that challenges theories of global corporate control over the media.

It is in fact very seldom the case that bloggers or internet communications hit the agenda of the big media and gain a political influence that is reported and debated in the more traditional public sphere. The many informal communities and forums of debate on blogs and on the internet may, however, influence the democratic debate and agenda by new means, as was seen in the very successful Obama presidential campaign in 2008, which organized networks of blogs and internet communication. Political organizations do take up new media and use them strategically, and independent organizations like, for instance, Moveon.org or Democracy.now are basically net-based grass-roots movements.

But a front-page story in the *Los Angeles Times* (30 September 2008), 'Wasilla gadfly swirls in a storm', is an interesting example of how a completely ordinary schoolteacher from Alaska can launch a political avalanche. The main character, the 57-year-old teacher Anne Kilkenny, simply reacted to debates among friends and colleagues about the Republican vice presidential candidate Sarah Palin, of whom she had knowledge from local political activities in her Alaska hometown, Wasilla. Instead of just talking about Palin, she sent a 24,000-word critique of her as a person and as a politician to 40 of her friends and told them that they could pass it on to anybody they knew. A few days later her email inbox was flooded with more than 13,000 emails, some critical, some supportive, and as a consequence of her friends posting her original mail on Facebook, blogs and websites, her name soon generated more than 550,000 Google hits.

Kilkenny was not an experienced and organized political activist with strong skills in internet communication. She was simply a person with

116

interesting and timely knowledge about a key figure in the public sphere, expressing her personal opinion to a close community. But the internet made it into an example of viral politics in a digital age, where new media and ordinary citizens can sometimes set an agenda and influence mainstream media and the more centralized public-sphere debate.

Whereas Kilkenny was just an ordinary, individual schoolteacher going viral almost by accident, Paul Thompson and his 9/11 Complete Timeline Project represent an instance of organized grass-roots online journalism, supported by a group of creative-commons journalists and historians, the Centre for Cooperative Research (see Thompson n.d.). Paul Thompson is an independent investigator who, in the months after 9/11, started wondering why some of the news stories about this event and the politics behind it did not add up. Over the next three years he started stitching together more than 7,000 news stories from mainstream media, simply putting them up for comparison on a timeline. Incredible patterns of contradictions came up, very revealing for top politicians and members of the Bush administration. In 2004 his book (Thompson 2004), based on the online timeline, appeared. What we see here is actually the power of persistent, systematic journalism and research on and through the internet, and also an example of how online journalism can succeed in setting an agenda for the mainstream media. The publication of the book is the final proof of that, but more important is the fact that the timeline became a major source of information for journalists in the established media, whether network TV or newspapers. The timeline also became a major resource behind the independent documentary film *Press 9/11 for Truth*, which deals with the famous Jersey girls, widows of 9/11 victims, and their search for answers.

Established political parties and institutions clearly already use many forms of internet communication, but it is also very well documented that Facebook, MySpace, YouTube and other sites are used by groups of citizens or individuals to further political issues. The *Los Angeles Times* (2 October 2008) reports on the front page of the California section that YouTube is a platform for debate in connection with sensitive issues like the present attempt to change the law allowing gay marriages. What is interesting is that, in this particular case, people are using home videos for political reasons. By following the YouTube slogan, 'Broadcast Yourself', they made a political statement and, by illustrating homosexuality openly, gave this political issue a new, personal dimension. The proposal to ban gay marriage has led to heated controversy in documentary form: some make videos that indicate that gay marriages are against nature and cause doom and disaster while others illustrate how gay couples actually live in order to challenge such stereotypes.

These testimonies of homosexuality give politics a personal, authentic dimension. But the problem with online media products and genres is that, to a large degree, it is much more difficult to trust them as their origin and context is often not rooted in any accountable institution. Keen puts in very directly:

> In the digital world's never-ending stream of unfiltered, user-driven content, things are indeed not what they seem. Without editors, fact-checkers, administrators, or regulators to monitor what is being posted, we have no one to vouch for the reliability or credibility of the content we read and see on sites like Xanga, Six Apart, Veoh, Yelp, Odeo and countless others. There are no gatekeepers to filter truth from fiction, genuine content from advertising.
>
> (Keen 2008: 64–65)

Keen illustrates his point with a number of examples of fraud, fiction posted as fact, and hoaxes: the slandering of electoral candidates by people with false identities posting lies on the internet; the infamous conspiracy movie *Loose Change*, which accused the Bush administration of orchestrating the 9/11 attacks and went to the top 100 on Google Videos in 2006, was seen by more than 10 million people, and then turned out to be fiction disguised as a documentary; the incident with the *Los Angeles Times* journalist Michael Hiltzik, who wrote the strident liberal and polemical blog 'Golden State' and invented internet characters who could defend his own views when he was attacked by conservatives. Keen's sceptical view of all this points to the fact that the huge aggregation of information data on the net, data that never goes away, threatens what he calls 'our collective intellectual history' (Keen 2008: 75). Online media makes it much harder to stop the spread of nonsense and misinformation. Even without sharing Keen's deeply conservative scepticism towards new media, it is clear that this new media environment puts much greater demands on the common trust and social pact underlying communication in a given society. Even in the advanced and global-network society, people do have to be able to have common frames of reference in their communicative space in order to be able to navigate.

Getting the stuff out there: Googling reality

In 1939, long before the digital revolution, Jorge Luis Borges wrote an essay called 'The Total Library', about a chaotic network of all texts in the world assembled and joined in one system (Keen 2008: 86). Borges' vision is now becoming a reality and one of the truly democratic, social and cultural benefits of the internet revolution is the open access to all sorts of media material normally difficult to get and, in the old media culture, spread through many institutions. Searching, for instance, for documentary material on a specific subject is now often just a click away, wherever you are in the world. Both on YouTube and on Google Videos, just two of the most popular sites, you cannot only find clips from all sorts of public and private sources, but also films and programmes that can be hard to get from the original source. Trying to get access to programmes from, for instance, public-service broadcasters like the BBC can be hard, although they are starting to go public with much of their stuff on open-access pages.

While broadcast media and mass media used to exist in linear time – publish and disappear or disappear into archives – most media today move towards total digital online existence with all output accessible with or without some sort of control. This clearly has consequences for holding the media accountable and for comparing media. Behind any public debate lies a vast digital memory bank that can easily be activated and used at any given moment. So, besides giving the ordinary citizen a potential new voice in the public sphere, the new media also give access to an almost endless pile of information and documentation. As we have seen already in the case of both Kilkenny from Alaska and Thompson and his group of journalists and historians, these potential new forms of democratic influence and control actually do sometimes pay off and influence the general public. But most of the time the information chaos and the vast amount of information on the digital platforms demand time and skills that will favour elite users.

Andrew Keen (2008: xv) takes a clear elitist approach to the new media and, to a large degree, sees them as giving rise to a 'digital mob', undermining quality media content. But he also acknowledges that the new media are part of a new media culture with much greater interactive possibilities than traditional media – possibilities the elites and the traditional media will also be sure to benefit from. His scepticism towards utopian ideas about how digital media will fix democratic deficits is worth listening to in order not to succumb to technological utopianism. There is real quality in the fact that, potentially, all global communications can be reached and used on the internet and that everybody can have a voice there. But in the end, maybe, in the global chaos of communication, nobody really listens, and trust in what is out there can be lost. Wikipedia has often been praised as a marvellous example of how the amateur as a collective voice can match experts. Maybe so, but, as Keen points out (Keen 2008: 186), one of the pioneers behind Wikipedia, Larry Sanger, got so fed up with the thousands of lunatics and anarchists vandalizing entries or disputing the, by any standard, very open editorial policy of Wikipedia that he left and in 2006 created Citizendium. In this project, Sanger created an online encyclopaedia combining the input of ordinary people with the input and decisions from experts and specialists. Citizendium seeks reliability and quality and asks everybody to contribute under their real name.

Online media in service of democratic movements

The internet and digital media in general have given rise to many utopian ideas about the development of a new, active democracy by the people and

119

for the people. From local communities to the European Commission, the establishing of e-portals for information and debate has been key. But all too often excessively high expectations have been put on the technological platform itself, and its infrastructure, and too little attention paid to the social and cultural context of the citizens and users. Communities, basically, cannot be created with technology if the social and cultural networks are not there, and if users do not see the benefits or are not motivated to use the technology.

However, even though many of these sites and utopian ideas have not proven very successful there is no need to underestimate the potentials for interactivity and engagement through digital media. Perhaps especially in countries like the US, where the public media sector is very small compared to the big, commercial players, the internet does seem to have some potentials that traditional media lack. Two examples are Moveon.org and Democracy.now, defined as political and civic organizations that aim to mobilize people to take active part in democracy and politics.

Moveon.org has supported both books and independent documentary film production, mainly based on the support of ordinary citizens. However, Democracy.now, seen in a new media perspective, is much more interesting, because it uses the internet, podcasting and web-TV, as well as more traditional media, and because the website is an example of well-developed alternative online journalism. Their daily news programme is shown on the web and on independent channels across the US and constitutes one of the very few dissident voices on national television. The Democracy.now website is highly professional and diverse in genres and formats, and it shows how media genres and technologies for production and distribution are being developed beyond their original forms.

Another, somewhat different, initiative is MediaChannel (http://www.mediachannel.org), a New York-based organization founded by Danny Schechter and Rory O'Connor:

> MediaChannel exists to provide information and diverse perspectives and inspire debate, collaboration, action and citizen engagement … The vitality of our political and cultural discourse relies on a free and diverse media that offers access to everybody. Journalists and media professionals, organizations and activists, scholars and citizens all need improved access to information, resources and opportunities to reach out and build connections. MediaChannel has been created to meet this need at the dawn of the new millennium.
>
> (http://www.mediachannel.org)

So what we see here is a movement of critical journalists and political activists trying to create an alternative to the dominant news agenda and mobilizing people by creating a higher media awareness. The new media environment is used for a very well-known critical and educational purpose.

Another good example is Michael Moore's use of Facebook as a mobilizing and organizing tool. It is easy to join as a fan and several times a week receive a fairly detailed email from him on some subject of political importance. His latest film, *Slacker Uprising*, was a real internet project and was launched in the US, on 1 October 2008, as an internet-download movie. Another example is Robert Greenwald's BraveNewFilm.org, a combination of an online journalistic site and a production and distribution site for critical, political documentary films. Greenwald's film, *Iraq For Sale: The War Profiteers* (2006), was basically financed by the web community of active individuals and organizations linked to BraveNewFilm and, through the website, debate and further distribution of the film was also made possible. It is, now, an institutionalized political factor in the US.

Old media and strategies for the digital future

Perhaps the most enduring part of the new media development is the merging of old and new media. This development comes in many forms: television stations developing huge online platforms with many different services; newspapers merging print media and visual media online; new internet-based channels giving a new space for professional producers on a digital platform. The two whizz-kids who started Skype, for instance, Niklas Zennström and Janus Friis, have now developed Joost.tv. The idea is to bring together TV productions, film productions, and so on, on a free and open platform on the internet – a kind of meeting of professionals and a new audience through the internet. The same idea in different forms has been developed by many channels all over the world, for instance SurftheChannel and Current.tv. It is also an idea taken up by artists and artist communities.

But the old TV stations are also learning a lesson. Where, before now, programmes would disappear from the public space after being shown once or twice, and then perhaps reappear published on video/DVD, it is by now pretty clear that we are moving towards the complete, digital archive of at least all public-service channels in Europe. At the same time, current programmes of any given day and week can be seen on the net. On many of these public-service channels television is merged with radio and print media in the form of online print journalism and blogs, and often visual material is linked to print material. On the internet we therefore clearly see a media hybridization where audio-visual media genres and programmes merge with traditional print-media formats and new digital formats.

It is also interesting to see broadcast stations positioning themselves on sites that reach young audiences, which the old media are otherwise in danger of losing altogether. If you go to channels on YouTube and select news and politics, you are presented with a large group of both American and European channels: RAI, FOX, BBC, Al Jazeera, CSpan, PBS, CNN, ZDF, France24, to name just a few. Along with these more established channels are a lot of channels made directly for YouTube, representing organizations and grass-roots movements of different kinds. The established broadcasters are not developing new channels for the YouTube audience but they organize and profile their material in new ways that match the overall layout of YouTube. In June 2009 the main Danish public-service channel DR, for instance, launched a new internet channel with the very streetwise name of Piracy TV (www.dr.dk/pirat), where they remix existing programme segments in a 'YouTube' format for the younger generation. Here it is possible to surf by category and to find short statements targeted directly at young people, and, of course, there is also a blog. Traditional broadcasters are gradually moving into the digital universe, trying to speak a new language to the digital generation.

If we look at the newspaper universe, it is equally difficult to tell what kind of media we are dealing with. The main product for the older consumer may still be the daily newspaper, but a newspaper today must primarily be seen as a multimedia platform. This is not just because many newspapers are involved in publishing, television, radio, and so on, but is also a result of development of the online newspaper as a multimedia phenomenon. Globally, one of the most developed newspapers online is the British *Guardian.* The interactivity of the site is amazing, not just because of the almost 50,000 different blog posts and comments it includes, but also because the site allows the user to navigate and link between clearly defined thematic fields. But what is of special interest here is the development of the newspaper towards documentary filmmaking and visual journalism.

The *Guardian*'s video site is organized in thematic blocks, following the general structure of the newspaper, so we have: national news, world news, sport, art, society, media, and so on. A closer look at the videos on the site reveals that they are not in any way innovative compared to ordinary television: they have the same content and the same format. The only difference is that we can navigate between clips and then email them, share them or make our own clips. Looking, for instance, at the art videos, it becomes clear that this site gives room for experimental language alongside normal informational material about art. And if we go to the site GuardianFilms we learn that in 2002 the newspaper established itself as a major producer of documentary films; a new space for independent film production and also for new talent:

> We concentrate our efforts on stories that other companies can't reach by harnessing the Guardian's exceptional journalistic base. Our specialist current affairs and news coverage has been internationally regarded for its journalistic rigour and tenacity. Our long-form

documentaries exhibit a diverse range of human interest stories, continuing the GuardianFilms interest to make 'films that make a difference'.

(http://www.guardian.co.uk/news/guardianfilms)

One example is *America's Forgotten War*, which can be viewed on the site and which offers links to other material related to the film's theme. You can also follow the making of the film through the director John D. McHugh's diary from the filming in Afghanistan and also read a blog made before, during and after the film. All in all, it is an example of the superiority of internet TV over broadcast TV, simply because it creates a much richer informational context around the film.

The equivalent Danish newspaper, *Politiken*, is not nearly as developed and ambitious, but does show ambition towards becoming a news channel with independent and original journalism. The main impression when watching Politiken.tv is that this is far from traditional TV news and is in many ways much closer to newspaper journalism: it is visualized talking heads. It is informational but not visually interesting or made with reports or documentary clips of reality; it is serious, no-nonsense news journalism, and in this way differs from the trend towards soft news and infotainment on TV channels. Other parts of the Politiken.tv site, however, are closer to the journalistic format of TV news. The news link and the focus link are news clips based on footage from national and international news agencies, but with editing and active material and interviews made by Politiken journalists. An example of the experimental nature of the site is a project with the Danish Film Institute called *Clips*, and the idea behind the project is to challenge some of the best Danish documentary filmmakers to use a 5-minute format and the website to create new and more visually challenging reporting on reality. It is art film and elite culture meeting web 2.0; it is a challenge to the amateurs dominating the new media videos; and it is a meeting between journalism and film art.[2]

Concluding remarks

It seems wise not to go completely utopian-wild or take a too gloomily pessimistic stance when considering the consequences for democracy. What we see shows real possibilities for a more active democracy, giving a voice to ordinary people, because the new media are much more accessible than traditional media and can spread messages with impressive speed. But there are very few indications of traditional media seriously losing power: on the contrary we increasingly see a merging of old media and new media; the merging of genres and formats on new platforms.

Looking at visual, factual and documentary formats, we see independent production and grass-roots organizations gaining new ways of producing and distributing their products. While it is obvious that the big players and distributors are still holding the reins we do see independent productions hit the mainstream media agenda and we do see examples of the mobilization of issues from user-driven public-sphere debate. But it is still the traditional channels and media that are setting the agenda. So the new media have created a new media culture with much potential, but we are not talking about one culture replacing another: we are talking about a slow transition with a strong merging of old and new, with a new positioning and organization of very old social and cultural agendas. Technology is important, but more important is the social context and the fundamental structure of human cognition and communication.

Notes

1 I am grateful to my PhD student Inge Sørensen for telling me about this BBC incident in a presentation at an internal seminar in Copenhagen in 2008.
2 A report on this experiment has been published in Danish, Bondebjerg and Jensen (2009).

References

Beattie, Keith (2004) *Documentary Screens: Nonfiction Film and Television*, New York: Palgrave.

Bondebjerg, Ib and Jensen, Klaus Bruhn (2009) *Clips – et medieeksperiment*, Report, University of Copenhagen.

Dovey, Jon (2000) *Freakshow: First Person Media and Factual Television*, London: Pluto.

Doxwise (n.d.) Official site, http://www.myspace.com/doxwise. Accessed 26 August 2009.

Doyle, Gillian (2002) *Media Ownership*, London: Sage.

Keen, Andrew ([2007]2008) *The Cult of the Amateur*, New York: Doubleday.

McNair, Brian (2006) *Cultural Chaos: Journalism, News and Power in a Globalized World*, London: Routledge.

Renov, Michael (2004) *The Subject of Documentary*, Minneapolis: University of Minnesota Press.

Thompson, Paul (n.d.) *Complete 911 timeline*, http://www.historycommons.org/project.jsp?project=911_project. Accessed 13 August 2009.

Thompson, Paul (2004) *The Terror Timeline*, New York: HarperCollins.

10

LIFESTYLE AS FACTUAL ENTERTAINMENT

Christa Lykke Christensen

The electronic lifestyle magazine

Public-service channels generally have undergone changes in programming during the last 10 to 15 years and this has also been the case with the Danish public-service channels, DR and TV 2. The early hours of prime time for four days of the week have gradually been filled with programmes concerned with so-called lifestyle matters. The programmes address home improvement, gardening, cooking, hobbies, holidays, personal appearance and health, and the formats range from the instructive do-it-yourself programme or the sceptical consumer programme, through programmes with the 'makeover' as their central dramaturgical logic, to programmes concerned with the presentation and updating of taste, where aspects of lifestyle are often integrated with traditional entertainment elements such as quizzes and competitions.

The early hours of prime time on Danish channels used to be dominated by comedy series, documentaries and quizzes but, since 2000, lifestyle programmes have gradually succeeded in displacing them while the elements of comedy, documentary, experiments, games and quizzes have been integrated into these programmes, which is one of the reasons they are labelled as a hybrid genre, under the heading of 'factual entertainment' (Hill 2005). My argument is that the very combination of factual, educational and entertainment television is the reason the programmes are as popular as they are, at least from the standpoint of ratings. The hybrid genres offer the viewers many and varied opportunities to connect with the programmes, and thus provide them with different ways of being entertained.

Lifestyle programmes on television are not unique media phenomena. They are part of what one may call late-modern makeover or improvement culture. Newspapers abound with lifestyle supplements, and lifestyle material is abundantly available on the internet – as a supplement to television programmes, among other things; moreover, the number of lifestyle magazines for men, women and children has risen throughout the last 10 years.

Compared to the print format of the lifestyle magazines, television programmes benefit from the possibility of constructing narratives, following ideas over time, realizing them in practical activities, and producing social actions with consequences to 'real' people. Humanized and dramatized content, involving 'ordinary' people placed where they belong in a private setting, furthers the entertainment value of the programmes. In comparison with print media, moving images stimulate sympathetic viewing, which creates the opportunity for emotional connection or rejection, related to the aesthetics of programmes. In itself, this may be considered to have a special entertainment value in viewers' experiences. Moreover, as Ouellette and Hay mention, television may have a greater impact than print magazines because it is easily accessible without much planning within the private space of the home, and because it has an established, central place in the rhythm of everyday life. Compared to television, magazines, newspapers and books require a different type of engagement on the part of the individual, who must seek them out on their own to a greater degree (Ouellette and Hay 2008: 73). In other words, lifestyle programmes on television are attractive because they are accessible, they are about 'real' people, and they represent a 'do-it-yourself' trend in the landscape of modern media.

Mediatization of everyday life

Most lifestyle programmes deal with everyday life. Usually, they take place in people's private homes, and show ordinary people occupied with ordinary things related to the home – for example, cooking, cleaning and decorating. I am interested in analysing how such programmes relate, how they contribute to ideas of everyday life, and in discussing the way in which television contributes a mediatization of that same life, which results in, among other things, a construction of everyday life as entertainment, denying housework as 'a form of labour, and constructing it as a "fun" leisure and lifestyle activity' (Hollows 2003: 229).

Inspired by Stig Hjarvard's general definition of mediatization (Hjarvard 2008: 28) as a process through which late-modern society is increasingly subjected to, or has become dependent on, the media and their logic, my argument is that, on the one hand, lifestyle programmes are preoccupied with concrete and recognizable aspects of everyday life: how to lay out a garden, how to cook good and healthy food, how to raise children, and so on. In that respect, lifestyle programmes authoritatively mirror factual, everyday activities and may in many ways be compared to educative programmes from the earlier days of public-service programming, when viewers were supposed to learn something useful from television. In that sense, lifestyle programmes are 'everyday television', that is, a window on the ordinary lives of ordinary people, providing viewers with knowledge, and giving them good advice so that they can better handle the frequent practical problems that arise in the normal run of things.

On the other hand, or rather in the very way television provides viewers with knowledge about everyday life, my argument is that everyday life becomes entertainment when subjected to the logic of television, resulting in, among other things, synonymity between everyday life and lifestyle. In other words, mediatization in this context means the 'lifestyling' of life. Lifestyle programmes do not describe everyday life in documentary terms, but actively produce particular ideas of it, determined by the format and the concept, and with regard to the entertainment value of the programmes. The 'style' element indicates that everyday life has to be considered as a specific set of aesthetically, and often normatively, reflected ways of doing things, anchored in the logic of recurrent alterations, innovations and stylings.

Lifestyle programmes circulate discourses on the importance of individual choice as crucial to the meaning of life. They are about how to make the most effective and professional choices about how to change or improve your individual life; choice, change and innovation are not necessarily motivated by particular ideological reasons, though visions of 'the good life' are communicated by lifestyle experts as 'tastemakers' (Philips 2005: 228), oriented towards individualistic, middle-class tastes and values. Change is considered *a good thing in itself*, and is often effectively visualized through aesthetically decorative changes. In accordance with expectations of individual citizens at a given social level, lifestyle programmes stimulate change concerning visible effects – as a sign of individuals' preparation and readiness for entrepreneurial activity, for willingness and interest in creating results, which may promote yet other activities. Ouellette and Hay describe the relationship between television and the citizen in this way:

> The citizen is now conceived as an individual whose most pressing obligation to society is to empower her or himself privately. Television assists by acting as a visible component of a dispersed network of supporting technologies geared to self-help and self-actualization.
>
> (Ouellette and Hay 2008: 3)

In this respect, mediatization means that television not only presents different aspects of everyday life and ways of improving it; it also creates the impression that everyday life means a daily, individual responsibility for practicing an aesthetic, self-reflective attitude, and readiness for recurrent change and innovation. Thus, television viewers are not only positioned as recipients and consumers of knowledge and entertainment, they are receiving a stimulus to always be prepared for change, and to be responsible for their own actions or, perhaps more importantly because of the potential for disaster, for the lack of any change.

Lifestyle as 'self-help'

In lifestyle media, everyday life, the home and the body are objects of reflection and considered as projects of self-actualization. Media users are regarded as needing to understand themselves as unique, individual personalities, constantly working on the 'self', and enhancing the quality of their lives; at the same time, lifestyle media have to ensure that this individual working on the self is legitimized within generally accepted normative standards, which make the individual recognizable to others as a modern subject, self-aware and, first and foremost, a selective consumer. In that way, lifestyle programmes may be considered as electronic versions of content that is figuring simultaneously on various media platforms, stressing everyday life as 'a site of perpetual "renovation"' (Lewis 2007: 286). They translate the tendencies of modern individualization, reflectivity and distinctions of taste into equivalent practices, thereby legitimizing the aspect of 'perpetual renovation', connected to distinctive consumption. Lifestyle programmes provide consumers with arguments for the positive and 'natural' aspects of individualization and reflectivity, and for the obviousness of working on the differentiation of taste. Lifestyle programming demonstrates that television channels also consider it their business to stimulate these tendencies. They comply with a viewer who, from a psychologically motivated point of view, is entertained by picking up such forms of knowledge and competences. On the other hand, this invests the educational dimension of public service with a marked instrumental aim.

From a gender perspective, it is interesting that the printed lifestyle magazine has become electronic. As Tania Lewis argues, the programmes have further anchored the ideas of traditional feminine competences, interests and domestic work in ideas of 'lifestyle' (Lewis 2007: 291). Lifestyle programmes have unambiguously exposed housework, connected to home, food and health, as interesting from an aesthetic point of view because of the attention paid to the potential of this work, in terms of style and taste. Some would call this development a feminization of television programming; I am more inclined to consider it a result of mediatization, because the traditional domestic world of women is staged in ways which optimize their potential for play and pleasure, and the idea of lifestyle, first and foremost, exposes everyday life as a starting point of 'fun', play and pleasurable visual potential for consumption. Therefore, everyday imagination (Prokop 1978: 97), connected to both ordinary housework and to pleasurable daydreaming, has not only been subjected to extensive media exposure that stages daydreaming as a public show; it has also become the object of professionalism, primarily provided by the numerous experts and professionals appearing on lifestyle programmes – connecting aesthetic imagination with professional modelling of taste and identity – and thereby also indicating its commercial potential.

Genre hybrids

It is difficult to give a precise genre definition of lifestyle programmes; partly because there are many different types of programmes, partly because the individual programme is itself a hybrid, composed of several elements from different genres. Some programmes – for instance, consumer programmes – strongly emphasize the informative aspects; some emphasize traditional entertainment elements, with a dramaturgical drive based on competitions and quizzes among experts and performers. Thus, 'lifestyle' on television is not to be categorized as one genre. Lifestyle programmes engage with viewers in different ways, function in various ways, and 'do' differently in relation to viewers.

Research on lifestyle programming also indicates the difficulties of a genre definition. Annette Hill makes some attempts to define the programmes (Hill 2005, 2007), explaining how the thematizing of lifestyle within a factual framework has had several definitions since it appeared on British television at the beginning of the 1990s, including leisure, infotainment, educational, lifestyle and reality programmes (Hill 2005: 41–56). This variety may be considered the outcome of the confusion caused by the number of factual experiments in the nineties which wrestled with 'reality' in new and often provocative ways. Hill defines lifestyle programmes in this way:

> There are two types of lifestyle: instructional and makeover programmes. Instructional programmes offer straightforward advice and are close to consumer programmes. Makeover programmes focus on the transformation of something, and are closer to constructed popular factual.
>
> (Hill 2007: 51)

While Hill makes a distinction between *instructional* and *makeover* programmes, her categorization does not take into account a specific category of programme that, at least in Denmark, has manifested itself as important. Besides programmes giving specific advice *and* makeover programmes there is a third category in which lifestyle is neither related to tips and handy advice nor has it to do with a makeover of a house, garden or body. It is a category of programme aimed at exposing various forms of lifestyle by looking inquisitively into people's homes, kitchens, gardens, and so on. Often, the viewers are offered a (simulated) visit to ordinary or semi-well-known personalities, and are guided through their private homes by so-called lifestyle experts, who express their knowledge of taste and style in relation to the specific home and its occupant. In such programmes, viewers are presented with private homes from the perspective that each home potentially holds forms of taste and lifestyle. These may be described as *expository* programmes. This category of programme takes for granted the viewers' knowledge of lifestyle, and their readiness with regard to the styling of life. In this way, programmes stimulate viewers' need for knowledge by playing with utopian ideas of improving lifestyle.

In order to define this category of programme, one may distinguish, as do Carlsen and Frandsen, between instructive and lifestyle programmes (2005: 12). They place programmes with different thematic matter (interior, body, food, etc.) in these two categories. The categorization is favourable since it suggests (at least) two strategies of communication and two notions of viewers: on the one hand, it suggests the educational, often didactic way of addressing the viewer expecting to be informed and to learn something from the programme. In such programmes, the host is often an outstanding figure with regard to performance and attitude. This is often the case in consumer programmes, for example *Rabatten* ('discount') (2002–), or in handyman series, for example *Ønskehaven* ('the wishing garden') (2008–).

Lifestyle programmes are, on the other hand, to a greater extent directed towards the value of experiences in watching design, food, fashion, and so on, and to a lesser degree are directed at practical advice. Typically, the host functions as co-viewer, or acts as 'a mediator between the participants of the program and between program and viewer' (Carlsen and Frandsen 2005: 18). Danish examples are *Kender du typen?* ('do you know the type?') and *Liebhaverne* ('prospective buyers'). By making more room for viewers' imagination and aesthetic judgement, the programmes call attention to the very fact that it is *possible* to learn and that life can be *better*; this contrasts with the instructive programmes, whose hosts and experts point out that the viewer *ought to* learn, and *how* the viewer should live. For Umberto Eco, texts of expository programmes seem more open than texts of instructive programmes, which are based more on instructive statements and results and final conclusions. In principle, expository programmes operate in an open structure, noting the importance of *possible changes* in preference to the results of such changes. Expository programmes, in a more abstract sense, appeal to a utopian dimension of viewer experience.

The tripartition of categories of programmes into instructive, makeover and expository functions pragmatically with respect to analysis, clarifying the different intentions of producer, and the different positions of viewer. In contrast to Hill's definition of genre, it makes it possible to classify the makeover as a category between instructional and expository programmes. It must be underlined that instructive programmes are also concerned with style and taste and, similarly, viewers may find it useful to watch expository programmes, though perhaps more abstractly. From a Danish historical perspective, the instructional programme was the first category to originate in a long public-service tradition of educational, factual programming. Thereafter the category of makeovers emerged, and then most recently the expository category of programmes. Although it represents a tendency, this is not an unambiguous development. It is difficult to delimit these categories unambiguously. Perhaps even the blurred boundaries between them are an advantage when we look at the great attraction of the programmes. Viewers may be satisfied with the fact that the viewer contract is often ambiguous. It admits several imaginative and emotional links to programmes, thereby enhancing their entertainment value.

Lifestyle as entertainment

According to Ellis, lifestyle programmes are popular because they give viewers insight into the everyday lives of other people (Ellis 2000) – speaking broadly of all categories of programmes. He does not mean that they contemplate wholesale voyeurism; rather, they give viewers a chance of getting an idea of what ordinary life is. As such, the programmes play a central role in television's support of an intimate relationship between television and the lives people are engaged in when they are not watching television.

> They sharpen awareness of all the subtle social distinctions that are conveyed by clothes, speech and lifestyle, and at the same time humanize them. They allow a small glimpse behind the designer labels and the style allegiances of public street culture, to see a more private side of consumerism, where commodities are infused with personal associations.
>
> (Ellis 2000: 112)

According to Ellis, television programmes are characterized by not only drawing attention to the meaning of social distinctions in the micro-cosmos of everyday life but they also humanize distinctions, showing a privatized manner of consumption by giving the viewer an insight into the way in which 'other people' practice consumption. But we have to specify and stress that lifestyle programmes are not documentaries, and that mediatized everyday life has some qualities which unmediatized reality does not have. That is, the glimpse we are allowed, of a more private side of consumerism, is made for television or, in Hill's words: 'constructed popular factual' (Hill 2007: 51). The constructed aspect is precisely the element that creates the entertainment aspect of the programmes. In order to entertain viewers, programmes are made entertaining, that is, they are made in ways that motivate viewers to be entertained.

Motivation

The previously mentioned three prototypes of lifestyle programme – the instructional, the makeover and the expository programme – address the audience in three different ways. Accordingly, the audiences are positioned differently. To provide a basis for discussing how an audience is entertained, I will take cognitive psychology as my starting point and state that, fundamentally, being entertained has to do with *motivation*. That is, it poses the question: what does the viewer gain from watching these categories of lifestyle programme?

However, when a person prepares to be entertained, and chooses a specific media product for this purpose, for instance a lifestyle programme, 'the desired experience ... lies in the future' (Vorderer et al. 2006: 6). That means that the person directs his or her activity towards a future psychological state that, so far, is only represented in his or her mind. Thus, entertainment can be defined 'as an intrinsically motivated response' (ibid.: 6) to certain media products. In order to determine what types of activities hold intrinsic interest for viewers of lifestyle programmes, we may use Ryan and Deci's cognitive evaluation theory (Ryan and Deci 2000). This is based on the assumption that humans have three fundamental needs, crucial for both an individual's intrinsic motivation and for his or her fundamental wellbeing. The three needs are *competence, autonomy* and *relatedness* – with the proviso that 'these needs materialize differently over a life span, in different cultures, situations, and even personalities' (Vorderer et al. 2006: 7).

The aspect of *competence* has to do with the feeling of being challenged – but not so radically that one feels overwhelmed and unqualified to meet the challenge – while seated before the screen. Being challenged must be in accord with the viewer's feeling of mastery. Being challenged means that you experience the sense of acquiring knowledge and information you did not have previously, or you did not know you would like to acquire.

> The enjoyment derived from mastery is not merely an affirmation of a routine and tested ability; it is a successful movement into a new area of competence. In terms of biological function, the subjective phenomenology of competence is a sign to the organism that it has mastered an adaptively significant challenge.
>
> (Vorderer et al. 2006: 14)

From the perspective of the phenomenology of the body, one may also say that the aspect of competence is realized in television programmes that stimulate and support dispositions of the 'I can/I know' aspect of the body (rather than the 'I think' aspect) (Thøgersen, on Merleau-Ponty 2004: 116). Stimulating the capability of the body by presenting socially meaningful relations between body, actions and objects (as often occurs in lifestyle programmes) may place viewers in a state of mind that they normally experience as pleasant and entertaining.

The aspect of *autonomy* has to do with the fact that viewers tend to see themselves as self-directed; as mastering their choices of entertainment products. The importance of choice has to do with the fact that media products are forms of simulation. 'Simulations model a phenomenon by use of substitute agents and objects, selectively conserving causal relations' (Vorderer et al. 2006: 14). Because of this selection, 'agents retain an autonomy over the model that is unattainable in real life' (ibid.). By pretending that a given lifestyle programme is real life, the viewer gets the feeling that he or she is the one who is mastering the need for information and competence. The autonomy aspect allows the viewer to both identify with agents and situations and to follow events at a distance. Thus, simulated realities create spaces for reflection and evaluation whereby autonomy is closely connected to the aspect of competence.

The third aspect, *relatedness*, has to do with the viewer's feeling of being together with somebody, or having an intimate relation to something. For example, from studies of parasocial interactions and relations (Horton and Wohl 1956), we know that media users often feel that they are in good company when they are watching television. Though they are watching television alone, they do not feel alone. In the case of lifestyle programmes, one may suppose that the focus on everyday life, the home and ordinary people improves the chances of relating, through identification, empathy or dissociation from the performers. Lifestyle programmes focus on private and personal matters in what Meyrowitz calls the area of *the middle region* (1986); they are preoccupied with issues of taste in a generally *feel-good* atmosphere, and viewers are expected to evaluate what they see as either demonstrating good taste or as distasteful. Several lifestyle programmes are positively concerned with the working-together aspect – for instance, in the renovation of houses and gardens. Thus, the viewers may be engaged in watching others manage collaborations related to practical activities and thereby reflect on whether they would have acted in similar or different ways. This is not only 'intimacy at a distance'; it is, as Thompson also stresses, a mediated quasi-interaction, which is non-dialogical and 'the form of intimacy established through it is non-reciprocal in character' (Thompson 1995: 219).

Lifestyle programmes as motivational factors

Cognitive psychology tends to examine these three elements of motivation in isolation, emphasizing that entertainment is 'a response to a certain set of opportunities, rather than a feature of a particular media product itself' (Vorderer et al. 2006: 3). I find this an unnecessary reservation. On the contrary, the three responses may actually be productive, with regard to analyses of lifestyle programmes (for example), which I consider as having the *potential to increase motivation*. I will outline how the three elements of competence, autonomy and relatedness find expression in the aforementioned three categories of lifestyle programmes. My intention is to draw attention to the sort of knowledge lifestyle programmes produce and circulate, and to discuss the fact that public-service channels find such knowledge important.

Regarding the attraction of the instructional programme, the aspect of competence supports the viewer's feeling of being capable and prepared to learn something from television. The motivation may be the expectation of concrete instructions and advice, which are demonstrated and communicated to the viewer, and, by extension, the ease and *the great efficiency* of problem-solving. The attraction may also lie in the confirmation of the perception that there is always a correct solution to a problem – which, from a viewer's perspective, may be experienced as agreeable. Moreover, programmes often produce competitions eliciting viewers' own proposals for solutions to given problems. Every programme always presents a winning solution, so the viewer may subsequently evaluate his or her own expectations and knowledge. In other words, the viewer may feel motivated by the feeling of being more or less skilled or competent than the programme.

Experts are important in all three categories of programmes but they play different roles which may entertain viewers in different ways. The expert in instructional programmes displays a specific form of expertise and knowledge. Generally, the expert is didactic, demonstrating how to do things – how to repair an old chair, how to be a good cook, how to weed the garden effectively, how to improve one's health, and so on. The knowledge of the expert is connected to practical activities performed in front of the camera, often in close-ups, so that the viewer acquires insight into the details of work processes. This corresponds to a particular aspect of knowledge: the 'knowing how' aspect. 'Knowing how' accentuates the active dimension of knowledge. It means that you know *what* to do and, equally important, that you have to realize your knowledge through activity. Looking at the experts, for example, in gardening and home-improvement programmes, the authority of the expert is founded in the fact that knowing and action amount to the same thing. The main discourse of the programmes is oriented towards the practical performance of knowledge. Thus the viewer is primarily met with the competence aspect – 'Could I do the same thing?' – but the aspect of autonomy also plays a role in the viewers' consideration of 'Would I ever do the same thing?'

For the second category, the makeover, the viewer's motivation may be stimulated by witnessing a possible transformation. In makeover programmes, it is demonstrated how, in very little time, an unpleasant 'before' situation may be turned into an absolutely much better 'after' situation – aided by quick solutions, well-chosen and infallible resources, and by the assistance of always optimistic and happy friends, neighbours and technically skilled people. Makeovers address viewers emotionally, pointing out the importance of the transformation to the one who is being transformed (Jerslev 2008). The moment of truth – the unveiling of a body or a garden, for example – may induce sentimental tears from both participants and viewers in response to the fantastic results or the thoughtfulness other people have shown the individual by contributing to the final result. Just as in unmediated life, viewers experience the ways in which the superficial worlds of things and emotional relations may be deeply connected. However, the advantage of televising this content, by virtue of its aesthetically enlarged tableaux, gives the viewer access to situations of non-reciprocal intimacy, and thus a more *effective* emotional response than in unmediated life. Thus, makeovers address the aspect of relatedness.

In makeover programmes, where bodies, houses, gardens, and so on are often radically changed, we also meet the kind of expert who uses his or her expertise, presented as technical skills. The expert is an expert by virtue of his or her practicable advice. The role of the expert is based on the idea that knowledge is legitimated in so far as it solves problems effectively. But, as Ruth Holliday says of the difference between programmes that demonstrate skills and the makeover: 'The pleasure of the new genre [makeover] is very much the pleasure of consuming a design idea. In earlier programmes the (relatively little) pleasure induced was the pleasure of learning skills – of production' (2005: 67). At the more general level of programme production, experts guarantee a quick and effective answer to a given problem so that the dramaturgical and narrative logic of the programme is followed, and the programme may reach an effective and satisfactory conclusion. Thus, the programmes also appeal to the aspect of competence, but in a more indirect way than do instructional programmes.

With the third category, the expository programme, the viewer is not necessarily interested in demonstrations of how to make everyday life easier and cheaper, nor in experiences of quick and ready-made solutions for changing their lives. Basically, the viewer already has a personal style, and knows how to arrange their lifestyle. Interest in these programmes is motivated by the desire to get an *update* on fashion and trends, originating from the experience that lifestyle is always about further refinement and styling. The general effect of the programmes is that elements of style and aesthetics play the most crucial role. The question is not how to get style or how to change life; rather, it is how to make further distinctions and qualify your present lifestyle. Generally, with regard to the motivational aspects, this category of programme is directed towards a knowledgeable audience, with the competence aspect as its motivation. Correspondingly, the experts are less didactic, just as the experts are less authoritative in the traditional way. These programmes are not concerned with leisure activities, hobbies, as something isolated from the rest of people's lives; they are about a whole way of life. When cooking is the subject, the entire context and lifestyle are taken into consideration: raw materials, primary production, food habits, the age and physique of participants, their economy and general health. Expository programmes have an integrative approach to everyday life. They operate with the ideals of harmony and balance in all aspects of life. The role of the expert is to communicate ideas and discourses on the 'good life', and to promote ethical and aesthetic questions and considerations, which may help the viewer to make the optimal choice. However, the principal effect of the programme is not that of *which* choices viewers have to make, but *that* the viewer feels obliged to reflect on the best choice. In that sense, the motivating factor of autonomy is addressed.

For this reason, the expert functions as *a guide*, rather than as a definitive authority who explains how to do something. The expert is more generally informative than instructive – and the ordinary people are integrated into these programmes as experts in their own right. The status of the participants as actors is emphasized, corresponding to the positioning of the viewer, who is similarly inscribed as an actor who is expected to take care of every aspect of life, and who expects this of him- or herself, too – which means that the viewer always reflects on their whole way of life. The expert is occupied with the communication of knowledge, primarily in the sense of knowledge as 'knowing that' – which means they know people's attitudes, consumer habits and the relationship between taste, style and social roles – and therefore they know why people do as they do when they further improve their lifestyles.

Expository programmes address the kind of media user that André Jansson characterizes as an exponent of 'an imaginative hedonism' (Jansson 2002: 430): that is, a viewer engaged in the symbolic dimensions and values of experiences and products, who demands aesthetic and mental stimulation to a higher degree than the practical advice and emotional influence. The imaginative hedonist is a sort of daydreamer, inspired by the desire for consumer products, home decoration, food, travel destinations, and so on – imaginations of new experiences, which are stimulated by mediated consumption. Thus, expository programmes also consider the aspect of relatedness, though primarily directed by a taste for things and atmosphere.

Guide to lifestyle

To sum up, all categories of programmes address the three motivational aspects of entertainment in different ways. In spite of the effectiveness and professionalism that is characteristic of mediated everyday life, or rather as a consequence of it – most clearly demonstrated in the quick changing of rooms, bodies and exercise habits – everyday activities are produced, and may be experienced by viewers as enjoyable entertainment. As Hill has demonstrated, viewers primarily watch lifestyle programmes in order to relax and to be entertained (Hill 2007). I am sure she is right, but I also find it interesting to examine more closely what it means to be entertained. From my perspective, the quality of entertainment has, first, to do with the fact that programmes stimulate viewers to acquire knowledge. Watching lifestyle programmes is experienced as a challenge, though for most viewers this comes at a minimal cost with respect to the feeling of competence that is achieved. Second, the programmes may outline what Richard Dyer calls a 'utopian sensibility' (Dyer 1992: 24). This sensibility is crystallized in the way in which lifestyle programmes communicate the idea that knowledge and work are synonymous with play. The element of play gives the viewer a desirable 'energy' and a feeling of being individually refreshed and invigorated. In this way, the professional element in its aesthetic form may promote the viewer's sense of both mastery and energy.

The boom in lifestyle television in the last 10 to 15 years is an example of the popularization of programming. It occurs through the transformation of 'citizens' into 'ordinary consumers', making room for them on television as 'important' and 'empowered' actors, on the basis of their private and every-day activities. Lifestyle television is purely *feel-good* television, which unpro-vocatively agrees with viewers' desires in pleasing ways. Thus, everyday life as presented by these programmes is synonymous with lifestyle. Discourses on 'the good life' are related to self-care, articulated around ideas of taste, status and consumption. Lifestyle television operates with an instrumental dimension of knowledge, following the fashion logic of innovation and updating. Deborah Philips says: 'If public broadcasting once saw its role as educative, that education has here become an instruction manual in the appropriate purchase and application of commodities for the home' (Philips 2005: 226). In public-service terms, one may say that the informative func-tion of television has been supplemented with the logic of updating, and with an optimization of the empowerment effect with regard to viewers. Oriented towards self-help, lifestyle television has become a consumer service that stimulates actions and imitations. Viewers seem to be amused.

References

Carlsen, J. and Frandsen, K. (2005) *Nytte-og livsstilsprogrammer på dansk tv*. Arbejdspapirer 133 fra Center for Kulturforskning, Aarhus: Aarhus University.

Dyer, R. (1992) *Only Entertainment*, London: Routledge.

Ellis, J. (2000) *Seeing Things: Television in the Age of Uncertainty*, London: I. B. Tauris.

Hill, A. (2005) *Reality TV. Audiences and Popular Factual Television*, London: Routledge.

Hill, A. (2007) *Restyling Factual TV. Audiences and News, Documentary and Reality Genres*, London: Routledge.

Hjarvard, S. (2008) *En verden af medier. Medialiseringen af politik, sprog, religion og leg*, Copenhagen: Samfundslitteratur.

Holliday, R. (2005) 'Home truth?', in D. Bell and J. Hollows (eds) *Ordinary Lifestyles*, Glasgow: Open University Press.

Hollows, J. (2003) 'Leisure, labour and domestic masculinity in *The Naked Chef*', *International Journal of Cultural Studies*, 6(2), pp. 229–48.

Horton, D. and Wohl, R. R. (1956) 'Mass communication and para-social interaction: observation on intimacy at a distance', *Psychiatry*, 19, pp. 215–29.

Jansson, A. (2002) 'Spatial phantasmagoria. The mediatization of tourism experi-ence', *European Journal of Communication*, 17(4), pp. 429–43.

Jerslev, A. (2008) 'Cosmetic surgery and mediated body theatre. The designable body in the makeover program *The Swan*', *New Review of Film and Television*, 6(3).

Lewis, T. (2007) '"He needs to face his fears with these five queers!". Queer eye for the straight guy, makeover TV, and the lifestyle expert', *Television and New Media*, 8(4), pp. 285–311.

Meyrowitz, J. (1986) *No Sense of Place*, Oxford and New York: Oxford University Press.

Ouellette, L. and Hay, J. (2008) *Better Living through Reality TV*, Oxford: Blackwell Publishing.

Philips, D. (2005) 'Transformation scenes. The television interior makeover', *International Journal of Cultural Studies*, 8(2), pp. 213–29.

Prokop, U. ([1976]1978) *Kvindelig livssammenhæng. Om strategiernes indskrænkethed og de umådelige ønsker*, Kongerslev: GMT.

Ryan, R. M. and Deci, E. L. (2000) 'Self-determination theory and the facilitation of intrinsic motivation, social development, and well-being', *American Psychologist*, 55(1), pp. 68–78.

Thompson, J. B. (1995) *The Media and Modernity. A Social Theory of the Media*, Cambridge: Polity Press.

Thøgersen, U. (2004) *Krop og fænomenologi*, Aarhus: Systime.

Vorderer, P., Steen, F. F. and Chan, E. (2006) 'Motivation', in J. Bryant and P. Vorderer (eds) *Psychology of Entertainment*, London: Routledge.

Part III

RECEPTION
Figures, experience, significance

11

TELEVISION USE IN NEW MEDIA ENVIRONMENTS

Barbara Gentikow

The ongoing processes of digitization and the convergence of information and communication technologies has been accompanied by controversial visions, not least of the future of television, which is still the leading medium in most households, on a national and global scale. These processes are often discussed generally and at large, and from a technologically deterministic perspective. Well-known people like George Gilder ([1990]1994) and Nicholas Negroponte (1995) have been predicting the end of television for a long time. The most seductive argument is that the one-way-flow of mass-media communication, not least broadcasting, is, allegedly, refused by contemporary television users just waiting for the chance to 'talk back'. Gilder has described this relation as a '"master–slave" architecture. A few broadcast centres originate programmes for millions of passive receivers, or 'dumb terminals' (Gilder 1994: 40). Thanks to new affordances provided by digital technology, audiences will finally be able to act, either by forgetting everything about television and using the networked computer[1] instead (the vision of Bill Gates) or by adopting new forms of participatory television and demanding more advanced interactive functions of the television set.

This type of argument confuses technological affordances with empirical use, or access with appropriation. As a result, changes in television technology are often ascribed quasi-automatic cultural and social changes, without taking into consideration two decisive factors: first, the empirical use of technologically new forms of television; second, the context of this use, that is to say (new) media environments which embed television viewing. This chapter focuses on both these aspects, by analysing findings from three empirical studies about television use conducted in Norway between 2004 and 2007.[2]

Media environments

Traditional studies of media use focus on people's relationship to a discrete medium or genre, like radio, newspapers, news or soap operas. This is also

141

due to the great bulk of empirical television studies. There is nothing wrong with this interest and perspective, but an alternative point of departure can throw an interesting light on hidden aspects of the use of media in everyday life. This life has for quite a time been called 'media saturated' or a life in media environments. Among the first researchers who described this situation were David Morley and Roger Silverstone; they open an essay from the beginning of the 1990s with these words:

> Television should now be seen, not in isolation, but as one of a number of information and communication technologies, occupying domestic time and space alongside the video-recorder, the computer and the telephone, as well as the Walkman, the answering-machine, the stereo and the radio.
>
> (Morley and Silverstone 1992: 201).

Almost two decades later, it is not difficult to see that households are characterized by an even stronger proliferation of information and communication technologies, due largely to the further development and adaptation of the networked computer and the unprecedentedly fast diffusion and widespread use of the mobile phone, not least in Norway. Thus, people use more media for much longer spans of time than ever before. This augmentation of mediated communication and information neither simply adds to the use of traditional communication technologies nor just obliterates them. More complex situations occur with digitization and convergences, such as parallel use of media, cross-media applications, the reception of media content from different platforms, new hierarchies of favourite media, but also surviving patterns of traditional use.

A useful study conducted in this spirit is Sonia Livingstone and Moira Bovill's *Children and their Changing Media Environment*. One of their main points is that 'children and young people construct diverse lifestyles from a mix of different media, rarely if ever making use of just one medium. For this reason, we stress the notion of the *media environment* ... ' (Livingstone and Bovill 2001: 7). One of the overall findings of the study is that this segment still prefers television as their main source of information and entertainment: 'the one most often chosen for excitement and for relieving boredom (ibid.: 312). But the study also documents an increasing competition for television users' time and attention. Our own small-scale studies of the use and evaluation of television from 2004 to 2007 in Norway show that time spent watching television is most heavily 'under attack' from the networked computer.

Television in transition

Norway is a small country[3] and the findings of our empirical studies should not be overestimated or even generalized. Generalization is not possible for other reasons as well: our data are predominantly generated by qualitative interviews. But the very interesting thing with Norway during this period is that while two thirds of all households had voluntarily and slowly adopted cable and satellite television from about 1990 to 2007,[4] the remaining third, still with analogue terrestrial television, had to connect rapidly between May 2008 and December 2009.[5] Thus, we could observe a quite dramatic process of final transition, with its dynamics, confusions and still-unclear outcome.

Transition is a highly interesting phenomenon,[6] in terms of ongoing changes where traditional and new technologies compete or struggle, with results still undecided. Transition is processual, open towards both 'the old' and 'the new', including grades of eager adoption of the new on the one hand and continuing sympathy for conservative patterns of behaviour on the other. This is in contrast to the rhetoric of revolutionary changes that presume that things are turned upside down and that new power relations rapidly establish. Television is a technology and a cultural form (Williams [1975]1990) and cultural changes like the diffusion and adoption of new technologies and techniques take time (Rogers 1962). Our findings do not support the conclusion that radically new patterns of watching television have been established, even if the media landscape in Norway has changed more radically than many of us (including our research group) expected.[7]

The most important technological shifts before digitization were the transition from black-and-white to colour, from mono to stereo sound, the invention of the VCR, the proliferation of channels and the transmission by cable and satellite in addition to antenna. These are, at least in some respects, minor details compared to ongoing changes like television on multiple platforms (predominantly web-TV and TV on mobile phones), the EPG,[8] and new techniques of storing programmes (on hard discs and PVR).[9] Not only do they amplify the traditional box in the corner, providing more channels and augmented perceptual qualities, the new devices make television more than a mass medium for just watching and listening. They 'mutate it in form' and 'at such rapid speeds that we no longer really know what "TV" is at all'. As a consequence, 'changes in the entire culture of "watching television"' might arise (Spigel 2004: 1–6).

Changes happen, and more are to come, without any doubt. But processes of transition are also characterized by resistance. One of the most radical visions was that people wanted interactive television because the internet had shown itself to be so successful in this respect. But television has an architecture of communication which is different from the internet, and people have used television's characteristic 'passive' or, as I call it, 'receptive' mode of interaction for a very long time. Habits, or what might be called the embodiment of media use (Gentikow 2005), can work quite strongly against the adoption of innovations. Television and radio are embodied as laid-back media, easy to use – also as a secondary activity.

A further hindrance against quitting traditional television-viewing is that digital technology also provides better television in terms of inviting audiences to enjoy it even more – 'just watching': sales of flat-screen TV sets, DVD recorders and surround-sound speakers have increased dramatically during the last three years in Norway.

The examples might illustrate the point that what we are dealing with is transition in terms of a struggle between traditional patterns of use and innovations – not the end of an old and the beginning of a decisively new era of watching television. One of the most peculiar features of the introduction of digital television in Norway is that it means big changes from a technological, economic and cultural perspective, but the act of watching television can still be performed in the same way as before.

Attitudes towards television in households with access to the internet

The media environment I want to focus on in this data analysis is households with access to the internet. In our first study, from 2004, 25 per cent of houses were connected to the internet, while all of our informants in the young-people study from 2007 had internet at home and used it actively on a daily basis.[10] Statistically, the penetration of internet at home in Norway is currently 87 per cent.[11]

There were relevant differences between media environments with and without a home computer in terms of evaluating and using television. My analysis concentrates on the following issues: (1) Interest in interactive and participatory television; (2) interest in 'personal television' or Me-TV; (3) other new ways of watching television; and (4) surviving conventional patterns of use.

Interest in interactive and participatory television

A definition of 'interactivity' and 'participation' in relation to television has to be short and pragmatic in the context of this analysis. Only quite rudimentary forms were available in the period under scrutiny. As to interactivity, it comprised functions like games, available by, for example, set-top boxes from Canal Digital, and the choice of camera angles in sport programmes (Player-Cam). These functions were not popular in households either with or without an internet connection, even if some informants were quite fascinated by the possibilities. But when it came to playing games, those with access to the internet very decidedly preferred playing games on that platform. Egil (35) makes this clear statement: 'I want to use interactive services and games on the computer only.'

Other 'interactive' functions, like programme information by the EPG, were used quite frequently both in households with and in those without internet access. But predominantly people in low-technology households would complain about malfunctions of the device and remark that they often prefer to read about the programmes in the newspaper. Only few had access to more advanced 'interactive' functions, like the recording of programmes on hard discs or PVR, and even fewer used them.

More generally, informants from households with access to the internet practiced a kind of division of labour between television and home computer. A kind of standard answer was that they use their PC when they want to be interactive, television when they want to relax. Thus, the two media are seen as different: television for easy reception of information and entertainment; the networked computer as a working station.

Another frequent moment of resistance against interactive television is the notion of television as not being a technology to handle actively. Fatima (22) puts it like this:

> I am not especially good at technology. I have learned to use the computer, for lots of things, but television ... I don't think of it in this way.[12]

Later in the interview she makes even clearer her conception of habitual differences: the television set is not a technological apparatus operated by a user, on the contrary, it serves the user.

Cross-media solutions are the simplest way of extending television to a two-way communication medium. In our case studies, participatory television was established by talking back via the mobile phone. The most successful technique of audience participation in Norway so far consists of sending text messages to ongoing TV programmes (typically talk shows) or voting for candidates in reality shows and contests like Melody Grand Prix. Most households in Norway have at least one mobile phone. In a more elaborated format, audiences can participate in shows explicitly made for text messages (SMS) and visual messages (MMS). These shows only present a minor studio programme, while personal statements, self-presentations (both verbal and visual) and chatting among participants from the audience is the core content presented on the screen. This type of SMS-TV can be classified as a new, user-generated television format. The most well known of these shows are *Svisj*, presented by the public-service channel NRK, and *Mess-TV*, presented by the commercial TVNorge.

A study by Gunn Sara Enli (2007) examines the format, partly from the point of view of producers, partly from a user perspective. SMS-TV is relatively popular, at least in quantitative terms. Enli quotes from a Norwegian survey which identifies a total of 22 per cent having used SMS and other cross-media platforms for audience participation. In my view, these are interesting facts but they hardly entitle us to talk about a 'participatory turn'. A turn in this case would mean that more than 50 per cent of television viewers changed from a 'receptive' to a 'participatory' mode. The purely quantitative results are also insufficient to give a picture of what people think of such participation.

Also our own participation study from 2005/2006[13] showed that many people had interacted with radio and television programmes in a broad range of forms but we found only few, if any, really dedicated regular users. One of our findings was that our informants have typically only tried it once, or a few times, and lost interest after that. This is a well-known way of using new communication technologies, motivated by fascination and curiosity. Far from all new options really get appropriated because many of them do not meet a real need.

Another finding was a very widespread and strong critique of this kind of participation. This critique is based not on the fact that people 'have their say' – on the contrary, this is quite generally seen as a positive possibility – but that the problem is that the participants cannot really express complex arguments in this short format, but are forced to 'be tabloid' (Hege, 24).

Several informants evaluate SMS-TV as 'only entertainment' or criticize it for exploiting or even abusing people. This is the main reason, for example, why Lasse (25) 'is not tempted to participate' himself; he is 'not eager to be part of public fun'. Others state that they would never participate but like to watch such shows for amusement (Kari, 20). Instead of acting as participants in a public debate, audiences are used as elements in entertainment shows (Bøe 2006: 45).

A very frequent critical argument was that people have to pay for it. As a result, many refuse 'to spend money on such rubbish' (Maria, 16). 'Wasting time and money ... This is sick' (Arne, 15); SMS-TV 'is a money machine for TVNorge' (Fred, 23).[14]

Summing up our main findings, let me quote two informants, both with access to the internet, who comment on 'interactive' and 'participatory' television. The first is Finn (25):

> Finn: For me, television is very much like a one-way-traffic, entertain-me tool. I do not believe that I would like to contribute with anything, I mean be interactive.
> Interviewer: Why is that?
> Finn: No, I think, it is not my job. I want to sit here, eat my food and look at that box, and that box has to entertain me.

Mehmet (29) tells this self-ironic story:

> Most of the time I am just a guy who watches TV. I take whatever they give me. Sometimes I look for something, but 99 per cent of the time I'm just watching ... It's exhausting to do anything more

with it. You need ... One of the biggest things about television is the couch-potato culture. That's why we're watching TV.

Interest in personalized television or Me-TV

Television's transformation from a mass medium into a personal medium is one of the main selling points for commercial actors in the new digital environment. A typical slogan is 'Watch what you want whenever you want.' It is a rhetoric of liberation (from the channels' programme schedules), personalization and self-realization, not untypically sold as a new, user-controlled 'democracy' versus the old sender-controlled 'dictatorship'.

There is a considerable amount of sympathy for such liberation and control among our informants. Older and younger males and females, criticizing widely and in an often harsh self-ironic manner, say how much they would like to watch more selectively; to use their time more reasonably.[15] Instead of just looking at what a channel provides, or zapping, always hoping for something better to come up, they believe that a more conscious choice of programmes, based on genuine personal interest, would be a more efficient way of using the box. Thus, there is considerable interest in recording and storing programmes to watch later, not least among informants with children or with late working hours. Several informants also mention the possibility of skipping advertisements with digital recorders: 'Very nice to kill advertising, with just pressing a button' (Niels, 44).

But there is a peculiar discrepancy between 'nice to have', or 'would like to have', and actual practice. Several informants report about huge archives of recorded or downloaded material 'which I never get the time to watch' (Odd, 47). Somewhat surprisingly, the widely bespoken Me-TV, in terms of 'watch what you want whenever you want' through new techniques of storing and later viewing, was not popular among our young informants. The question, 'How often do you use television for recording programmes' showed that 60 per cent never recorded programmes, 25 per cent did it rarely and 8 per cent once in a while.

Others say that they once recorded a lot but now do not because, with more channels available, 'you can always find a thing you missed on another channel, a week or so later' (Alex, 27). And some will not use storing and recording functions because 'it sounds very stressing ... to sit and plan and programme ... that's too tough, too structured ... I like to watch spontaneously' (Elin, 30). Some informants also explicitly refuse the slogan of more personal television use. Ole (34) says that channel proliferation and time-shift viewing 'will result in the fact that nobody watches the same programme any more. This means that the ... community thing disappears'.[16]

This 'community thing' disappears for other reasons as well. One is the well-known proliferation of channels and the installation of a television set in

147

several rooms of the house, not least in children's and young people's bedrooms. Nearly half of our young informants have a television set in their room and they mostly use it in a solitary way. Family television is 'out' for most of them, while watching together with friends is popular but obviously more a desire than a real practice.

Predominantly, the young people in our study used a wide range of audio-visual material, from their home computer, to their mobile phones and television. As a result, their consumption of pictures and sound was highly fragmented. There did not seem to be much shared audio-visual culture, at least not from television programmes.[17] The most popular genre for our young-people panel was television series, like *Friends*, *Prison Break* or *Grey's Anatomy*. But the top-rated favourites among these were characterized by strong segmentation. A graphic representation of our data would show a typical 'long tail' figure, with very few shows watched by many, and very many with only a few fan-viewers.[18]

Web-TV, as a new form of Me-TV, was just at the beginning of its implementation when we conducted our first study. But a few informants from the 2004 study commented on the new phenomenon. Victor (23), a fan of new communication technology, has discovered NRK's Web-TV[19] and praises it because of its high quality and because it does not cost anything. He has started watching earlier episodes of a popular Norwegian comedy from the archive, and he watches them on his widescreen television set, using a simple (SCART) cable connected to the computer. According to the questionnaire in the young-people study, 30 per cent of them noted that they used Web-TV at least occasionally.

There is considerable interest in more personalized ways of watching television and some of the (new) options to facilitate this have been adopted. Specifically, our young-people study, in which all had access to the internet, showed a tendency towards more individual viewing patterns, with a mix of audio-visual material from TV and from other sources and strong audience fragmentation in terms of a decrease of shared television programmes. But there is little evidence for an augmentation of recording TV programmes and watching them 'whenever you want'.[20]

Other new ways of watching television

One special way of watching television has been 'monitoring', that is to say the use of television as a secondary activity. Traditionally, monitoring has been understood to refer to simultaneous activities, like doing housework and listening to a TV programme, with glances at the screen when 'things happened'. But it can also refer to the parallel use of two media, like television and the newspaper. Predominantly, in our youth panel, we found a new technique of parallel activities. The young informants talked about doing school work on the computer while chatting with friends through

MSN Messenger, reading and sending text messages on their mobile phone and listening to music, all simultaneously. This seems to be quite a normal situation for this segment. Some of them say that, in addition, they watch television – for example, monitoring their favourite sitcom while using the networked computer. This constitutes a strong extension of parallel media use. Some might ask whether such a low involvement entitles being called 'watching television' at all.

An even more radical new way of using television is quitting it. Informants from both the first and the third study could say that they only watched television very rarely or had completely stopped watching. All of them had access to and used the networked computer. This pattern of use seems to correspond with one of the generalized claims about the future of television, that TV will be dead in a few years. The problem is that empirical studies still only find a small number of television viewers who really have stopped. So far, only 1–3 per cent of all households in Norway are estimated not to have a television.[21]

Our own studies revealed that four of the 45 participants from the first panel, and five of the 205 respondents in the quantitative part of the young-people panel reported that they do not watch television. These are low numbers, and were lowest in the youngest segment. And, when analysing the qualitative interviews and the answers to the questionnaire in context, we did not find a single person who has stopped watching television completely. There is always, later in the interviews or the questionnaire, a mention of an episode from a sitcom, of a football match or a film (watched, for example, at the home of friends). So, in reality, we have met nine informants who do not watch television regularly but none who has radically given up watching television.

Official statistics, at least from Norway, also show that time watching television has so far not decreased.[22] But there is, after all, an important caveat. It concerns time spent on television versus time spent on the home computer. Our young-people study showed that they actually used more time on the computer than watching television: an average of 84 minutes per day for TV, and 116 for the home computer. This corresponds with official statistics from the same period.[23] This 'dominance' of computer use in terms of investment of time may be an important indication for the future.

Surviving conventional patterns of use

There was broad sympathy for watching television in a traditional, purely receptive, way among our elder informants, mainly in the first study. The young-people study revealed both new patterns of watching television and very traditional television use. The most obvious new technique was the extended parallel media use, as described above. But, at the same time, many liked to just watch a TV programme. Asked to talk about a typical situation of watching television, they talked about coming home from school, getting rid of the satchel, lying down on the sofa in the living room or in the bedroom and watching one, two or more afternoon television shows. Even if many of them also downloaded series from the internet or liked watching them on DVDs, they were quite in favour of watching series when broadcast. They could look forward to a special day in the week when their favourite series was scheduled.

A pattern of watching that is both traditional and new is the home cinema. It typically consists of a big flat screen, at least five loudspeakers, preferably a subwoofer, and comfortable chairs to sit in. The sale of home-cinema equipment pretty well exploded during our research period.[24] Its attractiveness is mainly due to the considerably better quality of pictures and sounds, not least for people still connected to analogue antennae. When we asked our informants from the first study to tell us about their 'dream TV', it was not interactive, it was not participatory: nearly all of them described forms of home cinema.

The home cinema is a hybrid in terms of mediating shared culture and giving personal access to specific matters. It can be used for receiving broadcast programmes, watching stored material and playing games. But it is mostly marketed as a kind of Me-TV, 'delighting your senses'.[25] Spending time viewing DVDs or playing games means that the position of traditional television as broadcast programmes, shared by many or at least some others, is weakened. At the same time, the most traditional way of watching, 'passively' or 'receptively', is strengthened by home cinema. This may increase with the implementation of high-definition television, absorbing audiences even more pervasively. On the other hand, gaming increases possibilities for participation and interactivity as a new cultural and social practice. Thus, the home cinema both enforces traditional 'passive' reception and new user activities.

Households with a networked computer enforce very clearly the division of labour between the television as a machine of delivery of information and entertainment and the computer as a working station. But, paradoxically, they also reveal a pattern of convergence. It is a tendency towards looking at both television and the networked computer as machines of entertainment and information, or towards conceiving the use of both these media as purely receptive. The tendency is slight, but three relevant observations coincide.

The first is that some of the young people describe their use of a PC, typically a laptop and often wireless, literally as having the machine on their lap, sitting comfortably in the corner of a couch or in their bed. This does not resemble the description of working stations from our first study. It is, on the contrary, the kind of cosy, relaxed atmosphere which is typically ascribed to watching television.

The other finding is that a surprising number of our young informants use the PC/internet for 'reading', not for actively contributing to user-generated content. Besides 'communication with friends' (predominantly chatting by MSN Messenger), which a majority named as their most important activity, the informants ranked surfing websites and 'just looking' as number two; number three as 'information' (e.g. from Google and Wikipedia, often in relation to schoolwork); while 'contributions to own blogs and sites like YouTube' only figured as number six.[26]

The third observation is that our young-people study documented a desire, or even need, for easy and relaxed reception modes. Asked what they liked and hated most about television and the computer, a typical answer was that they were often irritated by malfunctions of the computer, including crashes, and that they sometimes had to 'fiddle' quite a lot in order to find what they were looking for, while television was easy to go to and to get 'served' things from. Things they did not like about television were, predominantly, 'bad programmes', advertisement breaks and that they could spend too much time watching. It may look like a declaration of sympathy for television as an alternative to the more troublesome operation of the computer and, more generally, a quite stressful everyday life.

In addition, some of our older informants with access to a home computer, like Karoline (26) from our first study, strongly underline how valuable it is to 'get things served':

I believe that we like not being able to make choices all the time. We can choose between more than enough things. It is good to be free from choices, just lie on your couch and receive ... It is very satisfying just to get things served.

A changing culture of mediated information and communication at home

From the perspective chosen for this data analysis, with media environments, innovation and transition as important key words, the following picture emerges:

A medium is not used in isolation from other media. In households with both a television and a networked computer, we observed that the two media 'affected' each other, reciprocally. Our data indicated that access to a home computer minimizes interest in interactive and participatory functions of the TV set. Even if some of our informants watch very little TV and use the computer instead, there is no strong evidence that the networked computer makes the television obsolete. Rather the contrary: television in digital environments can get more 'televisual'. The great popularity of the home cinema in Norway is a striking example, another indication of the sympathy of, not least, young people for 'just watching television' instead of fiddling

151

with the PC. Thus, television can be conceived of as a highly welcome alternative to the other, often more demanding, technologies at home. The future of television might be simply to be television, and nothing else.

From the perspective of innovation, the case of digitization of TV in Norway demonstrates very clearly that access does not equal appropriation. It was a striking finding that many members of households with more advanced television technology did not use the new options and sometimes were not even interested in them. Another important finding was that the occasional use of new functions (like SMS-TV) could produce quite high statistical ratings but did not tell us anything about whether people liked and really appropriated these functions.

On the other side, there are indications of changes due to new patterns of use. The fact that television is present on many platforms and that, vice versa, the TV set can work as a platform for other audio-visual material, does obviously result in a fragmentation of traditional media consumption. Shared experiences in terms of programmes watched and discussed by many have been decreasing for a long time already, but with the advent and application of more platforms, even fewer people seem to watch the same things at the same time.[27]

There is, without any doubt, a trend towards more personalized media use. This includes differentiations between media-rich and media-poor households, not least because media consumption depends increasingly on the will and ability to pay, be it for channel packages, broadband connections or the latest model of a mobile phone.

From the perspective of transition, our main finding is that television is still strong as a means of easy delivery of information and entertainment. The fact that the networked computer competes by offering important cultural resources, like giving access to more specific information, to participation and personal communication, is an interesting challenge. We will have to wait and see how television will cope with this increasing competition and how far audiences will be willing to leave their traditional receptive behaviour in front of the TV screen.

Notes

1 I use this term for defining the home computer with access to the internet. Sometimes I call it a home computer or just a computer.
2 The three studies were the following: (1) 'The interactive study' (spring 2004). This was a highly explorative qualitative interview study, with 45 participants, aged 18–61. The issue was a mapping of the field, with a focus on knowledge about digital television and interest in interactive functions; (2) 'The participation study' (winter 2005/spring 2006) comprised structured interviews with 32 informants (aged 15–73), focusing on experiences with and evaluations of new, participatory formats in television (and radio), such as SMS-TV;

(3) 'The young-people study' (autumn 2007) was a study of the use of TV and the PC/internet at home, conducted with a random sample of young people between 13 and 16, recruited at schools. The study included 20 qualitative interviews and a questionnaire, with 205 self-completed records. The three empirical studies were part of a four-year research project (2003–7), funded by the Norwegian Research Council. The overarching issue of the project was 'New media as cultural techniques and forums for communicative action. Empirical research and constituents of a theory' (see: http://www.kulturteknikker.hivolda.no).

3 With 4.8 million inhabitants, sharing 2.1 million households (Statistisk Sentralbyrå, January 2008).

4 More precisely, in 2006 Norwegian television households were divided as follows: 44 per cent with cable, 32 per cent with satellite and 28 per cent with analogue antenna (TNS Gallup/medienorge). In 2007, digital terrestrial television was introduced in addition, predominantly aimed at antenna households.

5 The analogue terrestrial network was switched off region by region, starting in Rogaland (with Stavanger as its capital) and finishing in Northern Norway.

6 See also the subtitle of the anthology *Television After TV* (Spigel and Olsson 2004): *Essays on a Medium in Transition.*

7 One of the most dramatic changes (which I cannot deal with in this context) is that the process of digitization in Norway meant the end of access to television by licence fees alone. After the final switch-off of the analogue terrestrial network everybody has to pay both licence fees (to the state) and more or less expensive fees for bigger and smaller channel packages, paid to commercial actors.

8 The Electronic Programme Guide allows orientation in relation to ongoing and upcoming programmes, selection of favourite channels, parental control, 'ordering' of programmes to be recorded on a hard disc or digital recorder, and other 'customized' functions. The EPG is the standard application for digital television in Norway. Compared to TiVo (employed in countries like the USA), it is far less advanced.

9 Personal Video Recorder. This advanced device for storing favourite programmes had largely not been introduced into the households we examined, but it has since become more popular.

10 This is mainly due to the introduction of the use of the networked computer at schools, including for doing homework. Another reason is that young people traditionally belong to the group of early adopters of communication technology. Thus, cable and satellite TV was most frequently installed in households with children and young people.

11 Source: Medienorge; see http://www.medienorge.uib.no/ ?cat=statistikkandmedium=itandaspekt=andqueryID=251.

12 A comment on all quotations from our interviews: The translation of oral data is problematic. It is nearly impossible to render 'the oral tone', with elliptical phrases, linguistic mistakes, creative innovations, slang, and so on.

13 This part of the empirical study was conducted by my colleague Lars Nyre. The data was analysed by a masters student, Torbjørn Bøe, who also did parts of the interviews; the main results are published in his masters thesis (Bøe 2006).

14 Enli also points at problematic aspects of this kind of participation (see Enli 2007: 18, 32ff and 220). But she insists in her thesis that a 'participatory turn' has taken place.

15 Some examples from the young-people study: 25 of the 205 informants responded to the open question: 'What do you not like about television?' with phrases like: 'It takes far too much time', '10 minutes easily turns into 4 hours' and 'I just hang in front of the screen for hours and am angry with myself afterwards.' In the qualitative part of the study, some of them also described parents, mostly fathers, as 'television slaves'. But they also criticized themselves, with phrases like: 'It's like being an addict'; 'It is a bit sick.'

16 Graham Murdock talks about 'self-enclosure' as a consequence of devices for personal programme selection (Murdock 2005: 228).

17 They shared more through and from the internet, predominantly by chatting with friends (via MSN), their favourite net activity, and by using social-networking sites like MySpace and YouTube.

18 Somewhat broadly watched were *Grey's Anatomy* (33 of our 205 informants named it as their first or second favourite), *One Tree Hill* (22), *Prison Break* (19), *Desperate Housewives* (16) and *Friends* (13). Thirteen other shows gathered 10 to 3 fans, and the rest of the programmes were only shared by two or even had just one informant.

19 The public-service channel NRK has quite an excellent website (http://www.nrk.no). It offers both a large archive of earlier programmes and updated news. It also has participatory functions, including message boards which facilitate comments by viewers.

20 According to statistics from spring 2008, less than 1 per cent of all television-watching is on recorded programmes. See Christian Thune Larsen: *Tidsforskjøvet TV-seing i Norge*, uke 1–7 2008; http://www.tns-gallup.no/?did=9077242.

21 The numbers vary according to various systems of measurement. Anyhow, they are very low, and there has not been a dramatic increase over the years which would correspond to the increase in internet access. There have always been about 1 per cent of households without a television in Norway. After the period of transition from analogue to digital TV there may be a significant increase in this figure since we still do not know how many households will refuse to sub-scribe to a digital package and, in practice, will have 'black screens'.

22 Time spent on watching broadcast television has gone up and down under the process of digitization in Norway. It fell slightly, from a historical peak of 166 minutes a day in 2004 to 154 in 2007, but increased to 174 minutes in 2008 (from TNS Gallup's TV-meter panel).

23 Source: Medienorge. According to this statistic, in 2007 young people between 13 and 19 years old spent 105 minutes a day on the home computer, while their 'television time' was 85 minutes a day.

24 According to statistics, by October 2005, 2 million people had installed home-cinema equipment (*Bergens Tidende*, 10 October 2005).

25 See for example an advertisement for Marantz, in *Digital Home*, February 2004.

26 This corresponds with an investigation made by Jakob Nielsen in 2006. According to him 'the law of participation' on the internet is 90-9-1, meaning that 90 per cent are lurkers (just reading and watching what others have created), 9 per cent contribute once in a while and only 1 per cent are really active and creative participants, or 'heavy contributors' (Nielsen 2006).

27 Meanwhile, there are still big audiences sharing, for example, the main evening news on the two main nationwide Norwegian channels (NRK and TV2),

entertainment shows (e.g. a series of Friday-night programmes on NRK) and films and series, predominantly when they are national productions. All of them can still gather 1 million viewers or more, which is quite a lot in a population of 4.8 million. The last gathering of a real mass audience was the Melody Grand Prix show (on NRK), which was won by the contestant from Norway (June 2009).

References

Bøe, T. K. (2006) *Hva synes publikum om å delta i medier? {What do people think of participation in media?}* MA thesis, Department of Information Science and Media Studies, University of Bergen.

Enli, G. S. (2007) *The participatory turn in broadcast television. Institutional, editorial and textual challenges and strategies.* PhD thesis: Faculty of Humanities, University of Oslo.

Gentikow, B. (2005) 'Limiting factors for embracing ITV. Television as a cultural form and the embodiment of media use'. *Proceedings EuroITV 2005*, 3rd European Conference on Interactive Television, pp. 61–67, Ålborg University.

Gilder, G. ([1990]1994) *Life after Television*. Revised edn., New York and London: W. W. Norton and Company.

Larsen, Christian Thune (2008) *Tidsforskjøvet TV-seing i Norge*, 1–7; http://www.tns-gallup.no/?did=9077242. Accessed 13 August 2009.

Livingstone, S. and M. Bovill (2001) *Children and their Changing Media Environments: A European Comparative Study*. Mahwah, NJ and London: Lawrence Erlbaum.

Morley, D. and R. Silverstone (1992) 'Domestic communication: technologies and meanings', in D. Morley, *Television, Audiences and Cultural Studies*, London and New York: Routledge, pp. 201–12.

Murdock, G. (2005) 'Building the digital commons. Public broadcasting in the age of the Internet', in G. F. Lowe and P. Jauert (eds) *Cultural Dilemmas in Public Service Broadcasting*, Göteborg: Nordicom, pp. 213–30.

Negroponte, N. (1995) *Being Digital*, New York: Knopf.

Nielsen, J. (2006) *Participation Inequality: Encouraging More Users to Contribute*, http://www.useit.com/alterbox/participation_inequality.html. Accessed 13 August 2009.

Rogers, E. M. (1962) *Diffusion of Innovations*, New York: The Free Press.

Schrøder, K. et al. (2003) *Researching Audiences*, London: Arnold.

Spigel, L. (2004) 'Introduction', in L. Spigel and J. Olsson (eds) *Television after TV: Essays on a Medium in Transition*, Durham, NC, and London: Duke University Press, pp. 1–34.

Spigel, L. and J. Olsson (eds) (2004) *Television after TV: Essays on a Medium in Transition*, Durham, NC, and London: Duke University Press.

Williams, R. ([1975]1990) *Television, Technology and Cultural Form*, London: Routledge.

12

THE GREY AREA. A ROUGH GUIDE

Television fans, internet forums, and the cultural public sphere

Peter Larsen

... this is a site about television, and the discussion should remain about television.

Television without Pity

Studies in the wake of Jürgen Habermas' *Strukturwandel der Öffentlichkeit* (1962) and its English translation *The Structural Transformation of the Public Sphere* (1989) tend to concentrate on the function of the *political* public sphere and seldom discuss its counterpart, the *cultural* public sphere. There is a similar pattern in recent discussions of new communication technology: the internet is described and discussed as an extension of the political public sphere, with focus on the possibilities for furthering deliberative and participatory democracy, while far less attention is paid to the transformation of the cultural public sphere brought about by the multitude of internet discussion arenas that have emerged during the 10–15 years, from the early Usenet groups and email lists to the current chat groups, blogs, message boards, and other forms of internet publishing.

The following is an attempt to throw some light on this immense and unruly field. After an overview and a brief analysis of communication within a sector of the computer-mediated cultural public sphere, I discuss the characteristics of such arenas in general and compare them to Habermas' description of the ideal cultural public sphere. My point of departure is those internet spaces in which television viewers discuss their favourite shows.

Television companies began establishing internet sites devoted to popular shows in the late 1990s. On such sites there would typically be a short presentation of the show, notes about current episodes, some promotional photos and links to the main actors' homepages. In parallel with these 'official' sites, a few eager fans of a given show would construct their own sites, with an extensive account of every single episode, gossip about writers and actors, lists of memorable quotes, and so on.

Page design as well as site topography and functionality have changed considerably since then. In particular, the introduction of various comments applications has opened up the possibilities for interactive exchange of opinions among site visitors. Today's official sites are elaborate, often lavishly designed constructions, and the fan sites have changed correspondingly into complex discussion arenas, in many cases hosted and maintained by internet marketing companies. In the following I concentrate on one such discursive universe, the one that has the US prime-time medical drama *Grey's Anatomy* as its centre.

An overview

Grey's Anatomy has run on the ABC network since 2005. The title is a reference to the classic medical textbook *Gray's Anatomy*, as well as to the main character Meredith Grey, who in the early episodes is a surgical intern at Seattle Grace Hospital. The show follows Meredith and her fellow interns, who in later seasons have become residents. Meredith's stormy relationship with the surgeon Derek Shepherd has been a central feature of the show throughout.

The official *Grey's Anatomy* site is nested within the ABC site (see References, below). On the homepage there is a trailer for the next episode plus links to actors' biographies, presentations of characters, summaries of prior episodes, podcasts about future episodes, promotional photos, competitions and tests, and an internet shop selling DVDs. The show also runs on several international television channels. Most of them have similar, if less complex, sites, usually with a common design.

The show is also presented and discussed on a number of *commercial sites* specializing in television and entertainment news. One example is Grey's Anatomy Insider, which is organized as a blog with production news and gossip about the cast. There are also links to quotes, a photo gallery, episode guides, characters, cast, and so on. Grey's Anatomy Insider is one of many similar sites nested within TV Fanatic, which is owned and operated by iScribe Ltd., 'an Internet marketing company that specializes in entertainment-themed websites' with the aim of establishing and maintaining 'high rankings in all major search engines'. Television without Pity is a commercial website of the same type. It started as a site with detailed and often highly ironic recaps of various television shows. In 2007 it was bought by the Bravo unit of NBC Universal and transformed into a more mainstream television and entertainment site. Its *Grey's Anatomy* section includes photos, videos, recaps, and forums.

In addition to the commercial sites there are a number of *amateur sites* constructed by fans of the show or of a particular cast member. Some fans also write fiction about the characters and publish their stories on sites like *Grey's Anatomy* Fanfic. Other fan sites present various types of visual art based on the show.

There are, in fact, so many commercial as well as amateur sites that a directory might be needed to get an overview, for example the quite homemade-looking Grey's Directory, an ever-growing site directory exclusively for websites dedicated to *Grey's Anatomy*. The directory is based on audience response about fan sites 'that will be updated regularly and that you've put a substantial amount of effort into'. In June 2009, the far from exhaustive directory lists 37 general fan sites, 25 message boards and discussion forums, and 45 fan sites dedicated to actors, actresses, or characters in the show.

Other fans have established more than 500 Facebook groups – in June 2009 there were, for example, Addicted to Grey's Anatomy (81,671 members, 9,609 wall posts, and a discussion board with 769 discussion topics), Bug Me During Grey's Anatomy And I'll Insert This Scalpel Into Your Spleen (124,469 members, 31,948 wall posts, and a discussion board with 2,609 discussion topics), and George From Grey's Anatomy Makes Me Happy! (417 members and 100 wall posts). There are similar group pages on MySpace.

All the types of sites mentioned above carry comments applications. Visitors are invited to comment on blog entries or to participate in ongoing discussions on message boards or 'forums'. The ABC screenwriters discuss the current episodes on the blog Grey Matter and viewers respond in the comments section. In addition the ABC site carries an open board with an endless number of threads; in June 2009 the most active thread had more than 20,000 posts. Message boards are also staple features on the other, commercial as well as amateur, sites. 'Join an existing topic or start your own to discuss all things *Grey's Anatomy*,' says the header of the Forums section on Grey's Anatomy Insider; in June 2009 there were seven 'main themes' in this section, and the most active, 'Episodes', had 166 topics and more than 11,000 postings.

Discursive communities

While some of posters on the commercial blogs are presumably professional 'content writers' hired to keep discussions going, most of the participants in this vast, diffuse discursive universe seem to be ordinary viewers, lay persons who just happen to have a strong interest in the show. They write primarily about the latest episode, the twists and turns of the narrative, the reactions of the fictional characters, but in some cases they engage in more open discussions of the show in general or of certain recurring themes. Most of the following examples are taken from posts discussing the opening episode of Season Five in October 2008.

Screenwriter Krista Vernoff's blog post about the opening episode drew around 270 comments. Most of the first ones are short exclamations of praise: 'I love love love loved this episode' or 'I loved this episode!! I loved everything about it!!! I laughed and cried all at the same time!! Well done!!!!' Many viewers also add what they wish or hope will happen in the following episodes: 'Loved the episode. I'm glad Mer stood up to Derek, and I'm glad he still loves her. I wish Dr Wyatt was still working with Meredith though.'

Some viewers write about how the current episode or the show in general relates to their own life and personal problems: 'This show, as odd as it sounds, has helped me through more times than I can count.' The portrayal of the therapist Dr Wyatt in the episode leads one viewer to write that she herself has 'just decided that therapy is ABSOLUTELY WHAT I NEED! This episode came at the most perfect time EVER! Thank you for this episode!! Your show never lets me down!' Another writes, 'I have a really really really good shrink! Just like Dr. Wyatt. Therapy changed my life and I'm much better now!'

It is not all praise. There is a fair amount of criticism voiced in the comments section. A major concern for many viewers is the lack of realism in the fictional universe. In the episode in question the hospital was flooded and the roof of one of the operating theatres caved in – which led one viewer to write:

> I mean PLEASE! Someone didn't check the ceiling before they used it? You could obviously see that water had collected up there. I would totally not want to be a patient in this hospital with incompetence like that … Ridiculous writing contrivance.

This observation sparks off a discussion in which other viewers draw on their own experiences of floods in hospitals: 'these things really DO happen' or 'the premise of a flood was not absurd. It happened to me as well. Not on such a grand scale but it was still a shocker … '.

Others use probability as a counter argument, for example a viewer who concludes that the flood was 'distracting, and unrealistic', not because floods do not happen in hospitals, but because this flood is 'put together with all of the OTHER freak, odd things in other epis' and 'it's unrealistic that in one hospital all of these odd ball things keep happening'.

The discussion of the flood points to a general pattern in viewers' approach to the show. On the one hand they often measure narrative events against standards of realism and probability, and they often write about – and identify with – fictional characters as if they were real-life people. On the other hand many viewers couple a realist approach with references to general narrative conventions and genre expectations, as, for example, did a poster on a Norwegian board who wrote that the show became more and more stupid towards the end of Season Three, particularly because of a new, romantic relationship between two central characters: 'I don't think there is any chemistry between them at all, it seems totally weird that there suddenly should be something between them.' She then offers a 'technical' explanation: such improbable developments always happen in shows that have run for a while – 'in order not to have too many minor characters to take into consideration, there is a "recycling" of boyfriends and girlfriends'. Another instructive example is a comment on Vernoff's blog post where a viewer simply marks her approach to the narrative universe with a slash: 'Hope Meredith/writers will reconsider Dr. Wyatt's return later, she is phenomenal.'

Posters on the 'unofficial', commercial message boards have the same *dual approach* to the narrative, for example on Television without Pity, where many viewers not only express wishes and hopes for the characters but also focus on the mechanics of writing the narrative and on generic demands ('I still think Mark's love interest is coming down the road, but adding Lexie into the mix gives all of these storylines more layers and drama').

A large portion of the posts on the unofficial boards are *interpretations* of events in the current episode, often with detailed reference to the characters' behaviour in earlier episodes and seasons, but, just as importantly, are discussions and interpretations of the producer's and the writers' intentions, usually based on close readings of remarks on the writers' blog or in the official podcasts. On Television without Pity there is actually a whole section called 'The Writers' Blog and Podcasts: We Could Do a Better Job', where posters argue against the writers and present alternative narrative solutions as well as general critical comments.

There are clear differences between the comment section on the official blog and the posts on the unofficial boards. The blog comments tend to have a relatively monologic character. They are primarily a string of spontaneous expressions of praise or disagreement which from time to time may turn into short dialogical discussions. The posters on the boards, on the other hand, usually engage in dialogue from the very beginning of a thread – 'What do you guys think of … ?' The same nicknames and avatars appear again and again, and there is also a certain tribal language signalling a community feeling and a sense of shared values, even if posters disagree about narrative characters and events.

Mapping the area

The blogs and boards concerning *Grey's Anatomy* are just one part of a larger conglomerate of internet spaces. All major television shows have viewers who follow and discuss the various episodes in similar spaces. How should one map this small section of the internet?

At the centre there is an *aesthetic object* – an audio-visual text, an episode in a television series about certain characters and events within a fictional universe. The audio-visual text refers to and draws on prior episodes in the series, and more generally it draws on a wide range of cultural and historical contextual information. In addition it belongs to a specific textual genre (prime-time medical drama) with its own set of standards and rules determining both semantic and syntactical structure. Around this text there is a 'grey area', a cluster of discursive internet spaces in which the textual object becomes an object of deliberation. Spaces like the writers' blog on the *Grey's Anatomy* site – the spaces closest to the institutions that produced the textual objects in the first place – present 'official' interpretations and explanations of the show and the episodes, prompting positive as well as negative reactions from viewers. At a greater distance from the institutional core is a multitude of discursive spaces in which viewers discuss the show and present their own, often alternative, views on various episodes.

Some of the comments and posts in these spaces are simple commentaries or simple evaluations ('I love/hate it'); others are critical evaluations based on reasoning ('I love/hate it because … '). A fairly large portion of them are attempts at interpretation: by writing in these spaces viewers try to develop an understanding of certain ambiguous events or characters in the narrative universe. In many cases they explicitly call on other participants to help them, and the threads often develop into long discussions of textual details.

The participants are *knowledgeable*. In their criticism and interpretations they not only draw on a vast and detailed knowledge of how plotlines and characters have developed over the years, they also evaluate the show against general narrative and specific generic conventions.

There is a clear sense of community among the participants. They are united as fans of a particular show, and they also express loyalty to the specific site where they post their comments. However, even though the discussion of a given show takes place on a multitude of sites in a multitude of separate spaces, each with a limited number of users, the participants in one space pay close attention to what is being discussed in other spaces. There are constant references to the themes that are up 'in the blogs' and 'on the boards', as for example when one viewer in the *Grey's Anatomy* community comments on Vernoff's blog post: 'With all the Meredith and Derek dismay and negativity (towards our girl Meredith) spread on the various related GA boards tonight for no real reason, I want to thank you', while a poster on Television without Pity writes: 'Wow, they are really pushing the whole Lexie/Mark thing in the blogs.'

Most of the boards, as well as the comments sections in the blogs, are moderated, and participants are required to follow certain *rules of discourse*. One example is the very long list of 'dos and don'ts' on Television without Pity. Some items deal with practical matters; others specify the ways in which posters are expected to engage in conversations and discussions. One of the founders emphasizes *relevance* and *substance* as fundamental criteria: 'this is a site about television, and the discussion should remain about television' – which means, for example, that participants are not allowed to promote personal websites, products, and so on, but also, more specifically, means that they should 'add something of substance to the conversation' and not start new threads unless they 'have something of substance to say'. Participants are recommended not to post on a given thread until they have 'read at least the last fifteen pages or days of content'. In addition there are a series of rules about *conducting a discussion*: arguments should be *impartial*, not personal; posters must 'know the difference between differences of opinion and personal attacks'; and there is no reason to 'post the same opinion over and over in the hopes of wearing other people down or "winning" a discussion'.

Other sites have similar rules. The *Grey's Anatomy* Wiki for example is 'a community for *Grey's Anatomy* fans to chat about the show' – which means: 'Shameless self-promotion and hawking of wares are strictly verboten, not to mention pathetic.' The site 'exists to support an organic and communal body of information' and the users are advised to 'Play nicely with others', to 'Act in good faith', and to 'Promote the community spirit … by enrolling others in the discussion, sponsoring a good debate, and setting a good, collaborative example.'

The idea of the public

The posters in these discursive spaces have obvious features in common with the publics of lay persons which Jürgen Habermas describes in *The Structural Transformation of the Public Sphere*. Let me briefly recapitulate his main points. He broadly defines 'the public sphere' (*Öffentlichkeit*) as 'the sphere of private people come together as a public' (Habermas 1989: 27); in a highly stylized historical analysis he traces the development in eighteenth-century Europe of a *cultural* public sphere in which lay persons engaged in critical discussions of 'the products of culture that had become publicly accessible: in the reading room and the theater, in museums and at concerts' (ibid.: 29); and he describes the subsequent establishment of a *political* public sphere in which private people contested the power of feudal authorities by means of public, critical reasoning on political issues, thereby preparing the ground for deliberative democracy. According to Habermas, the political public sphere was established by 'functionally converting' the cultural public sphere, a move that was possible because the cultural public sphere was 'already equipped with institutions of the public and with forums for discussion' (ibid.: 51).

The cultural public sphere was a public sphere 'in apolitical form' that served as a 'training ground for a critical public reflection' (ibid.: 29). Private people's discussions about cultural issues in coffee houses, salons, and various societies were based on three principles: (a) *disregard of the participants' social status*; (b) *critical discussion*; and (c) *inclusiveness* (ibid.: 36ff). Anyone who had the economic means to become a reader, listener, and spectator had, in principle, the right to participate in a critical discussion of 'areas that until then had not been questioned' (ibid.: 36). Social and economic power had, in principle, no influence; only the quality of the argument counted. These principles were not necessarily 'realized in earnest', but the *idea of the public* became institutionalized and 'thereby stated as an objective claim. If not realized, it was at least consequential' (ibid.: 36).

The fan communities in the grey area around a contemporary television show seem to revitalize this 'idea of the public' in a technologically new context. The discussions are, as our examples suggest, based on institutional criteria quite similar to those emphasized by Habermas: (a) the discussants are anonymous, writing under nicknames or pseudonyms; they may refer to their personal social experiences from time to time, but they seldom reveal their precise social status, and, even if they do, their status does not matter within this particular discursive space; (b) the individual episodes are criticized and problematized, often in direct opposition to the screenwriters' official intentions and interpretations; (c) the discussion groups are open and inclusive; anyone with internet access may join the party provided they obey the general rules of discourse. The rules are not meant to shut certain people out; they are merely aimed at keeping the discussion *relevant*, *serious*, and *civilized*.

Fan forums and ideal publics

There is a fair amount of critical discussion going on in the grey area around a contemporary television show, and the participants observe institutional rules that are similar to those of the ideal public sphere. On the other hand, this multitude of internet communities differs in significant ways from Habermas' ideal publics.

First of all, the fan communities are publics with a very limited aim: a group of fans who come together to share their thoughts on their favourite television show. Habermas voiced his doubts about political internet groups in a paper read to the ICA conference in 2006, saying that the 'rise of millions of fragmented chat rooms across the world' tends to lead to 'the fragmentation of large but politically focused mass audiences into a huge number of isolated issue publics' (Habermas 2006: 423).

His remarks apply to the cultural sphere as well. An internet fan community is quite clearly an 'issue public', a very near-sighted, *single-issue public* which will fall apart as soon as the particular show is taken off the air. In this perspective a public like the *Grey's Anatomy* fans have very little in common with the ideal Habermasian private people who come together on a regular basis to participate in an ongoing discussion of the larger issues of the times.

The internet fan communities are special-interest publics and are, as such, somewhat closer related to the *counterpublics* Oscar Negt and Alexander Kluge wrote about in *Öffentlichkeit und Erfahrung* (1972) or the *subaltern counterpublics* Nancy Fraser discussed in her essay on 'Rethinking the Public

Sphere' (1992). However, the posters in the internet fan communities do not participate in larger socio-political projects like Negt and Kluge's oppositional workers, nor are they engaged in collective identity formation like Fraser's subordinated social groups. If some of the posters were to open a discussion about being socially, culturally, and politically excluded, the topic would be deemed irrelevant. As Television without Pity puts it: 'this is a site about television, and the discussion should remain about television'.

In her essay Nancy Fraser also introduced the distinction between *weak* and *strong* publics. Weak publics are 'publics whose deliberative practice consists exclusively in opinion formation and does not also encompass decision making', while strong publics are the type of publics that appeared with the establishment of sovereign parliaments, 'publics whose discourse encompasses both opinion formation and decision making' (Fraser 1992: 134). The internet fan communities have no executive power and make no binding decisions of any kind. They are obviously not strong publics. Nor are they weak publics. In Habermas' ideal public sphere, conflicts of opinion are solved by the authority of the better argument; in the fan forums, conflicts of interpretation are merely stated, never solved. The forums are inclusive; the discussions are inconclusive: the posters are voicing opinions on their favourite television show, but their individual opinions are never summarized and formed into a 'public opinion'.

Deficient publics

To sum up: the internet fan communities are part of a fragmented public sphere; they are single-issue publics; the posters are not engaged in oppositional, collective social identity formation; they are weak publics, yes, actually too weak to even qualify as 'weak publics' in Fraser's terminology. They are 'odd publics', deficient publics.

However, this characterization is unfair for several reasons. First, the fragmented internet sphere is measured against the fairly simple model Habermas used to describe national, public communication in societies with limited means of communication at their disposal. Several critics have pointed out that his model is unable to account for the multitude and variety of public discursive spaces in complex media-driven societies. In the later work *Between Facts and Norms* (1996 [1992: *Faktizität und Geltung*]) Habermas acknowledged this criticism and presented a more nuanced view of the public sphere as 'a highly complex network that branches out into a multitude of overlapping international, national, regional, local, and subcultural arenas' (Habermas 1996: 373). Moreover, he tacitly introduced a distinction between *live* and *mediated* communication and described the public sphere as differentiated into levels 'according to the density of communication, organizational complexity, and range'. He placed the levels on an ascending scale

from the *episodic publics* found in taverns, coffee houses, or on the
streets; through the *occasional* or 'arranged' publics of particular presentations and events, such as theater performances, rock concerts,
party assemblies, or church congresses; up to the *abstract* public
sphere of isolated readers, listeners, and viewers scattered across large
geographic areas, or even around the globe, and brought together
only through the mass media.

(Habermas 1996: 373)

Still, it is difficult to make the internet fan forums fit into this expanded
model. Since the posters are 'scattered across large geographic areas', the
forums should evidently be placed at the highest, most 'abstract' level of
the scale. On the other hand, the posters are not brought together through
the mass media, and they are not isolated; they engage in interactive
conversation through the internet communication structure.

Obviously, Habermas' revised model should be further expanded to cover
computer-mediated communication as well. However, the more basic problem with viewing the fan forums as deficient publics is that they are measured against a normative conception of the public sphere in which political
communication and opinion-formation by means of rational-critical debate is
the main concern.

Within the Habermasian tradition, the political public sphere always
takes precedence over the cultural public sphere. In Habermas' own grand
narrative, the cultural public sphere is primarily an apolitical 'precursor'
that serves as a 'training ground for a critical public reflection' until the
proper institutions and forums of the political public sphere are in place.
'The public sphere in the political realm evolved from the public sphere
in the world of letters; through the vehicle of public opinion it put the
state in touch with the needs of society' wrote Habermas in *Structural
Transformation* (1989: 30–31). This is still his view in *Between Facts and
Norms*, where he defines the public sphere in complex societies as 'an intermediary structure between the political system, on the one hand, and the
private sectors of the lifeworld and functional systems, on the other'
(Habermas 1996: 373). In this view, the public sphere is 'a network for
communicating information and points of view (i.e., opinions expressing
affirmative or negative attitudes)' which are filtered and synthesized in the
communication process and coalesce into 'bundles of topically specified *public
opinions*' (ibid.: 360).

The cultural public sphere revisited

Measured against the ideal political public sphere, the television fans clearly
constitute an odd, deficient public. They discuss popular television shows,
not proper political topics. They communicate opinions, but not opinions

165

that can be synthesized into proper 'public opinions' and mediated into the political system.

However, if we view the posters as private people who come together to discuss cultural matters in public, there is nothing particularly odd or deficient about them. Not only do they conduct their discussions according to the institutional rules of Habermas' ideal public sphere, they have the same dual approach to cultural objects as the reasoning private people of the early cultural public sphere.

On the one hand the posters view their favourite show as a representation of a 'real' universe. They identify with the fictional characters, judge the probability of narrative events according to real-life criteria, and connect their experience of characters and events with experiences and situations in their own lifeworld. In some cases the vicarious experience of watching recognizable characters and events in the fictional universe prompts them to assess their own situation and to formulate individual desires and aspirations. By discussing the show with other viewers they are helped to understand their own lifeworld situation – not unlike the private people of the eighteenth century who learned to understand and manage their own personal relationships and private lives by reading literature and discussing their reading experiences in public (Habermas 1989: 50–51).

In addition, the posters view the show as an aesthetic construct. They evaluate individual episodes against general narrative conventions and specific generic expectations; they suggest what should be done to save problematic scenes or hopeless plotlines; they exchange views on general dramaturgy. By discussing and criticizing the show they evaluate the writers' craftsmanship, clarify genre boundaries, and mark which aesthetic devices and transgressions are acceptable and which are not – not unlike the private people in the eighteenth century whose practical criticism of new literature, drama, and music articulated emerging shifts in taste and helped establish new aesthetic criteria (Habermas 1989; 40–43; Morrow 1997).

When the discussions in the early cultural public sphere moved out of the salons and coffee houses and were institutionalized in print media like journals, magazines, and newspapers, and later on moved into broadcast media like radio and television, cultural criticism became a matter for pro-fessionals and the ideal open, interactive exchange of opinions and arguments was replaced by impersonal and asymmetrical one-to-many communication. The emergence of the interactive internet discussion arenas with their possi-bilities of instantaneous, many-to-many communication has to a certain extent solved this problem and revived private people's public discussion of cultural matters after a very long period of time.

'The Internet has certainly reactivated the grassroots of an egalitarian public of writers and readers', said Habermas at the ICA conference in 2006, but at the same time he emphasized that 'computer-mediated com-munication in the web' only has 'unequivocal democratic merits' in very special cases, for example when it 'undermine[s] the censorship of authoritarian regimes that try to control and repress public opinion' (Habermas 2006: 423).

The posters in the fan forums are one of these reactivated egalitarian publics of writers and readers. Evidently, these private people cannot be compared with traditional political publics. Nor can they claim unequivocal democratic merits by toppling authoritarian regimes. But their computer-mediated communication opens up a sphere for potential self-reflection and identity formation as well as for aesthetic judgement and taste formation. Which seems to be of no small merit.

References

Fraser, N. (1992) 'Rethinking the public sphere: a contribution to the critique of actually existing democracy', in C. Calhoun (ed.) *Habermas and the Public Sphere*, Cambridge, MA: The MIT Press.

Habermas, J. (1962) *Strukturwandel der Öffentlichkeit. Untersuchungen zu einer Kategorie der bürgerlichen Gesellschaft*, Berlin: Duncker and Humblot.

Habermas, J. (1989) *The Structural Transformation of the Public Sphere. An Inquiry into a Category of Bourgeois Society*, Cambridge: Polity (Translation of Habermas 1962).

Habermas, J. (1992) *Faktizität und Geltung. Beiträge zur Diskurstheorie des Rechts und des demokratischen Rechtsstaates*, Frankfurt a.M: Suhrkamp.

Habermas, J. (1996) *Between Facts and Norms: Contributions to a Discourse Theory of Law and Democracy*, Cambridge: Polity Press (Translation of Habermas 1992).

Habermas, J. (2006) 'Political communication in media society: Does democracy still enjoy an epistemic dimension? The impact of normative theory on empirical research', in *Communication Theory*, 16.

Morrow, M. S. (1997) *German Music Criticism in the Late Eighteenth Century. Aesthetic Issues in Instrumental Music*, Cambridge: Cambridge University Press.

Negt, O. and A. Kluge (1972) *Öffentlichkeit und Erfahrung. Zur Organisationsanalyse von bürgerlicher und proletarischer Öffentlichkeit*, Frankfurt am: Suhrkamp Verlag.

Negt, O. and A. Kluge (1993) *Public Sphere and Experience. Toward an Analysis of the Bourgeois and Proletarian Public Sphere*, Minneapolis: University of Minnesota Press (Translation of Negt and Kluge 1972).

Sites mentioned

Official sites

The official *Grey's Anatomy* site: http://abc.go.com/primetime/greysanatomy.
Official international *Grey's Anatomy* sites:
Australia: http://au.tv.yahoo.com/greys-anatomy
France: http://www.tf1.fr/greys-anatomy
Great Britain: http://www.livingtv.co.uk/shows/greys5
Norway: http://www.tv2underholdning.no/greys
Grey Matter. From the Writers of Grey's Anatomy: http://www.greyswriters.com.

Commercial sites

Grey's Anatomy Insider: http://www.greysanatomyinsider.com and http://www.iscribeltd.com.
Television without Pity: http://forums.televisionwithoutpity.com
Grey's Anatomy Fanfic: http://fanficga.1.forumer.com
Grey's Directory: http://greys.fan-sites.org
A Norwegian site: http://forum.kvinneguiden.no
Grey's Anatomy Wiki: http://www.thegreysanatomywiki.com

Rules of Discourse

Television without Pity Forums: http://forums.televisionwithoutpity.com/index.php?act=Help&CODE=01&HID=26
Television without Pity Forums, Dos and Don'ts: http://forums.televisionwithoutpity.com/index.php?showtopic=3150213
Grey's Anatomy Wiki, Code of Conduct: http://www.thegreysanatomywiki.com/page/Wiki+Code+of+Conduct

13

X FACTOR VIEWERS

Debate on an internet forum

Anne Jerslev

Introduction

The talent show *The X Factor*, which ran for the first time in the spring of 2008, has been hugely successful in Denmark, just like in other countries (cf. for example Hill 2007). *The X Factor* was broadcast by the Danish public-service channel DR1 and had an average share of 56.3 per cent and extremely high ratings, rising steadily from 1.3 million to as many as 2 million viewers during the finale, out of a population of 5.5 million people. Ratings were as high or even higher than the most popular programmes – the nationally produced drama series which usually top the ranking list – and it was covered extensively and debated avidly not only in the tabloids but in all media and on countless blogs and debate sites. An analysis of viewer attendance (from the first programme through the third live show) shows on average that more women than men watched the programme. Older viewers watched markedly less than average, even though this demographic group watches considerably more television. Among females, the age group 3–10 (Target Affinity 133.3 per cent), 21–30 (Target Affinity 136.9 per cent) and 31–40 (Target Affinity 139.7 per cent) were overrepresented. So, core viewers were between 31 and 40 years old, and in particular women of 21–40 years old; even girls below 10 watch *The X Factor*.

In this chapter I am going to discuss the debate on DR1's own *X Factor* site – a large debate site but only one of the hundreds of sites where the show was discussed. I want to outline what kinds of debates are taking place and discuss the kind of relationship between the writers/viewers and the programme that the debate both constructs and represents. How can we understand the writers' affective attachment to the programme and in what ways is the programme shaping the communal activities on the site? Hence, I want to take critical issue with Jenkins' (2006) ideas of *participation*. One difficulty with Jenkins' book is that he doesn't really define what he means by participation, except that it is a usually communal consumer/viewer activity which is significant to contemporary digital culture and has the web as its preferred meeting place; it is a kind of social interaction and a sign of the 'empowered consumer' (Jenkins 2006: 169), 'more open-ended, less under the control of media producers and more under the control of media consumers' (ibid.: 133) he contends, and, finally, it is 'a good thing' (ibid.: 248). Towards the end of *Convergence Culture*, Jenkins asks whether he is granting too much power to these communities (ibid.: 246). However, as his point is that the particular fan communities he has been studying since *Textual Poachers* (1992) have become a common part of popular culture in the age of media convergence, his question is rhetorical; the internet is a 'vehicle for collective problem solving' and 'public deliberation' (Jenkins 2006: 169). But looking at the debate on the Danish *X Factor* site I want to point out that questions of interactivity and participation are more complicated than that. Of course voting is a participatory strategy. And there are recurrent manifestations of an awareness of being part of a community on the site. Nevertheless, the question remains: What actually is the relationship between the programme and the debate forum and what kind of discussion takes place? Are debates on the site public deliberations, as Jenkins has it, or are they rather – and merely – affective opinion exclamations? What kind of participation are we talking about?

X Factor discussions: affective performances

I have selected debates from two specific days as my object of study, one from the day of, and the day after, the second audition show and one from right after the broadcast of the second live show. Altogether around one thousand comments were posted on the two days. It appears from Figure 13.1 below that at no other time was the activity as intense as on 15 February; there were more than three times as many contributions as on any other day during the entire broadcast of the show.[1]

One reason for this remarkable divergence is probably that the 'bad judge', Thomas Blachman, had been especially rude towards one of the acts, whom he had despised throughout the show. Another reason for the sudden intense activity on the forum was that, for the first time, the consequences of the format's casting of the judges as not only experts but also coaches, with each their individual performer or group to support and each their interests in who should move on in the competition, was recognized. Or, at least, viewers interpreted the evening's final judgement as a result of subjective interests, and not of informed and objective evaluations on the part of the judges.

Debates on the two dates diverge, as one takes place before the live shows started. However, what is similar is the degree of viewer commitment. Posts and comments are, in general, extremely noisy and passionate; they are either addressing aspects of the programme or other writers on the forum. The way of communicating is dramatic and expressive. As with other internet debates,

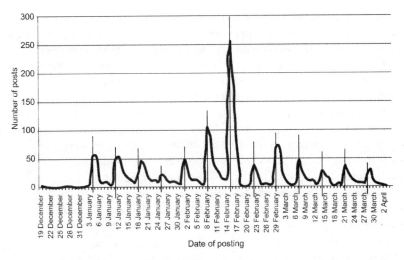

Figure 13.1 Debates about *X Factor*. Thin vertical lines indicate dates of broadcasting.

there is an abundance of exclamation marks and capital letters (Hougaard 2000) through which writers communicate affective states of being; hence, most of the texts could be described as *affective performances*. Only about half of the posted comments were remarked on, and only a few posts got more than three comments or caused extended debate. In general there is not much argument on the forum and there is not much deliberation. Many writers primarily seem eager to raise their own voice, either in confrontation or in a more friendly tone. Writers who have chosen not to start a new post but to comment on an already established one may also just voice their individual opinion, which might just as well be completely detached from the previous comment. Writers can expand on previous comments by referring to other posts or, in general, 'the debate', 'people', thereby constituting themselves as members of the community. Comments thought to be trivial are answered with irony or disdain. Factual questions are posed now and then, and they are always answered − for example questions about the title of the programme's background music or the brand name of some piece of clothing worn by a participant or a judge. But most comments are elaborations on 'I agree' or 'I disagree' statements. 'I disagree' statements are often quite aggressive, thus discussion on this public debate forum has a tone different to that of most communication on personal blogs, where visitors acknowledge that they have been invited into a public–private space.

On the first of the chosen dates discussions divided into the following three topics: (1) the judges and in particular judge Thomas Blachman's unruly behaviour towards contestants, (2) whether contestants ought to know the rules of the game they had voluntarily entered, and (3) the judges' evaluation of participants. The first two topics were just as eagerly discussed five programmes later. In addition, writers discussed (3) their preferred act/ whom they wanted to win and (4) the judges' professionalism. Throughout the programmes, debates were either about the behaviour of judge Thomas Blachman; about participants as either manipulated victims or agents who could be held responsible for having chosen to apply; *or* about who should win and who was voted out. Hence, debates were either about *ethical conduct*, either in the programme or on the debate forum, or they were about the rules of the game. In *The X Factor*, these ethical dramas were primarily staged and enacted through the performance of the 'bad guy' judge and, on the web, through the many discussions of *moral behaviour*, of *fairness* or not in the elimination process and the *reliability* of the judges' explanation of their decisions.

The X Factor : a makeover talent show and a forum for passing judgement

The X Factor can be defined as a particular kind of *makeover show* (Bratich 2007; Dover and Hill 2007; Heller 2007; Ouellette and Hay 2008); it is fundamentally a show about bodily and behavioural *quick-change* (Sobchack 2000) and a particularly successful and entertaining example of contemporary television's 'focus on behaviour' (Palmer 2003: 21), on *processes of transformation and education*.

Just as with similar entertainment programmes like *American Idol* and *Pop Idol*, but also programmes like *America's Next Top Model*, *Project Runway* and *The Apprentice*, *The X Factor* belongs to the reality TV subgenre of *makeover television*, 'to the extent that experts, teachers, and judges seek to transform raw human potential into coveted opportunities for self-fulfilment through the realization and expression of talent' (Ouellette and Hay 2008: 127). Or, in Couldry's (2004) words, the makeover takes the form of a process of *celebrification*. Participants in *The X Factor* undergo a transformation on many different levels. They go from being ordinary, everyday people into being celebrities and, thus, from unformed bodily 'raw material' into stylized and posing media personalities. With the help of coaching and support from the experts they go from amateurish singers to performers ready to conquer the professional and competitive world of the music industry. And even if they don't land the record contract, they have already landed a place in the spotlight for at least a short while.

Just as in other makeover shows, we are told that the outer transformation is no end in itself; more importantly, it facilitates inner growth. The finale contestants again and again pointed out that they were now where they had *always* wanted to be. When asked how she felt standing before a live audience in the Danish town hall square and singing to thousands of people just a few nights before the grand final, finalist Laura stated that, to her, it was a dream come true. Thus, even if she were not to win the competition, *self-fulfilment* was sufficient reward for having participated.

The photographs of the nine remaining contestants posted on the X Factor site just before the first live show were proof that they had singing talent, but also that they had the most 'potential to display the signs of transformation' (Palmer 2003: 180). The press photographs functioned ritually as both evidence and promise of the successful celebrification process, their transformation from ordinary people into celebrities. Like in cosmetic surgery makeover shows (cf. Jerslev 2008; Pitts-Taylor 2007) the process of transformation released what had been lying there, dormant, all the time. Like the doctors, the musical experts called forth the contestants' potential. Hence, the photographs were, at once, evidence of the new and improved self and strategic self-representations, iconic representations of a certain uniform appearance necessary in order to succeed in the marketplace in the 'era of the lottery of fame' (Andrejevic 2004: 10). The stylized, retouched photographs of commodified bodies were evidence that the programme's sought-after 'X Factor' was not an attribute of the self but a prerequisite for the construction of a *media self* (cf. Couldry 2004; Palmer 2003). Being selected to continue in the competition meant the contestants not only having shown the right kind of talent and having demonstrated that they were capable of transforming themselves, it meant that they had the potential to perform their transformed selves in the media.

Categorizing *The X Factor* as a talent makeover show makes Ouellette and Hay's idea of (reality) television as a 'common and regularized technology for self-fashioning' (2008: 117) pertinent to *The X Factor* as well (cf. also Ouellette 2004; Palmer 2002). Reality TV in general may be regarded as a resource for education relating to the strategic management and empowerment of self; talent-development shows in particular (like *The X Factor*) teach us lessons in the strategic performance of self and how to make our individual talent and our bodily appearance into a valuable asset in popular culture. However, as pointed out by Anna McCarthy (2005), people do not necessarily *learn* to act, to judge or decide in particular ways by reality TV's performances of conduct. Makeover programmes may play a pedagogical role but their games of strategic self-management could as easily be considered not worth learning or straightforward examples to follow by viewers. However, the X Factor debate shows that viewers accept the programme's invitation to launch debates *about* conduct and to *pass judgements* on everyone and everything going on in the show. What seems to affect viewers and make them rush to the debate forum is mostly that their sense of justice and the fair treatment of others is challenged. In response to reality TV's 'steady stream of ethical dramas' (Jenkins 2006: 84), they put forward their own view upon everyday morality without hesitation, both in relation to interpersonal conduct and to the conduct of the media. Thus, it seems to me that the debate site is more a forum for judgements and exchange of opinions than deliberation.

Half of the approximately 270 posts completed on Friday, 15 February were about the night's live broadcast. The revelation of who was voted out took place just before 9.30pm so comments were posted more or less immediately after the show finished. This eagerness can thus be seen as an indication of a strong attachment to *The X Factor*, made possible by the programme's participatory strategies; the *competition*, the viewer *voting*, the *elimination*, the *provocative performance* by one judge and finally the *series format* engaged viewers who each hold their own strong opinions both about the outcome of the competition and about the performance.

It seemed that viewers were rushing to the digital environment first and foremost to express their own opinions and exchange opinions with other viewers. The often quite rough tone in the forum indicates that it is used as a space where it is possible to pass judgement in a way that is socially unacceptable elsewhere. Just as Thomas Blachman does not care about good conduct, so many writers use the forum for affective outbursts, which may not be permitted in their everyday social life. The following comment is not unusual for the X *Factor* debate:[2]

GO THOMAS GO THOMAS GO THOMAS
THOMAS RULES.
ALL YOU FUCKING NEGATIVE PEOPLE.PULL YOURSELVES TOGETHER.THAT YOU ARE SO NAÏVE TOWARDS REA-LITY JUST SHOWS THAT SOMETHING IS WRONG WITH YOUR SENSE OF REALITY AND BECAUSE YOU CANNOT SING YOURSELF YOU HAVE TO TAKE IT OUT ON SOME-ONE ELSE.!!
GROW UP.!!!

The debate forum thus seems to establish an affective judgemental environment where people are allowed to speak their mind about the programme and about moral topics and are answered accordingly. But hardly anyone is asking others about their opinion. Again, the site is more of an affective outlet for the manifestation of strong opinions than for deliberation.

Debates after the second audition show[3]

Judge Thomas Blachman, the subject of four out of five posts, is basically defended in two ways: (1) most admirers think that his *rudeness is entertaining*; he is *honest* and *straight* and *contestants should thank him*. He dares say what other people – friends and family – should have told them a long time ago, that they have no singing talent. A recurrent argument is that harm is done to participants not by the judge but by parents who have not taken responsibility and given their children a realistic view about themselves. (2) Another way of defending Blachman is to argue that *he is just putting on an act, playing a role* written for him by the format. Blachman is *supposed* to be mean and therefore he cannot be scorned. In this view, Blachman's conduct is not about honesty but about performance. He is sincere in the performative way Paddy Scannell (1996) defines sincerity: not necessarily saying what you mean but meaning what you say.

Critics, on the other hand, evaluate Blachman's behaviour as unacceptable. He is arrogant and condescending and abuses his power as a judge. Even though he may be right in his judgements, his way of treating participants is way off. Again and again writers condemn Blachman (and the programme) for inappropriate conduct; for appealing to the lowest instincts in people.[4] And, again and again, writers refer to egalitarian discourses in a democratic society. No matter how widely opinions diverge, there should be a mutual performance of respect because everyone has an equal right to voice their opinion, but Blachman disrespects this basic rule. *The X Factor* is 'humiliation TV' (Hill 2007) according to many writers, and they are not comfortable with what is going on.

To admirers, people could learn from Blachman. In a post called 'Stop whining!', 'Ole U' asks below the headline 'It is possible to be honest without dragging people through the mud': 'Why should he absolutely slate people. Is this the way we should learn to talk to each other?' But the immediate response is, 'No ... but it is about time that we start to be a little honest and critical towards each other'. Another way of making a similar statement is to compare *The X Factor* with a Danish talent show called *Scenen er din* ('the stage is yours') where judges were very nice to all participants:

> In *Scenen er din* there was no evaluation at all. Everybody got four or five stars no matter how terribly they performed for nobody should be rubbed up the wrong way and no one was supposed to be sad. Therefore it was so shocking to a lot of people that you are actually evaluated in a programme like the *X-Factor*! That you are not just told that 'the mere fact that you participate makes you a winner' but you are actually taken up on your singing talent. Why don't we move on from this sloppy 'we are all equally talented at everything' mentality and realize that this is not true. When you decide to run for the first prize you have to remember that they are the judges and this is business and entertainment. They are not your overbearing parents or kind teacher.

Admirers of Blachman's elitist conduct thus value singularity and individuality and assert that some people are more talented than others. Participants have to accept that a talent show is based on the market's competitive rules and values, where the less talented lose. The (social) democratic idea of equality is connected to a particular soft Danish mentality, as is stated in the above comment, as in many other comments where Blachman is praised as the impersonation of liberal values.

The debate abounds with celebrations of the right to *free choice*. Writers remind people who disapprove of Blachman and who voice their anger towards a TV channel that permits his rude manners that they have the choice to turn off the TV or switch channels. Writers feeling sorry for participants who must endure his offensive behaviour (and the other judges' barely concealed laughs) are reminded that contestants have registered of their own *free will*. Since they have had the opportunity to watch similar shows over several seasons, they should know rules number one and two of the game, which are that you may not be treated nicely and you may not make it to the makeover part of the show.

So whereas critics of Blachman's conduct angrily maintain that he is humiliating participants and lacks empathy with ordinary people's vulnerability in exposing themselves on TV, admirers think participants, by enrolling in the game, are 'giving up their rights as ordinary people' (Hill 2007: 197). Blachman is creating great entertainment and so are many participants with their freakish and awkward behaviour and lack of talent.

A few writers stated that the initial part of talent shows is by far the funniest. For example, one writer argued that the best thing about talent shows is really only the first rounds, before all the freaks are sorted out. Basically, the rest of the acts are pure mediocrity and quite boring. It's the freak show that is awesome.

Whereas only a few writers talked explicitly about unpleasant feelings of embarrassment when watching the most awkward acts, many described their laughter and amusement – they had 'a laugh'. But the two things may very well be connected. Laughter may result from embarrassment. A stage performance is a social exchange between (social) actors and audiences. Viewers laugh because participants are obviously not obeying the expected rules of access to or behaviour on the stage. Laughter thus signifies knowledge of proper conduct and communicates an awareness that the person it is directed towards does not have such knowledge.

'Embarrassment is a social reaction', as Michael Billig puts it (2005: x). Billig's main point, in line with Henri Bergson's, is that ridicule and laughter are central to the maintenance of the norms of conduct in social life. He argues that what he calls *disciplinary laughter* is a negative reaction to inappropriate behaviour – contrary to *rebellious humour*, which 'mocks the rules and the rulers' (Billig 2005: 207). Although we are, of course, talking about parasocial interaction, it seems as if ridicule's disciplinary laughter is what many *X Factor* viewers described in their comments on the website. Their laughter is the laughter of embarrassment. But, as Billig emphasizes, disciplinary laughter is not just conservative and rebellious humour liberated; laughter may have different functions for different viewers and the two sorts of humour may mix. Laughing may be regarded as a demonstration of good citizenship and self-governance on the part of the one who is laughing. But some of the people presented in the audition programmes seemed to care so little about taste and social behaviour, and to be so beyond understanding conduct as a civic – and mediatized – obligation, that laughing can also be understood in a different manner. To many writers, the most conspicuous 'freaks' are heroes, and laughing can here be understood as a break from reality – and reality TV's pervasive staging and offerings of guides of conduct.

Altogether, this mixture of anger, irritation, ridicule and laughter created a strong attachment to the programme, so strong that viewers rushed to the site to give vent to their feelings. To some writers anger was overruling other emotions and their loyalty to the programme vanished; they stated furiously that they would not watch the programme again. Even though there were not many statements like these, they became somewhat more frequent as the audience started voting and might have to face up to the fact that their favourite is eliminated. To others, their emotional experience and moral opinions and their desire to share them with other viewers seemed to be the motivating force for participating in the internet community.

Debates after the second live show[5]

One writer confessed after the second live show that 'After the evening's "show" I really feel like going out and set whole neighbourhoods on fire ... arrgggg ... '. Another wrote, 'I got so angry that I had to rush in here and participate in a debate.' So, whereas laughter and amusement were often referred to in comments about the show after the second audition (apart from angry reactions to judge Blachman), reactions of anger and disappointment prevailed after the second live show.

Thomas Blachman is still a hot issue a month later. There are still heated arguments about his deviant behaviour; he is still defended as a laugh by admirers and he is still hated by a lot of writers who aggressively accuse him of being anything from a narcissist to a psychopath. In contrast to the comments from the earlier date, there is much discussion about who can sing and who cannot. Writers are articulating their opinions authoritatively, as experts: they seem never to be in doubt about how to judge participants' singing talent.

Thus, three quarters of the comments after the second live show are about the result, the final voting out by the judges of a young black man called Frederik, with much self-confidence and stage presence, in favour of three young men who had been in the same position the week before and were obviously very emotional and nervous. There is much condescending, prejudiced and sexualized reference to the three young men as 'faggots', 'homos', 'drama queens', and so on. Primarily, though, writers were debating how to understand the show's end result. One argument was that, beyond doubt, Frederik was the best – so how could the judges be so wrong? The answer was that the judges played tactically and, consequently, the question was posed whether they had been forced to do so by the programme-makers and the Danish public-service channel. Only in passing were writers reminding each other that they, or 'Denmark' as it was also phrased, had created this unhappy situation themselves by not voting for Frederik in the first place.

'Chris' writes below the headline 'What happens, Frederik is out?'

> This is unbelievable – one would think this was a put-up job ... No doubt Frederik was the perfect performer. I refuse to watch the *X-Factor* after this. Suddenly it has become so untrustworthy. It is just because no one wants to vote home his own candidate.

Likewise, 'Emma Jensen' writes below the headline 'What happens to DR!?'

> What the hell is going on? Why is Frederik voted home? Did DR botch the votes or what? Because after having seen all these comments I think that most of Denmark and most *X-Factor* viewers have voted for Frederik.!!

The two comments are quite typical of the debate. Suddenly, the consequence of the tension-creating rule of the game – that judges are also mentors – is played out. Subsequently, the debate in a sense turns the role of the expert upside down. Debate-forum participants act as experts and condemn judges for playing tactically and destroying their own trustworthiness – because they chose the wrong winner. And some writers come up with a conspiracy theory: the powerful institution Denmark's Radio has manipulated the programme by ordering the judges to vote in a certain way. And who knows whether the programme-makers have also manipulated viewer votes?[6] In both cases, viewers are questioning the voting procedure as a tool for viewer participation and democratic decision-making.

The conspiracy theory, on the other hand, acts as a kind of populist counter-attack or revenge on the programme-makers and the TV channel. Many writers express with great conviction the idea that they can read the tactical game, hence the questioning headlines are more like exclamations of outrage. They have lost the belief that they participate in a fair game and the programme has lost its credibility. Viewers are outraged because this means that voting becomes pointless and the feeling of having the power to support your preferred winner is a fraud. This twist certainly adds to the possibility of creating conflict and debate on the site and thus reinforcing viewer participation on the forum. On the other hand, it may also be that, if there is no other strong attraction, some of the people most strongly attached to the programme stop watching.

An *X Factor* participatory community?

People now simply have to buckle their helmets! X-Factor is a TV programme. It is not your heart medicine, your oxygen mask or your pacemaker etc. Calm down for God's sake. Enjoy the show; enjoy one and a half hours of entertainment. Say, 'well, okay' when it is over and look forward to next Friday.

This comment sums up neatly the heated activity on DR's *X Factor* debate forum. The internet debate about *The X Factor* constitutes an *affective environment* where writers' attachment to the programme is both enacted and communicated. Comments are often emotionally tense; capital letters and exclamation marks emphasize strong opinions and create a sense of *presence*, which seems to be crucial to the debate forum as an affective community. People rush 'in here' to voice their opinion and they often show an awareness of being in a community. The *X Factor* forum clearly demonstrates how participating in a debate community on the internet is both an important way of processing media experiences and a way of voicing comments about the moralities of everyday life.

An interesting observation is that members of the community often use phrases and words exactly as they were said and used in the programme so, in a certain sense, the debate *doubles* the programme. As such there is no remarkable 'adding' and 'expanding' to the programme or 'writing over' the show by the community, as Jenkins would have it (2006: 257). Whereas Jenkins uses the term *deliberation* for participatory communal activities on the internet and thus hints at a public-sphere theoretical framing, in the case of the *X Factor* debate it would be more correct to understand participation as simply a *digital feedback structure*, a media-updated version of what took place in the theatre in the eighteenth century, where the audience commented immediately and loudly on the play.

In general, writers are not particularly interested in the makeover 'narrative'. Instead they go into the many ethical questions the programme raises and they discuss them again and again. Also, there is a lot of debate about power relations between the programme and the viewers. Are viewers real participants and does voting matter at all? Hence, the power balance is not a given in the debate forum and the arguments about hidden agendas imply that, to some writers, the media institution, DR, will always overrule 'the people'.

Some writers think that the programme has an obligation to protect the weaker part, 'ordinary people', when they participate as social actors in a programme. Others apply liberal thoughts to the programme as a space for exercises in self-government: people are there on the stage of their own free will and being laughed at is their own responsibility. There is a lot of debate about good conduct and the psychological and social qualities necessary to function in a competitive society. Debates are thus also very much about *media participation*, about the terms and rules of interaction. I agree here with Jenkins (discussing *American Idol* and participation) that debates about voting are debates and negotiations about 'the terms of audience participation' (Jenkins 2006: 91).

The debate on the internet forum demonstrates that strong disagreements create vivid activity and a sense of community, and vivid activity may in turn support attachment to a programme. The debates also demonstrate that creating loyal viewers is no uncomplicated task. On the one hand, the debate forum on Denmark's Radio's *X Factor* site can be regarded as an extension of the programme, a public display of the successful working of the programme. The *X Factor* debate site is not communicatively united by deliberation. Neither is it, as a public debate site, structured by the intention of coming to a mutual understanding – or mutual discussion – of the subjects that are preoccupying everyone. Rather, what seem to a large extent to guide communication are confrontative practices, affective outbursts, a liberal idea of the individual, and self-representation as more important than deliberation and the collective.

On the other hand, the *X Factor* debate forum raises important questions about not only social conduct but also the conduct of media institutions. The site is an active environment for the voicing of opinions about the relationship between the media and their users, and the debate demonstrates that the relationships between media institutions, media programmes and viewers are no simple givens. Viewing *The X Factor* involves a continuous negotiation of meaning, of values and power relations, and, finally, at least for some of the writers, a dilemma about staying or leaving.

Notes

1 The diagram is provided by my research assistant, Aske Kammer, on the basis of all debate posts on the DR website's debate forum collected from http://www.dr.dk/xfactor. Debates on the site are organized from when the latest comment in each post is written. This means that the graph does not show duration of posts, only when they ended. However, posts are in general quite short and the majority seem to have been started on the same day. If writers want to air their opinion of a participant they usually start a new post instead of finding one which is already debating the act.
2 It is followed by four comments, which are equally rude.
3 There were 86 posts; altogether around 270 comments.
4 One of the recurrent angry comments is that DR also misuses the licence fees paid by the Danish viewers as their tax money by broadcasting a programme like *The X Factor*. This kind of programme has got nothing to do with the channel's

public-service obligations. Not only debate-forum writers but also conservative media debaters aired this opinion vehemently.

5 There were 270 posts; altogether around 710 comments.

6 On a few occasions a DR website editor posted a comment. He repeated the DR1 *X Factor* policy that, as in other countries, the programme-makers reveal nothing about the number of SMS votes and how many voted for which contestant.

References

Andrejevic, M. (2004) *Reality TV: The Work of Being Watched*, Lanham, Boulder, New York, Toronto, Oxford: Rowman and Littlefield Publishers, Inc.

Billig, M. (2005) *Laughter and Ridicule. Towards a Social Critique of Humour*, London, Thousand Oaks and New Delhi: Sage Publications.

Bratich, J. Z. (2007) 'Programming reality: Control societies, new subjects and the power of transformation', in D. Heller (ed.) *Makeover Television. Realities Remodelled*, London and New York: I. B. Tauris.

Couldry, N. (2004) 'Teaching us to fake it: The ritualized norms of television's "reality" games', in S. Murray and L. Ouellette (eds) *Reality TV. Remaking Television Culture*, New York and London: New York University Press.

Dover, C. and Hill, A. (2007) 'Mapping genres: Broadcaster and audience perceptions of makeover television', in D. Heller (ed.) *Makeover Television. Realities Remodelled*, London and New York: I. B. Tauris.

Heller, D. (2007) *Makeover Television. Realities Remodelled*, London and New York: I. B. Tauris.

Hill, A. (2007) *Restyling Factual Television: Audiences and News, Documentary and Reality Genres*, London and New York: Routledge.

Hougaard, Tina Thode (2000) 'Interaktionelle særtræk i chat'. http://www.nordisk. au.dk/forskning/publikationer/artikler/chat.pdf. Accessed 14 August 2009.

Jenkins, H. (1992) *Textual Poachers: Television Fans and Participatory Culture*, New York and London: Routledge.

Jenkins, H. (2006) *Convergence Culture: Where Old and New Media Collide*, New York and London: New York University Press.

Jerslev, A. (2008) 'Cosmetic surgery and mediated body theatre: The designable body in the makeover program *The Swan*', *New Review of Film and Television*, Vol. 6, No. 3, pp. 323–41.

McCarthy, A. (2005) 'The Republic of Tyra', *Flow TV*, Vol. 2. No. 1. http://flowtv. org. Accessed 14 August 2009.

Ouellette, L. (2004) '"Take responsibility for yourself": *Judge Judy* and the neoliberal citizen', in S. Murray and L. Ouellette (eds), *Reality TV. Remaking Television Culture*, New York and London: New York University Press.

Ouellette, L. and J. Hay (2008) *Better Living Through Reality TV*, Malden, Oxford and Victoria: Blackwell Publishers.

Palmer, G. (2002) 'Big Brother: An experiment in governance', *Television and New Media*, Vol. 3, No. 3, pp. 295–310.

Palmer, G. (2003) *Discipline and Liberty. Television and Governance*, Manchester and New York: Manchester University Press.

Pitts-Taylor, V. (2007) *Surgery Junkies. Wellness and Pathology in Cosmetic Culture*, New Brunswick, New Jersey and London: Rutgers University Press.

Scannell, P. (1996) *Radio, Television and Modern Life*, Oxford and Cambridge: Blackwell Publishers.

Sobchack, V. (2000) 'Introduction', in V. Sobchack (ed.) *Meta-Morphing. Visual Transformation and the Culture of Quick-Change*, Minneapolis and London: University of Minnesota Press.

14

THE DIGITALLY ENHANCED
AUDIENCE

New attitudes to factual footage

John Ellis

The excessive 'manipulation' of photographs was a pervasive fear of the closing years of the twentieth century. The arrival of digital photography seemed to threaten the evidential status of photography in the eyes of both popular and academic commentators (see Brand et al. 1985). Cases of image manipulation were widely debated, citing both the routine practice of 'retouching', and some flagrant examples of falsified photographic evidence. MIT's William J. Mitchell sounded this alarm in 1994:

> The growing circulation of the new graphic currency that digital imaging technology mints is relentlessly destabilizing the old photographic orthodoxy, denaturing the established rules of graphic communication, and disrupting the familiar practices of image production and exchange. This condition demands, with increasing urgency, a fundamental critical reappraisal of the uses to which we put graphic artifacts, the values we therefore assign to them, and the ethical principles that guide our transactions with them.
>
> (Mitchell 1994: 223)

More extreme responses included this from a British philosopher:

> There are good reasons, however, for thinking that digital images are not really photographs. The causal process that defines photography underpins the treatment of photographs as evidence of what they depict. The possibility of precisely and systematically breaking that causal relation to the world makes digital imagery sufficiently different from traditional photography to suggest calling such a picture a 'photograph' is little short of intentional ambiguity.
>
> (Friday 1997)

Digital image technologies seemed to challenge the status of photos as evidence, the 'causal process' that links the photograph to a moment as its visual imprint. Digital processes seemed to make it too easy to alter or improve images, or to 'manipulate' them.

In the end, though, photography was just too useful a tool to be abandoned in the face of such strictures. The digital has not destroyed the evidential qualities of the photographic. The popular consumption of visual images and, indeed, of digitally recorded moving images and sounds, has adapted to these new circumstances. Photographic material is now subject to a double examination of its status as evidence. When it matters (which is definitely not the case with many photos and much footage), the contemporary viewer will tend to examine images as evidence both of events and of an activity of image creation. Images are subject to a double test of their qualities as evidence: first for what they show, and second for the activities which brought them into existence as images. 'How did they get those pictures?' 'Is that a plausible angle?' 'Was anything set up?' 'Was anyone exploited?' These are the kinds of questions that we now ask of images that seek or are given the status of evidence. We will even ask: 'Should the photographer have been taking photographs rather than intervening in the events?'

The transformation of image recording wrought by digital technologies has been a complex process. The easy availability of digital photographic and recording devices has been as important in this as their revolutionary potential for image manipulation. The worried commentators of the 1990s concentrated on the malleability of the photographic, and missed the democratization of the photographic processes that were also to be enabled by digital technologies. Digital technologies have provided easy and readily available ways of recording images and sound (cameras, mobile phones, and so on); of editing them (FinalCut and other packages); and disseminating them on the internet (YouTube, MySpace, and so on).

Digital technologies have made the recording and dissemination of moving images and sound a mass activity in the developed world. Flowing from this process, new forms of audio-visual communication have developed, and with them, significantly, new attitudes to the audio-visual. With widespread use has come widespread scepticism. I believe that we are seeing the emergence of an increasing sophistication of attitudes towards the truth claims of moving image and sound. These attitudes are our best defence against the activities of manipulation that were identified by the doomsayers of the 1990s. Since the middle of that decade, controversies about the nature of still and moving images have multiplied.[1] They have taken a variety of forms:

- *Problems around trust in factual TV programmes.* The UK saw a major controversy about fakery in documentaries, both by programme-makers and their subjects. (Ellis 2005)

- *The revelation that published news photographs had, in fact, been faked.* In 2004, the editor of the UK *Daily Mirror*, Piers Morgan, was sacked after publishing photos, which turned out to be faked, of British soldiers abusing an Iraqi prisoner.[2] Competing newspapers made the most of his downfall.

- *Controversies about the activities of paparazzi photographers.* Paparazzi were prosecuted for their activities around the 1997 death of Princess Diana in a road accident which some deemed them to have caused.[3] In 2009, all photographers were forbidden by a British court from coming within 100 metres of the UK home of singer Amy Winehouse.[4]

- *Condemnation of the publication of 'inappropriate' photographs.* The New York *Daily News* was widely condemned for Todd Maisel's photo of a severed hand, index finger pointing, lying on the tarmac (Girardin and Pirker 2008), as were other papers for the picture of the so-called Falling Man, both images from 9/11.

- *Controversies around the press photography of extreme circumstances.* In 1994 press photographer Kevin Carter committed suicide, two months after receiving the Pulitzer Prize for his photography of a Sudanese child dying of hunger as a vulture looked on. One press critic wrote: 'the man adjusting his lens to take just the right frame of suffering might just as well be a predator, another vulture on the scene'. (Girardin and Pirker 2008: 249)

- *Scandals around amateur photography of extreme acts.* Photos of torture and humiliation were taken at Abu Ghraib prison in Iraq by members of the American military, and circulated privately as trophies. Their revelation by the press provoked both outcry and prosecutions.

At stake in all these cases are two interconnected issues: the activity of taking photographs and the circulation of photographic material with particular 'truth claims' attached. Debates and scandals around the activity of photography centre on the ethics of taking photographs in particular circumstances. Sometimes the photographer is accused of acting as a bystander rather than intervening in the situation. In other cases the presence of a camera is judged, by those debating the results, to have incited the actions which are photographed.

Problems around the truth claims of photographs centre on their nature as evidence. They tend to deduce whether any fakery has taken place from detailed examination of the photographs and footage themselves. Indeed it is relatively easy to find examples of the public disputation of photographic material, as they are often fuelled by a competitive press eager to prove that rival publications have been hoodwinked. Such stories sell newspapers and promote the image of the print press as relentless seekers after truth. Detailed evidence was produced for the two cases cited above (the 1999 documentary crisis and the 2004 *Daily Mirror* photos) in authoritative newspapers which interrogated details of the images. In the case of the *Daily Mirror* photos, it was proved that the type of vehicle in which the abuse was taking place was not used in Iraq. As for some of the footage in the faked documentary *The Connection*, it was shot in the director's hotel room rather than a 'secret location to which the crew were taken blindfold' as stated in the programme's commentary. In the cases of other programmes caught up in the controversy, the activity of filming was interrogated for its plausibility: was it really likely that a documentary crew would have been filming a couple when the wife suddenly woke in the middle of the night; or how much pressure seemed to have been put on interviewees to perform in particular ways?

At the heart of this development is a sceptical public, knowledgeable about the practical and ethical issues surrounding photography and film. Contemporary publics know more about the processes behind image production because they have experienced them for themselves. Just as the computer has made a routine event out of the once exclusive craft skill of high-quality word processing and document creation, the emergence of digital image technology has spread the potential for high-quality moving-image recording and dissemination. Hitherto rare experiences have become commonplace as a result of mass consumer digital technologies: particularly the experiences of filming, being filmed and seeing the results on a screen. Before the 1990s, such experiences were confined to the privileged few who worked within broadcasting or had the honour of appearing on TV, or within the relatively closed circuits of home filming on Super-8 film or VHS video. The division between the amateur and the professional pervaded every area of moving-image production and dissemination. Now we need a new term to describe those who routinely produce such material but without the aim of being a 'film-maker': perhaps we should talk of someone as 'a filmer',[5] just as computing discourse talks of 'users', making no binary distinction between the amateur and the professional. Nowadays we are both: our skill levels may differ but it is impossible to be highly skilled in all areas; every professional is an amateur in another area.

It is necessary to use a new term like 'filmer' since mass consumer digital technologies have brought moving-image experiences to very wide publics. Filming is used for all kinds of mundane purposes, in relation to work, leisure and all the areas in between. All kinds of image-capture devices surround us (particularly in the UK, with its dense population of surveillance cameras). The occasional controversies around 'amateur' material posted on sites like YouTube or circulated by email demonstrate how widespread the generation of moving images and recorded sound has become.[6] The experiences of filming and being filmed, as well as of the distribution of the resulting material, have become more casual and mundane than at any previous moment in the development of moving-image culture. Every stage of the process has been made available through low-cost devices, often with surprisingly good picture quality (the sound, though, is quite another matter). Image capture goes on everywhere: in DIY stores and at rock concerts, at traffic accidents and in classrooms. Image dissemination requires little more than an internet connection, and image sharing is even simpler as every camera has a digital display screen. Anyone who wants to can see what they have just shot, and show it around to others. The acts of image capture and image projection can be performed using the same device, as was the case at the dawn of cinema, with the Lumière brothers' first cameras.

The flip-up digital display screen has also altered the experience of producing images for all users, both 'amateur' and 'professional'. Images can be seen as they are being captured. The digital screen that has replaced the viewfinder of analogue devices will display the image as it will later exist, while it is being recorded. Analogue viewfinders always provided an approximation, and were only accessible to one individual at a time, who jammed their eye to an eyepiece in order to see this approximation. The digital screen allows more than one person to see the image, permitting a more collective approach to film construction. It has also had an impact on the work of the lone (or almost lone) documentary film-maker by altering the relationship between the filmer and those being filmed. As many documentary film-makers will attest, it is much easier to engage directly with a subject when eye contact can be maintained without the camera being in the way. Without the need to use an eyepiece, a discreet check of the digital screen is all that is necessary. The new intimacy and casual nature of contemporary documentaries attests to this: what we witness is more genuinely a one-to-one encounter between filmer and subject than has hitherto been possible. This experience has changed for those with professional intentions, and, crucially, their experience is now not substantially different from that of anyone else with a digital image-capture device. The experience of being filmed by both professional and non-professional filmers has altered. Filming has become a more casual process, more akin to an intimate conversation than the quasi-religious confessional endured by those interviewed by the multi-person crews needed to shoot with 16mm and one-inch video.

Digital technologies have altered factual-filming relationships while making them familiar to a very broad public. The distinctions between amateur and professional remain in the area of actual film creation, however. There are fundamental differences, both in the intentions behind any act of filming and in the means of dissemination of the results. It remains a different class of activity to make a documentary for broadcast and to make a recording for YouTube circulation. Different rules apply, and different expectations are held by viewers of the two media. The closest the two media get is in the status of social-campaigning videos on YouTube, and the status of highly first-person documentaries on TV. However, in normal practice, the distinction between amateur and professional intentions remains relatively clear. Attitudes to factual filming, however, have undergone a real revolution. Familiarity with the activity of filming and being filmed has bred a generalized suspicion or scepticism about factual footage. This scepticism frames the modern activity of viewing and interpreting documentary material, and fuels many of the debates about documentary and news footage.

Suspicion of photography

The growth in all forms of photographic activity, enabled by digital technologies, seems to have reawoken long-held anxieties about photography. Photography allows all kinds of activity in relation to individuals, from the creation of memories through a constant requirement to 'look one's best' to the pervasive presence of surveillance cameras. Photography has produced a heightened awareness of being watched, evidenced in phenomena as diverse as an abiding fascination with celebrities caught unawares and the real concern about surveillance cameras in public, business and institutional spaces. We are increasingly aware of being watched, and the fact that watching requires particular forms of performance of the self. We have learned what cameras require and how to provide it. In early TV gameshows involving 'ordinary' members of the public and early news 'vox pops', many of the citizens involved seem to have problems with even the most basic aspects of performance: how to stand, how formal their speech needed to be, etc. It seems that awareness of the need for performance and of the necessary modalities of performance were much more rare than they are in nowadays (see Ellis, forthcoming). To know these skills for oneself is also to be aware of them in the behaviour of others. From this familiarity emerges the frequent perception that individuals in documentaries are 'playing up' for the camera, or are behaving in ways that are somehow 'not true' to themselves.

We also know that, however good our performances may be, the camera can still catch us unawares. From the unconscious blink as the image is captured to transient grimaces frozen for ever, almost everyone has experienced the feeling of photography traducing how they might wish to appear. This feeling is as old as Kodak itself. Newer is its extension to the domain of the moving image and recorded sound. We may be able to come to terms with the strange sound of our own recorded voices compared to the sounds that resonate in our heads as we speak. But the strangeness and awkward fascination that we experience on seeing our own videoed images is far harder to dispel. Photography appears to us as a treacherous activity: it produces both good and bad images, desired and undesirable images, of ourselves. In revealing ourselves as other, it destabilizes our perceptions of our selves. Our attempts to manage this process involve forms of performance, negotiation and even pretence. Our increasing everyday encounters with photography and recording now involve far more than simply 'saying cheese' in a formal photographic setting. Photography, and particularly moving-image recording, has developed at such a rate that different generations have contrasting attitudes and approaches to it. While middle-aged people are still concerned at the possibility of being shamed by a TV appearance, younger generations have a more acute sense that any such appearance will be ephemeral and that any embarrassment will consequently be temporary: so why not 'go for it'?

Digital camera technologies have made the experience of being 'the other side of the camera' more routinely available. Kodak made the experience of being photographed commonplace; the Handycam and its successors have brought the experience of being a filmer into everyday life. So most people now know about the delicate negotiations that take place in getting someone to appear on camera; how difficult it is to get them to do what you want; how uncomfortable it sometimes feels to point a camera at someone, to ask them intrusive questions, to catch them unawares. Picking up a moving-image camera is a transformative experience: it catapults the individual into a role that they often feel unprepared to take up. No longer involved in the flow of events as a simple participant, the individual becomes something else as well. The camera gives the power to comment, it becomes an extra participant in the events, a focus for all kinds of hitherto submerged interpersonal dynamics. Amateur footage usually appears intensely ritualized as a result. It is easier to adopt standard roles than to work through the emotions stirred up by the presence of the camera in the hands of a family member (or an interloper). The film *Capturing the Friedmans* captures much of this dynamic, from the adoption of TV modes as a communal family disguise to the decision of David Friedman to document the process of the family breaking down during the trial of the father and younger brother Jesse.[7]

We now are familiar with both what it feels like to photograph and to be photographed. We know the processes of performance and the difficulties of adopting the position of the filmer. We know the problems and vagaries, too, of the subsequent uses of the material. Indeed, many of our anxieties relate to the subsequent uses of photos and recordings. They can easily be made 'just for fun', but they are a record, and a physical entity that can have a career of its own. The evidence of this is everywhere, unavoidable. Local-newspaper users in the UK have developed a curious habit of taking out display adverts for relatives' birthdays, illustrated with 'embarrassing' childhood pictures. Parents checking Facebook for their children's back-packing whereabouts sometimes come across photos not intended for their eyes. Sex tapes exposed on the internet sometimes break (or indeed make) the careers of celebrities or politicians. Photographs and recordings are born in an intimate moment, but grow up quickly and take on a life of their own.

Anxieties haunt photography and recording, anxieties about the moment of making recordings and the subsequent uses to which they can be put. As recording becomes more commonplace, these anxieties have developed into a more sophisticated public attitude towards the consumption and use of recordings. The public for TV and internet moving images has become more sceptical around any material that claims to be 'factual', and more appreciative of the skills involved in manufacturing the modern fictional spectacle. A connoisseurship has developed, which asks 'How did they do that?' In relation to fiction, this enables the extension of the fiction itself into 'Making of' materials. In relation to factual footage (documentary and news), it has produced a more sceptical viewing public, to which professional film-makers and broadcasters have adapted their practices. Many of the ethical concerns that were once the subject of abstruse debates between journalists and documentary film-makers now have a much wider currency. A public that is aware of the processes of obtaining footage now routinely ponders the nature of the shooting relationship. They assess what each side wanted from the filming and, in the case of documentaries like Molly Dineen's *Geri* (about the former Spice Girl Geri Halliwell as she reinvents her career), the film actively concerns itself with the same question.[8] Viewers will speculate among themselves about the nature of the editing and possible omissions of important material. When the issue is sufficiently important, they will scan the footage closely for tell-tale details in the background which might indicate that an alternative version of events could be constructed. All this activity is essentially the same as that undertaken by professional organizations concerned with the truthfulness of the footage: whether journalists wanting to catch out documentarists, or broadcasters trying to assess the nature of the 'user-generated content' that comes their way.

Audio-visual hearing and seeing

The growing consciousness of the ethics of recording and photography is accompanied by an emerging appreciation that looking and listening is not at all simple. We know that image and reality are different things, so the old beliefs in the reality of the image are tempered by a growing understanding of what is involved in accessing and using recorded images and sounds. The current moment, with its proliferation of screens of all kinds, is the site of a growing awareness that the viewing relationship is not as simple as that of providing a window on the world or a panorama, as TV used to claim. Still less can we believe that our media are telling it like it is. In the consumption of recordings of real events, something is lost and something is gained. We are increasingly aware that this gives our moving images a double status. They are at once imprints of the real and constructed texts or documents (as is, indeed, implied by the word 'documentary').

The experience of watching these documents of the real is one of participating to some extent in three different experiences at the same time. The first is that of experiencing events directly, of being a part of what is going on. Recorded images and sounds certainly provide sense impressions that resemble those of someone actually present within an event, but equally they deprive us of other sensory data which those present would use to understand their predicament. There is no sense of smell, of touch; no awareness of the temperature and humidity of the air, of the nature of the space as crowded and confined or empty and remote. We see and we hear, but we know that these senses alone can be deceptive. As viewers of a text, we may well be able to work out some of these factors from internal evidence (beads of sweat, shivering, etc.), and we may even have them drawn to our attention. We cannot judge how important they may be to the way that events turn out, or to the truthfulness or otherwise of the characters. Beads of sweat on a person's brow could indicate the stress of lying, the stress of being forced to reveal something against his or her will, or the lack of air conditioning. We experience through seeing and hearing, but at the cost of losing other elements of the experience.

The viewer of recorded images and sounds also experiences the position of a bystander at events. We watch and listen, but do not participate. The events we see are of interest but do not directly involve us. We are not called upon to take any action. But unlike the bystander at an event, we could not take any action even if we wanted to. Our separation is enforced and absolute. On the other hand, the position we are given is more than that of a simple bystander. A bystander is limited to one physical position. The viewer of filmed footage is given a privileged view compared to such a bystander. Cameras reframe events, microphones pick out particular material from the overall sound, cutting recombines fragmentary views into a synthetic whole. Through the screen, we become privileged bystanders at events, the point to which they seem to be addressed and the place where they end up making sense. Our privileged position comes at a cost: we are bystanders who cannot intervene. We cannot offer help or comfort or congratulations.

The third element of this distinctive audio-visual experience of events is that of the construction of those events for our consumption. The privileged bystanding enjoyed by the viewer of footage of the real is a construction. It is the result of a process of production which is increasingly well understood. Media organizations, preoccupied with branding in a crowded market, are increasingly explicit about their orientation and news values. Fact and commentary are more closely intertwined as a result, further encouraging viewer scepticism. News itself becomes the story as soon as any scandal breaks: attempts to suppress revelations or bad news often intensify the scandal. In short, we know that the footage that we see comes from somewhere in particular. It has been gathered and assembled by individuals working in organizations with particular aims and characteristics. This is as true for clips on YouTube as it is for a BBC documentary or a film by Michael Moore. We do not simply see footage and hear sounds: we are addressed by them. We recognize the terms of that address as belonging to specific individuals and specific institutions. Usually there will be more than one set of terms in any one broadcast: we are addressed by a series of attempted communications by journalists, by broadcasters, and by the persuasive voices of others that they present within 'their' material. Any broadcast text is an assemblage of communicative attempts, not all of which are successful in their aim to communicate. As bystanders, after all, we can choose to ignore if we want.[9]

Conclusion

The audio-visual experience is a distinct form of experience, sharing some characteristics of direct experience and bystanding, but also involving a privileged synthetic view of events that is always the product of a particular organization and the individuals working within (or against) it. The growing public knowledge of what it is like to photograph and be photographed encourages an awareness of the nature of the viewing experience as well. The result is a rising scepticism about the audio-visual products we consume, and in particular those which claim any factual or evidential status. This is the result of the spread of digital recording technologies and opportunities for digital viewing. Such scepticism was not necessarily anticipated by critics writing less than 20 years ago. Yet it can be seen at the heart of many of the current conflicts about the use of imaging technologies. During the spring of 2009, conflicts around the policing of the G20 summit in London involved both sides using recorded images to prove versions of the events. Surveillance by the police was matched by successful sousveillance by protesters who demonstrated that a different angle revealed very different aspects of police behaviour. Similarly, a running battle over photography and the right to privacy is taking place involving both celebrities objecting to the activities of paparazzi and those who object to the imposition of surveillance cameras in public spaces. Digital image production has not flooded the market with faked photos. It has brought about a scepticism about the truth claims of all and every image by a public who feel empowered to 'make up their own minds'.

Notes

1 Controversies about still images tend to be international as the circulation of press images is globalized. However, most controversies about moving-image material for broadcasting, outside news material, still tend to be limited to national contexts.
2 See BBC News, 14 May 2004; http://www.guardian.co.uk/media/2004/may/14/pressandpublishing.iraqandthemedia.
3 Photographers Fabrice Chassery, Jacques Langevin and Christian Martinez were at one point condemned by French courts to a prison sentence but eventually had to pay symbolic damages of €1 for invasion of privacy.

4 See the *Guardian*, 2 May 2009, p. 11.

5 I first came across this term in French, in an issue of the revue *Communications* in which social scientists and anthropologists interrogate their routine use of video as a research tool. They do not claim to be film-makers in the traditions of Jean Rouch or Frederick Wiseman: they do not create for an audience. However, they are using film in a sophisticated way as a tool in their research. Hence they needed a term to describe their status: 'un filmeur' was the elegant solution. *Communications 80*, Editions du Seuil, Paris, 2006, ed. Daniel Friedmann.

6 For instance, private sex tapes revealed online, 'happy slapping' footage of street attacks filmed on mobile phones, and so on.

7 For a discussion of this film, and the seemingly endless audience commentaries it has provoked, see Thomas Austin, *Watching the World, Screen Documentaries and Audiences*, Manchester University Press, Manchester, 2007.

8 For a discussion of this film, see Stella Bruzzi, *New Documentary* (Second Edition), Routledge, London 2006, pp. 199–206.

9 For a more detailed discussion of these issues, see John Ellis, 'Mundane witness', in *Media Witnessing: Testimony in the Age of Mass Communication*, eds Paul Frosh and Amit Pinchevski, Palgrave Macmillan, London, 2008.

References

Austin, Thomas (2007) *Watching the World: Screen Documentaries and Audiences*, Manchester: Manchester University Press.

Brand, Stewart, Kelly, Kevin and Kinney, Jay (1985) 'Digital retouching: The end of photography as evidence of anything', *Whole Earth Review*, July, pp. 42–49.

Bruzzi, Stella (2006) *New Documentary* (Second Edition), London: Routledge.

Ellis, John (2005) 'Documentary and truth on television: The Crisis of 1999', in J. Corner and A. Rosenthal (eds) *New Challenges in Documentary*, Manchester: Manchester University Press, pp. 342–60.

Ellis, John (2008) 'Mundane witness', in Paul Frosh and Amit Pinchevski (eds) *Media Witnessing: Testimony in the Age of Mass Communication*, London: Palgrave Macmillan.

Ellis, John (forthcoming) 'The performance of self on television: The case of ITV's first game show', in Gilles Delavaud and Denis Marechal (eds) *Television: The Experimental Moment*, Paris: INA.

Friday, Jonathan (1997) 'Digital imaging, photographic representation and aesthetics', *Ends and Means*, Vol. 1 No. 2, Spring 1997, University of Aberdeen, available at http://www.abdn.ac.uk/philosophy/endsandmeans/vol1no2/friday.shtml. Accessed 19 August 2009.

Girardin, Daniel and Pirker, Christian (2008) *Controverses: une histoire juridique et ethique de la photographie*, Lausanne: Actes Sud/Musee de l'Elysee, pp. 249, 286–89.

Mitchell, William J. (1994) *The Reconfigured Eye: Visual Truth in the Post-Photographic Era*, Cambridge, MA: The MIT Press.

15

DIGITAL MEDIA, TELEVISION AND THE DISCOURSE OF SMEARS

Todd Gitlin

A prologue on indeterminacy

Thinking about the no longer exactly new but certainly absorbing digital media, and what they portend for political life, I confess I am caught between two impulses, like a hungry donkey midway between two haystacks. I could fancy up the point by saying that they are two theories, and there are certainly theoretical loadings to my impulses, but impulses they remain. When we think about the future, after all, our reasoning and seasoning, and what we blithely call our knowledge, may be our engines, but impulses are our fuel.

One of my impulses says that screened media in the digital age represent a change in the quality of human experience. Although the change is neither simple nor uniform, its lineaments are unmistakable. Its central element consists of this compound: the sheer proliferation of media in intensifying competition for the attention of publics; the media's non- or post-linearity; the mounting ratio of the visual and aural to the written; the public hunger for sensation and disposable emotion; the growing portion of the waking day devoted to media, whether in casual contact, deep attention or simultaneous connection; the erosion of mass media by less-than-mass, segmented, niche or point-to-point media; the displacement of the slow by the fast, the black-and-white by the colour, the simple screen by the split screen, and so on. This ensemble generates a phenomenology in which media images and sounds show up as discontinuous blips or, in sum (if there is a sum), a 'blooming, buzzing confusion' (William James) distinctly conducive to political disengagement, or fragmenting party loyalties, or intensified culture wars, or *something*.

The other impulse clears its throat and points out that these developments arrive in the thick of an essentially a- or anti-political culture that has long assimilated political discourse into a culture of entertainment. Consumerism, as the historian Gary Cross has put it, 'won the century' – the twentieth century (Cross 2000). On the whole, it defeated civic republican-ism and radical change. It is what Americans, though not only Americans, and however true or false their consciousness, have come to want. It gives them pleasure as well as utility. In the United States, at least, disposable emotion, sensation and speed, in combination with the rest of the consumed world, have been characteristics of mediated life for centuries, perhaps increasingly so (see Gitlin 2002). (My impulse calls up a corollary impulse here: that a similar process now operates to varying degrees in most of the other democracies; but I toss this out as a lazy hypothesis, not even a working one.) This preference for the quick and stimulating is nowhere more evident than in the American nation, the first to be more or less born bourgeois. As Daniel Bell (1976) wrote, the American nation state was founded on this very principle: the denial of the primacy of politics for everyday life. Its constitutional foundation was premised on the over-whelming value of freedom *from* the federal state. Private life deserved to be protected from the government. Civic republicanism has laboured under this burden since the growth of the market in the nineteenth century.

In such a setting, American institutions have long cultivated the media of sensation. By the early nineteenth century the daily press was flourishing as a medium of sensation. Photography conveyed impressions for rapid delectation. Especially after the Civil War, with the rise of department stores, magazines, and then film and radio, images for consumption rhymed with consumer goods. Over the course of the twentieth century, voting par-ticipation generally declined, though with upticks during periods of social mobilization in the 1930s and 1960s. Though waves of political engagement wax and wane, it is a fair generalization that Americans have to be coaxed into politics from their preferred default position – withdrawal into the pleasures, burdens and other preoccupations of private life. My second impulse therefore protests that when politics is filtered into everyday life, it arrives not as Deweyan discourse conducted in Habermasian coffee houses but in the form of flickering images and sound bites, jolts delivered to flat screens in elevators and bars, to car radios and via podcasts, to laptops at Starbucks.

Both impulses have their merits. There are continuities and dis-continuities. Very well – isn't history like that? But is there any way to discern where media proliferation, fragmentation and acceleration are tending, and how they are guiding politics? Anticlimactically, I think not.

For one thing, however continuous and discontinuous the digital onslaught is with the preceding history of political culture, the digital onslaught is relatively recent. A better word is 'emergent'. If we had been writing on this subject 10 years ago, we would have missed cellphone cameras, iPods and iPhones, BlackBerries, Kindles, Google, blogs, Wikipedia, Facebook and Twitter. If we had been writing in 2003, we would still have missed Twitter, Facebook and other social-networking sites, YouTube, the Howard Dean campaign, *The Huffington Post*, and the crash and burn of George Allen's 2006 Virginia Senate campaign because of a video that was shot and uploaded to YouTube by an operative in his opponent's campaign.[1] (In the video, Allen, a conservative darling and a front-runner for the Republican presidential nomination in 2008, used a racist term to describe the operative.) Myself, I am probably missing the Next Big Thing – as a relatively late adopter, it won't hit me till around 2012.

Moreover, history has an annoying way of confounding 'if.then.' claims. Too much happens at once to permit the keenest observer to trace out the significance of any particular thread. Too many times the beat of the butterfly's wings interacts with other forces, shallow or deep, and the whole ensemble induces a hurricane. How much of Barack Obama's triumph rested on his specific talents – not least his speaking out against the Iraq war in 2002 – and how much on the eight years of George W. Bush's rule that ushered Obama to this rendezvous, as FDR said, with destiny? Don't we learn from the massacres of September 11, 2001, that events are hostage to what Richard Slotkin has called 'wild history'? With the proliferation of the means of history-making – and I mean the technological as well as organizational means – it becomes difficult, maybe impossible, to distinguish structures from agents and techniques.

Such indeterminacy makes us nervous. No wonder. As analysts of media we are, like it or not, authorities, and we like to be authoritative. But we are guilty of a collective hubris. We like to think that we recognize the forces at work. Our professional pride demands that we offer prognoses. We're paid to know, after all – not to confess, or boast, that we *do not* know. We think we can master the future by imagining that we see it. But we do not see it. Our claim to intellectual mastery is an illusion.

Or, in the memorable words of a contemporary sage: 'As we know, there are known knowns. There are things we know we know. We also know there are known unknowns. That is to say, we know there are some things we do not know. But there are also unknown unknowns, the ones we don't know we don't know.' Thus spoke Donald Rumsfeld on 12 February 2002. Even that expert judgement understated the problem, as his subsequent career displayed.

The discourse of digital smears

All this said, I want to offer the proposition that digital media lend themselves to a discourse of insinuation, which is in turn a way station heading towards a discourse of smears. This is so whether or not we find the historical continuity half full or half empty.

In his conference paper (Schudson 2009), my colleague Michael Schudson itemizes some of the ways in which the campaigns have lost control over the imagery, slogans and other discourse features that circulate, mutate, combine and recombine, delineating, in toto, a compound 'text' that forms a penumbra around the 'official' campaign. Since the 2004 presidential primaries – when Howard Dean, the former governor of one of the smallest of the United States, catapulted to the front ranks of Democratic contenders largely on the strength of his online organization, and later the right-wing Swift Boat campaign helped torpedo the candidacy of John Kerry – the intertangled, interactive totality of our manifold paramedia has morphed into an ever-more bustling social phenomenon. I use 'paramedia' here to refer to the breakdown of barriers among informal, post-it-yourself blogging and email crusading, cable television news networks canvassing the internet for usable material, and the like. In 2008, the paramedia surged with a rumbling torrent of anecdotes, rumours and falsehoods, many of them featuring ephemeral characters – what Bill Wasik (2009), in *And Then There's This: How Stories Live and Die in Viral Culture*, calls 'nanostories' – extending, like some spliced-together nightmare, across a period of some *two years*. I speak of the dozens, perhaps hundreds or even thousands of circulating email chain letters, YouTube, Comedy Central and Saturday Night Live videos, local attack videos and audio downloads that go nationally, even internationally, 'viral', many of them ending up as sound-bite clips that spread through voracious cable television and eventually through broadcast as well as talk radio – some promoted directly by campaign headquarters, some by arm's-length supporters, some by comedians, and some by God knows whom; some circulating for days, others for weeks, others for months; some bobbing up, then subsiding, then bobbing up again; some fermenting up into mainstream media, some less so or not at all.

It is not clear who to credit, or blame, for the observation that the term 'originality' is synonymous with faulty memory. Suffice to say that there are precedents for the style of political discourse that has emerged in the era of the nanostory. In the relatively recent past, the phrase that famously grasps the ephemerality of celebrity, the '15 minutes of fame' immortalized (!) by Andy Warhol in 1968, shrank to 'flavour of the month' (or more compressed yet, FOTM), or even 'flavour of the week', as news cycles accelerated. The declining length of television sound bites, based on the idea that the audience at large is unwilling to pay attention to more protracted statements, has been a subject of alarmed commentary for more than two decades now (see Gitlin 2002: 95–97). Television documentaries shrank first into television 'newsmagazines' and then, in turn, into skeins of snippets, attention to them in turn weakened by the news ribbons of headlines 'crawling' across the bottom of cable-channel screens. In bestselling novels and magazines, sentence length has diminished over the course of recent decades (ibid.: 98–103). These are examples of the chicken–egg cycle, in which the popular taste for speed is fed by the familiarity of speedier transitions (from image to image, from subject to subject, from screen to screen, from screen item to screen item), a speed-up that is in turn fed by the popular taste for speed ... and so on in the sort of supply–demand loop that recurs throughout the history of popular culture. But even the more ephemeral nanostory, especially in the form of the 'pseudo-scandal' named by the historian Sean Wilentz (2002), is not new either. American political history stretching back into the late eighteenth century is replete with the scandalous microstories of earlier days – which diffused more slowly, of course, in the era of newspapers that had to be delivered by stagecoach, but nonetheless did diffuse, sometimes spiking in prominence during political campaigns. The fetish of the new is not new.

Speed is only one characteristic of a discourse of insinuation; the shape of the map is another. The public-discourse world now boasts multiple points of entry. If it was ever appropriate to call it a 'sphere', implying a nicely, symmetrically, smoothly curved domain, it no longer is so (Gitlin 1998).[2] The shape of public discourse may well have become not only much bumpier but less predictable. In any event, for our purposes, it does not exactly matter whether the central staffs of political campaigns have lost control, whether control has been dispersed or diffused, or whether the central apparatuses have successfully encouraged auxiliary efforts to influence the candidate or tar the opponent. Suffice to say that accusations of evildoing or bad conduct, whether accurate, scurrilous, both or somewhere in between, have never been easier to circulate.

A case study in the circulation of falsehood

In America, no national political campaign or substantial battle over legislation is complete without eruptions and cascades of falsehood – from the Right. (Unsubstantiated and/or nonsensical stories popular on the Left, including the rumour that '9–11 was an inside job'[3] or that Sarah Palin's daughter Bristol, and not the governor herself, gave birth to the baby Trig in 2008,[4] proved unable to cross the barrier to mass media.) The institutional means for the circulation of smears, once confined to the more polemical newspapers, even more marginal tracts, and right-wing radio – not negligible channels by any means – have proliferated to include the 24-hour Fox News Channel, nationally syndicated right-wing talk radio and right-wing blogs. In recent years, this ensemble has devoted itself to promoting – among many others – the charge that John Kerry lied about his Vietnam war experiences (Gitlin 2004); that Barack Obama is a Muslim;[5] that Obama was not born in the United States and is therefore ineligible to be president (Smith 2009); that Obama's health-care reform programme provided for the determination of end-of-life medical care by 'death panels' (Weiner 2009). There is no better way to convey the flavour of their operations, and their ability to cross the barrier into mainstream discourse, than with a case study. The quality of today's paradiscourse is best exhibited in action.

Here are the dramatis personae: The man who claims to have first circulated the meme[6] that Barack Obama was secretly a Muslim is a fringe anti-Semite. Sean Hannity is the second most popular host on Rupert Murdoch's cable channel, Fox News (where he was paired until recently with a bland liberal, Alan Colmes). He is, by himself, also one of the top-rated radio talk-show hosts. On Sunday nights, also by himself, Fox News gave him an hour for 'specials', to do with what he would. Fox management was pleased enough with Hannity to have just offered him a renewal through the year 2012.

On Sunday night, 5 October 2008, Hannity narrated an hour-long hatchet job on Barack Obama, complete with a soundtrack of the sort more usually found in C-pornography, featuring prominently, as a major witness testifying to Obama's iniquity, one Andy Martin, described by Fox News' chyron as 'author and journalist', and, though not identified as such on Fox, perennial political candidate in four states. Hannity called him an 'internet journalist'. On air, Martin made what Hannity called 'the explosive claim that Obama's role as a community organizer was a political staging ground perpetuated by the unrepentant terrorist William Ayers'. Ayers, a former leader of the Weather Underground of 1969 and thereafter, is now an education professor in Chicago. He and Obama participated on a foundation board, and lived in the same Chicago neighbourhood, where Ayers and his wife, the former weather presenter Bernardine Dohrn, hosted a fund-raising party when Obama was beginning his career in electoral politics. Allegations of Ayers' sinister relation to Obama circulated for more than a year, rearing their heads into the mainstream media during the Democratic primary season.

As for Sean Hannity's star expert Andy Martin, he has been crawling beneath the rocks for quite some time. According to no less a source than the Unification Church's impeccably right-wing *Washington Times* of 22 December 1999:

> In 1986, when Mr. Martin ran as a Democrat for Connecticut's 3rd Congressional District seat under the name 'Anthony R. Martin-Trigona,' his campaign committee filed papers saying its purpose was to 'exterminate Jew power in America and impeach U.S. District Court of Appeals judges in New York City.'

The *Washington Times* reporter, Ralph Z. Hallow, went on:

> A Connecticut federal judge finally barred him from filing any more federal lawsuits without permission. The judge said Mr. Martin has pursued legal actions with 'persistence, viciousness, and general disregard for decency and logic.'

And:

> In a New York bankruptcy case, he referred to a judge as a 'crooked, slimy Jew.' During the bankruptcy dispute, he filed a civil-rights lawsuit claiming Jewish bankruptcy judges and lawyers were conspiring to steal his property. He asked a court to bar 'any Jew from having anything to do with plaintiff's property.' In another motion in the case, he wrote: 'I am able to understand how the Holocaust took place, and with every passing day feel less and less sorry that it did, when Jew survivors are operating as a wolf pack to steal my property.'

Still according to Hallow, Martin 'ran for the Republican nomination for governor of Florida ... in 1990. The Florida Republican Party disavowed him because he previously ran for office as a Democrat and because of his anti-Semitic statements.'

Martin, it turns out, is one of the most litigious individuals in America, so he leaves a paper trail (and no doubt spreads fear among mainstream journalists). In a document included within in a lawsuit against the liberal watchdog group Media Matters for America, Martin claimed that 'African-American judges ... circle the wagons and try to protect Barry [Obama]'. He said that the actions of an African-American judge who presided over the case 'show that African-Americans are willing to corrupt and abuse their public offices to defend their own sleazy candidate for office'.

More recently, Martin claimed, contrary to fact, that Obama, whom he called a 'media witch doctor', had 'locked his granny away and refused to allow her to be seen' in order to 'pretend he has no white relatives'.

Martin was Sean Hannity's idea of a reliable source. None of the above-mentioned items in Andy Martin's curriculum vitae were announced to Hannity's two million viewers. But my real point, for analytical purposes, is that once a meme is 'out there', even critics run the risk of reinforcing it, in the fashion of 'Have you stopped beating your wife?'

From Hannity, Martin's accusation migrated into *The New York Times* (Rutenberg 2008), where, under the bland headline 'Obama's Personal Ties Are Subject of Program on Fox News Channel', the reporter Jim Rutenberg quoted Martin as saying that the anti-Semitic sentiments cited by liberal bloggers were forged. By whom? With what motive? Rutenberg did not say. Nor did he wonder why the above-quoted remarks were reported in the *Washington Times* and never retracted.

Notice how the fetish of objectivity leads to the ready transmission of nonsense. Here's an important dimension of the discourse of insinuation: it percolates easily from the fringe into the mainstream. Once there, the insinuation is treated as, perhaps, 'controversial', 'questionable',[7] 'a matter of opinion', but it continues to bounce around through media as a 'question' that has been 'raised'. The question, having been 'raised', becomes legitimate, so that other journalists may speak of 'questions having been raised' about X. Lazy, rushed reporting – another feature of the torrential culture of news – elevates the importance of the initial charge even in the course of rebutting it, or, as in Rutenberg's case, blessing it with weak curses. For Rutenberg writes that Martin's 'accusation that Mr. Obama's work as a community organizer in Chicago was "training for a radical overthrow of the government"' is 'unsubstantiated'. Why 'unsubstantiated' rather than false, and indeed slanderous? Is the claim that the moon is made of green cheese 'unsubstantiated'?

'Mr. Martin said he was careful not to present his theories about Mr. Obama as proven fact', Rutenberg says, going on to quote Martin as follows: 'That is my opinion – expert opinion – if you will. I don't pretend to be an exclusively fact-based reporter, though I try as hard as I can to get the facts.' He doesn't explore the question of whether Martin is qualified to offer 'expert opinion'. He doesn't ask at what he is 'expert'. He doesn't distinguish between grounded opinion and arbitrarily made-up opinion and contrary-to-fact opinion. We are in the realm of the self-parody of 'objective journalism': some say there was a Holocaust, some deny it; everyone has an opinion. If your doctor offers you an opinion, you assume it is grounded in fact. Once you learn that the doctor is an unlicensed quack, however, you discount the opinion and flee to another doctor. Ignorant and credulous viewers need to be told explicitly, unequivocally, that the first doctor is a charlatan. I take this communication to be the moral responsibility of a professional.

I am making no claim about the efficacy of corrections, especially in a time when the media suffer a loss of authority that is partly caused by political rebellion and partly by a generalized withdrawal of trust. It is beyond us to know with any degree of certainty what the impact of insinuation is on the population. The same doubt applies to the impact of corrections. There are too many cross-cutting, confounding variables in play.

But I think it is demonstrated that digital media lend themselves to a discourse of insinuation and falsehood. They specialize in the production of impressions. Impressions circulate easily. This is partly because they are compressed in space and time. They grab – and are meant to grab – the attention of distracted, torrentially drowned media multitaskers, especially the young. They grab attention through condensation, ready symbolization, reduction. They are sensational – they are intended to arouse sensation, and up to a point, they do. Like the advertising that has circulated for decades, they aspire to 'break through the clutter' produced by the sum of all other attempts to 'break through the clutter produced by the sum' ... and so forth. In an attention economy, the point is to drive traffic. Insinuation – the art of leaving the not-quite-said almost said, so that the thought seems to complete itself – insinuation drives traffic. It is not as if media do this in a vacuum. In daily discourse as well, there is a premium on slogans that establish you as knowing. 'D'oh.' 'As if.' 'Not.'

What else isn't new?

Now, there was no golden age when impressions did not matter. As Pericles, Aristotle, Cicero, Patrick Henry, Lincoln, Woodrow Wilson and Martin Luther King knew, rhetoric is the production of impressions. Today's para-media are the updated, heavily visual updates. Perhaps they amount to Pamphlets and Handbills 2.0. Newspapers and magazines have always used headlines, typography, drawings and photographs – in recent years supplemented by pull-quotes, cover banners and the like – to inject impressions into the public domain. To underscore the parallel, let me dwell for a moment on the classic case of the American presidential election of 1828, which pitted the incumbent John Quincy Adams against the former general and senator Andrew Jackson.

The press of 1828 was a party press, and it was vicious. The pro-Adams press dwelt on the charge that when Jackson had married his wife Rachel, *37 years earlier*, she was still married to her first husband. Evidently, at the time of their marriage, Rachel believed she had been divorced for, shortly after Rachel had separated from her former husband, he had written her to say that he had secured a divorce. Believing the divorce complete, Jackson and Rachel married in 1791. When the legal divorce agreement was concluded, in 1794, they remarried. These charges rattled around for decades. Jackson fought duels over them. Now, in 1828, the Adams press convicted her of adultery and bigamy. One Adams supporter, Charles Hammond, publisher of the *Cincinnati Gazette*, asked: 'Ought a convicted adulteress and her paramour husband to be placed in the highest offices of this free and Christian land?'

Meanwhile, Jackson supporters charged that Adams, while serving as Minister (Ambassador) to Russia, had procured an underage servant girl for the Czar. They also accused Adams of using public funds to buy gambling devices for the presidential residence. (These turned out to be a chess set and a pool table.)

Rachel Jackson suffered a heart attack and died on 22 December 1828, after her husband's victory in the election and before his inauguration. As for the public life of the nation, the two major consequences of the election of 1828 were that the National Bank was dissolved and many thousands of Indians, Native Americans, were expelled from their lands. The point is obviously that the tenor of a campaign may have little or nothing to do with its stakes.

Political territory is not only a minefield, it is full of boomerangs, inadvertencies, and recoveries. It is worth noting about 1828 that the Adams supporters also called Jackson a jackass – perhaps they were making a lame pun on his name. In 1837, in his second term, a political cartoon showed Jackson riding a donkey that represented the Democratic Party. Thirty-three years later, in 1870, the great cartoonist Thomas Nast, in *Harper's Weekly*, borrowed the symbol. Other cartoonists followed. The Democrats themselves have played with the symbol for decades. In Denver, outside the stadium, Democratic Party operatives were proudly if bemusedly selling T-shirts that read: 'DID ANYONE EVER WANT A NICE PIECE OF ELEPHANT?'

To return to my analytical as well as prophetic indeterminacy: the politics of insinuation and falsehood is a staple. I do not believe it is uniquely American, either, though the personification of American politics in the person of the president, which undermines the importance of ideological politics, accentuates it in the United States. The ability of a fringe anti-Semite and racist to gain access to a television network with two million viewers is no small thing, even if, in the omnibus spirit of populism, one characterizes it as 'fairness and balance', or 'access' for 'other voices'.

What is not evident is how digital media's availability for the circulation of insinuations or downright smears is correctible without a massive infringement upon First Amendment liberties. The customary European laws against certain forms of public speech are inconceivable in the United States. Almost the entire direction of American civil-liberties law for a century has been to the contrary. I should restate the point in positive terms: it *is* evident that such availability under the law qualifies as a structural element of the American media universe.

But then, democracy has always been an arena for damage as well as mobilization, and there are no technological fixes for moral problems.

Notes

1 http://www.youtube.com/watch?v=r90z0PMnKwI/.

2 My own neologism, 'public sphericules', is also inadequate for this reason. See 'Public Sphere or Public Sphericules?' in James Curran and Tamar Liebes, eds, *Media, Ritual, and Identity* (London: Routledge, 1998).

3 For example, '9/11 Was an Inside Job,' viewed 20 August 2009 at http://www.911sharethetruth.com.

4 *Vanity Fair*, 'The Authoritative Trig Palin Conspiracy Time Line', 5 September 2008, viewed 20 August 2009 at http://www.vanityfair.com/online/politics/2008/09/the-authoritative-trig-palin-conspiracy-time-line.html.

5 'Is Barack Obama a Muslim?' viewed 20 August 2009 at http://urbanlegends.about.com/library/bl_barack_obama_muslim.htm.

6 I use the word 'meme' because it has made itself a place in popular parlance – indeed, attributing this 'making of a place' to 'it' already presupposes that 'memes' are 'it's', active things with lives of their own – although the depersonalization of the process, and the attribution of force to slogans, catchwords, and so on, is, in my view, a scientistic attempt to liken cultural moves to genetic

processes, 'memes' to genes, making culture look naturalistic. The dehumanization of culture is a category error and a tribute to moral evasion. Still, the meme is out of the barn, so I will play along for now and use the term.

7 Almost a year later, Rutenberg (this time writing with Jackie Calmes) had recourse to 'questionable' in a *Times* article on the health-care imbroglio (11 August 2009): 'The White House on Monday started a new Web site to fight questionable but potentially damaging charges that President Obama's proposed overhaul of the nation's health care system would inevitably lead to "socialized medicine," "rationed care" and even forced euthanasia for the elderly.' On the inevitability of 'socialized medicine' and 'rationed care', a weak but non-empty claim of questionability could be made, but about the charge of 'forced euthanasia', the correct term would have been 'false'. See my 'Questionable', available at http://tpmcafe.talkingpointsmemo.com/2009/08/11/questionable.

References

Bell, Daniel (1976) 'The End of American Exceptionalism', *Public Interest*, Vol. 41 pp. 193–224.

Cross, Gary (2000) *An All-Consuming Century*, New York: Columbia University Press.

Gitlin, Todd (1998) 'Public Sphere or Public Sphericules?' in James Curran and Tamar Liebes, eds, *Media, Ritual, and Identity,* London: Routledge.

Gitlin, Todd (2002) *Media Unlimited: How the Torrent of Images and Sounds Overwhelms Our Lives,* New York: Metropolitan.

Gitlin, Todd (2004) 'Swifter Than Truth', *American Prospect,* November, http://www.prospect.org/cs/articles?article=swifter_than_truth. Accessed 20 August 2009.

Rutenberg, Jim (2008) 'Obama's Personal Ties Are Subject of Program on Fox News Channel', *New York Times*, 7 October 2008, http://www.nytimes.com/2008/10/07/us/politics/07fox.html?_r=1&oref=slogin. Accessed 26 August 2009.

Schudson, Michael (2009) 'The New Media in the 2008 U.S. Presidential Campaign: The New York Times Watches Its Back', *Javnost – The Public*, Vol. 16 No. 1, pp. 73–86.

Smith, Ben (2009) 'Culture of Conspiracy: The Birthers,' *Politico*, 1 March http://www.politico.com/news/stories/0209/19450.html. Accessed 20 August 2009.

Wasik, Bill (2009) *And Then There's This: How Stories Live and Die in Viral Culture,* New York: Viking.

Weiner, Rachel (2009) 'Palin: Obama's "Death Panel" Could Kill My Down Syndrome Baby', *The Huffington Post*, August 7 http://www.huffingtonpost.com/2009/08/07/palin-obamas-death-panel_n_254399.html. Accessed 20 August 2009.

Wilentz, Sean (2002) 'Will Pseudo-Scandals Decide the Election?' *The American Prospect*, November 30 http://www.prospect.org/cs/articles?article=will_pseudoscandals_decide_the_election. Accessed 20 August 2009.

Part IV

CRITICAL PERSPECTIVES

16

THE COST OF CITIZENSHIP IN THE DIGITAL AGE

On being informed and the commodification of the public sphere

Peter Golding

How comforting it would be to see in every technological advance the promise and delivery of social improvement. As scientific and technological achievements have accelerated, and as we have become ever-more accustomed to technical progress providing the means and the challenges for societal development, the notion that new technology might leave us, socially or culturally, no better or even worse, can seem perverse. Communication technologies have provided just such a host of promises and presumptions, and have also been the cause of many such unrealized hopes or realized disappointments.

In recent times the phenomenal growth of digital technology and the communications possibilities that have come with it, especially the exponential growth of the internet and mobile communications, has fed an almost limitless enthusiasm for the social gains that must ensue. In particular it has been expected that new and extended forms of sociability would rapidly develop, that greater, more frequent and more intense social intercourse would foster greater social cohesion, and that barriers to social inclusion erected by problems of physical isolation or limited mobility would be swiftly eroded by the reach and potential of new communication technologies. That this is often and valuably true cannot be denied, though nor can the many negative and disappointing outcomes that such technologies have bequeathed (Golding 2000).

This chapter is addressed to one such promise: the expectation that the growth of digital media would enrich and enhance democracy, by generating wider choice and accessibility of political information, and by providing the means for a more informed and engaged citizenry. The argument is persuasive and important. While effective democracy rests on the presumption that citizens engage with the political process, and do so in an informed and

207

egalitarian manner, it has long been recognized that opportunities to interact with institutions and processes of power are differentially available to different groups and classes, who remain variably able to turn the wheels of power, or to empower themselves by being informed about issues and information in ways that they are able not just to share with others but to use as the key resource for political mobilization and organization that engaged citizenship requires. Such shared information, in turn, enlarges the opportunities for citizens to act meaningfully, and to participate fully in what becomes, de facto, a digital assembly, constructing in large-scale, complex and populous societies what was once only possible (though only for a fraction of the population, the majority being excluded by status or gender) in the small city state of the Athenian polis.

This ideal is of enormous promise, and its potential as an outcome of qualitative changes in the forms of communication available in a digital society should not be questioned lightly. However, in this chapter, five current and serious reservations about the forms of digital development in major Western countries (with examples mainly provided from the United Kingdom) are discussed. These are the availability and range of political information in the public domain; the growing fragmentation of audiences; the commodification of cultural goods and the ensuing unequal access to relevant information; the limited form of political narrative, especially the presumption of causality in contemporary journalism; and finally the enduring implications of the 'digital divide', despite its regular dismissal as a diagnosis.

The growth of political information

Broadcasting has increasingly diversified and expanded as a form of communication, and most people have more access to more channels and output than at any time in the past. But this has not necessarily brought with it a growth in information about the main events and processes that govern people's lives. In a report issued at the end of the century, Barnett and Seymour concluded that many major areas of current-affairs programming – foreign affairs, economic activities, industry and business – were disappearing from current-affairs television in the UK (Barnett and Seymour 1999). Their analysis pointed to a decline in political and economic issues in current affairs on the main commercial channel, ITV1, from 13 per cent of the total in 1977 to 4.5 per cent in 1998, while there had been a similar decline in coverage of industry and business. International affairs had more or less disappeared from all channels, and generally their research suggested that 'softer' current-affairs programming, presenting issues such as consumer affairs and crime (which had trebled in coverage in the previous decade), was increasing at the expense of the 'harder' subject matter traditionally considered to be core current-affairs programming.

Many other studies have pointed to similar trends. The regulatory agency, Ofcom, has shown in more recent audits that current affairs is increasing again, and moving back into peak hours. Nonetheless, their study of 2006 showed that nearly 60 per cent of current-affairs programming on the five main terrestrial channels was shown outside peak hours, and that 'only a very small amount of the output during this period (3%) was dedicated economics/business current affairs' (Ofcom 2006). In asking audiences about their reception of current-affairs broadcasting they also found that 'viewers tended to define current affairs programming quite widely', citing examples such as the comedy quiz show *Have I Got News for You* and the celebrity chef Jamie Oliver's campaigning series *Jamie's School Dinners*, as programmes that they felt had current-affairs values. Even the BBC governors recognized that seekers after current-affairs TV would need to search it out. Their own review concluded that, while 'The BBC is serving committed viewers quite well, and audiences to its regular strands are steady ... most are shown either off-peak on BBC One or on BBC Two, so do not reach a Mainstream audience. Despite this, they regularly have a huge impact on the areas they report on. The lack of a regular, high profile peaktime offering on BBC One means that the BBC is serving the mainstream less well' (BBC Governance Unit 2005). Many studies of specific issues have also expressed worries about the evacuation of policy issues from mainstream broadcasting. In a study of documentary television, Nason and Redding again note the return in quantity of such programming in recent years after long and continuous decline, but that this has been mainly through the rise of more entertainment-oriented genres in the specific field they are concerned about: international, and especially development, issues. The raw numbers of hours have been increased by 'internationalising' entertainment and consumer genres. They note that 'Reality TV', putting British people into constructed environments located in developing countries, gets more television hours than the actual realities of life for the majority of the world's people. At the same time, holiday shows, travel challenges and 'docu-soaps' – all of which mainly feature British people being confronted by foreign environments – also rose, to dominate factual international programming. The number of developing-country factual programmes in 'harder' categories like 'history', 'politics', 'development, environment and human rights' and 'conflict and disaster' fell further – to unprecedented low levels (Nason and Redding 2002).

The same concerns apply to mainstream broadcast news. As a 2007 report by Ofcom pointed out, 'Economic circumstances make it much less likely that commercial broadcasters would choose to carry news for the UK nations and regions at anything like its current level, in the absence of effective regulatory intervention ... '. Thus 'the unprecedented availability of such a huge range of traditional and new sources of news opens up possibilities for real diversity of opinion to be heard – although, so far, the potential is far from being fully deployed or used', because 'in general, news outlets of all kinds often tell the same stories, from the same perspective, using much the same material' (Ofcom 2007). It came as no real surprise that in late 2008 it was announced that regulatory requirements on the major broadcasters to deliver both children's services and regional news were being relaxed.

But if provision is less rich than once it was, or perhaps as we might imagine it once was, are audiences being left distraught and hungry for more? In fact, audiences for news have been steadily declining – by about 25 per cent in the last 40 years in the UK, while in the USA television audiences for news have reduced from about 90 per cent of the total audience in the 1960s to 30 per cent by 2000. At the same time, readership of newspapers has been declining fast as readers either switch to newer forms of news consumption (though only to a very limited extent, as we shall see) or simply become less and less engaged with matters of public debate and policy relevance. This is especially true for younger readers. Lauf has shown that 'analysis of audience data from nine EU member countries in 1980, 1989 and 1998 indicates that the decline is mainly due to both age and cohort effects. As in the US, young people do not read current affairs news daily any more' (Lauf 2001). But this is not, of course, purely a cohort phenomenon. A study by the Newspaper Association of America shows that the percentage of American adults reading newspapers during the week fell from 58.6 per cent in 1998 to 48.4 per cent in 2007 (Newspaper Association of America 2009). In the UK, analysis undertaken for the House of Lords Select Committee on Communications showed a similar decline in readership. While the population actually increased, the proportion of the population reading any one of the top ten national daily newspapers fell by 19 per cent from 1992 to 2006 (a fall from 26.7 million to 21.7 million), and an even greater proportionate decrease was evident for Sunday papers (Select Committee on Communications 2008).

Three caveats are usually entered against such data. First, it is suggested that this decline was transitional, and that recent provision has increased. After all, the volume of UK national news on the five main channels increased by 80 per cent between 1994 and 2003, though mainly due to the growth in daytime and weekend news. However, much analysis shows that this is only because of the rise of more 'infotainment' forms of factual and policy provision. Secondly, it is suggested that any lament about this apparent decline in provision is but the distress call of a disappearing generation, which cannot understand the new forms of political engagement in which drama, soap opera, consumer programmes and entertainment more generally, especially where they invite participation or even adjudication by audiences, represent a new form of politics and democratic expression unfamiliar to those regretting the disappearance of more traditional forms. This is not the place to argue this analysis in detail, save to note that even were it true, it describes not the supplementation of mainstream and traditional forms, but their displacement. Finally, it is suggested that new forms of communication, notably the internet, deliver news and 'current affairs' material to audiences and readers, who far from having abandoned such fodder have simply transferred their attention to newer forms of delivery. Nonetheless television remains the main source of news for 65 per cent of UK adults, and the use of the internet for news consumption is often exaggerated.

That last proposition is worth pausing over, for the argument that 'the Internet will provide' is frequently at the centre of enthusiastic appraisal of the contribution of new communication technologies to the utopia of an informed citizenry. Internet availability and use has undoubtedly grown, and continues to do so. But broadband access in the home remains, to date, limited in many countries. Broadband subscriptions per hundred people in OECD countries in late 2008, according to the most recent summary (OECD 2009), range from 37.2 in Denmark to 10.5 in Poland. The internet, even where available and used, is not used particularly for access to news and related forms of information. Surveys of internet use often overstate the enthusiasm and regularity of such use – the figures published by the UK government, for example, define regular use of the internet as having accessed it at any time in the three months prior to interview, despite which, in 2009, over 10 million adults remained defined as having never accessed the internet. Of those who had, the overwhelming use was for email, finding out about goods and services, and increasingly for buying things (Office for National Statistics 2009). A recurrent habit of typing in one's credit-card data seems a rather meagre indicator of enhanced democratic engagement. So too in the USA, the evidence suggests that growing internet availability has done little if anything to wean audiences off TV news as their source of choice. As Jackson suggests, summarizing many studies, 'nearly 66% of adult Americans got most of their news from television in 2006 ... researchers found that despite the vast number of Internet service provider news sites, political Web sites, and other online sources, Americans were relying heavily on the legacy broadcast media' (Jackson 2009).

For some, the internet is positively unattractive. Many are deliberately and assertively non-users, with a recent UK report suggesting as many as 17 million people in the UK aged 16 or over do not in any way use the internet. The report also suggests that despite rising Internet use 'only 4 per cent of Internet users who read a newspaper said they only read it online', which the report suggests shows that online news is complementing rather than substituting more traditional media (Dutton et al. 2009). While the internet has been eagerly appropriated by legislators, keen to demonstrate their familiarity and involvement with new media, or even genuinely convinced that new forms of interactive engagement with their constituents were becoming possible, the evidence in the UK suggests that

> MPs [Members of Parliament] are using the Internet primarily to inform their constituents rather than engage with them. The most

widely used digital media are those which are mainly passive in nature, such as websites. Interactive forms of media which could be used by MPs to develop a two-way dialogue with their constituents, such as blogs and social networking, are used much less commonly. Where these tools are used, it is often in passive 'send' mode with few MPs exploiting their full interactive potential.

(Williamson 2009)

Beyond all this, the evidence of growing use, as yet uncertain and unconvincing, nonetheless poses questions about the impact of internet use and the availability of democratic effects – notably the growth of an informed citizenry. If internet use supplants rather than supplements prior information-seeking resources, its impact will be truncated. Pew research in the United States concluded that 'the coaxial and digital revolutions and attendant changes in news audience behaviors have had little impact on how much Americans know about national and international affairs' (Pew Research Center 2007). The research found no association between the kinds of sources enjoyed and people's knowledge of political leaders and events.

Of course the growth of the internet has had an impact not just on the consumption but on the production of news. While this is not the place to explore the implications for journalism of the growing use of the internet as a resource for information or journalistic practice (see Allan 2006), it is necessary to note how far the range and diversity of journalism can be affected by new technologies. Bird has noted how, despite the possibilities inherent in non-professional use of internet communication, in the recent past many newspapers have been closing down due to the competition of online news, while others, like *The Christian Science Monitor* (which simply dropped its weekday edition entirely), have moved almost exclusively to online formats. In the US, newspaper revenues dropped by over 18 per cent in the third quarter of 2008 (Bird 2009). In 2007 US newsrooms lost 2,400 journalists, a 4.4 per cent drop from the previous year. In 2008 the largest newspaper publisher in the country, Gannett, announced layoffs of 3,000 people, 10 per cent of its workforce. Time Inc. cut 600 jobs (Mosco 2009). CBS announced major news layoffs in April 2008, ordered up to 5 per cent job cuts at several of its local stations, and also moved ahead with plans for layoffs in network news (Jackson 2009: 160). ABC announced comparable cuts in 2008, and News Division President David Westin stated that he planned to eliminate more jobs in the future. NBC cut 700 news positions between 2006 and 2008.

The production of news in broadcast and other newsrooms also changes in form and character. In his indictment of UK journalism, Davies argues that using the internet makes journalism both more hasty and more passive, so that what he disparages as 'churnalism' becomes ever-more dependent on websites, and ever-more subject to pressures to 'break the news' first, even celebrating such triumphs in microseconds, at the expense of accuracy, while 'adopting the writing style of a robot' (Davies 2008: 71). At the same time, resources are cut but the demands for more and more material to fill more and more time accelerate.

Thus our first reservation about the flowering of democracy in the digital age derives from the diminishing range and availability of all forms of policy and political information from the mainstream media, the evident reduction in news audiences, and the as yet unconvincing evidence that the exponential growth of the internet compensates for these shifts.

Audience fragmentation

The ideal democracy assumes a shared culture and a universal integration of members of a community, however large and geographically dispersed, in some form of common set of understandings. Sociology through the ages has sought to understand the forms and limitations of these cultural forms, whether in concepts like Durkheim's *'conscience collective'* or the emerging definitions of society, as sociology began to define its terms and presumptions, in notions like Tönnies' *Gemeinschaft* and *Gesellschaft*, attempting to understand how the complexities of the modern division of labour nonetheless create, indeed presume, a balance between the self-interest of the individual and the perceived common good that generates the binding energy of a social formation. Interestingly, diagnoses of the ills of contemporary society have been fascinated by the return of social fragmentation and isolation, from Riesman's concept of the 'lonely crowd' to, more recently, the argument that social capital is disappearing, and we are increasingly 'bowling alone', separated from the ties of friends, community and neighbours, and especially of democratic association, by the collapse of civic society and the assertion of individualism (Putnam 2001).

For our present purposes the question is how far this is reflected in the fragmentation of media audiences. Paradoxically the explosion of information channels and media creates the possibility for a narrowing of their interest range in each case, fostering fragmentation of audiences and specialized consumption. What emerges is a 'special-interest mosaic', conglomerating in ever-smaller niche collectivities of interest around special concerns or activities. In a fascinating exploration of this theme Prior argues that new communication technologies increase the effort required to seek information beyond an individual's immediate interest, while lowering the cost of obtaining views and information consonant with existing interests and beliefs. Prior's empirical work suggests growing inequalities of political knowledge as a result of new technologies, and identifies growing political-participation gaps between those focused on entertainment and more politically engaged consumers (Prior 2007).

Table 16.1 Growth of multi-channel TV sources in the UK

Year	Cable	Satellite	Dtt	Total
1992	409	1893	-	2302
2002	3794	5732	794	10,320
2009	3585	9440	14,808	22,471

Source: http://www.barb.co.uk.

Table 16.2 Annual percentage share of viewing

Year	BBC1	ITV1	Others
1990	37	44	-
2000	27	29	17
2008	22	18	39

Source: http://www.barb.co.uk.

Certainly we have seen a massive growth in the use of cable and satellite as means of obtaining broadcast programming. In the UK by late 2009 almost 40 per cent of households were receiving free-to-view digital television on their main set. Almost 37 per cent were by then receiving satellite television, and cable television in the UK was in 13.2 per cent of homes (Ofcom 2009). Tables 16.1 and 16.2 show how rapidly the fragmentation of UK television audiences has advanced. In Table 16.1 we can see how from 1992 the number of households receiving television via cable or satellite grew from 2.3 million to 13 million in 2009. In Table 16.2 we can see how the audience share of the two major terrestrial channels declined from an 81 per cent share in 1990 to 40 per cent in 2008. It is hard to see evidence in such data for the survival of a shared common media culture which might form the foundation for that discursive sharing which is the currency and core of a societally integrated experience.

Surveys by the UK regulator Ofcom confirm that audiences for the major channels continue to decline while those for entertainment genres increase further. The growth of special channels and services is almost entirely within the entertainment sector. In 2007 Ofcom awarded 143 television licences. Factual channel licence applications fell from 18 in 2006 to just 4 in 2007. Audience fragmentation is a universal phenomenon where technologies advance the delivery systems available. In a review of Nielsen audience data in the US, Webster notes that 'Audience fragmentation is more advanced than is generally recognized. Polarization, the tendency of channel audiences to be composed of devotees and nonviewers, is also evident, though modest. Contrary to the "law of double jeopardy," there are now many examples of both small-but-loyal and small-but-disloyal audiences' (Webster 2005).

Thus the notion of a shared cultural experience being the unique outcome of a national broadcast or media diet is increasingly subject to the growing fragmentation of audiences. While diversity and specialization of delivery offer choice and complexity for the discerning consumer, they also signal the impossibility of seeing media output as a common culture of information and opinion for the shared consumption of a unified citizenry. This is further intensified by the commercial and commodified character of information.

Commodified culture and the 'knowledge society'

Where information is available at a price rather than uniformly and freely accessible then its consumption and use will be parallel to the array of disposable incomes, and the inequality of access to material resources, that characterize a society. The increasing integration of news with the entertainment industry speeds this process (Franklin 1997; Thussu 2007). At its most stark this produces a simple but direct clash of values. 'When the news media are expected to be purveyors of the public interest while pursuing profits for their corporate owners, the result often is a clash of capitalist and journalistic imperatives' (Jackson 2009). With the growth of pay-per-view systems and increasing competition for the attention and payments of consumers, this has enormous implications for people's capacity to obtain information, and, as we shall see below, is exacerbated by the very differential availability of communication resources at different levels in the income structure. The most assertive statement of this conflict emerged from James Murdoch, the son of News Corporation Chairman Rupert, and himself Chairman and Chief Executive, Europe and Asia, of the corporation. In his 2009 MacTaggart Lecture to the annual gathering of UK broadcasting's great and good he argued quite simply that '[w]e should ... trust consumers, embrace private enterprise and profit, and reduce the activities of the state in our sector ... The only reliable, durable and perpetual guarantor of independence is profit' (Murdoch 2009). The comparison between the annual cost of a Sky fee (roughly £600 p.a. for a basic package) and the BBC license fee (£142.50) was not mentioned, nor the growing evidence of disengagement from news broadcasting as it slid further into the maw of entertainment-led provision.

This raises considerable concerns about the supposed emergence of a 'knowledge society'. If there has been a decline in the ready availability of political and related information, and widespread evidence of a decline or at least stasis in political knowledge, then the notion of a 'knowledge society' becomes problematic. Barabas and Jerit have examined how far even a growing volume of coverage can have an impact on people's capacity to be informed. In their view '[w]hat would seem to be the most obvious determinant of media effects – the volume of coverage – is not the only or even the most important predictor of knowledge. The breadth of coverage and the

215

prominence of a story are equally powerful predictors of knowledge' (Barabas and Jerit 2009). In other words, as coverage becomes thinner and less information-rich, no amount of availability can compensate for the loss of real information available. Many have seen wider and more worrying developments arising from the diminishing availability of well-resourced, fully elaborated information based on evidence, argument and reason. At its most alarmed this diagnosis detects the emergence of an increasingly unknowing culture, in which irrationality and myth become dominant in the absence of widely available information and evidence (Thompson 2008; Wheen 2004).

One consequence, and a matter for much comment, is the evidence of growing consumer-citizen disenchantment with the political process, as the marginalization and cost of political information becomes both a cause and an effect of disengagement. This is most often noted among younger groups. In the last five years in the UK the number of 16–24 year olds who say they only follow news when something important is happening has risen from 33 to 50 per cent. At the same time TV news viewing has dropped in this age group, and is now at an average of roughly 45 minutes per week (Ofcom 2007). The view that 'much of the news on TV is not relevant to me' has increased in particular (from 44 to 64 per cent). Attempts to lure such audiences back have been in vain, despite the introduction of the 'news bunny', a live mascot who mimed the news behind the newsreader, and even, in 2004, the UK's first naked news reader, on *Get Lucky TV*. Inevitably, charges of 'tabloidization' have followed, with clear and insistent evidence of this trend over time, as also in newspapers (McLachlan and Golding 2000).

The evidence of disengagement is strong. The Hansard Society conducts annual surveys to track this trend in the UK. Their 2009 survey finds that nearly half the public (47 per cent) say they are 'not very' or 'not at all' interested in politics, while more than half claim to know 'not very much' or 'nothing at all' about politics (Hansard Society 2009). The most obvious consequence, if not necessarily the most significant, is the fall over time in voter turnout at elections (see Table 16.3).

Table 16.3 Turnout at selected UK general elections

Year	Turnout %
1950	83.9
1959	78.7
1966	75.8
1979	76
1987	75.3
1997	71.4
2005	61.4

Source: Electoral Commission 2005.

The same trend is evident in European elections. In the UK, turnout fell from 56.8 per cent in the 1994 election to 45.5 in 2004.

News, of course, is not the only form of information that both resources the actions and knowledge of the citizen and has also become increasingly commodified as a product to be purchased in the marketplace. The most obvious example beyond the news media is higher education.[1] The rise of 'borderless education' and the virtual university, and the wariness of governments drawn into ever-rising financial support for the growing higher-education sector, has increasingly driven universities in most industrial countries into commercialization of what they do and how they deliver it. Barnard notes that 'In the USA, 77 per cent of the 12.2m distance learning course enrolments for 2006/07 were completely online ... During the autumn term 2006, almost 3.5 million students in the USA were taking at least one online course and the number of online students more than doubled during a four year period' (Barnard 2009). These institutions are often massive. Examples are the University of Phoenix (the largest private university in North America and the top recipient of federal aid in 2008, receiving US$2.8 billion. Owned by the Apollo Group Inc. it trades on the NASDAQ) and Capella University Online (owned by Capella Education Company and traded on the NASDAQ since 2006, with trading revenues of $272 million in 2008, and a 25 per cent year-on-year growth rate for the last five years). An interesting third example is Kaplan University, which is owned by the Washington Post Company. The financial success of Kaplan, providing nearly half of the parent company's revenue in 2007, has led to the Company redefining itself as an education and media company. The University had 37,000 students enrolled in 2007, mainly on business and law courses.

The commercialization of universities focuses on the delivery of goods (qualifications and accreditation) for payments (fees), and distills the essence of education into the transmission of useful knowledge that can be traded for such accreditation, and thus used as a voucher and passport to improved employment opportunities (see also Bok 2003; Washburn 2005). The consequence, as in the commodification of news and entertainment, is its differential availability to audiences with different levels of disposable income, and its dilution as a resource for the exercise of active citizenship.

Explaining causes

The fourth concern about the impact of digital provision on an enriched democratic debate is the outcome of enlarged provision and competitive drive on the narrative which underpins journalism and the news. At the heart of this is what I have called 'the culpability model' in which the news narrative, espcially of social problems and issues, crystallizes around a simple linear account relating, first, the problem, second, and very quickly, the identification of a culprit, and thus, finally, a solution involving the replacement or reprimand, whether symbolic or real, of the culprit. Journalists remain the major users of Mills' first canon of explanation, and the pressures of time and of audience retention discussed above intensify these trends. Once a problem is reported it attracts an instant identification of a culprit. Examples of instant identification of culprits are legion, of course; the case of the 'unabomber' in the United States being one such (Wardle 2003). In the UK, regular cases involving complex domestic difficulties that result in the death or serious injury of a child have provoked routine demonization of social workers, as those involved are placed in the stocks of front-page accusation (Golding 1991). The coverage of the complex and extraordinary meltdown of financial institutions and, in some accounts, of the very fabric of Western capitalism, in the Credit Crunch of 2008–9, was ever eager to identify rogue bankers whose greed and failings could readily explain the causes of the crash, implying instant and relatively simple remedies. Media research has frequently focused on this tendency as 'personalization' in politics: the need to attach faces and personalities to more complex processes to make them comprehensible to audiences. But beyond this is a fundamental simplification of narrative that raises questions about the implications for democratic understanding of broadening and numerically growing items of news and 'sound bites'.

Thussu provides a particularly interesting example of this in coverage of the November 2008 terrorist attacks in Mumbai. He notes how swiftly news reporting of the events was anxious to seek culprits and simple explanations, in what he describes as 'fevered speculation'. He argues that the amalgamation of news with entertainment in the Indian media meant that 'in a market-driven broadcasting environment, the urge to present sensation and spectacle rather than cover substantive stories is almost a commercial imperative' (Thussu 2009).

Thus the integration of news and entertainment, and the explosive growth in volume but perhaps not complexity, of information provision, raise questions about the implications of digital multiplication for the contribution of digital media to democractic enrichment. This brings us to our final concern.

Digitization and social division

The concept of the 'digital divide' has been subject to repeated attack since its application to the discovery that the rapid spread of new communication technologies was not following the simple 's-shaped' curve of previous generations, in which early adopters found themselves soon caught up by late adopters, as technologies such as domestic 'white goods' became more familiar and moved from being luxuries to becoming staple household necessities. Because the new technologies were themselves rapidly changing, requiring recurrent expenditure and consumer investment, and because they entailed substantial expenditure on 'software' or accessories of varying kinds, the advantages of the better-off remained intact, and the digital divide stubbornly persisted. Nonetheless, opposition to the simpler formulations of the digital divide have continued to suggest, first, that this is simply a transitional phase en route to near universal ownership and access, and, secondly, that the division should better be understood as multi-dimensional, resulting not just from differential ownership of hardware and equipment, but from inequities of skill, digital literacy, opportunity and motivation (these issues are explored in Murdock and Golding, forthcoming).

In fact the evidence increasingly shows that diffusion of the internet is becoming more, rather than less, polarized by family income. Examining US data on internet access and use, Martin and Robinson found that 'the odds of access increased most rapidly for individuals at highest family income levels and most slowly for individuals with the lowest income levels' (Martin and Robinson 2007). In the UK, home access to the internet has certainly continued to rise, so that by 2009 18 million households had some form of internet access, of which the majority had broadband access. Nonetheless, the divisions of ownership across households in different income bands have continued to be palpable, as illustrated in Table 16.4.

As these data show, among poorer households computer access is still only available to a minority, and this remains true even in the third least poor quintile. Among the poorest 10 per cent of households in 2009 fewer than a quarter had internet access. The same gradient is apparent for other communication goods, even though social need among those with limited or no opportunities for travel or for effective contact outside the home might well be assumed to be greatest. That this division is so stubborn raises important doubts about the potential for digital technologies, increasingly market-oriented and available only at a price which has to compete with many other pressing demands on household incomes, which are themselves increasingly differentiated, to contribute to the universal provision of information and symbolic resources that are the lifeblood of democracy.

Table 16.4 Ownership of communications goods by income group (UK, 2007) % in each income group

	Home computer	Internet connection	Telephone	Mobile phone	Satellite receiver*	DVD player
All households	70	61	89	78	77	86
Poorest 10 per cent	35	24	72	60	56	67
Third decile group	45	36	87	67	71	78
Fifth decile group	72	60	89	85	80	90
Richest 10 per cent	97	95	98	91	87	97

Note: * includes digital and cable

Conclusion: the policy response

There remain, then, a number of doubts about the current capacity of digital communications to enrich the broadcasting environment in such a way as to ensure the enhancement and renewal of democratic debate and participation. This is not to sound an incontrovertibly pessimistic obstacle to welcoming the potential of such technologies. But it does at least require pause before undue euphoria. The promise is of hugely improved opportunities for participation and engagement, as people become more informed and increasingly better equipped to undertake their role as citizens in a vibrant and mature democracy. This chapter has addressed a number of reservations that suggest this optimism, if not misplaced, should at least be subject to critical appraisal. The increase in broadcast provision has not always, nor inevitably, led to more and better political information for audiences. The internet is not used especially for information-seeking, and is only very differentially available in ways that directly mirror income inequality. Audiences, far from increasingly sharing a common cultural experience, are becoming more fragmented, and even polarized. Cultural resources for citizenship, whether those provided by the old or the new media, or in institutions like education, are becoming commodified in ways that make market opportunity rather than social membership the criterion for obtaining them. As journalism becomes increasingly entangled in the provision of entertainment forms, simplification of journalistic narrative poses obstacles to the analysis and complexity which democratic understanding so often requires. Finally, the much derided digital divide seems obstinately characteristic of the diffusion of new communication technologies.

Many of these difficulties are rooted in the familiar contradiction between construing audiences as either consumers or as citizens. On the one hand they are selecting and purchasing cultural goods and services in the marketplace in ways that reflect their needs and shape provision. Alternatively, they are provided with access to a comprehensive set of symbolic resources that are, in effect, a cultural commons, allowing all to engage with the democratic process in a fully informed and participatory manner. This dilemma was at the core of an assessment of the regulator's role undertaken by the UK regulator, Ofcom, in 2008. In attempting to consider the problems of serving these two needs Ofcom finds itself uncomfortably squaring a circle:

> Ofcom believes that the interests of consumers are usually served by promoting competitive markets, although regulatory intervention is also needed to protect consumers from harmful practices and ensure that they have the information they need to make informed choices. Citizens' interests are also served by the market, which has an

important role to play in delivering innovative services and increased choice.

(Ofcom 2008: Paragraph 2.4)

Thus the role of the regulator, rather than recognizing any fundamental contradiction between liberating the market for the consumer and protecting the interest of the citizen, is, in fact, to assume they are complementary interests. 'Ofcom's role in furthering the interests of consumers involves making markets work better ... ' (ibid.: Paragraph 5.1). The report struggles to keep these two objectives in tune, but not entirely convincingly:

> Ofcom's role in furthering the interests of citizens involves ensuring that people have access to the services, content and skills needed to participate in society, and that they are protected appropriately. To some extent, the market will deliver these aims, so meeting the needs of society will certainly not always require regulatory intervention.
>
> (ibid.: Paragraph 2.27)

The debate inherent in this report will clearly continue, as digital broadcasting, and the new media more generally, demonstrate both the potential for fully liberating and excitingly progressive enrichment of democratic society, but also the daunting prospect of a narrowed and technologically enhanced inhibition of participation and engagement. Neither path is inevitable, and technology is neither the cause nor the reason for either. Understanding and then addressing both the possibilities inherent in new communication technologies and the political and social action required to realize those potentialities will, as always, determine our future.

Note

1 This section draws on research by my doctoral student and colleague Sarah Barnard. See Barnard (2009).

References

Allan, Stuart (2006) *Online News: Journalism and the Internet*. Milton Keynes: Open University Press.

Barabas, Jason and Jerit, Jennifer (2009) 'Estimating the causal effects of media coverage on policy-specific knowledge', *American Journal of Political Science* 53 (1), pp. 73–89.

Barnard, Sarah (2009) 'Virtual universities and the commodification of higher education'. Unpublished work.

Barnett, Steven and Seymour, Emily (1999) 'A shrinking iceberg travelling south: Changing trends in British television: A case study of drama and current affairs', Campaign for Press and Broadcasting Freedom, London.

BBC Governance Unit (2005) 'Governors' genre review: Current affairs television', BBC, London.

Bird, S. Elizabeth (2009) 'The future of journalism in the digital environment', *Journalism* 10 (3), pp. 293–95.

Bok, Derek (2003) *Universities in the Market Place – the Commercialisation of Higher Education*. Princeton, NJ: Princeton University Press.

Davies, Nick (2008) *Flat Earth News*, London: Chatto & Windus.

Dutton, William H., Helsper, Ellen J. and Gerber, Monica M. (2009) 'The Internet in Britain 2009', Oxford Internet Institute, Oxford.

Electoral Commission (2005) 'Election 2005: Turnout – how many, who and why?' The Electoral Commission, London.

Franklin, Bob (1997) *Newszak and News Media*, London: Arnold.

Golding, P. (2000) 'Forthcoming features: information and communications technologies and the sociology of the future', *Sociology* 34 (1), pp. 165–84.

Golding, Peter (1991) 'Do-gooders on display: Social work, public attitudes, and the mass media', in Bob Franklin and Nigel Parton (eds) *Social Work, the Media and Public Relations*, London: Routledge, pp. 88–104.

Hansard Society (2009) 'Audit of political engagement 6: The 2009 Report', March 2009, Hansard Society, London, http://www.hansardsociety.org.uk/blogs/publications/archive/2009/04/01/audit-of-political-engagement-6.aspx. Accessed 1 September 2009.

Jackson, Pamela Taylor (2009) 'News as a contested commodity: A clash of capitalist and journalistic imperatives', *Journal of Mass Media Ethics* 24 (2), pp. 146–63.

Lauf, Edmund (2001) 'The vanishing young reader: Sociodemographic determinants of newspaper use as a source of political information in Europe, 1980–98', *European Journal of Communication* 16 (2), pp. 233–43.

Martin, Steven P. and Robinson, John P. (2007) 'The income digital divide: Trends and predictions for levels of Internet use', *Social Problems* 54 (1), pp. 1–22.

McLachlan, Shelley and Golding, Peter (2000) 'Tabloidisation in the British press: A quantitative investigation into changes in British newspapers, 1952–97', in Colin Sparks and John Tulloch (eds) *Tabloid Tales: Global Debates over Media Standards*, New York and Oxford: Rowman and Littlefield, pp. 75–89.

Mosco, Vincent (2009) 'The future of journalism', *Journalism* 10 (3), pp. 350–52.

Murdoch, James (2009) 'The absence of trust – MacTaggart lecture 2009', Edinburgh TV Festival, Edinburgh, http://www.centreforjournalism.co.uk/blogs/james-murdoch-mactaggart-lecture-full-text. Accessed 1 September 2009.

Murdock, Graham and Golding, Peter (eds) (forthcoming) *Digital Dynamics*, Cresskill, NJ: Hampton Press.

Nason, Sarah and Redding, Don (2002) 'Losing reality: Factual international programming on UK television, 2000–2001', 3WE, London, available at http://www.ibt.org.uk/3WE/Research/LosingRealityTop.htm. Accessed 30 August 2009.

Newspaper Association of America (2009) 'Readership Trends', NAA, Washington.

OECD (2009) 'OECD Key ICT indicators', OECD, http://www.oecd.org/document/23/0,3343_en_2649_34449_33987543_1_1_1_37441,00.html. Accessed 1 September 2009.

Ofcom (2006) 'The Provision of Current Affairs', London: Ofcom.

Ofcom (2007) 'New News, Future News: The challenges for television news after Digital Switch-over', London: Ofcom.

Ofcom (2008) 'Citizens, Communications and Convergence', London: Ofcom.

Ofcom (2009) 'Digital television update – 2009', London: Ofcom.

Office for National Statistics (2008) 'Family spending 2007', London: ONS.

Office for National Statistics (2009) 'Statistical bulletin: Internet access: Households and individuals 2009', London: ONS.

Pew Research Center (2007) 'What Americans know: 1989–2007', Washington: Pew Research Center.

Prior, Markus (2007) *Post-Broadcast Democracy: How Media Choice Increases Inequality in Political Involvement and Polarizes Elections*, New York: Cambridge University Press.

Putnam, Robert D. (2001) *Bowling Alone: The Collapse and Revival of American Community*, New York: Touchstone Books.

Select Committee on Communications (2008) 'The ownership of the news', House of Lords, London. HL Paper 122–I.

Thompson, Damian (2008) *Counterknowledge*, London: Atlantic Books.

Thussu, Daya (2007) *News as Entertainment: The Rise of Global Infotainment*, London: Sage.

Thussu, Daya (2009) 'Turning terrorism into a soap opera', *British Journalism Review* 20 (1), pp. 13–18.

Wardle, Claire (2003) 'The "Unabomber" vs. the "Nail Bomber": A cross-cultural comparison of newspaper coverage of two murder trials', *Journalism Studies* 4 (2), pp. 239–51.

Washburn, Jennifer (2005) *University Inc. The Corruption of Higher Education*, New York: Basic Books.

Webster, James G. (2005) 'Beneath the veneer of fragmentation: Television audience polarization in a multichannel world', *Journal of Communication* 55 (2), pp. 366–82.

Wheen, Francis (2004) *How Mumbo-Jumbo Conquered the World*, London: Harper Perennial.

Williamson, Andy (2009) 'MPs online: Connecting with constituents – A study into how MPs use digital media to communicate with their constituents', Hansard Society, London.

17

NETWORKING THE COMMONS

Convergence culture and the public interest

Graham Murdock

Casting around for a potent metaphor that captures the way two decades of marketization have accelerated the commercialization of public culture, a number of commentators have compared it to the enclosure of common land that began with the new agricultural entrepreneurs of Tudor England erecting fences around previously open spaces and aggressively protecting their extended possessions, with additional penalties for trespassing (see Murdock 2001). For the critical lawyer James Boyle, the corporate push to extend the terms and reach of commercial copyright and impose tougher sanctions on unauthorized use is a 'second enclosure movement' fencing off 'the commons of the mind' (Boyle 2008). Since 1978 the period before copyrighted material passes into the public domain in the United States has almost tripled, from 32 years to 95 years, producing a swelling chorus of critics claiming that 'copyright has become too strong' (Vaidhyanathan 2006: 43). For Lawrence Lessig, another major dissenting voice, by outlawing the remixing and reuse of a wide range of cultural materials the current copyright regime 'makes it difficult, and sometimes impossible, for a wide range of creativity that any free society – if it thought about it for just a minute – would allow to exist legally' (Lessig 2008: 18). It is a dramatic narrative with strongly drawn protagonists and a clear central conflict, but it has little or nothing to say about the role of cultural provision underwritten by government, and funded mainly or solely out of central and local taxation.

The contested commons

The cultural domain is formed by the intersection of three economies: of commodities, public goods and gifts (Murdock 2007). Each contributes to the cultural commons, but on radically different terms.

The commodity economy operates through the price system and advertising subsidy. For a wide range of cultural goods or services, access is conditional on paying the price producers demand. This has two consequences. First, by excluding those unable to afford the sums asked it makes economic capacity a major determinant of cultural experience. Second, it constructs that experience around private ownership and personal pleasure. Cultural commodities either cannot be shared (as with a cinema seat) or can only be shared in limited ways. Family members and friends can watch subscription television services together and paperback books can be sold to second-hand dealers or donated to charity shops. These restrictions do not apply to free-to-air commercial television services since the costs are borne by advertisers paying for access to audiences, but this subsidy carries cultural costs.

By giving advertisers guaranteed access to screen time on payment of a fee it extends unique privileges to a particular world view. Audiences are hailed as consumers in the advertising breaks that interrupt programmes, in the sponsorship material that surrounds them and, increasingly, in the product placements that furnish studios and locations and are integrated into the flow of on-screen dialogue. Foregrounding product promotion squeezes the space available for other voices, other identities, other ways of looking. Diversity of expression is further restricted by advertiser demands for audience maximization and the pressure this exerts on creative choices by favouring variations on already popular themes and genres rather than risky experiments with minority or unfamiliar forms. This disincentive to challenge pre-existing tastes and preconceptions has long been regarded as a 'market failure', even among dedicated supporters of private enterprise. As one of the most influential early British manifestos for greater competition in broadcast markets pointed out: 'There will always be a need ... for programmes of a public service kind supported by people in their capacity as citizens and voters but unlikely to be commercially self-supporting in the view of broadcasting entrepreneurs' (Home Office 1986: 133).

Public-service broadcasting, which developed in the years after the First World War, was designed to address this shortfall in market provision. It arrived to find an extensive array of cultural resources supported by the public purse already in place. Some were institutions: public libraries, museums, galleries and adult-education centres. Others were public spaces: parks, recreation grounds, sports fields, city squares and piazzas. Taken together they made up a public cultural commons offering an array of opportunities for acquiring new knowledge and skills, deliberating on issues of the day, developing self-expression, staging self-organized cultural activities and accessing professionally produced art, music, literature and performance. The history of its modern formation is coterminous with the account that Jürgen Habermas offers of the development of the public sphere, which he sees as made up of two separate systems: a political public sphere and a literary public sphere. His major concern is with the constitution of democratic participation as a grounded practice, rooted in collective deliberation on public issues. His historical account nominates newspapers free of state control as the key informational and analytical resource for deliberation, and the coffee houses of London as prototypical arenas for its everyday enactment. At the same time he sees the 'heart to heart' interaction between novelists and their readers as the central imaginative space for cultivating self-knowledge and empathy (Habermas 1991: 50). These qualities, in turn, are essential preconditions for the openness, respect and willingness to change one's mind when given good reasons that effective deliberation requires. Despite the importance of expressive and creative activity to democratic politics, Habermas has never explored its organization in any detail. Other writers have set out to develop more comprehensive conceptions of this second, 'cultural', public sphere, but it remains a fuzzy conception that includes commercial enterprise alongside public provision. This has the effect of blurring the differences in the way each constitutes cultural life and cultivates identities and dispositions.

Where the commercial cultural commons privileges personal possession and satisfaction and the role of the consumer, the public cultural commons promotes shared use and invites participants to think of themselves as citizens, coupling the right to participate fully in social and cultural life with the injunction to contribute to the vitality of communal provision. Its rationale is providing cultural resources for citizenship rather than profit maximization. Realizing the goals of open and equal access and shared use was no easy matter, however. First, because public cultural facilities were concentrated in specific geographical sites they were only available to those who could afford to travel to them. Second, attempting to generalize access to unique or scarce resources created its own problems. Someone else may have borrowed the library book. Crowds gathered around a famous painting or exhibit obscured a clear view and militated against full enjoyment.

Broadcasting offered a technological solution to both these problems. No matter how large the audience for a particular programme might be, everyone with the appropriate receiving set and aerial could access it at the same time without interfering with anyone else's enjoyment. These qualities of being non-excludable and non-rival applied equally to commercial and non-commercial services and defined both as public goods in the terminology of economics. What distinguished the public-service variant was its concern with the 'public good' as an ethical ideal and its commitment to enhancing the quality of collective life by providing comprehensive symbolic resources for citizenship. To this end, it took on the roles of every other public cultural arena and wrapped them up into a continuous stream of programming. It presented itself as a concert hall, theatre, debating club, adult-education service and library of the air.

From the outset, however, there were continual conflicts over which voices and expressive forms were to be included and which ruled inadmissible, which were to be celebrated and which dismissed. Some of these struggles took place within the cultural establishment, between the academy and the avant-garde, the old guard and the young lions, the metropole and the regions, but the most entrenched division was between professionals and amateurs. Those who made their living from producing or commenting on legitimated expressive forms claimed privileged access to broadcasting's institutional spaces largely excluding the activities of non-professionals. Amateur performances featured in talent shows and vernacular narratives provided much of the raw material for documentary and feature programmes, but what was broadcast was only a tiny fraction of the mass of amateur creativity taking place on a daily basis, from brass bands to local choirs, amateur photographers, Sunday painters and part-time writers. With the rapid growth of docusoaps and 'reality TV', the last two decades have seen an increasing amount of air-time given over to ordinary lives, but, with the rare exception of programmes where professional producers have ceded or shared editorial control, the orchestration of voice and visibility has remained firmly in the hands of professionals.

Over the last decade, however, broadcasting's central position in the organization of the contemporary cultural commons has been increasingly challenged by the rapid expansion of the internet, particularly by its most extensively available domain, the World Wide Web. The increasing speed and processing power of laptop computers and broadband connections, combined with the internet's migration to mobile phones and other digital devices, has substantially increased the range and flexibility of Web use, providing a platform for an upsurge of vernacular creativity and peer-to-peer exchange. As Clay Shirky notes, 'Never have so many people been free to say and do so many things with so many other people' (Shirky 2008: 122–23). As he points out, however, online exchange relations operate at various levels requiring different degrees of commitment from participants. The least involving is sharing, typified by blogging, the videos put up on YouTube, and the personal advice and opinions on travel, hotels, books, and so on contributed to grass-roots recommendation sites. Sharing is primarily a form of self-expression and display. The next stage on is cooperation, where participants contribute to making a site easier or more pleasurable for others to use by, for example, adding keyword tags to the personal photographs posted on the file-sharing site Flickr. This extra effort may or may not provide a basis for the additional investment demanded by truly collaborative projects. The example most commented on so far is the Open Source movement, in which computer programmers cooperated to develop a range of free software tools as alternatives to the products sold by Microsoft and other commercial corporations. Their robustness was guaranteed by the open invitation issued to anyone able to improve the existing programme. The same principle of inviting 'anyone to initiate an entry ... and to keep editing and altering whatever is already there' (Runciman 2009: 14) also underpins another frequently quoted example of online collaboration: Wikipedia.

These various forms of Web-based sharing, cooperation and collaboration make up a third cultural economy, an economy of gifts, based not on the price system or advertising payments (as with commodified culture) or on subsidies from taxation (as with public goods) but on the principle of reciprocity, and the expectation that time and labour donated will be matched by other participants.

Romantic accounts of this emerging economy, and the cultural commons of gifts that it supports, see it as entirely open and inclusive, a spontaneous explosion of popular creativity and grass-roots collectivism. As the Open Source movement illustrates, however, amateur involvement sits alongside initiatives that are more usefully seen as a democratization of expertise. For Linus Torvalds, the main initiator of the Linux open-source operating system, computer programmers have an 'ethical duty ... to share their expertise by writing free software and facilitating access to information and computing resources wherever possible' (Torvalds 2001: vii). Although Wikipedia currently has over 2.8 million entries in its English-language edition, fewer than 2 per cent of users have ever contributed (Shirky 2008: 125). These instances are closer to established models of 'mass' communication than to genuine reciprocity in action. A more collaborative pattern of relations between amateurs and professionals is provided by the online newspaper *Oh MyNews*, one of the most successful examples to date of citizen journalism. Originally launched in South Korea but now with international editions, it relies on a network of non-professionals for stories but retains a full-time editorial team. A similar division of labour was developed within the BBC for the Video Diaries project. The original footage was shot by amateurs on their topics of choice but the editorial process was overseen by professional programme-makers.

These variations in the terms of online participation have not curbed the enthusiasm of more utopian commentators. For Kevin Kelly, the founding executive editor of *Wired*, '[w]hen masses of people who own the means of production work towards a common goal and share their products in common, ... contribute their labour without wages and enjoy the fruits free of charge, it's not unreasonable to call that socialism' (Kelly 2009: 122). If we look again at the examples cited above, however, we see this vision of 'digital socialism' punctured by the familiar dynamics of 'free' market enterprise.

The fact that contributors to free sites are unpaid does not mean that there are no personal rewards for their efforts. A study of the photos of a parade in New York posted on Flickr revealed that half of the 3,000 images came from the 10 most active users and 1 in 12 from just one person (Shirky 2008: 123). This unequal distribution is typical of social media websites more generally and alerts us to a hidden economy of returns. As Marcel Mauss argued, in his classic meditation on gift relations, gifts are 'not freely given [but] made with a view to maintaining a profitable alliance'

(Mauss [1950]1990: 73). This point applies with particular force to digital exchange. As the general creative economy moves increasingly towards free-lance working, so visibility and social connections become more and more important in securing employment. 'In the economy of ideas that the web is creating, you are what you share – who you are linked to, who you network with' (Leadbeater 2008: 6). Interventions by freelance cultural workers and those cherishing hopes of making a living in the creative industries may occupy a central position in online exchange, but for some commentators the real significance of digital networks still lies with the proliferating mass of amateur contributions.

For John Hartley, far from being trivial and marginal, the online creative activity of 'millions of teenagers – extending to whole populations – forms the enabling infrastructure' (Hartley 2009: 70) of an emerging knowledge economy in which the locus of innovation is moving decisively from a 'closed expert value chain controlled by "industry" [to] a complex open system in which everyone is an active agent' (ibid.: 63). This vision of a people's capitalism conveniently ignores the fact that the internet has expanded within the same time frame as the concerted global push towards market-ization and an unprecedented consolidation of corporate reach and power in the cultural sphere (see Murdock and Wasko 2007). These developments are increasingly intertwined.

Cultural production has been seen as central to post-industrial capitalism for some time, but the financial crisis of 2008 has invested its development with a new sense of urgency. Faced with the decimation of traditional man-ufacturing and the collapse of trust in a pivotal area of the service sector, exploiting competitive advantages in communications and the arts has moved rapidly up the list of priorities for both governments and enterprises. As Stephen Carter, the British minister responsible for this sector, told a journalist in the autumn of 2008:

> We're as good at the poetry as we are at the pipes [and given] that in the short, and possibly medium term, the financial services sector is going to take some time to restructure, from a UK plc perspective, this important sector becomes relatively an even more important sector.
> (Gibson 2008)

This altered context has given an added impetus to corporate efforts to exploit the business opportunities presented by digital exchange networks. The result is what Henry Jenkins has dubbed 'convergence culture'.

Capitalizing on convergence

Jenkins sees this new culture being formed at the point where 'top-down decisions made in corporate boardrooms by companies wishing to tap their cross-media ownership' intersect with, or 'converge' with, the 'bottom-up decisions made in teens' bedrooms' (Jenkins 2006: 1). The result, in his account, is an entirely virtuous business circuit. Media conglomerates exploit 'branded properties' such as Harry Potter across a range of 'platforms' and commodities – books, films, toys, video games, merchandise – providing multiple 'raw materials which fans then want to recombine in new ways and thus generate new forms of cultural expression' (ibid.: 2). 'Shrewd companies [then] tap this culture to foster consumer loyalty and generate low cost content' (Jenkins 2001: 93). To assist them in this, Jenkins has established a Convergence Culture Consortium at MIT offering 'companies looking to understand new strategies for doing business in a converging media environment ... insights into new ways to relate to consumers, manage brands, and develop engaging experiences' (Convergence Culture Consortium 2009: 1).

Music companies, who have been hit particularly hard by illegal downloading, have been experimenting with new ways of managing their brands by 'monetizing' online access to their catalogues. Spotify, for example, has built up a customer base of 2 million British users for its music-streaming service. The music companies license their content for a small fee and users enjoy free access in return for accepting ads. Music companies are also striking deals with Internet Service Providers and mobile-phone companies to develop unlimited download services over their networks (Wray 2009: 11). Other corporations are experimenting with harnessing the intrinsic satisfactions of sharing ideas and experiences over digital networks in their marketing campaigns. Unilever, for example, signed a deal with Christine Dolce, who appears on MySpace as ForBiddeN, to promote their male deodorant, Axe, by targeting the 90,000 'friends' linked to her site. The promotional interactive game she hosted attracted 75,000 MySpace users. Facebook, another major social-networking site, has launched 'engagement ads', encouraging users to invite friends to become fans of a brand and cementing loyalty through exclusive advertiser-created gifts. The intention is to get 'brands to interact with consumers in the same kind of way consumers interact with each other' (Brand Republic 2008). In pursuit of this aim, Proctor and Gamble have launched Tremor, a network of carefully selected young people who are involved in product development and are encouraged to publicize new brands on their own websites and in everyday conversation. They are not paid for their participation. They are rewarded with exclusive previews and samples of new products and the sense of being 'insiders' and 'in the know'. They are not obliged to tell anyone that they are working for the company. This is a specific instance of the more general strategy of viral marketing, where promotional messages are transmitted from person to person. Altered advertisements are another case in point.

The chocolate manufacturer Cadbury recently promoted a product line with a television ad showing a gorilla drumming to a well-known rock song.

It was immediately posted across a range of file-sharing sites, both in its original form and in altered variants produced by fans. Although all these activities violated copyright, the returns to the corporation in terms of increased visibility and an enhanced image of the brand as cool and of the moment were both very substantial and cost-free.

Corporations are also experimenting with ways of co-opting user creativity into the production system itself. John Fluevog, a manufacturer of expensive shoes, for example, invited customers to submit ideas for new lines. The originators of designs selected for production would not receive any payment but would have the symbolic reward of seeing their names emblazoned across the finished shoes (Tapscott and Williams 2008: 129). While this arrangement gives young designers wanting to break into the market an opportunity to showcase their talents, the returns to them are more than outweighed by the benefits to the company of 'outsourcing' the costs of research and development.

Connectivities

In his analysis of the shifting distribution of power in contemporary capitalism, Manuel Castells has no hesitation in placing control over symbolization and communication at the centre. His central argument is simple and familiar. Force by itself is never enough to secure popular consent and compliance on a durable basis. This requires command over the terms of reasoning and hope and, since communications media are the primary source of the narratives, information and imagery which shape everyday thinking, 'communication networks are' by definition 'the fundamental networks of power-making in society' (Castells 2009: 426). One can take issue with his underestimation of the role of force, both military and economic, in shoring up existing arrangements and inequalities, but he is right to argue that cultural life has become a central site of struggle between competing identities, explanations of the present, and proposals for the future.

The main parties to this contest do not act alone, however. Rather, Castells argues, 'Networks of power in various domains are networked among themselves. They do not merge. Instead, they [practice] cooperation and competition simultaneously by forming ad hoc networks around specific projects' (ibid.: 426). To operate successfully, however, these coalitions need to be effectively coordinated. Consequently, for Castells, 'in a world of networks' one of the key capacities is 'the ability to connect and ensure the cooperation of different networks by sharing common goals and combining resources, while fending off competition from other networks by setting up strategic cooperation' (ibid.: 45). He dubs the agencies who take on this role 'switchers', and offers an extended analysis of the way Rupert Murdoch moves between power blocs, cementing connections that deliver competitive advantages to his own News International Corporation while, at the same time, securing an overall operating environment that benefits commercial entrepreneurship in general.

This analysis raises the intriguing question of whether it is possible to locate a 'switcher' within the public cultural domain capable of taking the lead in constructing a networked public commons that can match the range and reach of the commercialized commons. I want to suggest that it is, and that public-service broadcasting is the most plausible candidate (Murdock 2005), but before exploring this argument in more detail we need to look at the ways public cultural institutions have responded to the rise of the internet.

Net gains

As we noted earlier, the ability of public cultural institutions to make their holdings and expertise as widely available as possible has historically been limited by time and space constraints. Museums and libraries are only open at certain times and can only be accessed by travelling to a particular location. In the early 1950s, Andre Malraux, later to become France's longest-serving Minister of Culture, published a book entitled *Museum Without Walls*, celebrating the role of postcard reproductions in extending popular access to the works of art held in museums. Digitalization has the potential to move public cultural holdings outside institutional walls and promote open, flexible access on an unprecedented scale. By allowing all public cultural institutions to follow broadcasting in becoming non-excludable and non-rival, it lays the basis for an economy of public goods in the full sense of the term. Materials that have been consigned to basements for lack of space can now be displayed online in their entirety. Fragile objects can be viewed in virtual form without damaging them. Recordings of historic performances can be downloaded at any time. The curatorial expertise and contextual information formerly confined to printed catalogues, programmes and written archives can be made readily accessible. Full realization of these possibilities is still some way off. Digitalization is expensive and its pace depends on the funds available. But the internet is not simply an enhanced means of distribution, it is also, crucially, a space of interactivity, and the websites established by public institutions are already experimenting with developing new relations with their users.

Convergence cultures are formed at the points where cultural economies intersect. Most commentators have followed Henry Jenkins in focusing on the way commercial corporations are busily forging new relations between the economy of commodities and the economy of gifts. The first step in building a public cultural commons for the digital age is to develop a counter set of relations linking the new online gift economy to the economy of public goods. Public broadcasting has been in the vanguard of this effort. The BBC offers an instructive instance. Promoting sharing has become increasingly central to its audience-building strategies. Viewers and listeners

are urged to contribute their comments to the message boards around programmes, to send in eyewitness accounts and photographs of events, and
to post video diaries of their lives and aspirations. These interventions
may also form the basis for genuinely collaborative activity in which the
news coverage or documentation offered on the Corporation's website combines professionally crafted material and expert analysis with grass-roots
contributions. Commemoration of the First World War for example,
involved viewers and listeners donating family photographs and personal
diaries to an online archive.

Reconfiguring convergence on an institution-by-institution basis is necessary for developing a revivified public cultural sphere, but it is not sufficient
in itself. Dispersed initiatives need to be connected up.

Connecting the public commons

Public cultural institutions have tended to develop in parallel rather than in
combination. They have drawn on dedicated forms of training and expertise
and generated exclusive practices. This professional separation has been
reinforced by the intensifying competition for public and private funding.
The compulsory licence fee that funds the BBC is unusual in being a hypo-
thecated or 'earmarked' tax that cannot be used for any other purpose.
Funding for other public institutions comes out of general taxation and has
to compete with other demands on the public purse. As these demands
have escalated, squeezing cultural funding, commercial subsidy has become
increasingly important as an alternative source of support. While corporate
sponsorship underwrites acquisitions, exhibitions and performances that
would not be possible otherwise, by integrating them into strategies for
enhancing public relations and brand awareness, it detaches them from
the culture of public goods and repositions them within the culture of
commodities.

The leading commercial internet search engine, Google, is currently digi-
talizing the entire collections of a number of the world's leading libraries,
including the New York Public Library. The resulting archives, which none
of these institutions could afford to generate themselves, offer readers
unprecedented flexibility in locating, retrieving and using materials.
Providing a text is out of copyright, it can be accessed in its entirety without
payment. But if it is still covered by copyright, readers are only allowed to
see extracts and anyone wanting the full copy is directed to libraries or
retailers where it can be borrowed or purchased in the normal way. This
produces the paradoxical situation in which access to the original copies
is limited by geography but unlimited at the point of use while virtual
access is infinitely mobile but use is conditional on the ability to pay.

There is no question that public funding will be squeezed still further in
the coming years as governments struggle to reduce the very high levels of

public debt incurred in bailing out banks and shoring up the 'real' economy. It is against this background that the BBC has been developing a series of partnerships and collaborations with other cultural and media institutions. Some of these moves, like the decision to share video news clips with leading national newspapers, are damage-limitation exercises designed to head off mounting criticism that the success of its website is stifling commercial initiatives with less secure funding and that its commercial ventures, such as it recent acquisition of the *Lonely Planet* travel guides, constitute unfair competition. On the other hand, the collaborative arrangement being developed with other major public cultural institutions, including the Arts Council, the National Theatre, the British Library and the British Museum, suggests that the BBC is taking on the role of 'switcher'. As the Corporation's creative director, Alan Yentob, has noted, acting 'as a broker in these times' is 'the next stage for us' (Thorpe 2009: 1). There is also scope for new interventions in the organization of deliberation on key public issues. The *GM Nation?* debate offers an instructive case study.

Launched by the British government in June 2003 as a month-long exercise in sustained public consultation and discussion, the initiative generated deliberation across a wide range of sites. In addition to the four national meetings organized by the Steering Board and the 40 public meetings sponsored by local councils or national organizations, there were over six hundred meetings organized by local community groups and a dedicated official website offering information and opportunities to register views. This diversity of on- and off-line activity was reproduced in the contributions made by public broadcasting. There were editions of the main discussion programme formats dedicated to the issue. Viewers and listeners were invited to contribute comments and arguments to two major domains on the BBC's website. There was even an episode of *The Archers*, the long-running radio soap opera set in a rural community, that staged a debate among the residents in the village hall. There was, however, little or no cross-fertilization between these various inputs. The key challenge for the future 'is to find creative ways of linking argumentation on-air and on-line with deliberations taking place off-line and live in a multiplicity of venues' (Horlick-Jones et al. 2007: 158).

In taking on the role of 'switcher', connecting up key nodes of public knowledge, expression and deliberative activity, the BBC, and public-service broadcasting institutions in general, enjoy four substantial advantages. First, given that viewers will have to embrace digital technology when governments switch off analogue signals, and that the new sets will be internet-enabled, television offers new opportunities to extend access and address the digital divides that have historically characterized Web use. Second, although continually contested, the funding base of public-service broadcasting has tended to be more secure than other public cultural institutions. Third, the cultural resources provided by broadcasting remain central to most people's everyday symbolic experience. As the success of the BBC's website and iPlayer, which allows viewers to stream programmes over the internet for up to a week (and sometimes longer) after their initial broadcast, demonstrate, the solution to audience migration from off-air transmission to Web-based engagement is to move online. Fourth, and perhaps most importantly, public-service broadcasting enjoys high levels of public trust.

Trust provides the essential basis for another key aspect of managing 'switching' and convergence effectively: acting as a trusted gateway and navigation aid to Web-based resources. Public broadcasters are ideally placed to become the portal of choice for users wishing to locate the non-commercial resources they need to pursue issues raised by programmes or Web postings or their own concerns and experiences. These resources would be drawn from public cultural institutions and civil-society organizations and provide access to the widest possible range of reliable information free from commercial promotion, authoritative analysis and contextualization, debate and critique, and professional and vernacular creative expression. To compete effectively with commercial provision, however, a public portal would need to facilitate personalization so that users could link it with their own email and social-networking sites. As the head of Yahoo Europe noted, launching his company's new-look homepage, which incorporates these facilities, 'one size fits all no longer works' (Clark 2009: 42).

Enemies of promise

Any proposal to extend the range of activities public-service broadcasters engage in will be fiercely resisted by corporate interests. Time spent with public cultural institutions is time lost to product promotion. The more people gain from public services the more likely they are to support public investment, and the more tangible the idea of the common good becomes. The more often they are invited to contribute to collective cultural life and benefit from other people's gift giving the less often they are likely to think of themselves primarily as consumers. The battle lines are already drawn, with mounting calls for the further privatization of public cultural assets, the redirection of public subsidy to commercial enterprise, the introduction or reintroduction of charges for access, and the end of net neutrality, so that public communication over the internet no longer enjoys equal status with the commercial traffic generated by paid-for services (such as film and video on demand) and is relegated to slower lanes on the digital highway. Castells is right to argue that 'preserving a free internet' as the essential 'foundation of a new public space' for the digital age is a central struggle of our time (Castells 2009: 414–15). This is not simply because the internet massively extends popular access to information, voice and expression. What is needed is not simply a new public space but a new public cultural commons built around the intersections between the established economy of public goods and the emerging economy of gifts. Public-service broadcasting has an indispensable role to play in securing and fostering these connections.

Acknowledgements

My thanks to all those participants in the 'Television and the Digital Public Sphere' conference in Paris, 22–24 October 2008, who commented on an earlier version of the material presented here, and to friends at Fudan University, Shanghai, who commented on some of the arguments I developed as a result.

References

Boyle, James (2008) *The Public Domain: Enclosing the Commons of the Mind*, New Haven: Yale University Press.

Brand Republic (2008) *Facebook to Trial 'Engagement' Ad Format*. http://brandrepublic.com/News/841192/Facebook-trial-engagement-ad-format. Accessed 2 September 2008.

Castells, Manuel (2009) *Communication Power*, Oxford: Oxford University Press.

Clark, Nick (2009) 'Yahoo joins battle with Google after EU revamp', *The Independent*, 24 July, p. 42.

Convergence Culture Consortium (2009) 'Welcome to the MIT convergence culture consortium'. http://www.convergenceculture.org. Accessed 18 July 2009.

Gibson, Owen (2008) 'Credit crunch makes digital strategy more critical say Carter', *The Guardian*, 20 October.

Habermas, Jürgen (1991) *The Structural Transformation of the Public Sphere: An Inquiry into a Category of Bourgeois Society*, Cambridge, MA: The MIT Press.

Hartley, John (2009) *The Uses of Digital Literacy*, St Lucia: University of Queensland Press.

Home Office (1986) *Report of the Committee on Financing the BBC*, London: HMSO Cmnd 9824.

Horlick-Jones, Tom et al. (2007) *The GM Debate: Risk, Politics and Public Engagement*, London: Routledge.

Jenkins, Henry (2001) 'Convergence? I diverge', *Technology Review*, June, p. 93.

Jenkins, Henry (2006) 'On convergence culture'. Available at www.bigshinything.com/henry-jenkins-on-convergence-culture. Accessed 14 August 2009.

Kelly, Kevin (2009) 'The new socialism', *Wired*, 9 July, pp. 120–25.

Leadbeater, Charles (2008) *We-Think*, London: Profile Books.

Lessig, Lawrence (2008) *Remix: Making Art and Commerce Thrive in the Hybrid Economy*, London: Bloomsbury.

Mauss, Marcel ([1950]1990) *The Gift: The Form and Reason for Exchange in Archaic Societies*, London: Routledge.

Murdock, Graham (2001) 'Against enclosure: Rethinking the cultural commons', in David Morley and Kevin Robins (eds) *British Cultural Studies: Geography, Nationality and Identity*, Oxford: Oxford University Press, pp. 443–60.

Murdock, Graham (2005) 'Building the digital commons: Public broadcasting in the age of the internet', in Gregory Ferrel Lowe and Per Jauert (eds) *Cultural Dilemmas in Public Service Broadcasting*, Goteborg University: Nordicom, pp. 213–30.

Murdock, Graham (2007) 'Digital technologies and moral economies', in Virginia Nightingale and Tim Dwyer (eds) *New Media Worlds: Challenges for Convergence*, Melbourne: Oxford University Press.

Murdock, Graham and Wasko, Janet (2007) *Media in the Age of Marketisation*, Cresskill, NJ: Hampton Press Inc.

Runciman, David (2009) 'Review of *The Wikipedia Revolution* by Andrew Lih', *London Review of Books*, Vol. 31, No. 10, 28 May, pp. 14–16.

Shirky, Clay (2008) *Here Comes Everybody: The Power of Organizing Without Organizations*, New York: The Penguin Press.

Tapscott, Don and Williams, Anthony D. (2008) *Wikinomics: How Mass Collaboration Changes Everything*, London: Atlantic Books.

Thorpe, Vanessa (2009) 'BBC to throw open its archive of film and radio treasures', *The Observer*, 19 July.

Torvalds, Linus (2001) 'Preface' to Pekka Himanen, *The Hacker Ethic and the Spirit of the Information Age*, London: Vintage, pp. vii–xii.

Vaidhyanathan, Siva (2006) 'Copyright jungle', *Columbia Journalism Review*, September/October, pp. 42–48.

Wray, Richard (2009) 'Monster of Rock sound upbeat at last', *The Observer Business and Media*, 19 July, p. 11.

18

SMART HOMES

Digital lifestyles practiced and imagined

Lynn Spigel

In the midst of the current housing crisis and economic collapse, it may well be odd to speak about housing, even less the high-tech smart home with its equally high-ticket price. The smart home began to emerge as a semi-practical housing form in the 1980s, but its cultural form dates back to a longer history of 'homes of tomorrow', predicated on automation and technological gadgets.[1] Today, the fates of architecture, home technologies and residential real estate are increasingly intertwined, not just through corporate mergers, but also through speculative fictions as well as artistic and popular practices that form a cultural context for our imagination of home, technology and everyday life.

The smart home is a networked home where artefacts, spaces and people interact within the house and, via the internet and mobile technologies, from remote locales. Although smart homes are designed in numerous parts of the world, my focus here is on US examples, which are largely orchestrated through global corporations such as IBM, Panasonic, Intel, Microsoft and Philips, and through university initiatives. Today, at a time when 'Some 63% of adult Americans have Broadband Internet connections at home' (Horrigan 2009), smart homes are increasingly targeted at people with internet services and also with the digital literacy and economic means that often go along with that. And note that while Broadband Internet households are growing among numerous populations, adults who are under 65, more highly educated, and in higher income brackets are more likely to have it in their homes, and Broadband is less common in African American households (Horrigan 2009: 36).

But smart homes are not just corporate constructs aimed at high-end consumers. They are also cultural forms that express and promote social identities and lived experiences. Smart homes, to borrow Michel de Certeau's terminology, are 'spatial stories' for the emplotment of alternative futures and possible worlds (De Certeau 1984). In so far as smart homes also

reimagine the logics of architectural time (issues of permanence, imperma-
nence and, more important to my inquiry, the time-shifting dynamics of
contemporary culture), they also serve as time machines through which daily
rhythms of labour and leisure are being reclocked, and where life-cycle issues
(such as childcare or aging) can be rethought in spatial terms.

Throughout the twentieth century, the technologically enhanced 'house
of tomorrow' has been a key vehicle through which visionary architects –
often in conjunction with corporations – have imagined a better world.
Notable US examples range from Buckminster Fuller's automated Dymaxian
house, first exhibited in 1927, to the corporate display homes of General
Electric and Westinghouse in the 1930s and 1940s, to MIT's futuristic
Monsanto House, first on exhibit in 1957 in the Tomorrowland section of
Disneyland. (For histories of homes of tomorrow, smart homes and architectural utopias see Allon 2004; Boyce 1993; Colomina 2007; Heckman
2007; Haddow 1999; Horrigan 1986; Riley 1999; Scott 2007; Spigel 2001,
2005.) Despite the rhetoric of the technological sublime common to these
visionary homes, stories about futuristic homes gone awry have been a
mainstay of popular culture. Think, for example, of Buster Keaton's *The
Electric House* (1922) where Keaton is outdone by a set of domestic contrivances including an escalator-like smart staircase on which he hilariously
tumbles and a smart pool in which he nearly drowns. Similarly, Warner
Brothers' 'Merrie Melody' *Dog Gone Modern* (1939) features two cartoon dogs
who visit a home of tomorrow only to be assaulted by an assembly of robot
sweepers, overambitious dishwashers and sentient napkin folders, which
inflict all kinds of harm and humiliation on the unsuspecting canines.
Science-fiction stories present comparable tales, but rather than laughter they
provoke uncanny terror. Famously, in Fritz Lang's *Metropolis* (1927), the
home of Joh Fredersen (the uber-capitalist ruler of a futuristic city) has
an electronic surveillance screen from which he surveys his underground
workers. Post-war American science fiction further developed the genre. Ray
Bradbury's 'There Will Come Soft Rains' (1950) features a sentient home
where a lonesome toaster and sorrowful stove mourn their missing residents,
who have died in a nuclear blast. *Forbidden Planet*'s (1956) space-age dream
house turns out, in the tradition of false utopias, to be a mad scientist's trap.
The Stepford Wives (1975) depicts a seemingly ideal suburban community
that turns out to be a corporate plot in which sinister husbands turn their
women's-lib-inspired wives into docile housewife robots. Not surprisingly,
in this regard, while today's consumer magazines, corporations and smart
home designers project utopian futures, films like Disney's *Smart Home*
(1999), Steven Spielberg's *AI* (2001) and Jon Favreau's *Iron Man* (2008)
continue to present uncanny visions of smart homes in corporately engi-
neered futures.

It is this theoretical, imaginary dimension of the smart house that interests
me most. Because I am concerned both with practical inventions and

innovations, as well as theoretical speculative designs (some by architects more associated with avant-garde art installations than with actual buildings), what follows is an analysis of some of the central dynamics at play in the digital culture of home.

Lifestyle loops

Unlike an Orwellian surveillance screen or a Foucauldian panopticon, the smart home is essentially an architecture of feedback where humans and artefacts communicate in what might be called a cybernetic *lifestyle loop*. As in Bruno Latour's 'actor-network' theory, in the smart home technological artefacts and human agents are not conceived in binary terms or top-down relations of control, but rather as components in feedback circuits, as equal partners in mutual force fields of action and reaction (Latour 2005). The smart home creates a circuit of communication in which the classic Marxist binaries of subject–object – or humanist binaries of man vs. machine – no longer apply. If everyday life is commodified, this occurs through the feedback among and between artefacts and humans rather than through the classic Marxist explanations of alienation, the commodification of labour, or commodity fetishism per se. In the smart house, relations between people and things extend past the emphasis on acquisition and display associated with modern homeownership, and towards post-human relational bonds, including caregiving and the reproduction of the life-cycle. For example, in smart homes a fridge can call the market to order your tuna when it runs out; a smart toilet can monitor your urine and send the results to your doctor; a smart picture frame (containing a photo of your mother) can monitor her heartbeat (even if she lives miles away); and a smart closet not only hangs up your clothes but also acts as your personal wardrobe consultant by telling you what not to wear.

Although commercial gimmicks abound, the most interesting digital designs are rooted in pro-social goals that have been central to housing utopias for over a century. Care for the elderly and green architecture rank high among these aims, and numerous designers imagine a more inclusive set of family structures, with gay couples populating the homes. But while engineers and designers often have pro-social intentions, smart homes are predicated on corporate synergies, branding and especially lifestyle marketing. With dream kitchens, elaborate home theatres, and surveillance systems as their most advertised features, smart homes maintain long-standing middle-class housing ideals of luxury and privacy. Indeed, as I have argued elsewhere, smart homes (at least the ones that appear most often in consumer magazines) are often physical embodiments of 'yesterday's future' (Spigel 2001). They recall the baby-boom era, space age, family consumer-oriented future first imagined by Disneyland's Tomorrowland or TV shows like *The Jetsons*. In its contemporary manifestation, the smart house is also a response to the neoliberal post-welfare state that encourages lifestyles that sustain themselves with little or no public intervention. For example, even if smart homes offer designs beneficial to elderly populations, this is still a private (and expensive) solution to the substandard nursing homes in the public sector, and these private solutions still beg the question of who can afford them. The smart home's lifestyle loops are therefore not just rooted in consumer taste, but also in governance and policy decisions that help to regulate people's life choices. Lifestyle loops are thus a contradictory product of both market and social values – values that at times converge, but also often clash in a variety of contradictory impulses.

A prime example of these contradictory impulses is found in MIT's House_n, which is designed by architecture professors Kent Larson and Chris Luebkeman and sponsored by a consortium of corporations including, for example, Dow Chemical, Sylvania Electronics and Allstate Insurance. On its inaugural website (in the early 2000s), House_n promoted itself both as an ancestor of, and also in comparison to, older modernist homes of tomorrow. Comparing House_n with Le Corbusier's designs (and echoing Le Corbusier's 1919 statement, 'The problem of our epoch is the problem of the house'), the website positions the home as a social experiment. (The website states: 'The problem of our epoch is the problem of the electronically mediated house.' – MIT n.d.). According to Larson and his fellow designers, the mass-customized digital home offers consumers a variety of lifestyle choices and socially responsible goals (in a corresponding project called PlaceLab, for example, MIT researchers are engaged in experiments with smart technologies that control childhood obesity and help develop memory and mobility tools for aging populations). Nevertheless, Larson acknowledges the fundamental commodity logic of his housing future. 'High-tech companies', he notes, 'are looking to the home as the next big market ... They're realizing they'll never successfully sell all the gadgets they envision unless there's a more sophisticated infrastructure in the home to plug them into – which means new ways of building' (Larson in Hull 2002).[2] The heart of House_n is a chassis with an 'infill' of sensing devices like LEDs, speakers, displays, heat sensors and cameras that can be plugged in at any point and upgraded as new technologies become available. In this way, the home is designed as a sustainable future with technological updates and opportunities for shopping in mind.

In addition to new ways of building, House_n offers new ways of marketing and buying a home. Speculating on how homebuyers of the future may design their own houses, Larson writes:

> The home industry may look something like this in a few years: By 2015, savvy well-capitalized companies from outside of the housing industry have taken over the market, and speculative developers have all but vanished. A young couple looking to build a new home

begins the process at one of a number of Internet home sites, where they play design games and select from options presented to them ... Systems from one manufacturer are now interchangeable with another ... They learn that Ikea Systems has expanded their kitchen and home furnishing product line to include low-cost kit home components with Scandinavian detailing and energy saving technologies; BMW has developed sleek, modernist, high-tech house components ... and Home Depot and Martha Stewart have partnered to offer fully furnished reproduction historic homes.

(Larson 2000)

Personalized modular design and mass customization therefore produces an entire lifestyle loop in which each brand builds on the other.

At a more abstract level, the smart home's lifestyle loops are rooted in new modes of non-standard architecture, which as architecture theorist Mario Carpo writes, represent 'the latest avatar to date of the digital revolution in architecture, now [in 2008] early in its second decade'. 'In its simplest definition', Carpo continues, 'Nonstandard serialization means the mass production of nonidentical parts.' As opposed to mechanical mass production, which 'generates economies of scale on the condition that all items in the same mechanically mass-produced series be identical, as in a traditional assembly line', new 'digital technologies applied simultaneously to design and manufacturing may generate the same economies of scale while mass-producing a series in which all items are different, but different within limits.' Both physically and ideologically, non-standard digital production allows for greater diversity, but some critics reject it for encouraging artificial demand for styles that go beyond necessity and for promoting marketing gimmicks that foster desire for diverse forms that are nevertheless essentially more of the same (Carpo 2008: 134).

Even if they acknowledge that there are limits to digital diversity, the key terms among digital home designers are 'variation' and 'adaptability'. The 'n' in House_ n is scientific shorthand for 'variable', and Larson sees this as one of the home's key assets. Ruminating about the advances of House_n, Larson argues that the twentieth-century homes of the future, such as Fuller's Dymaxion house with its centrally located 'brain', were doomed because they were 'single purpose structures with a single form driven by one ideology' that was forced on residents (Larson in Hull 2002). As opposed to this, Larson boasts that House_n's adaptive systems adjust to residents' personal tastes and life-cycles. Like Amazon.com or TiVo, House_n will let you know what products you'll like and it will even purchase them for you. Explaining this logic, Larson goes back to his imaginary house-hunting couple:

Living in their new home takes some getting used to. With sensor arrays and digital displays embedded into most surfaces, the home begins to discover their patterns of activity and tries to anticipate what they might need or want. At first, it gets it only about half right, but within several weeks it begins to fit like a glove. It adjusts the ambient light for reading a book in the afternoon, keeps tuna fish on hand in the pantry, monitors their nutrition, and suggests new films that they may enjoy. It becomes a companion of sorts.

(Larson 2000)

As the term 'companion' suggests, the smart house expands previous affective bonds between humans and their homes by turning the home into a sentient agent that virtually befriends the resident.

More generally, the smart home's lifestyle loop is based on new forms of post-human family relations where humans and artefacts are networked together in the performance of family roles associated with caretaking, relationship-building and affection. In another iteration of the impulse, Panasonic's smart house, on view at Panasonic's Tokyo headquarters from 2003–4, was a consumer showcase for these new bonds between humans and things. Upon entering the living room, the visitor sees what looks like a virtual fish tank, but is really a large glass table full of intelligent 'fish' agents that are designed to develop relationships with residents and adapt to their needs. Later in the decade, Panasonic's Eco & UD (Universal Design) House (also on view at its Tokyo headquarters) offered a blend of green architecture, adaptable environments and high-end gizmos (like a 103-inch plasma TV), and for the more middle-class market the company advertises 'bio-concept' appliances that form emotional bonds with humans. As Panasonic claimed on its promotional website, 'We especially focus on "Brand Loyalty" and try to create new values for home appliances ... new sensuous values such as affection, loyalty and loveliness that put new life "Bio" into home appliances'.

However constrained by lifestyle marketing and branding, smart-home enthusiasts tend to see their homes not as palaces of consumption, but rather as spaces for production. Comparing House_n with its predecessors, House_n Technology Director Stephen Intille claims, 'The popular vision of the house of the future is where you hardly have to get up from your easy chair. That's not ours at all. We want the house to enable you to lead a more active and richer life – and encourage you to do things, not to have them done for you' (Intille in Hull 2002). Whereas Jean Baudrillard and Paul Virilio have argued that audio-visual media and telerobotics have rendered human bodies 'superfluous', 'disabled' and increasingly sedentary, smart home engineers and promoters posit just the opposite (Virilio 1989; see also Virilio 1997; Baudrillard 1987). For today's digerati, interactivity has become the buzzword for a kind of common-sense, taken-for-granted future where social ills are remedied by technologies that stimulate us to action.

Nevertheless, interactivity is not just a new democratic utopia empowering consumers to talk back or act up. Instead, as Mark Andrejevic argues, the business community uses interactive media technologies and services as a way to offload the work of market research onto consumers themselves (Andrejevic 2007). Andrejevic calls attention to how, under the banner of interactivity, people who use devices like DVRs or participate in online services or even chat rooms are often also submitting themselves to new forms of observational feedback. In his view, the current enthusiasm for interactivity is traceable back to the dawn of Taylorism and especially to the science of public opinion and market research, which encouraged people to respond to and be observed by autonomous and anonymous measurement techniques. Today these architectures of observation and feedback are incorporated into televisual devices like TiVo or services like Amazon.com, and – more importantly for my purpose here – market research and observational science are being hardwired into the architecture of the home. In the smart home, the entire house – theoretically at least – doubles as a market-research lab that tracks your preferences and habits. As Andrejevic suggests, these modes of interactive market research are not simply a doomsday Orwellian nightmare of surveillance and control. Instead, feedback is based on a dynamic relationship between the science of market research and our idealization of and pleasure in interactive communication. In other words, we like it that the DVR manages our programme choices and records them for us; but we may not fully grasp (or else we disavow) the ways in which such devices are also busy counting us and selling our personal information.

In the world of theoretical architecture and museum installations, architects are commenting back on the interactive home and its lifestyle loops through speculative designs for the future that often (playfully) point to the social contradictions entailed in the new forms of everyday feedback and adaptive systems that smart homes employ. In their design for the Phantom House (2007), an unbuilt adaptive home commissioned by *The New York Times Magazine*, the architectural firm Diller, Scofidio + Renfro imagine the human–artefact relation in terms of what they call 'soft ownership', in which the home 'is connected to larger economic and ecological systems in a production–consumption cycle'. The architects promote soft ownership as a means of using a feedback loop to achieve – ironically – a back-to-nature 'ethos'. According to the architects, the Phantom House negotiates the seemingly opposite goals of consumerism and environmentalism:

> While the environment movement focuses public consciousness to the delicate and vulnerable state of our environment, 'green' architecture is hardening into a new orthodoxy characterized by a lifestyle of guilt and sacrifice. Green architecture often stands at odds with the American Dream and the promise that a lifetime of

hard work will be rewarded with prosperity and material comforts. Do we have to accept a reversal of this dream to be good global citizens?

Answering their own rhetorical question, the architects propose to build 'a green architecture that satisfies our quest for the good life while compensating for it'. A fantastic counterpart to the more mundane (if equally high-end) vision of Panasonic's Eco & UD House, the Phantom House conjures up a strange mix of ecological ethics and luxury lust. The sketches recall the mid-century glass homes (also situated in nature) of Philip Johnson, Mies Van der Rohe and, in particular, John Lautner, whose 'California moderne' glass homes hung off the Hollywood Hills. Built into the side of a mountain, the Phantom House's spectacular glass façades open onto breathtaking desert and swimming-pool views. The home is populated with retro-style moderne furnishings and martini-drinking couples (some same-sex) who seem to be living in a 1960s issue of *Architectural Digest*. Yet despite the moderne retro-style look, the Phantom House is built with today's eco-cybernetics in mind. The architects go on to explain that their single-family house 'is a living, thinking organism; a sophisticated desert dweller that dynamically adapts to its harsh and variable environment'. Comprised of twin glass domiciles, the Phantom House has two levels, which mirror each other and reduce the need for 24/7 climate control.

Promoting the house as an adaptive sentient agent that takes on the code of its residents, the architects explain: 'A comfort shadow tracks the movements of inhabitants and anticipates their needs and preferences. Body and house become an intertwined single organism; energy salvaged from domestic activities is banked and used for domestic services as needed.' The Phantom House even has a smart bed with 'transducers in the mattress to collect and convert excess human energy into electricity stored in the house's rechargeable battery' (Diller, Scofidio and Renfro n.d.). In the Phantom House, sleep becomes the literal reproduction of labour power, recalling the virtual world in *The Matrix* (1999), where humans do not even know they are being drained and controlled. In fact, despite the Phantom House's prosocial back-to-nature values and the super-sunny, retro-moderne lifestyle, there is (as the 'Phantom' name implies) something haunting about this house, with its perfectly controlled climates and feedback-produced lifestyle loops, which suggests its uncanny dystopian underside (see also Vidler 1994). In other words, as a speculative fiction, like Donna Haraway's cyborg, the Phantom House is an ironic and monstrous form, expressing and instructing us to consider the future in all its hybridity and complexity (Haraway 1985).

Just as the Phantom House negotiates the contradictory ideals of environmentalism and consumerism, other speculative designs play with social contradictions between privacy and communitarian values that have been key concerns of housing utopias throughout the twentieth century. For example, Gisue Hariri and Mojgan Hariri's speculative design for the Digital House (unbuilt, 1998), which was commissioned by the magazine *House Beautiful*, uses plasma and liquid-crystal walls developed at NASA to cover the home with a smart skin that allows residents to transcend the domestic wall of inside/outside, public/private. The smart skin develops community relationships, and the home even welcomes in a virtual chef who will cook for you and your virtual guests. Similarly, Michael Trudgeon and Anthony Kitchener's 'Hyper House Pavilion 5' (unbuilt, 1998) transmits a programmed message to neighbouring homes on its electrochromic glass skin (Riley 1999). In these designs, human residents become entirely redundant as the home performs the ideals of community and neighbourliness for them.

Insofar as these designs are intended less as lived spaces than as meta-theoretical commentary on the future, the architects often describe their buildings as ways to provoke discomfort and anxiety about the entire concept of home (as opposed to the romantic ideal of home as safe haven). An Iranian émigré, Gisue Hariri comments on the contradictions of the digital world and sees her Digital House as a response to this. When asked about the possible downside of technological lifestyles encapsulated by her Digital House, Gisue says, 'I feel coming from a background that is very experience orientated, very tactile, very earthy, yes, we will definitely lose all that, and it's going to be a pity. But I see it [as] part of an evolution, and we will gain other things ... I am very, very optimistic about it.' She adds, 'We are dealing with things that to me are magic! These are things that if you read in a book, you would think it would never happen. And to have that in my lifetime, it's like when the first light bulb was invented and people didn't have to light candles! ... Otherwise we'd all still be farmers ... and I would have a burqa on!' (cited in Ballen and Hauge 2009). These contradictions – of both loss and liberation – via digital technologies inform other architectural projects similarly based on the paradox of being at home with, and yet feeling displaced by, the technological future.

The vision of privacy and public life inscribed in smart homes is very different from that of older social systems where production and consumption – work and leisure – were split across city and suburb. Corporate sponsors and architects think that the infrastructure of tomorrow's home will be wired to decentralized virtual workplaces and to the service economy of goods, conveniences and entertainment. Speculative designs like the Digital House and the Phantom House disintegrate boundaries of home, office, store, factory, nature, restaurant, school and community. Meanwhile, consumer magazines offer their own, more practical, versions of this merging of place. As a 2008 issue of *Home Entertainment* declares, with internet access, flat-screen TVs and professional espresso machines, kitchens are morphing into multipurpose home-entertainment centres and business hubs and even 'begin to take on the look and feel of a small café or coffee shop' (Mills 2008).

In their use of media and technology to bring the outside in, smart homes build on Raymond Williams' seminal concept of *mobile privatization* – a phenomenon he tied to the simultaneous rise of privatized suburban housing and mobile industrial cities in the late nineteenth century. The advent of telecommunications, Williams argues (1975), offered people the ability to maintain ideals of privacy while providing the mobility required by industrialization and urbanization, and broadcasting in particular held out the promise of bringing the public world indoors. As I have argued elsewhere (Spigel 2001), the rise of portable and remote technologies in the 1960s inverted these terms, allowing for new possibilities of *privatized mobility* in which consumers (of portable TV sets) were advised to bring TV outdoors and to engage with TV in active, even athletic ways (so, for example, advertisers showed images of TV sets on the beach, in cars or at picnics, with viewers on the go, driving, even swimming, or just enjoying TV outside the family space).

Smart homes and devices extend such fantasies of mobile privatization and privatized mobility. Ads for mobile technologies promise the dream of carrying around our private life (whether entertainment or work-related data) on smaller and smaller devices, while entertainment Web services like Hulu allow us to stream TV and movies (as their ad promises) 'anytime, anywhere'. With cellphones, PDAs, cloud computing and the like, people can experience being at home while in public and we also experience being in public while at home. In March of 2008 the Pew Research Center found that '62% of all Americans are part of a wireless, mobile population that participates in digital activities away from home or work' (Horrigan 2008). Place-shifting, in other words, now occupies the lives of the majority of the US population. As David Morley (2000) argues, the home is being 'dislocated' and disconnected from its physical and psychical place. So, too, the home is being 're-clocked' as traditional work schedules are reorganized in the digital world.

In this context, smart home designers conceptualize domesticity as a site of perpetual preparedness where residents are ready to 'work' or 'play' when keyed into the home's systems. In their sketches for the Phantom House, Diller, Scofidio and Renfro plot out an hour-by-hour schedule of human–artefact energy-producing frenzy (the architects use words like 'nervous' and 'agitated' to describe states of mind in this ironic nature retreat). Laptops are everywhere, and the energy-sucking bed has two flat screens next to it (one projects the stock report, the other *Casablanca*). In Hariri and Hariri's Digital House, 'transient spaces' (or hallways between rooms) have liquid-crystal walls and digital-image environments that are designed so that residents can make valuable use of time spent walking from one room to the next. As with the Phantom House, in the Digital House even sleep is transformed into usable time. The bedrooms are equipped with dream-recording devices that provide a transcript of the dreamer's unconscious. Similarly, Diller and Scofidio's Slow House (unbuilt, 1999) is a hybrid vacation-workplace. Situated on the relaxing Long Island Sound, the house projects the spectacular vacation view back to the residents' Manhattan apartment, thereby blurring the spaces of leisure and labour. In the architects' words, the Slow House is designed to provide an 'escape from escape, that is, to connect at a moment's notice back to the sites of anxiety' in the city (cited in Riley 1999). The ultimate paradox, then, is that the luxury home is now the ultimate work terminal.

Conspicuous production

In his *The Theory of the Leisure Class* (1899), Thorstein Veblen famously conceptualized class in relation to its performative dimensions of 'conspicuous consumption' and 'conspicuous leisure' – the acts of displaying property and time as a luxury accumulated via privilege. If conspicuous consumption described the dynamics of class, labour and leisure in the era of industrialization, the post-industrial digital home is more aptly understood through the related concept of *conspicuous production*. In the smart house, residents display their social privilege via their ability to work – seemingly all the time.

Corporations promote the lifestyle aesthetic of conspicuous production in ads for home-based digital technologies. Rather than the image of upscale leisure that accompanied the sale of new technologies in the first half of the twentieth century, advertisers offer consumers the dream of super-productivity – even when at rest. Consumer magazines depict residents who are able to multitask across an array of leisure and labour activities. The founding text – or at least the earliest I have found – comes from a 1996 issue of *Wired Magazine* that presents on its front cover Microsoft guru Bill Gates floating in his swimming pool (in smiley-face swimming trunks) while hooked into work via his cellphone. As a high-tech CEO (and by 2005 himself a proud owner of one of the first smart mansions), Gates is the perfect representative for this new lifestyle aesthetic of conspicuous production. In the 2000s, this image has become something of a viral visual icon, replicated in numerous ads and magazine articles that show images of men (and sometimes women) phoning (or emailing) into work while sitting near or floating in pools. For example, a 2003 cover of *Digital Home* shows a classically beautiful couple in swimwear at the poolside while talking on mobiles and working on laptops. Similarly, a photo spread in a 2001 issue of *Broadband House* shows a family busy at work and play, with the father in a pool while on his cellphone and the mother and children variously engaged in digital work and leisure pursuits. Coming from the point of the view of the mother, the pull-quote reads, 'We're rehearsing the future. We're always experimenting with ways to use technology to increase our productivity.'[3] Conspicuous production means that leisure is not just 'time off', but rather part of the job.

This contemporary proliferation of work/play images and the lifestyle aesthetic of conspicuous production take place at a time when people are asked to work more hours and in more locations and when the eight-hour work day, breadwinner commuter dad and the stay-at-home mom are no longer the rule. In 2002, dual-income families with children made up more than twice as many households as did traditional nuclear families (in which mothers stay at home); even double-income families with no children outnumbered the traditional family by almost two to one.[4] Meanwhile, studies show that people are relying on broadband internet connections to bridge the geographies of domestic space and workplace. In 2008, The Pew Internet and American Life Project observed 'Some 45% of employed Americans report doing at least some work from home and 18% of working Americans say they do job-related tasks at home almost daily.' 'Networked workers who use the internet or email at their job report higher rates of working at home' and 'Overall, 56% of Networked Workers report some at-home work and 20% say they do so "everyday or almost every day."' So, too, 'Networked workers … are more likely than average Americans to have access to a wide array of technological assets outside the workplace' that enable work not just at home, but on the go (Madden and Jones 2008).

While the smart home is symptomatic of, and conducive to, the changing nature of work and leisure, it is still a place where gender plays a major role. As with previous waves of technological and media innovation, the smart home is still replete with gendered ideologies and practices. Like previous houses of tomorrow, the smart home is promoted as a utopian refuge for women. But whereas the first home appliances of the twentieth century (washing machines, stoves, dishwashers) were advertised as labour-saving devices that would provide women with unbridled leisure time (see Cowan 1983), advertisers for contemporary smart homes promise that intelligent agents will make it possible for women to multitask – to be dutiful mothers and successful career people at the same time.

For women, the imagery of conspicuous production is often accompanied by related images of *conspicuous reproduction*. Magazines and adverts depict women engaged in all kinds of tele-work at home while posed with their children and performing caretaking roles. Women are shown cradling babies while working on laptops, texting into work while cooking a meal, or lounging on sofas while telemanaging a team of employees at a remote locale. The difficulties of juggling a professional career with mothering (or other caretaking roles) are magically solved through smart home devices.

For men, smart homes are figured in somewhat different terms. Given that domestic space has traditionally been associated with women's work, smart home promoters have to persuade men that the home is in fact a masculine place to be. Accordingly, ads often show men in 'macho' postures, aiming remote controls like guns at wide-screen TVs, monitoring surveillance systems, playing games with buddies, and even, in the more fantastic versions, jumping into (virtual) sports matches they watch on TV. Although advertisers do depict scenes of domesticated family men, they balance these with images of men who have prestige jobs, mobile lifestyles, and/or dominion over their professional careers. Moreover, when men are shown sharing space with children, they typically are not doing traditional forms of women's housework (cleaning, feeding kids, etc.). Instead, fathers are in charge of technology (installing the network or building home theatres) or else at play (watching TV or playing games with kids). And unlike multitasking moms, when men are shown working they are typically focused on the task, often alone in offices or dens away from the family.

Home offices designed for men typically eschew domestic decoration (associated with femininity) in favour of minimalist modernism, or else men's spaces have a rustic caveman feel, using dark woods to connote outdoorsy, rugged masculinity. In his Seattle-based smart house of 1995, Bill Gates installed electronically enhanced walls that generated the look and feel of rustic wood while providing the high-tech capabilities needed for his smart den (Zion 1998). In the Tokyo-based Panasonic House 2000, masculinity was an essential part of the floor plan. As one reporter described it, 'Panasonic's study looks every inch a guy's room, emphasizing multimedia and the glory of lording it over the entire household at the flick of a switch. There's even a bottle of whisky perched within easy reach' (Lytle 2003). Here, as elsewhere, the man's room is represented in ways that connote traditional ideals of male mastery over space as the smart dad controls the home both through his remote access to it and his remote accessibility within it.

Certainly, for some people the advantages of working at home are real. But the promotional materials gloss over the tensions inherent in smart lifestyles. According to the 2008 Pew research, when speaking of computer and mobile technologies '49% say these technologies make it harder for them to disconnect from their work when they are at home and on the weekends'. Research also suggests that computer use leads to family conflicts, with families vying over workspace and screen time (Frohlich et al. 2003). And while smart home promoters offer women an idealized view of multitasking and career–caretaker job juggling, studies indicate that women feel the strain. In her ethnographic study of computer-owning households in Western Sydney, Elaine Lally (2002: 159) found that 'some of the gendered meanings of new technologies are translated from the technology's previously established business and educational settings'. For example, women are more likely than men to do 'pink-collar' secretarial tasks, such as word processing for the family, so this office work is now added to the caretaking role (Lally 2002). In her study of women and home computers, Catherine Burke found that women feel both guilty and anxious about the anger they perceive to be directed at them by partners and children when they focus on work at home (Burke 2003: 332–33). As such studies suggest, the smart home is giving way to domestic anxieties, anxieties that now surface in the stories we tell about home and the popular practices that comment back on the smart way of life.

The great iPhone massacre

Despite all the promotional rhetoric and utopian predictions, the smart home – as I have already indicated – is also an uncanny and paranoid architecture that takes its place in the longer history of dystopian science fiction. Today, smart homes appear in stories not just about technology out of control, but also about a whole set of cultural anxieties, particularly in the realm of family life, sexuality and gender. Films like *Smart House* and *AI* present smart homes that may look cool but turn out be chilling images of family life in the future. In addition to Hollywood examples, tales of smart terror are also appearing on digital share sites, where a burgeoning group of DIY video-makers are engaged in their own brand of 'rage against the machine'. In particular, YouTube features a new viral video genre of gadget destruction footage that is appearing in amazing volume. The genre typically contains the following features: (1) boys or men commonly featured as central protagonists; (2) a domestic setting, often a kitchen but sometimes a suburban yard, garage, driveway or street; (3) a media technology, often a valuable piece of smart technology – for example an iPod, cellphone, flat-screen TV or laptop; (4) a ritual 'sacrifice' of the artefact.

One of the most professionally executed of these is the 'Will It Blend?' series, in which a man dressed in a lab coat puts all sorts of desirable goodies (including remote controls and cellphones) in a blender. Some of the more garden-variety examples show boys in kitchens microwaving iPods ('Death to My iPod') or in bed breaking cellphones ('How to Break a Cellphone') or in yards killing TV sets with spud guns ('Spudgun vs. TV'). Perhaps the videos are just a pretence for seeing oneself doing something cool on the internet. But I also think this viral video genre serves as an interesting cultural expression of anxiety, not just about smart technologies and the corporations that make them but also about masculinity in relation to the emerging work and domestic environments of digital culture, as well as the temporal, spatial and social dislocations associated with the smart way of life. The fact that the heroes are usually boys or young men, coupled with their curious use of kitchen appliances to 'cook' machines or their desire to devour cellphones in bed, suggests a deviant domestic practice in the traditionally female space of the home. If, as Andreas Huyssen argues in his essay on Fritz Lang's *Metropolis* (Huyssen 1987), stories about technology out of control are historically related to fears of women out of control, these videos take the culture of domesticity and the new logics of conspicuous production and turn this into an occasion for *conspicuous destruction*.[5]

I could not help thinking, while I watched about 50 of these viral videos, of Robert Darnton's essay 'Worker's Revolt: The Great Cat Massacre of the Rue Saint-Séverin' in which he asks why male labourers in an early modern printing shop found the massacre of the precious cat belonging to their boss's wife so funny. Reading an account of the event, Darnton argues that the joke had to do with the workers' outrage at their boss and their pleasure in seeing him (through the symbolic massacre of his wife's cat) cuckolded and emasculated (Darnton 1984). Although Darnton privileges a reading about class and labour exploitation, he doesn't explore the tale for its troubling gender and misogynist meanings – elements that seem just as important to that story as to the viral video technology massacres of today.

In thinking back to 'The Great Cat Massacre' for its possible explanatory power, I wondered if the cat massacre story was in some ways an early modern predecessor of the technology massacres now on YouTube. I then came across a particularly prolific viral video-maker who produces both technology massacres and cat massacres (albeit he only kills his wife's kitsch statues of cats). In other words, the genres – at least in this video-maker's mind – are related. This brand of technological torture, which takes place in the 'feminine' domestic space of the home, seems, in this sense, part of a much older cultural activity in which rage against industrialization and human exploitation is expressed through the ritual sacrifice of the fetishized object of desire symbolically associated not only with corporate control over life but also with fears of femininity and domesticity – so much so that the home becomes a site of terror and torture (an uncanny scenario so obvious I will not belabour the point).

While I am not celebrating this form of viral video-making, I do find it important to recognize that there is a 'low-end', popular corollary to the building and marketing of smart homes, an end which often rejects the futures imagined by engineers, designers, architects, popular magazines and their clients, patrons and publics. The smart home and its related devices are often stubbornly refused, and the feeling of being NOT at home with the future is, I think, just as important to consider as the designs and aspirations for it.

As the 'great technology massacre' on YouTube suggests, no position on the future is ever 'pure' and no environment (whether physical or virtual) is a perfect world for all. Writing in the 1990s, when cyberspace was being touted as new utopia of disembodied identities and democratic participation, Kevin Robins observed that rather than dream of a utopian virtual public sphere where all strife is erased, we should approach the virtual world as an actually existing 'world we live in' – a world of struggle, conflict and necessary negotiations among differently situated and desiring publics (Robins 2007). And, as Elizabeth Grotz argues in her discussion of virtual architecture, despite some notable exceptions, utopia was largely a man-made concept and, in architecture, it has not been very kind to women, or to most populations. As she suggests of the dreams of egalitarian utopias, 'Egalitarianism consists of extending to women, or to other cultural minorities, the rights accorded to the dominant group; it does not consist of rethinking the very nature of those rights in relation to the very groups it was originally designed to exclude or constrain' (Grotz 2001). So, in this sense one can certainly wonder whether the inclusion of same-sex couples or the technological fix offered to aging populations or toxic environments can in themselves redesign everyday life in ways that go beyond inclusion in someone else's (expensive) dream.

Despite this cautionary note, and as should be obvious, it does seem to me that smart homes are worth thinking about. Smart homes are not just homes with media; they are themselves communication media that narrate visions of a better world. As such, they offer opportunities to reinvestigate stubborn conflicts and social contradictions, including the persistent dilemma of uneven access to decent shelter that governs any consideration of home – smart or otherwise. In the context of the current economic crisis, these problems of housing will hit home for more and more people, and, in this context, perhaps we will be compelled to think more often and more wisely about how to build a smart future.

Notes

1 In 1986 the National Association of Home Builders offered a tour of a smart home that was a prototype for the alliances between the home-building industry and digital communication technologies.
2 In the summer of 2004, MIT House_n and TIAX opened The PlaceLab, a residential observational research facility with occupants located in Cambridge Massachusetts.
3 *Wired*, June 1996, cover; *Digital Home*, August 2003, cover; Cleaver 2001–2. For more on conspicuous production see Spigel 2005.
4 AmeriStat Staff, 'Traditional Families Account for only 7 Percent of U.S. households.' Population Reference Bureau, 2003. Online at http://www.prb.org/Articles/2003/TraditionalFamiliesAccountforOnly7PercentofUSHouseholds.aspx. Accessed March 2004. The major increases in dual-income couples occurred between the mid-1970s and the mid-1990s. US Department of Labor Statistics, Monthly Labor Review, July/August 2007, p. 37. Online at http://www.bls.gov/cps/demographics.htm#families. Accessed 16 July 2009.
5 I am currently thinking about these YouTube videos with my colleague Max Dawson, to whom I owe the term 'conspicuous destruction'.

References

Allon, Fiona (2004) 'Ontologies of Everyday Control: Space, Media Flows, and Smart Living in the Absolute Present,' in Nick Couldry and Anna McCarthy (eds) *Mediaspace*, London: Routledge, pp. 253–74.

Andrejevic, Mark (2007) *I Spy: Surveillance and Power in the Interactive Age*, Kansas: University of Kentucky Press.

Ballen, Sian and Hauge, Lesley (2009) 'Gisue Hariri,' *New York Social Diary*, http://newyorksocialdiary.com/node/4102. Accessed 20 May 2009.

Baudrillard, Jean (1987) *The Ecstasy of Communication* (trans. Bernard and Caroline Schutze, ed. Sylvere Lotringer), New York: Semiotext(e).

Boyce, Robert (1993) *Keck and Keck*, Princeton, NJ: Princeton Architectural Press.

Burke, Catherine (2003) 'Women, Guilt, and Home Computers,' in Joseph Turow and Andrea L. Kavanaugh (eds) *The Wired Homestead: An MIT Sourcebook on the Internet and the Family*, Cambridge: The MIT Press, pp. 332–33.

Carpo, Mario (2008) 'Nonstandard Morality: Digital Technology and its Discontents,' in Anthony Vidler (ed.) *Architecture Between Spectacle and Use*, Williamstown, MA: Clark Art Institute and Yale University Press.

Certeau, Michel de (1984) *The Practice of Everyday Life* (trans. Steven Rendall), Berkeley: University of California Press.

Cleaver, J. (2001–2) 'Say Hello to the House of Tomorrow', *Broadband House* (Winter): 56–63.

Colomina, Beatriz (2007) *Domesticity at War*, Cambridge, MA: The MIT Press.

Cowan, Ruth Schwartz (1983) *More Work for Mother: The Ironies of Household Technology from the Open Hearth to the Microwave*, New York: Basic Books.

Darnton, Robert (1984) 'Worker's Revolt: The Great Cat Massacre of the Rue Saint-Séverin,' in *The Great Cat Massacre: And Other Episodes in French Cultural History*, New York: Vintage, pp. 75–107.

Diller, Scofidio and Renfro (n.d.) http://www.dillerscofidio.com. Accessed 10 September 2008.

Frohlich, David M., Dray, Susan and Silverman, Amy (2003) 'Breaking Up is Hard to Do: Family Perspectives on the Future of the Home PC,' in Turow and Kavanaugh (eds) *The Wired Homestead*, Cambridge MA: The MIT Press.

Grotz, Elizabeth (2001) *Architecture from the Outside*, Cambridge, MA: The MIT Press, p. 147.

Haddow, Robert (1999) 'House of the Future or House of the Past: Populist Visions from the USA,' *Architecture and Ideas* 1:1 68–79.

Haraway, Donna (1985) 'A Manifesto for Cyborgs: Science, Technology and Socialist Feminism in the 1980s,' *Socialist Review* 15:2 65–108.

Hariri, Gisue and Hariri, Mojgan (n.d.) *Hariri & Hariri – Architects*, http://www.haririandhariri.com. Accessed 25 August 2009.

Heckman, Davin (2007) *A Small World: Smart Houses and the Dream of the Perfect Day*, Durham, NC: Duke University Press.

Horrigan, Brian (1986) 'The Home of Tomorrow, 1927–45,' in Joseph J. Corn (ed.) *Imagining Tomorrow, History, Technology, and the American Future*, Cambridge, MA: The MIT Press, pp. 137–63.

Horrigan, John (2008) 'Mobile Access to Data and Information,' Pew Internet and American Life Project, March 5, http://www.pewinternet.org/Reports/2008/Mobile-Access-to-Data-and-Information.aspx. Accessed 9 April 2008.

Horrigan, John (2009) 'Home Broadband Adaptation 2009,' Pew Internet and American Life Project, June 17, http://pewresearch.org/pubs/1254/home-broadband-adoption-2009. Accessed 30 July 2009.

Hull, Peter (2002) 'Living for Tomorrow,' *Metropolis Magazine*, December, online at http://www.metropolismag.com. Accessed 3 March 2004.

Huyssen, Andreas (1987) 'The Vamp and the Machine', *After the Great Divide: Modernism, Mass Culture, Postmodernism*. Bloomington: Indiana University Press, pp. 65–81.

Lally, Elaine (2002) *At Home with Computers*, Oxford: Berg.

Larson, Kent (2000) 'The Home of the Future,' *A+U* 361 June, http://architecture.mit.edu/house_n/web/publications/publications.htm. Accessed 5 June 2007.

Latour, Bruno (2005) *Reassembling the Social: An Introduction to Actor-Network Theory*, New York: Oxford University Press.

Lytle, Mark (2003) 'House: The Digital Homes of Our Dreams,' *Digital Home*, Spring, p. 78.

Madden, Mary and Jones, Sydney (2008) Madden Pew Internet and Life Project, 'Networked Workers,' 24 September, http://www.pewinternet.org/Reports/2008/Networked-Workers.aspx. Accessed 10 March 2008.

Mills, Karen (2008) 'Tech Kitchens,' *Home Entertainment*, 27 November, http://www.hemagazine.com/node/Tech_Kitchens. Accessed 1 February 2009.

MIT (n.d.) House_*n*, http://architecture.mit.edu/house_n. Accessed 25 August 2009.

Morley, David (2000) *Home Territories: Media, Mobility and Identity*, London: Routledge.

NYT (*The New York Times*) (2007) 'An Eco-Architecture for the Future,' *The New York Times Magazine*, 20 May, pp. 85–90.

Riley, Terence (1999) *The Un-Private House* (exhibition catalogue). New York: Museum of Modern Art.

Robins, Kevin (2007) 'Cyberspace and the World We Live in,' in K. Robins, *Into the Image*, London: Taylor and Francis.

Scott, Felicity (2007) *Architecture or Technotopia: Politics after Modernism*, Cambridge, MA: The MIT Press.

Spigel, Lynn (2001) 'Yesterday's Future/Tomorrow's Home,' in L. Spigel, *Welcome to the Dreamhouse: Popular Media and Postwar Suburbs*, Durham, NC: Duke University Press, pp. 379–408.

Spigel, Lynn (2005) 'Designing the Smart House: Posthuman Domesticity and Conspicuous Production,' *European Journal of Cultural Studies*, 8:4 403–26.

US Department of Labor (2009) 'Where People Worked, 2003–7,' Issues in Labor Statistics, Summary 09–07, June, http://www.bls.gov/opub. Accessed 17 July 2009.

Veblen, Thorstein ([1899]2008) *The Theory of the Leisure Class*. London: Oxford University Press.

Vidler, Anthony (1994) *The Architectural Uncanny: Essays on the Modern Unhomely*, Cambridge, MA: The MIT Press.

Virilio, Paul (1989) 'The Last Vehicle,' in Dietmar Kamper and Christoph Wolf (eds) *Looking Back at the End of the World* (trans. David Antal), New York: Semiotext(e).

Virilio, Paul (1997) *Open Skies* (trans. Julie Rose), London: Verso.

Williams, Raymond (1975) *Television: Technology and Cultural Form*, New York: Schocken.

Zion, Adi Shamir (1998) 'New Modern: Architecture in the Age of Digital Technology,' *Assemblage* 3,565.

19

TELEVISION AS A MEANS OF TRANSPORT

Digital teletechnologies and transmodal systems

David Morley

In 1933 the art historian Rudolf Arnheim proposed that the new invention of television was best understood metaphorically, in relation to questions of physical transport – as a 'means of distribution' – but of images and sounds, rather than of objects or persons. To this extent, he argued, television is fundamentally related to modes of transport such as the motor car and the aeroplane – but in this case as a 'means of transport for the mind' (Arnheim 1933, quoted in Rath 1985: 199).

In making this argument, Arnheim, if inadvertently, comes close to Marx's understanding of 'communications' as properly being understood to comprise the movement of objects, persons and messages. Marx's analysis sought to combine the virtual with the actual: the analysis of the media industries with those of physical transport (De la Haye 1980). This multi-modal approach represents a link which has been sundered in the contemporary development of media studies, as a discipline which nowadays attends only to the symbolic dimensions of communication.[1]

Evidently, Arnheim's argument works at the level of metaphor by trans-posing the function of physical modes of transport to the virtual sphere, where the entities being transported – images and ideas – are themselves immaterial. Indeed, if we trace the etymology of the word 'metaphor' we find that its original Greek meaning is precisely to 'transport' or 'carry across' – in this case to transfer significance, by using a figure of speech in which a name or descriptive term is transposed from one realm of meaning to another. My own concern here is simply to indicate, schematically, what kind of analytical benefits might accrue from the restoration of the broken linkage between the analysis of symbolic and physical modes of communication represented in this metaphor.

Digital teletechnologies and the 'death' of geography

Over the last decade it has come to be widely presumed that one of the principal effects of the new digital teletechnologies (technologies of distance) of our age is the 'death of geography' (Meyrowitz 1985; Wark 1994). According to this view, we all now live in a cyber world of placelessness, as these technologies have 'overcome' the problem of distance to such an extent that material geography now counts for very little as a determinant of social or cultural life.

However, a revisionist position has more recently been articulated which disputes these idealist presumptions (Hannam et al. 2006; Urry 2008) and argues that, while the new virtual dimensions of our world are of considerable consequence, material geography, far from being 'dead', still requires our close attention. This is so, not least because, in the first place, the internet itself has a very real geography (Crampton 2003; Zook 2005); moreover, rather than simply 'bringing us all together', these technologies both create new unities ('technozones') and divide them from others by inscribing them in technological form (Barry 2001). For example, statistically speaking, the principal use of email is not, in fact, for long-distance communication, but between people in the same organization who are already geographically proximate (often in the same building), and the most successful of the social-networking websites increasingly function by articulating the virtual with the actual world, rather than by substituting the former for the latter. Thus, in the light of these considerations, rather than thinking about cyberspace in the abstract, as some unitary new sphere, we might be better advised to investigate the specific ways in which the virtual is integrated with the actual in different material cultures (cf. Miller and Slater 2000).

Reinterrogating transport geography: 'the box that changed the world'

If we understand a metaphor as a container for the transport of meanings, and if, following Marx, we are concerned to re-define the analysis of communications so as to include transport, we can also apply the metaphor in another context: in relation to the container box (known in the vernacular of the transport industry as a 'can' or 'box') which provides the basic form of that industry today. The box itself is a totally banal object: so simple in its standardized dimensions and construction, and so ubiquitous in the contemporary world, that it is almost invisible to us, precisely because we are surrounded by it. As one of the characters in William Gibson's novel *Spook Country*, puts it, 'he [had] read the names on individual boxes ... Hanjin, Cosco, Tex, K-Line, Maersk Sealand', but another character notes that 'she'd never really thought about them before; you glimpse them from freeways sometimes, an aspect of contemporary reality so common as to remain unconsidered, unquestioned. Almost everything, she supposed, travelled in them now' (Gibson 2008: 294, 176).

The box functions (literally) as the foundation of the multi-modal transport system on which the time–space compression of the global economy depends, combining the great economy of water shipment with the speed and flexibility of methods of overland transport, while minimizing handling costs. It has had tremendous economic impact, in so far as it has enabled the drastic reduction in transport costs which has been the key driving force in the expansion of international trade and the process of globalization over the last 50 years. By reducing these costs, containerization radically expands the geographical scale of markets – allowing products to be carried vast distances at such low costs that they can still be sold more cheaply than comparable goods made locally (Cudahy 2006; Donovan and Bonney 2006; Levinson 2006).

At the same time, the basic concept – a standardized container capable of being moved across different systems of transportation – is so simple that this humdrum object might be thought barely to qualify as a significant form of technological advance. The 'invention' of containerized transport systems is sometimes attributed to the 'hero figure' of Malcolm McLean of Sea-Land Transport, who first used containers in ports on the east coast of North America in 1956. But containerization was not a new idea, and McLean did not invent it. He was simply the first to see that a whole new transport system could be built around the simple concept of goods being transported from door to door, from origin to destination, across a variety of modes of transport, in a closed box – and he constructed a whole industry around this pre-existing technology.[2]

However, besides its practical purposes, the box also functions, metonymically, as one of the key symbols of the age, to 'represent' the whole process of long-distance transportation which lies at the heart of the global economy.[3] To this extent, we need to address not only its practical functions (or, in technical terms, its 'affordances') but also its symbolic significance as a 'global icon' of our era. Alan Sekula has noted that, if Marx saw the commodity as the container of 'dead labour', and if the slave ship was perhaps the first 'container ship' – functioning, literally, as a floating means of transport for potential labour power – then the container box can itself perhaps be seen as the 'coffin' of remote labour power performed elsewhere, in dispersed long-distance production chains, and delivered to markets anywhere across the globe.[4] A number of commentators have recruited the container box to a similar status to that given by McLuhan to electronic technologies of communication. Thus they argue that today 'the rapidity and low cost with which shipments can now be moved around the world is doing for goods and materials what the electronic media did for visual and aural representations ... McLuhan's global village of images of information and ideas is paralleled by containerization's global village of goods' (Donovan and Bonney 2006: xxiii; 211).

Of course, all of this is to speak only of those uses of the box which conform to the intentions of its designers. As we well know, the box, like any other technology, is capable of being used in a multiplicity of ways. It can be transformed into a variety of forms of living accommodation or workspace – e.g. as emergency housing in the rich West (as in New Orleans after Hurricane Katrina). It functions as the routine basis of self-build forms of vernacular architecture in the Third World – like that of the *gecekondu* areas of Istanbul or of the parts of Lagos explored by Rem Koolhaas and his colleagues (cf. Koolhaas 2004; Morley 2007). It provides the physical basis for the 'largest market' in the world – the 'Seventh-Kilometre' market outside Odessa in the Ukraine, composed entirely of discarded containers.[5] Within the art world, following the path-breaking work of Dick Hebdige and Kim Yosuda in Santa Barbara, containers have been utilized for a variety of purposes. There have now also been a number of 'Container Art' exhibitions – e.g. at Kaohsiung in Taiwan in 2007 and in Genova in Italy in 2008 – which have offered critical commentary on the place of the container within the economy and ecology of the contemporary world. There is even an artist, Yvan Salomone, whose work focuses exclusively on the representation of container ports.[6]

BBC.co.uk/thebox: dramatizing globalization[7]

In this context I want to explore the significance of an imaginative project which brings together the issues of digitalized communication and transport. In August 2008, the BBC sponsored and 'branded' a shipping container, to which was attached a GPS transmitter, which allowed its progress to be monitored over the course of a year, as it criss-crossed the globe. The beauty of the project lay in its very simplicity: on the one hand, at a literal level, the GPS facility allowed those who followed its progress on the BBC's website to track it (and its changing contents) online, and thus to get a vivid sense of the geographical scale and complexity of the flow of international trade. At the same time, the box functioned not simply as a vehicle for its material contents, nor just descriptively as an 'object lesson' (*sic*) in transport geography, but also metaphorically, as a vehicle for generating a variety of detailed individual stories about the world economy and globalization, delivering multi-platform content for the BBC's television, radio and online audiences.

In effect, the project took the armchair-documentary genre to a new level, whereby the online viewer was like a participant in a live experiment about the geography of globalization, watching the unforeseen developments revealed by this particular case study. The capacity offered by the GPS, linked to the website, to track the box's progress live, day-by-day, introduced a series of revealing 'microcosmic' glimpses of the complex macrodynamics which determined the path and speed of its journeys. As Michel Callon and Bruno Latour note, even the longest journey is ultimately built out of – and dependent on – the effective functioning of an indeterminate number of micro-linkages (Callon and Latour 1981).[8] The slightly fortuitous element in the narrative was that the experiment took place in remarkable circumstances: as the global economy collapsed during the box's round-the-world journey, the project was able to dramatize the dynamics of global trade more effectively than can possibly have been imagined in advance by its planners.

In mid-September 2008, just as the Credit Crunch began to bite in the UK, the box began its journey by train from Nuneaton Station in the British Midlands. It was then transferred by truck to a warehouse in Paisley, near Glasgow, where it was loaded with a consignment of 15,120 bottles of 12-year-old Chivas Regal whisky. At that stage, with their exports in the first half of 2008 having gone up 14 per cent, the Scottish whisky manufacturers were still very optimistic about their prospects, despite the overall downturn in the global economy. The next stage of the box's journey took it, again by road, to the Greenock Ocean Terminal, where it was put on a container ship, the *Vega Stockholm*, which took it to Southampton. There it was reloaded, along with about 1,500 other boxes, containing everything from German chemicals to frozen pork, onto the MV *Copenhagen Express*, whose ultimate destination was Shanghai.

The ship travelled down through the Irish Sea, across the Bay of Biscay, through the Gibraltar Straits, and across the Mediterranean to the Suez Canal. This was a crucial stage of the journey, as the canal route saves the 20-days' sailing time otherwise involved in the circumnavigation of Africa. However, even as the box passed through the canal in early October, serious concerns were beginning to emerge that shipping going this by route was increasingly threatened by Somalian pirates operating at the southern end of the Gulf of Aden. The significance of this story was well confirmed in subsequent months, in which the re-emergence of piracy in this region led to a series of international crises. As a result of these developments, the cost of insuring ships passing through the Gulf of Aden has increased to the extent that some shipping companies are now even considering taking the long route around Africa, via the Cape of Good Hope, rather than running these risks. As we see from this example, the path of globalization can never be assumed to run smooth: even the decreases in journey times facilitated by a nineteenth-century invention such as the Suez Canal cannot necessarily be assumed to hold good for the future.

The box then made its way down the Red Sea, across the Indian Ocean to Singapore, arriving in mid-October. By the time the box arrived there, the global economic slowdown had cut into shipment volumes across the industry, with Singapore especially hard hit, freight rates falling to six-year lows and local shipping companies seeing their share prices in freefall. Further anxieties, at this stage of the journey, concerned the fact that the Malacca Straits, like the Gulf of Aden, have, in recent years, also seen an increasing number of 'ship-jackings' by hi-tech pirates, who themselves make very effective use of exactly the same GPS transmitters installed on the box for the purposes of the BBC project – evidently, GPS itself, like any technology, is a double-edged sword, which can be used for a variety of legal and illegal purposes.

At this stage the project also ran aground on the classic experimental dilemma, whereby the experimenter's methods begin to affect the results of the study. The normal situation on board a container boat is that the crew are largely ignorant of the specific contents of the boxes on board. However, in this case, the situation was transformed by the fact that relatives of the crew, monitoring the BBC website, had informed them that one of the boxes on board contained a large quantity of very high-quality whisky – a revelation which the ship's captain took in good humour, although he did maintain that, as a result, he would institute 'extra security'. However, despite the captain's levity, it should be remembered that pilfering – especially of alcohol and tobacco – was such a serious problem in the previous era of 'break-bulk' loose cargo transportation that the savings enabled by containerization of cargo were, in fact, a substantial motivating force in the abandonment of the old, more vulnerable methods of shipment. Indeed, before containerization, the standing joke in the port of New York was that a longshoreman's wages were '$20 a day and all the whisky he could carry home' (Donovan and Bonney 2006: 111).

From Singapore, the box travelled up through the South China Sea, arriving, in late October, at the end of a journey of 10,000 nautical miles from Greenock, at Yangshan port in Shanghai, which is already one of the biggest ports on the planet (though soon to be exceeded in size by the terminal now being built on an artificial island in the East China Sea). However, only a month after leaving Southampton, the extent of the global crisis was now becoming clearer. Within the shipping industry itself, falling demand meant that the costs of box transport, for any given journey, had fallen by a third compared with the previous year. Moreover, within China, while companies such as Marks & Spencer had just opened their first large stores, targeting China's emerging middle class, in the hope that export sales there might support their falling profits at home, it was already clear that Chinese consumers were also reining in their spending, given their anxiety about their own financial futures.

In Shanghai, the box was loaded with a variety of cheap Chinese consumer goods (manufactured in a factory in nearby Ningbo) such as plastic spray bottles, digital bathroom scales and metal measuring tapes, for sale in a chain of DIY stores in the US. In recent years, most of China's export trade in manufactured goods has travelled in container boxes along this route and the exporters have developed particularly close linkages with American mass retailers such as Wal-Mart, whose logistics of 'just-in-time' supply mesh very effectively with the computerized inventory-control systems of containerization.

However, while the flow of exports from China across the Pacific to the west coast of America has been the fulcrum of global trade over the last 10 years, China too was, by the spring of 2009, also experiencing the effects of the global downturn in terms of falling orders (reduced by 70 per cent in some cases) for exports to the United States, Europe and Japan. This, of course, also turned out to have major ramifications for China's internal labour market, in so far as many of the workers in the factories making these consumer goods were migrants who had arrived in the cities during the boom, but were now themselves fearful of losing their jobs because of the global crisis.

Having spent approximately a month in China, the box left Shanghai in late November on a ship bound for Sendai in Japan, and then on to Los Angeles, a journey of around 12 days. By the time of its arrival in Los Angeles, the world economy was in even deeper trouble and, within the shipping industry, charter rates for container ships had plummeted further. In the boom years, companies had built bigger and bigger ships in the expectation that demand for transportation was set to continue to increase indefinitely. However, in the context of the economic downturn, the industry now faced a crisis of oversupply. Moreover, if the port of Los Angeles had in those years been the crucial nexus between the emerging system of Asian mass production and American mass consumption, that relationship itself was clearly in crisis, one of the signs of which was the mountains of empty containers now growing along the portside in Los Angeles. Given that America has very little to export that Asia wants to buy, rather than send the containers back empty, as had been done for some time, they were now simply being abandoned at the port – and the long shadows which the mountains of empty containers cast brutally symbolized the crisis which had marooned them there.

From Los Angeles, the box travelled by rail across to the west coast, via Pennsylvania, arriving in mid-December at the aptly named 'Big Lots' import company, on Long Island just outside New York, which has a chain of more than 1,300 stores across the United States, and specializes in selling cheap imported goods from the Far East to working-class American consumers. The company's hope was that, even in a collapsing market, these 'good value' cheap goods would hold their own better than most.

However, at this point in its journey, the economic crisis meant that the box was marooned in a container park in Trenton, New Jersey for a considerable period before acquiring a viable load for its onward journey. At the same time, the GPS tracking device fitted to the box malfunctioned and needed to be returned to England for repair. As is so often the case in stories concerning technology, it is the point at which the system breaks down which is most revealing – in this case about the difficulties of maintaining the effective functioning of the kind of online tracking system on which the design of the BBC project was premised. The fault proved hard to repair and for the rest of the box's journey, the 'mapping' facility on the website only functioned intermittently, or at best retrospectively, which deprived the user of the (somewhat magical) sense of immediacy that had contributed greatly to the appeal of the project.

In fact, the box did not leave New York until late January 2009, when it was loaded with an eclectic mix of items ranging from replacement ink cartridges for pens to spearmint flavouring and additives to polyester fibre. It arrived at the port of Santos in Brazil (the busiest container port in South America) in late February, after its 21-day journey from New York. Once again, it transpired that the box had arrived in a difficult economic situation: notwithstanding Brazil's overall economic successes in recent years, the port had already suffered a 15 per cent decrease in trade in the previous six months. It was thus some time before the box acquired a viable load for the next stage of its journey, when it left Santos in March on the *NYK Clara*, bound for Japan, via the Cape of Good Hope, Singapore and Hong Kong. When it arrived in Yokohama port, in Tokyo Bay, in April, at the end of its long journey from Brazil, with a cargo of foodstuffs, it was clear that the global downturn was now affecting Japan just as much as it had Brazil.

Indeed, in a particularly ironic turnabout, it transpired that while Japan was still happy to import foodstuffs from Brazil, the government was now keen to encourage the many Brazilian migrant workers, who had been enticed to come to work in Japan in recent years, to go back home. Many of them were in such straitened circumstances that they had little option but to accept the Japanese government subsidies that would, in effect, 're-export' them to Brazil now that they constituted an unwanted category of surplus labour. What was strikingly revealed here, as in the case of the 'internal' migrants in China who had left the countryside to work in the cities during the boom years but now faced unemployment there, are the complex forms of indetermination (and contradictions) between the different 'regimes of mobility' of labour and of commodities.[9]

Such are the trials of globalization in a period of downturn. After half a century of consistent annual growth, the volume of cargo carried by container ships decreased for the first time in May 2009. While the project was planned when global trade was booming, the story of the BBC box's journey, marooned as it has been – for lack of demand – at various stages of its journey, has precisely mirrored the declining fortunes of the global shipping industry. If, as Roland Buerk notes in his report from Shanghai, the box is now looking a little battered, and its paint a little faded after its long journey, that would seem a fitting symbol for the state of the global economy.

Globalization, convergence and standardization

However, beyond detailing the journalistic output and originality of the BBC project, I also want to make this 'box' the grist to a rather different mill by returning to some of my earlier themes concerning the definition of the field of communication studies. The principal issues here are how we should understand the relations of communications and transport and, more particularly, how we might re-integrate the material dimension of communications into the field, which, as I indicated earlier, presently tends to be conceived of as if 'communications' should refer exclusively to the symbolic realm of the movement of information and messages.

If we begin with the question of globalization, it is worth observing, with Alan Sekula (1995), that most people talk as if globalization is all about email and air transport, and that in most conceptions of globalization, maritime space is a forgotten area. However, the long-distance production and supply chains on which the global economy is now premised entirely depend on the transport of both 'intermediate' (parts) and finished goods over long distances.[10] From the point of view of media and communications studies, one of the most interesting things about the container industry is that the transformations it has gone through, over the last 50 years, since the standardized container box was first invented, offer an uncannily exact 'pre-echo' of the more recent transformations of the communications industries in the era of digitalization.

The key point about containerization in the transport industry is that, just like 'convergence' media in the digital era, it is a transmodal system, in which the same unit (the containerized box of a standard size and shape) can readily be moved across different systems of transportation – rail, road or sea. To this extent, the experience of the coming of the container box in the transport industry has clear parallels with the more recent transformation of the communications industries, once they too began to move to a transmodal, multi-platform configuration, based on a standardized form – in their case, digitalized units of information which can readily be transposed across different media platforms. Furthermore, this means that when we speak of convergence, as we have done within media studies in recent years, we must recognize that we have much to learn from the previous experience of 'transmodality' of the transport industries.

By the 1950s, it was already clear to many people in the shipping industry that, just as Henry Ford had revolutionized motor manufacturing by standardizing the assembly process, they now had to standardize the process of handling goods on ships, crucially by loading all goods into containers of a uniform size, so that machinery could then be developed to automate the process (Donovan and Bonney 2006: 74). The key to efficient shipping clearly lay in standardizing the unit of transport, but different shipping companies had opted for boxes of different sizes, leading to bitter conflicts, which were only resolved in 1965 when the International Organization for Standardization established the cross-industry standard box sizes which still dominate the industry today.

In this context, Andrew Barry (2001) has detailed the crucial role of the establishment of technical standards in the creation of entities such as the EU's 'single market' and has highlighted the inevitably political nature of the battles which have preceded the establishment of agreed standards in many technological fields. In the media field, one might think of parallels with the 'standards wars' between Betamax and VHS formats for control of the home video market – or of contemporary struggles over different possible standards for the next stage of high-definition TV and blu-ray technology.

Technological innovation and regulatory contexts

However, if the analysis of technical forms of standardization benefits from consideration of these parallels between different industries' experiences of the same basic processes, the further issue concerns the relationship between technological innovation and the changes in regulatory contexts which make particular technologies both feasible and (potentially) profitable.

Within transport studies, the story of containerization is sometimes constructed as a matter of technological determinism – in which, as I noted earlier, this 'invention' is held to have 'changed the world'. However, the crucial issue was not simply the invention of the box itself but, rather, the new context provided for that invention by the deregulation of the transport industries, which increasingly allowed cross-industry forms of ownership that had previously been outlawed under monopoly legislation. It was not the container box alone, as a particular technological innovation, which created globalization. Rather, it was the development of multilateral trade frameworks such as the General Agreement on Tariffs and Trade, designed to lower trade barriers across the globe, which created the deregulated context in which containerization became viable as the technology at the base of the freight transportation system – which then did transform the global economy (Donovan and Bonney 2006: 209).

If, today, transmodal transport systems are established all over the world, in the USA, where the containerization revolution began, freight transportation has always been heavily regulated by the Interstate Commerce Commission. The commission 'saw its task as defining and policing the boundaries that separate rail, truck and water transportation. Each of these modes of transportation was to concentrate on providing the services for which it was best suited'. To this extent 'in transportation, modalism became the industrial equivalent of nationalism in international politics' and the ICC saw an important part of its anti-monopoly role as blocking emergent ownership structures which attempted to straddle different modes of transport. However, McLean famously saw the ship as 'just another piece of highway to transport goods on' and regarded the regulatory roadblocks that then separated different transportation modes merely as temporary obstacles to be overcome. Nonetheless, these obstacles stood for a considerable time, until the final deregulation of the American transport industries in the Reagan years. Although various forms of intermodal service were gradually developed, throughout the sixties and seventies, it was not until the eighties that the Interstate Commerce Commission's regulatory grip on the transport industries was decisively loosened.[11]

The parallels with our concerns in media and communication studies of the relation of digital technologies of 'convergence' to the deregulation, during the same period, of the structures within which the media had until then developed, are clear enough. To put it more concretely, in relation to the UK, rather than thinking about how technologies of digitalization 'caused' the development of convergence media we might perhaps better look to the deregulation of these industries from the 1980s onwards as the key causal factor. That process of deregulation permitted forms of cross-media ownership which would previously have been outlawed by anti-monopoly legislation. Without that transformation, the 'economies of scope' now available to multimedia companies (to redeploy the same content across a variety of media platforms) would simply have been illegal, whether or not the technology necessary for the task was available. In short, what is needed here is a more complex model of the dynamics of the interactions between technical innovation, invention and implementation, in the broader context of the role of regulatory structures in setting parameters to what technologies can be profitably developed at a given moment (Winston 2006; Curran forthcoming).

Redefining media and communication studies

Evidently, one of the main burdens of my argument is to criticize any narrowly focused, technologically deterministic approach which concentrates its attention on the history of the 'internal logics' of technological progress, whether in the realm of material transport or the media. Regrettably, a number of contemporary accounts of the development of 'digital media' display exactly this deficiency. Evidently I would support the arguments many of the other authors in this collection, who critique perspectives which regard digitalization as the harbinger of some 'Year Zero' in matters of communication. Centrally, we must attend to the simultaneities and symbioses achieved in the relations of older and newer media (the obvious example being a person on a train, looking in a newspaper, to see what they might watch on television when they get home …).

As indicated earlier, my own main interest lies in the better integration of the analysis of physical transport with that of symbolic communication and my key point of reference lies with Marx and Engels' definition of communications as the study of the movement of 'information, people and commodities' (De la Haye 1979). However, in closing, I would like to push things one stage further, by also arguing in favour of what I would call a 'non-media-centric' form of media and communication studies (cf. Morley 2009). A communications studies with a narrow focus on the latest technological developments is clearly inadequate; one with a longer historical perspective, which attends to the articulation of the older, material technologies and the newer, virtual ones is clearly better; one which attends to both the virtual and material dimensions of the movements, not only of messages and persons, but also of objects and commodities – and to the disjunctures between these different regimes of virtual and actual mobility (Appadurai 1997, 2006) – will surely serve us best.

Notes

1 But see the work of Parks (2005) and Larkin (2008) as well as Morley (2009) for an emerging focus on questions of communications infrastructures.
2 cf. M. Rosenstein, quoted in Donovan and Bonney 2006: 51. For a fascinating account of one of the precursors of 'containerization', systems of transport based on the barrel ('the perfect marriage between high art and utilitarian function ... beauty and strength') see Chapter 8 of Murray (2007).
3 Cf. Barthes (1972) and Ross (1996) on the 'superlative objects' of an age – e.g. the motor car, the TV set and the fridge as the key symbols of post-war modernity.
4 Alan Sekula, verbal contribution to discussion at 'The Travelling Box: Containers as a Global Icon of our Era', University of California Santa Barbara Conference November 2007.
5 See the report 'Ukrainian Mall not for the Dainty', International Herald Tribune 19 May 2006.
6 Dick Hebdige and Kim Yosuda collaborated at UCSB in 2006–7 using abandoned container boxes from the port of Los Angeles for their students to 'customize' both as studio spaces and as site-specific sculptural exhibits. The documentation of the Kuohsiung and Genova container art exhibitions can be found at http://container.khcc.gov.tw/home01.aspx?ID=1 and http://www.containerart.org/eng/ecosystems_genova.html. (Accessed 28 August 2009.) For the work of Yvan Salomone see Dean and Millar (2005: 166–68).
7 Full details of the box's travels, as well as short reports and videos, can be found at the web address in the subheading. In the narrative account given in this section, I rely heavily on the various reports on the project posted on the BBC website by, among others: Jeremy Hillman, Hugh Pym, Nils Blyth (all at the BBC's London offices), Christian Frazer (Middle East Correspondent), Jonathon Gordon (Singapore), Quentin Somerville and Chris Hogg (Shanghai), Matt Frei (Los Angeles), Greg Ward (North American Correspondent), Gary Duffy (San Paolo) and Roland Buerk (Tokyo). This account also draws on an interview conducted as the project was nearing its conclusion (in September 2009) with

Jeremy Hillman who, as Head of BBC Business News, conceived the original idea and managed it throughout.

8 See also McKenzie Wark's *Dispositions* (2002), in which he traces the narrative of his own movements over a nine-month period, not only through time but also across space (using a personal GPS device), which offers an interesting parallel to the BBC project.

9 See Appadurai (1997 and 2006) on the potential disjunctures between 'ethnoscapes', 'financescapes' and 'technoscapes'.

10 As Marc Levinson notes, the majority of the containers imported through Californian ports are carrying 'intermediate goods' – 'factory inputs that have been partially processed in one place and will be processed further somewhere else' (Levinson 2006: 268).

11 Donovan and Bonney (2006: 25–27, 46, 172–73).

References

Appadurai, A. (1997) *Modernity at Large*, Minneapolis: University of Minnesota Press.

Appadurai, A. (2006) *Fear of Small Numbers*, Raleigh, Durham, NC: Duke University Press.

Arnheim, R. (1933) *Film as Art*, London: Faber and Faber.

Barry, A. (2001) *Political Machines*, London: Athlone Press.

Barthes, R. (1972) *Mythologies*, London: Paladin.

Callon, M. and Latour, B. (1981) 'Unscrewing the Big Leviathon' in K. Knorr-Cetina and A. V. Cicourel (eds) *Advances in Social Theory*, London: Routledge & Kegan Paul.

Crampton, M. (2003) *The Political Mapping of Cyberspace*, Edinburgh: Edinburgh University Press.

Cudahy, B. (2006) *Box Boats*, New York: Fordham University Press.

Curran, J. (forthcoming) 'Technology Foretold' in N. Fenton (ed.) *New Media, Old News*, London: Sage.

De la Haye, Y. (ed.) (1980) *Marx and Engels on the Means of Communication*, Paris: International General Books.

Dean, T. and Millar, J. (2005) *Place*, London: Thames and Hudson.

Donovan, A. and Bonney, J. (2006) *The Box That Changed the World*, New Jersey: Commonwealth Business Media.

Gibson, W. (2008) *Spook Country*, London: Penguin Books.

Hannam, K., Sheller, M. and Urry, J. (2006) 'Mobilities, Immobilities and Moorings' *Mobilities* Vol. 1.1.

Koolhaas, R. (ed.) (2004) *Mutations*, Bordeaux: ACTAR.

Larkin, B. (2008) *Signal and Noise*, Raleigh, Durham, NC: Duke University Press.

Levinson, M. (2006) *The Box: How the Shipping Container Made the World Smaller and the World Economy Bigger*, Princeton, NJ: Princeton University Press.

Meyrowitz, J. (1985) *No Sense of Place*, New York: Oxford University Press.

Miller, D. and Slater, D. (2000) *The Internet: An Ethnographic Approach*, London: Berg Publishing.

Morley, D. (2007) 'Istanbul Tales' *Soundings* Issue 37.

Morley, D. (2009) 'For a Materialist, Non-Media-Centric Media Studies' *Television and New Media* Vol. 10.1.

Murray, S. (2007) *Moveable Feasts: The Incredible Journeys of the Things We Eat*, London: Aurum Press.

Parks, L. (2005) *Cultures in Orbit: Satellites and the Televisual*, Raleigh, Durham, NC: Duke University Press.

Rath, C. D. (1985) 'The Invisible Network' in P. Drummond and R. Paterson (eds) *Television in Transition*, London: British Film Institute.

Ross, K. (1996) *Fast Cars, Clean Bodies*, Cambridge, MA: The MIT Press.

Sekula, A. (1995) *Fish Story*, Rotterdam: Witte De With Centre For Contemporary Art.

Urry, J. (2008) *Mobilities*, Cambridge: Polity Press.

Wark, M. (1994) *Virtual Geography*, Bloomington: Indiana University Press.

Wark, M. (2002) *Dispositions*, Applecross, WA: Salt Publishing.

Winston, B. (2006) *Media, Technology and Society*, London: Routledge.

Zook, M. (2005) *The Geography of the Internet Industry*, Oxford: Blackwell.

INDEX

271